Lecture Notes in Computer Science 1497

Edited by G. Goos, J. Hartmanis and J. van Leeuwen

Springer
Berlin
Heidelberg
New York
Barcelona
Budapest
Hong Kong
London
Milan
Paris
Singapore
Tokyo

Vassil Alexandrov   Jack Dongarra   (Eds.)

Recent Advances in Parallel Virtual Machine and Message Passing Interface

5th European PVM/MPI Users' Group Meeting
Liverpool, UK, September 7-9, 1998
Proceedings

 Springer

Series Editors

Gerhard Goos, Karlsruhe University, Germany
Juris Hartmanis, Cornell University, NY, USA
Jan van Leeuwen, Utrecht University, The Netherlands

Volume Editors

Vassil Alexandrov
University of Liverpool, Department of Computer Science
Chadwick Building, Peach Street, Liverpool L69 7ZF, UK
E-mail: vassil@csc.liv.ac.uk

Jack Dongarra
Univesity of Tennessee and Oak Ridge National Laboratory
107 Ayres Hall, Knoxville, TN 37996-1301, USA
E-mail: dongarra@cs.utk.edu

Cataloging-in-Publication data applied for

Die Deutsche Bibliothek - CIP-Einheitsaufnahme

**Recent advances in parallel virtual machine and message passing
interface** : proceedings / 5th European PVM-MPI Users' Group
Meeting, Liverpool, UK, September 7 - 9, 1998. Vassil Alexandrov ;
Jack Dongarra (ed.). - Berlin ; Heidelberg ; New York ; Barcelona ;
Budapest ; Hong Kong ; London ; Milan ; Paris ; Singapore ; Tokyo :
Springer, 1998
   (Lecture notes in computer science ; Vol. 1497)
   ISBN 3-540-65041-5

CR Subject Classification (1991): D.1.3, D.3.2, F.1.2, G.1.0, B.2.1, C.1.2,
C.2.4, C.4

ISSN 0302-9743
ISBN 3-540-65041-5 Springer-Verlag Berlin Heidelberg New York

© Springer-Verlag Berlin Heidelberg 1998
Printed in Germany

Typesetting: Camera-ready by author
SPIN 10638910   06/3142 – 5 4 3 2 1 0   Printed on acid-free paper

Preface

Parallel Virtual Machine (PVM) and Message Passing Interface (MPI) are the most commonly used tools for programming based on the message-passing paradigm.

This volume consists of 49 contributed and invited papers presented at the Fifth European PVM/MPI Users' Group Meeting held in Liverpool, UK, September 7-9, 1998. The conference was organised jointly by the High Performance Computing and Communication group, the Computer Science Department, University of Liverpool, UK, and Oak Ridge National Laboratory, USA. A special session on tools for PVM and MPI was organised by EuroTools Working Group.

The first four conferences of the series were held at the University of Rome, Italy (1994), ENS Lyon, France (1995), TU München, Germany (1996), and the Institute of Computer Science and ACC CYFRONET in Krakow, Poland (1997).

This conference was a forum for users and developers of PVM, MPI, and other message-passing programming environments as well as developers of tools for PVM and MPI. The meeting permitted a useful interaction between the groups and provided a forum for exchanging and developing new ideas in parallel computing.

The main topics of the meeting were the latest extensions and improvements to PVM and MPI, tools for PVM and MPI, performance and evaluation of PVM and MPI, algorithms using PVM and MPI, applications in science and engineering based on the message-passing paradigm, interfaces for PVM and MPI, HPF/MPI extensions, and implementation issues. The conference included 2 tutorials on advanced usage of PVM and MPI, 19 invited talks, and 39 contributed oral presentations.

The drawing up of the interesting programme was due to invaluable suggestions of the members of the EuroPVM/MPI98 Programme Committee. Each contributed paper was refereed by at least two referees.

The conference was sponsored by EuroTools Working Group within the ESPRIT programme of the EC, FECIT (Fujitsu European Centre for Information Technology) Ltd., IBM (UK), NAG Ltd., NA Software Ltd., Progress Computer Systems Ltd. and DEC (UK), SiliconGraphics (UK), and The University of Liverpool.

Finally, we would like to express our gratitude to our colleagues from the Department of Computer Science at Liverpool, who assisted in the organisation of EuroPVM/MPI'98.

July 1998   Vassil Alexandrov
                                                                          Jack Dongarra

Programme Committee

Vassil Alexandrov	University of Liverpool, Liverpool, UK
Marian Bubak	Institute of Computer Science, AGH, Krakow, Poland
Jens Clausen	Technical University of Denmark, Denmark
Mike Delves	NA Software, Liverpool, UK
Jack Dongarra	University of Tennessee and ORNL, USA
Graham Fagg	University of Tennessee, USA
Afonso Ferreira	INRIA, Sophia-Antipolis, France
Al Geist	Oak Ridge National Laboratory, Oak Ridge, USA
Alan Gibbons	The University of Liverpool, UK
Rolf Hempel	C&C Research Labs, NEC Europe Ltd., Germany
Thomas Ludwig	Technical University of Munich, Germany
Emilio Luque	Universitat Autonoma de Barcelona, Spain
Thomas Margalef	Universitat Autonoma de Barcelona, Spain
Graham Megson	University of Reading, UK
Benno Overeinder	University of Amsterdam, The Netherlands
Andrew Rau-Chaplin	Dalhousie University, Halifax, Canada
Yves Robert	Ecole Normale Superieure de Lyon, France
David F. Snelling	Fujitsu European Centre for Information Technology, UK
Vaidy Sunderam	Emory University, Atlanta, USA
Bernard Tourancheau	Universite Claude Bernard de Lyon, France
Marian Vajtersic	Slovak Academy of Sciences, Bratislava, Slovakia
Roland Wismüller	Technical University of Munich,Germany
Zahari Zlatev	National Environmental Research Institute, Denmark

Referees

Cliff Addison	Fujitsu European Centre for Information Technology,UK
Marian Bubak	Institute of Computer Science, AGH, Krakow, Poland
Jens Clausen	Technical University of Denmark, Denmark
Mike Delves	NA Software, Liverpool, UK
Frank Dehne	Carleton University, Ottawa, Canada
Ivan Dimov	CLPP, Bulgarian Academy of Sciences, Bulgaria
Jack Dongarra	University of Tennessee and ORNL, USA
Graham Fagg	University of Tennessee, USA
Afonso Ferreira	INRIA, Sophia-Antipolis, France

Al Geist	Oak Ridge National Laboratory, Oak Ridge, USA
Alan Gibbons	The University of Liverpool, UK
Rolf Hempel	C&C Research Labs, NEC Europe Ltd., Germany
Thomas Ludwig	Technical University of Munich, Germany
Emilio Luque	Universitat Autonoma de Barcelona, Spain
Thomas Margalef	Universitat Autonoma de Barcelona, Spain
Graham Megson	University of Reading, UK
Benno Overeinder	University of Amsterdam, The Netherlands
Ray Paton	University of Liverpool, UK
Andrew Rau-Chaplin	Dalhousie University, Halifax, Canada
Yves Robert	Ecole Normale Superieure de Lyon, France
Wojtek Rytter	University of Liverpool, UK
David F. Snelling	Fujitsu European Centre for Information Technology, UK
Vaidy Sunderam	Emory University, Atlanta, USA
Bernard Tourancheau	Universite Claude Bernard de Lyon, France
Marian Vajtersic	Slovak Academy of Sciences, Bratislava, Slovakia
Roland Wismüller	Technical University of Munich, Germany
Zahari Zlatev	National Environmental Research Institute, Denmark

Invited Speakers

Cliff Addison (Fujitsu European Centre for Information Technology, UK), Mark Baker (University of Portsmouth, UK), David Beagle (DEC, UK), Shirley Browne (University of Tennessee, USA) Karsten Decker, (CSCS/SCSC, Switzerland), Mike Delves (NA Software Ltd., UK), Mishi Derakhshan (NAG Ltd.), Ivan Dimov (CLPP, Bulgarian Academy of Sciences, Bulgaria), Hubert Ertl (GENIAS GmbH, Germany), Markus Fischer (University of Tennessee, USA), Al Geist, (Oak Ridge National Lab, USA), Andrew Grant (SiliconGraphics, UK), William Gropp (Argonne National Laboratory, USA), Werner Krotz-Vogel (Pallas GmbH, Germany), Graham Megson (University of Reading, UK), Wolfgang Nagel (TU Dresden, Germany), Vaidy Sunderam (Emory University, USA), Richard Treumann (IBM Server Group, Poughkeepsie, USA) Zahari Zlatev (Danish Environmental Research Institute, Denmark).

Acknowledgements

EuroPVM/MPI'98 would not have been possible without the enthusiastic support of Khalil Rouhana, DG III, European Commission; Roland Wismüller, Technical University of Munich; our colleagues from Oak Ridge National Laboratory, and the Department of Computer Science at Liverpool and our sponsors.

Warm thanks to Ken Chan for his invaluable work in editing the proceedings; to Thelma Williams for dealing with the financial side of the conference, and to Katrina Houghton, Ray Paton, Nia Alexandrov, Keith Taft, and Jose Libano Alonso for their contribution to the organization of the conference.

Table of Contents

1. Evaluation and Performance

On-Line Performance Monitoring Using OMIS
M. Bubak, W. Funika, K. Iskra, R. Maruszewski   3

Performance Analysis of Task-Based Algorithms on Heterogeneous Systems
with Message Passing
A. Clematis, A. Corana   11

Automatic Detection of PVM Program Performance Problems
A. Espinosa, T. Margalef, E. Luque   19

Evaluating and Modeling Communication Overhead of MPI Primitives on
the Meiko CS-2
G. Folino, G. Spezzano, D. Talia   27

A Parallel I/O Test Suite
D. Lancaster, C. Addison, T.Oliver   36

Improving the PVM Daemon Network Performance by Direct Network
Access
R. Lavi, A. Barak   44

SKaMPI: A Detailed, Accurate MPI Benchmark
R. Reussner, P. Sanders, L. Prechelt, M. Müller   52

2. Extensions and Improvements

MPI on NT: The Current Status and Performance of the Available
Environments
M. Baker   63

Harness: The Next Generation Beyond PVM
G.A. Geist   74

Advances in Heterogeneous Network Computing
P. Gray, A. Krantz, S. Olesen, V. Sunderam   83

MPI_Connect Managing Heterogenous MPI Applications Interopration and
Process Control
G.E. Fagg, K.S. London, J.J. Dongarra   93

An Active Layer Extension to MPI
M. Chetlur, G.D. Sharma, N. Abu-Ghazaleh, U. Kumar V. Rajasekaran,
P.A. Wilsey   97

Interconnecting PVM and MPI Applications   105
P.D. Medeiros, J.C. Cunha

WMPI - Message Passing Interface for Win32 Clusters   113
J. Marinho, J.G. Silva

A Java Interface for WMPI
P. Martins, L.M. Silva, J. Silva   121

3. Implementation Issues

Porting CHAOS Library to MPI
M. Bubak, P. Łuszczek, A. Wierzbowska   131

Athapascan: An Experience on Mixing MPI Communications and Threads
A. Carissimi, M. Pasin   137

Developing Message-Passing Applications on MPICH under Ensemble
Y. Cotronis   145

The NAG Parallel Library and the PINEAPL Project
M. Derakhshan, A. Krommer   153

High Performance Fortran: A Status Report or: Are We Ready to Give Up
MPI?
M. Delves, H. Zima   161

On the Implementation of a Portable, Client-Server Based MPI-IO Interface
T. Fuerle, E. Schikuta, C. Loeffelhardt, K. Stockinger, H. Wanek   172

Distributed Computing in a Heterogeneous Computing Environment
E. Gabriel, M. Resch, T. Beisel, R. Keller   180

Rank Reordering Strategy for MPI Topology Creation Functions
T. Hatazaki   188

Scalable and Adaptive Resource Sharing in PVM
M. Kemelmakher, O. Kremien   196

Load Balancing for Network Based Multi-threaded Applications
O. Krone, M. Raab, B. Hirsbrunner   206

Creation of Reconfigurable Hardware Objects in PVM Environments
G.M. Megson, R.S. Fish, D.N.J. Clarke   215

Implementing MPI with the Memory-Based Communication Facilities on
the SSS-CORE Operating System
K. Morimoto, T. Matsumoto, K. Hiraki   223

PVM on Windows and NT Clusters
S.L. Scott, M. Fischer, A. Geist   231

Java and Network Parallel Processing   239
N. Stankovic, K. Zhang

4. Tools

A Tool for the Development of Meta-Applications Supporting Several
Message-Passing Programming Environments
R. Baraglia, R. Ferrini, D. Laforenza, R. Sgherri   249

Cross-Platform Parallel Debugging and Performance Analysis Tools
S. Browne   257

Debugging Point-to-Point Communication in MPI and PVM
D. Kranzlmüller, J. Volkert   265

Monitoring PVM Programs Using the DAMS Approach
J.C. Cunha, V. Duarte   273

Functional Message Passing with OPAL-MPI
T. Nitsche, W. Webers   281

An MPI-based Run-Time Support to Coordinate HPF Tasks
S. Orlando, R. Perego   289

Dynamic Visualization and Steering Using PVM and MPI
P.M. Papadopoulos, J.A. Kohl   297

A PVM-Based Library for Sparse Matrix Factorizations
J. Touriño, R. Doallo   304

On-Line Monitoring Support in PVM and MPI
R. Wismüller   312

5. Algorithms

Coarse Grained Parallel Monte Carlo Algorithms for Solving SLAE Using PVM
V. Alexandrov, F. Dehne, A. Rau-Chaplin, K. Taft   323

Parallel Quantum Scattering Calculations Applied to the Dynamics of Elementary Reactions
A. Bolloni, A. Riganelli, S. Crocchianti, A. Laganà   331

On the PVM Computations of Transitive Closure and Algebraic Path Problems
K.J. Chan, A.M. Gibbons, M. Pias, W. Rytter   338

Implementation of Monte Carlo Algorithms for Eigenvalue Problem Using MPI
I. Dimov, V. Alexandrov, A. Karaivanova   346

Running an Advection-Chemistry Code on Message Passing Computers
K. Georgiev, Z. Zlatev   354

A Model for Parallel One Dimensional Eigenvalues and Eigenfunctions Calculations
A. Laganà, G. Grossi, A. Riganelli, G. Ferraro   364

Sparse LU Factorization with Partial Pivoting Overlapping Communications and Computations on the SP-2 Multicomputer
C.N. Ojeda-Guerra, E. Macías, A. Suárez   371

Use of Parallel Computing to Improve the Accuracy of Calculated Molecular Properties
E. Ramos, W. Díaz, V. Cerverón, I. Nebot-Gil   379

A New Model for the Analysis of Asynchronous Parallel Algorithms
J.L. Roda, C. Rodríguez, F. Sande, D.G. Morales, F. Almeida   387

Portable Randomized List Ranking on Multiprocessors Using MPI   395
J. L. Träff

A Parallel Algorithm for the Simultaneous Solution of Direct and Adjoint Multigroup Diffusion Problems
E. Varin, R. Roy, T. NKaoua   403

Author Index   411

Part 1
Evaluation and Performance

On-Line Performance Monitoring Using OMIS

Marian Bubak[1,2], Włodzimierz Funika[1], Kamil Iskra[1], Radosław Maruszewski[1]

[1] Institute of Computer Science, AGH, al. Mickiewicza 30, 30-059 Kraków, Poland
[2] Academic Computer Centre – CYFRONET, Nawojki 11, 30-950 Kraków, Poland
email: {bubak,funika}@uci.agh.edu.pl, {kiskra,ortokbld}@icslab.agh.edu.pl
phone: (+48 12) 617 39 64, *fax:* (+48 12) 633 80 54

Abstract. This paper presents the motivation of development and functionality of a tool for on-line performance monitoring developed using an independently operating monitoring facility built according to OMIS requirements. The tool is based on previously developed one for off-line performance analysis. The monitoring facility's operation has been modified by adding a request distributor as an intermediate layer for handling user's requests. The request distributor and the monitoring facility communicate using two-directional asynchronous communication built on top of Sun RPC.

1 Introduction

Recent advances in parallel distributed systems and parallel programming have resulted in the growth of interest in message passing paradigm for solving complex computational problems on networks of workstations (NOWs) which now constitute a popular class of distributed computer systems [1, 2]. Compared with massively parallel systems, understanding what causes poor performance of a parallel program on NOWs is a more complicated task due to interaction of a number of performance factors.

To a large extent, the difficulties of understanding application's behavior stem from the limited functionality of existing tools which support performance monitoring and analysis [3]. Whereas there is a large number of off-line tools, there is a shortage of interoperable on-line tools, mainly due to the lack of versatile mechanism of interaction between a monitoring system with well-defined interface and a performance tool. This situation will possibly improve thanks to the recent emergence of the OMIS specification [4, 5].

In the paper, an approach to the adaptation of an off-line performance monitoring facility [6, 7] for on-line performance monitoring is described. To accomplish this, OMIS specification is used. The on-line tool is built based on an existing off-line performance analysis tool. A number of modifications to the existing mechanisms and the introduction of new mechanisms are presented. The current state of the work is presented as well as the perspectives of extension of the tool functionality.

2 Related Work

The tools which are used to support performance analysis of parallel programs can be divided into those on-line and off-line ones. Operation of off-line tools is mainly based on a trace which is generated during an application's run. Whereas in case of off-line tools the user has to predefine the goals of measurement and therefore the instrumentation scope, on-line tools provide a means by which the user can control monitoring, collecting and presenting performance data in real-time or quasi real-time.

In comparison to off-line tools, on-line ones have to meet a larger set of requirements, one of them being the possibility to manipulate an application's execution. This implies a higher extent of complexity of developing such a tool. On-line monitoring should provide getting a flexible user-driven real-time insight into an application's behaviour rather than setting up a number of measurement goals in the pre-run fixed mode only. Due to the complexity of on-line monitoring system, on-line tools are significantly fewer than off-line ones.

Generally, such an on-line tool uses dedicated non-portable mechanisms of interaction with operating system, application programming interface and hardware. Let alone vendor-supplied on-line tools, we will mention two examples of public domain tools: *XPVM* [8] and *Paradyn* [9]. *XPVM* provides monitoring PVM programs based on the instrumented communication functions library, but it can be neither extended nor controlled as to the extent of intrusion induced thus disabling to get a realistic time-bound picture of an application's execution. *Paradyn* is a powerful approach using on-line manipulation of object code and search-based mechanisms for isolating poor performance. However, getting conventional performance displays with *Paradyn* is virtually impossible due to the lack of extendibility and interoperability.

To remedy this condition, a standardised mechanism of interaction is introduced with OMIS specification [4]. The main advantage of OMIS is its versatility which is provided using a unified set of monitoring service requests common to most software and hardware environments as well as a possibility to add new services specific to particular environmental conditions like PVM and MPI.

3 Use of Off-Line Tool Monitoring Mechanism for On-Line Operation

The on-line flexible tool should provide the possibility of real-time observation and manipulation of a program run. To minimise efforts to develop a monitoring facility for PARNAS/OPM (PARallel iNstrumentation and Analysis System, On-line Performance Monitoring tool), we decided to use the current monitoring facility, which constitutes a part of an off-line performance analysis tool [7].

The off-line tool mentioned enables:

– instrumenting the source code of an application for tracing or profiling by substituting original function calls for instrumentation functions (e.g. Tpvm_* instead of pvm_*) or by wrapping with instrumentation function calls [7],

– collecting performance data with the monitoring facility, which synchronizes time-bound data for logged events, watches *host-add*, *host-delete*, *task-spawn* and *task-exit* function calls as well as controls tracing operations during a program's run,
– performance analysis and visualization based on the data collected.

The use of the monitoring facility mentioned above to build an intermediate layer between a GUI-driven performance tool and a monitoring facility in *client–server* mode seems to be natural due to the existing mechanism of interaction between an application and the monitoring facility. When developing a specialized on-line version of monitoring facility, OMIS specification was used to standardize the operation of the intermediate layer mentioned.

For building an on-line performance tool we needed to adapt the monitoring facility so that it could provide performance data and to *on-the-fly* manipulate an application's execution. A mechanism of interaction between the performance tool and the monitoring facility needs to be built, which stems from the way in which OMIS establishes a request for *information services* to get any information about a process's state – the process should be asked for these data.

4   Operation of PARNAS/OPM

4.1   Structure of PARNAS/OPM

The structure of the on-line performance tool is shown in Fig. 1. The tool level is divided into two layers: the one of the *on-line monitoring facility* (OMF) as a *server* and that of the *graphical performance tool* (GPT) as a *client*. GPT is extended with *request distributor* (RD) which plays the role of a mediator between a human-driven graphical interface of GPT and OS-bound OMF. RD and OMF are built according to OMIS requirements. The structure presented below is a simplified version of the general operational scheme of OMIS compliant monitoring system (OCM) [4].

4.2   New Mechanisms

Instrumentation function calls as mentioned above are used in twofold way:

– **first**, each instrumented function can involve a function call for checking whether a request from the monitoring facility has arrived. In our tool, most such requests ask processes for various performance data, like the CPU load on a node or the number of page faults since process started. Such data can usually be collected with a few simple system calls and are immediately returned to the monitoring facility;
– the **second** benefit comes from the fact that these functions allow to implement an event service which traces function calls. This service allows a client of the monitoring facility to perform certain actions once an application's function has started or finished its execution. The implementation of this

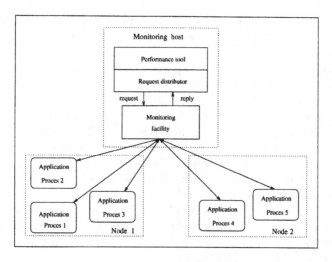

Fig. 1. Structure of on-line performance tool using OMIS-compatible monitoring facility

mechanism requires establishing communication from the monitoring facility in the direction of application processes. This requirement is due to the necessity to inform the application processes about what function calls the OMIS client is interested in. So setting up communication mechanism from the monitoring facility towards application processes is indispensable.

When choosing the way how to implement the communication in this direction, a problem occurs: whether PVM mechanisms or some other way should be used. The first way will necessarily induce the risk of mixing up monitoring requests with normal application communication. Whereas a *message-tag* attribute can be used to distinguish between application messages and monitoring requests, this method fails at pvm_recv with "-1" as the source identifier. Here, the instrumentation functions turn out to be of help by enabling the determination whether this message is a request or normal message using pvm_bufinfo. Unfortunately, this method cannot be applied in all cases, e.g. pvm_precv immediately places the message arrived into the user's buffer as opposed to other communication functions. In this case, pvm_recvf function can be used, which allows to redefine the comparison function used for accepting messages. This way, messages from the monitoring facility can be skipped.

Communication between OMF and GPT does not use PVM mechanism. Instead, two-directional asynchronous communication is built on top of Sun RPC. This way, the possibility of idling due to the execution of more complicated requests by application is avoided.

The most difficult part of the OMIS layer is handling "Omis_request". Such a request is a string containing calls to various OMIS services which should be executed. The request can be conditional, in which case it is not executed immediately, but each time when a condition defined in the request is met. When the execution of a request is completed, an Omis_reply object is passed to the client. This object contains result strings and status codes generated by the invoked services.

Handling OMIS requests involves parsing, checking for correctness and execution. All these operations are done by RD. The way a request is executed depends on the type of the request (conditional or unconditional) and the services used. For example, a request ": proc_get_info([], 0x200)" is to be parsed, checked whether known services were used, checked for correctness of parameter types, etc. Once this has been done, the request can be handled as unconditional and executed immediately. Next, tokens are expanded, in this case an empty list should result in inserting all the tokens of this type (here, all the processes constituting the virtual machine).

RD sends the request to OMF, which, in turn, sends corresponding requests to all the processes specified. An application process receives a request within instrumentation functions (e.g. Tpvm_*). The request is then processed resulting in a response sent back to GPT via OMF.

OMF fills in the proper fields of the Omis_reply object with responses incoming from application processes, and as soon as the object is ready, the reply will be returned to the user via RD, this way completing the "Omis_request" execution. This scheme is quite sophisticated due to the necessity to handle a number of requests at the same time, which results in a need for an identification mechanism, queueing intermediate results, etc.

5 Monitoring Overhead

Like other software monitoring system, PARNAS/OMF causes intrusion of application execution. Intrusion occurs due to execution of additional code connected with event processing within instrumented program as well as to service request/reply data transfer on the network. One of the advantages of PARNAS/OMF is the possibility to select objects to monitor with turn off/on option as well as the limitation of volume of data to be processed and transferred to ten-odd bytes. In the current implementation of PARNAS/OMF, the communication layer of the monitoring system is realized on top of PVM. In this context, a sample instrumentation code implanted into an application includes pvm_send(), pvm_nrecv() and cca twenty C instructions. Experiments on SUN4 IPX workstations with 40 MHz processor and 48 MB RAM show that the latter component of the instrumentation code, i.e. event processing code executes cca 30 μs, while data transfer with PVM 3.4 resulted in the following performance: with normal mode 0.995 ms for pvm_send and 0.104 ms for pvm_nrecv, whereas with DIRECT option 1.451 ms for pvm_send and 0.093 ms for pvm_nrecv.

It may be deduced that the normal mode of message passing is more effective in terms of pvm_send time, whereas pvm_nrecv operation is faster with DIRECT option. Summing up the time spent in the message transfer and instrumentation code connected with event processing results in cca 1.15 ms overhead per event for the workstation mentioned above.

6   Implementation Stage

So far, main efforts were focused on the implementation of the internal OMIS mechanisms, which are indispensable for handling requests. Now, a list of implemented information and event services includes: pvm_vm_get_node_list, pvm_vm_get_proc_list, node_get_info, proc_get_info, thread_get_info as well as proc_has_terminated, thread_has_started_lib_call and thread_has_ended_lib_call. As soon as the implementation of lacking internal mechanisms such as conditional requests is complete, the list of services implemented will significantly increase.

Although easy to read for casual readers, the OMIS description is sometimes ambiguous or incomplete for those who develop a tool which is supposed to be OMIS compliant. Since we are trying to keep the conformity of the tool to OMIS, its description should be improved to eliminate the incompleteness as to the following:

1. basic symbols of the parser such as "integer" or "string" are defined in 7.2.1 of OMIS as corresponding to the C programming language. A major concern is to what extent should they conform to each other? Are hexadecimal or octal integers supposed to be accepted, or should escape sequences such as "\n" be expanded as in C?

2. in 9.2.3 of OMIS, available event context parameters for pvm_send in thread_has_{started,ended}_lib_call service are enumerated. This is supposed to explain the general concept, but handling more sophisticated calls such as pvm_mcast, where one of the arguments is an array, is unclear. Admittedly, the authors will specify of each PVM call in the next version of OMIS.

3. handling possible errors as defined in 7.1.3 of OMIS turned out to be incomplete when implementing asynchronous communication. Sometimes, messages may not arrive at destination process. This situation requires applying a kind of time-out, after which a message "request timed out" should be returned. An error message like OMIS_TIMED_ERROR should be defined in the OMIS description.

Another problem is connected with omis_fd() function. This has to be able to return int that is an open file descriptor via which events are incoming. This function and select function enable waiting for events from several sources, which is important in interactive applications with a graphical interface. As mentioned earlier, the communication between GPT and OMF is built on top of Sun RPC. It turned out that communication via Sun RPC requires a set of file descriptors whose number varies with time. Due to this, we had to change the type of the value returned by omis_fd to fd_set, and to place the function call before each call of the select(2) function as opposed to 7.1.6 of the specification, where an example with a single call is shown. More generally, this peculiar behavior of Sun RPC makes incorporation of graphical interface a difficult task, since XtAppAddInput cannot be used. Currently, we use XtAppAddWorkProc, which allows us to poll for OMIS requests, but its functionality is inferior to XtAppAddInput.

7 Results and Conclusions

The implementation of PARNAS/OPM on-line performance tool with OMIS made it possible to adapt a monitoring facility used for an off-line performance analysis tool to build up an on-line performance monitoring tool on top of an independent interoperable monitoring facility. One class of performance views enables to observe the current states of application processes and inter-process communication relations as well as to trace the run of application which may be useful while debugging a program as shown in Fig 2. Another class of views allows to get snapshots of node and process usage.

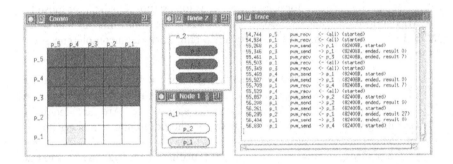

Fig. 2. Performance views with PARNAS for a parallel program solving traveling salesman problem with genetic algorithms

So far, the monitoring facility implemented is centralised, which may be acceptable for a moderate number of hosts in an execution configuration. Larger configurations would necessitate developing a distributed monitoring system. On-going work is aimed at completing the functionality of the monitoring facility and request distributor as well as enhancing the performance tool's capabilities.

Acknowledgements. We would like to thank Dr. Roland Wismueller (LRR–TUM) for his significant help while our making acquaintance with OMIS and fruitful co-operation. We are also grateful to Dr. Thomas Ludwig (LRR–TUM) and Dr. Vaidy Sunderam (Emory University) for valuable comments on on-line monitoring issues during EuroPVMPI'97 Conference. We appreciate discussions and comments of Prof. Jacek Mościński.
This work was partially supported by KBN under grant 8 T11C 006 15.

References

1. Strumpen, V., Ramkumar, B., Casavant, T.L., Reddy, S.M.: Perspectives for High Performance Computing in Workstation Networks, in: *Liddell, H., Colbrook, A., Hertzberger, B., Sloot, P., (Eds.): Proc. Int. Conf. High Performance Computing*

and *Networking, Brussels, April 15-19, 1996,* Lecture Notes in Computer Science 1067, pp. 880–889, Springer, 1996

2. Viersbach, U., Hesse, M., Zellermann, G., Schlanke J.: Parallelization: Readiness of Workstation Clustering for Computer Aided Engineering, in: *Bubak, M., Mościński, J., (Eds.): Conf. Proc. High Performance Computing and Networking on Hewlett-Packard Systems HiPer'97, Kraków, November 5-8, 1997,* pp. 95, ACC CYFRONET-KRAKÓW, 1997

3. Pancake, C. M. , Simmons, M. L., and Yan, J. C., (Eds.): Special Issue on Performance Evaluation Tools for Parallel and Distributed Systems of *IEEE Computer,* November 1995, Vol. 28, No. 11

4. Ludwig, T., Wismueller, R., Sunderam, V., and Bode, A.: OMIS – On-line Monitoring Interface Specification (Version 2.0), Shaker Verlag, 1997, Aachen, vol. 9, LRR-TUM Research Report Series
   `http://wwwbode.informatik.tu-muenchen.de/~omis/OMIS/Version-2.0/version-2.0`

5. Ludwig. T. and Wismueller, R.: OMIS 2.0 – A Universal Interface for Monitoring Systems, in: *Marian Bubak, Jack Dongarra, Jerzy Wasniewski (Eds.): Recent Advances in Parallel Virtual Machine and Message Passing Interface. Proceedings of 4th European PVM/MPI Users' Group Meeting, Cracow, Poland, 3-5 November 1997,* Lecture Notes in Computer Science 1332, pp. 267-276, Springer, 1997

6. Bubak, M., Funika, W., Mościński, J.: Monitoring of performance of PVM applications on virtual network computer, in: *Waśniewski, J., Dongarra, J., Madsen, K., and Olesen, D., (Eds.): Applied parallel computing – industrial computation and optimization, Proc. Third International Workshop, PARA'96, Lyngby, Denmark, August 18-21, 1996,* Lecture Notes in Computer Science 1184, pp. 147-156, Springer, 1996

7. Bubak M., Funika, W., Mościński J.: Evaluation of Parallel Application's Behavior in Message Passing Environment, in: *Marian Bubak, Jack Dongarra, Jerzy Wasniewski (Eds.): Recent Advances in Parallel Virtual Machine and Message Passing Interface. Proceedings of 4th European PVM/MPI Users' Group Meeting, Cracow, Poland, 3-5 November 1997,* Lecture Notes in Computer Science 1332, pp. 234-241, Springer, 1997

8. Kohl, J.A., and Geist, G.A.: The PVM 3.4 Tracing facility and XPVM 1.1. in: *Proceedings of the 29th Hawaii International Conference on System Sciences,* Hawaii, 1996

9. Miller, B.P., Callaghan, M.D., Cargille, J.M., Hollingsworth, J.K., Irvin, R.B., Karavanic, K.L., Kunchithapadam, K., and Newhall, T.: The Paradyn Parallel Performance Measurement Tool, *IEEE Computer,* vol. 28, No. 11, November, 1995, pp. 37-46

10. Maillet, E. and Tron, C., "On Efficiently Implementing Global Time for Performance Evaluation on Multiprocessor Systems", *Journal of Parallel and Distributed Computing,* vol. 28, July 1995, pp. 84-93

Performance Analysis of Task-Based Algorithms on Heterogeneous Systems with Message Passing

Andrea Clematis[1] and Angelo Corana[2]

[1] IMA-CNR, Via De Marini 6, 16149 Genova, Italy
E-mail: clematis@ima.ge.cnr.it
[2] ICE-CNR, Via De Marini 6, 16149 Genova, Italy
E-mail: corana@ice.ge.cnr.it

Abstract. We address the problem of performance analysis and prediction of a class of parallel applications on heterogeneous systems. Our attention is oriented towards workstation networks programmed using message passing libraries. Particularly, we consider a switched Ethernet-based network and we use PVM as parallel tool, adopting the master-worker model with the task farm paradigm.

The simulation applied to the matrix multiplication example yields results in good agreement with the experimental ones.

The model makes possible to estimate the computation and communication times and the idle time due to unbalancing, provided that the computation and communication complexity at the task level is known. In this way we are able to evaluate how the efficiency varies with the task granularity and the degree of heterogeneity of the network.

The analysis can be easily modified to copy with other message passing environments.

1 Introduction

Networks of workstations (NOW) represent a widely available platform to execute with good performance parallel applications provided that the communication to computation ratio is low enough.

NOWs are in most cases heterogeneous systems, since the various processors are in general different. Moreover, the computational nodes and the interconnecting network are often shared with other users and applications. These facts require that the performance metrics employed for dedicated homogeneous systems are modified and generalized [4, 8, 7, 1, 2].

PVM [6] is one of the most used parallel frameworks for the development of portable parallel applications with the message passing model, and it is widely employed in networked environments.

In this work we present a simple method to analyze and predict performance of a given parallel application on a heterogeneous NOW with message passing, using the PVM communication library. In particular, we consider a master-worker computational model with the task farm paradigm running on a switched Ethernet-based NOW.

2 The computing environment

2.1 System architecture

We consider an heterogeneous network of q workstations connected by a switched Ethernet. Of course our analysis can be applied to others switched networks (e.g. fast-Ethernet).

We assume that heterogeneity can be expressed by a single parameter, representing the speed of each node relatively to a reference machine (that not necessarily is one of the q nodes) and measured for the application under investigation. Let s_i, $i = 1, \ldots, q$ be the relative speeds of the various machines. If a machine is not unloaded but the load remains constant during the whole execution, its speed can be considered to be a fraction of the speed of the unloaded machine.

We assume that communication speed is the same for all nodes, since they belong to the same local network and the physical bandwidth of the various links is the same. Our analysis can be easily extended to the case of mixed networks (for examples Ethernet and Fast-Ethernet) by assigning the proper communication speed to each pair of nodes.

2.2 The parallel framework

In the PVM communication library [6, 5] primitives are available to pack and unpack data in the send and receive buffer and to send and receive packed messages.

As a first approximation, communication time in PVM can be modeled in the usual way as a linear function of message length [5]

$$t_{comm} = \alpha + \beta \cdot L \tag{1}$$

where α is the latency (we assume for α the average value over the NOW), β is the communication time per byte and L is the message length in bytes.

Similarly, the time for packing/unpacking messages on the i-th node can be modeled as [5]

$$t_{pk}^{(i)} = \alpha_{pk}^{(i)} + \beta_{pk}^{(i)} \cdot L \quad i = 1, \ldots, q \tag{2}$$

with $\alpha_{pk}^{(i)} \simeq 0$ and $\beta_{pk}^{(i)} = \beta_{pk}/s_i$, denoting with β_{pk} the value on the reference node. The time for packing/unpacking is greater if the encoding of data in a machine independent format is required; if all machines involved in communication support the same data format no encoding is needed, and β_{pk} is greatly reduced.

2.3 Task farm applications

Since in parallel applications on heterogeneous systems a good balancing is of basic importance in order to achieve a good efficiency, the master-worker computational model with the pool of tasks paradigm [5] is a simple and effective approach, that guarantees a good dynamic load balancing, irrespective of the computing power and the load factors of the various machines.

The applications we consider consist in the processing of a domain of size N, and can be divided into n independent tasks, each corresponding to the processing of a subdomain of size $m = N/n$. The master generates tasks and collects results; the workers concurrently process the various tasks and produce the partial results. As a worker terminates the current task it receives a new one from the master. So, computation is completely asynchronous and each worker proceeds at its own rate (Fig. 1).

```
send a task to each worker;   //initialization phase
while WorkToDo {
  Receive.Result       //receive results from worker
  Schedule.NextTask    //select the next task
  Send.Task            //send task to available worker
}
collect remaining results     //termination phase
and terminate workers
```

Master pseudo-code

```
while WorkToDo {
  Receive.Task         //receive task from master
  Execute.Task         //execute current task
  Send.Result          //send results to the master
}
```

Worker main loop

Fig. 1. Pseudo-code of a task farm application

We assume that: 1) for a given N, the total computational work does not depend on the number of tasks; 2) the various tasks require the same amount of computation and the same amount of communications; 3) to process a task, each worker does not communicate directly with the others but only receives input data from the master and sends results to the master.

This computational scheme is quite general and can be used in various applications, like linear algebra, terrain analysis and time series analysis [3].

3   Performance analysis and modeling

Let p be the number of workers. There is a worker process per node; the master process can either share a node with a worker process $(p = q)$ or run on a dedicated node $(p = q - 1)$.

For a given application and a given task granularity, let t be the CPU time needed by the reference processor to process a task and t_i^c the time needed to move the data involved with each task from/to the master.

The total time spent by each worker is

$$T_i = n_i \cdot (\frac{t}{s_i} + t_i^c) + I_i \quad i = 1,\ldots,p \tag{3}$$

where n_i denotes the number of tasks executed by the i-th worker and I_i takes into account the possible idle time at the end of computation due to unbalancing. Of course we have

$$n = \sum_i n_i \tag{4}$$

With this notation we can express the sequential execution time on the reference node as

$$T_{seq} = n \cdot t \tag{5}$$

and the parallel time as

$$T_{par} = T_1 = T_2 = \cdots = T_p \tag{6}$$

In a quite general manner we can suppose that to process a task the data flow between master and worker is of N_{inp} bytes of input data and N_{res} bytes of results. Of course we can have the particular case of results that remain local to each worker and that only at the end of the computation must be collected by the master; in this situation we can assume $N_{res} = 0$ at the task level.

In order to model performance, we need the analytical expression of N_{inp} and N_{res} as a function of the task size.

Considering that with PVM we usually pack into the same message buffer different types of data and we perform one single send for the input data and one single send for the results, using eqs. (1,2), we can express the communication times at the task level as

$$t_i^c = t_i^{inp} + t_i^{res} \tag{7}$$

with

$$t_i^{inp} = \alpha + (\beta + \beta_{pk}^{(mst)} + \beta_{pk}^{(i)}) \cdot N_{inp} \tag{8}$$

and

$$t_i^{res} = \alpha + (\beta + \beta_{pk}^{(mst)} + \beta_{pk}^{(i)}) \cdot N_{res} \tag{9}$$

where mst denotes the master process.

Since normally $\beta_{pk} << \beta$, we can consider $t_i^c \simeq t^c$ constant for all workers.

These timings refer to the basic situation depicted in Fig. 2, with no overlap between communication and computation.

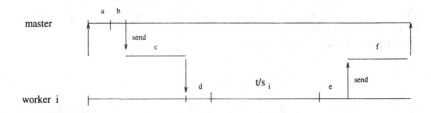

Fig. 2. Computation and communication times at the task level. The different segments represent: a = time to unpack results on master; b = time to pack input data on master; c = communication time for input data; d = time to unpack input data on worker; e = time to pack results on worker; f = communication time for results; t/s_i is the task computation time

In this simple model we suppose that communications occur without conflicts on the network. The switched network assures that conflicts are limited to the link between the master and the hub. Assuming that

$$t^c << \frac{t}{s_i} \qquad (10)$$

and considering that the computation is fully asynchronous, the probability of such conflicts is sufficiently low to be neglected at a first approximation. Taking the effect of conflicts into account requires a much more complex model.

We note finally that some modifications can be made in the basic scheme of Fig. 2 to overlap some communication overheads with computation. The simplest one is the immediate service of the worker request on the master, delaying the unpacking of results; a more complex improvement is the adoption of a double buffer technique, which can in some situations give an almost complete overlapping of communications with computation. In general we can represent by t^c the fraction of communication time not overlapped with computation.

¿From eq. (3) we can define a local efficiency of worker i as the ratio between the computation time

$$T_i^{comp} = n_i \cdot \frac{t}{s_i} \qquad (11)$$

and the elapsed time, obtaining

$$\eta_i = \frac{1}{1 + s_i(R + \frac{I_i/n_i}{t})} \qquad (12)$$

where $R = \frac{t^c}{t}$ can be considered the communication to computation ratio on the reference node.

Using eqs. (5,6,4,11) we can obtain the speed-up

$$SU = \frac{T_{seq}}{T_{par}} = \sum_i s_i \cdot \eta_i \qquad (13)$$

and using eqs. (11,5,13) we can find the fraction of the total tasks carried out by the i-th worker

$$\frac{n_i}{n} = \frac{s_i \cdot \eta_i}{\sum_i s_i \cdot \eta_i} \qquad (14)$$

In the ideal case ($R = 0$ and $I_i = 0$, $i = 1, \ldots, p$) all the local efficiencies are unitary, so the speed-up reduces to the sum of the relative speeds, and each worker executes a number of tasks proportional to its relative speed.

We can therefore define a global efficiency η as

$$\eta = \frac{SU}{SU_{id}} = \frac{\sum_i s_i \cdot \eta_i}{\sum_i s_i} \qquad (15)$$

4 An example: matrix multiplication

To test our model we choose a simple application, the matrix multiplication ($C = A \times B$); here a task consists in multiplying m rows of A by the whole matrix B, which is kept local to each worker to reduce communications.

We note that in this case we have

$$t = N^2 \cdot m \cdot \tau$$

τ being the time to carry out one floating point addition and one floating point multiplication on the reference machine, and

$$N_{inp} = N_{res} = N \cdot m \cdot 4$$

The test program is implemented using the C language and PVM v. 3.4.

We apply the described model to predict the behaviour of matrix multiplication on a network of 13 heterogeneous workstations connected by a switched Ethernet. The workstation models include SGI O2, Sparc-Ultra, Sparc-20, Sparc-10, Sparc-1, and HP-715/33, thus leading to very different speed values. Using these computing nodes we set-up 12 configurations with different total computing power and different degree of heterogeneity. Table 1 summarizes the relative speed of different workstations with respect to the first machine (SGI O2), the considered configurations and the total computing power for each of them.

The trials are executed on dedicated nodes and with a low-medium traffic on the network. We measure on the network the values $\alpha = 1$ $msec$ and $\beta \simeq 1$ μsec.

Using the model it is possible to investigate the optimal task grain. In most applications it is necessary to evaluate a trade-off between communication cost

Table 1. The first row summarizes the relative speed of the nodes of the network; the config. row summarizes the considered configurations (each configuration includes all the nodes up to its column); the last row summarizes the total available power for the corresponding configuration

s_i	1	1	0.55	0.45	0.3	0.3	0.25	0.2	0.15	0.15	0.1	0.1	0.05
Config.	-	C1	C2	C3	C4	C5	C6	C7	C8	C9	C10	C11	C12
$\sum_i s_i$	-	2	2.55	3	3.3	3.6	3.85	4.05	4.2	4.35	4.45	4.55	4.6

and unbalancing, with fine grain providing good balancing figures, and coarse grain improving communications. In the example under consideration computation is dominant and hence the balancing parameter is the most relevant to obtain good performance. Table 2 summarizes the measured and predicted efficiency for the configurations of Table 1, in the case of two matrices of 600x600 double precision elements, with a granularity $m = 3$ (i.e. 3 rows for each task).

Table 2. Simulated vs. measured efficiency for different configurations

Config.	C1	C2	C3	C4	C5	C6	C7	C8	C9	C10	C11	C12
meas. η	0.91	0.91	0.92	0.90	0.92	0.89	0.90	0.87	0.85	0.82	0.83	0.81
sim. η	0.94	0.94	0.93	0.93	0.94	0.93	0.92	0.90	0.88	0.86	0.86	0.72

The results show a good agreement between the model and experiments. It is useful to notice that the simulated results normally provide a slightly optimistic efficiency value, due to a small underestimate of the communication cost. In a case (configuration C12) the model is pessimistic. This is due to an over-scheduling of tasks on the slowest node in the simulation which increases unbalancing and then worses performance.

It is important to point out that the model is useful to estimate trends while it may fail in estimating discrete values. Key aspects are the relative speed measurement and the network parameters set-up. A small change in relative speed may affect simulated results in a heavy manner, especially for highly heterogeneous networks and coarse grain computation, since it may lead to more or less favourable schedules. Moreover, it may be quite difficult to evaluate relative speed values exactly, since many different factors, both at the application level and at the architectural level, can affect them. However, in most cases speed approximations are sufficient since the main interest is in trends, which may be identified by repeating, with small perturbation of relative speeds, critical simulations.

5 Conclusions

We propose a simple model to analyze and predict performance for a class of parallel applications running on heterogeneous networks of workstations with PVM as parallelization tool. Precisely, we deal with data parallel applications executed using the pool of task paradigm and the master-worker computational model.

This computational scheme is simple but it often occurs in real applications. Moreover, it permits a straightforward but effective analysis, able to provide insight into the behaviour of the application varying the task grain and some node and/or network parameters.

The model is tested using the matrix multiplication and a satisfactory agreement is obtained between simulated and experimental figures of performance.

We plan to carry out other experiments with different NOWs and/or applications in order to further asses the reliability of the model.

References

1. Clematis, A., Corana, A.: Modeling performance of heterogeneous parallel computers. Technical Report ICE-CNR n. 3/97 (1997), submitted to Parallel Computing
2. Clematis, A., Corana, A.: Performance analysis of SPMD algorithms on a network of workstations with virtual shared memory. In: D'Hollander, E., Joubert, G., Peters, F., Trottemberg, U. (eds.): Parallel Computing: Fundamentals, Applications and New Directions. Proc. Parallel Computing 97 (ParCo97). Elsevier (in print)
3. Corana A.: Computing the correlation dimension on a network of workstations. Concurrency, Practice and Experience (to appear)
4. Donaldson, V., Berman, F., Paturi, R.: Program speedup in a heterogeneous computing network. J. Parallel and Distributed Computing 21 (1994) 316-322
5. Schmidt, B.K., Sunderam, V.S.: Empirical analysis of overheads in cluster environments. Concurrency, Practice and Experience 6 (1994) 1-32
6. Sunderam, V.S., Geist, G.A., Dongarra, J., Manchek, R.: The PVM concurrent computing system: Evolution, experiences, and trends. Parallel Computing 20 (1994) 531-545
7. Yan, Y., Zhang, X., Song, Y.: An effective and practical performance prediction model for parallel computing on nondedicated heterogeneous NOW. J. Parallel and Distributed Computing 38 (1996) 63-80
8. Zhang, X., Yan, Y.: Modeling and characterizing parallel computing performance on heterogeneous networks of workstations. In: Proc. Seventh IEEE Symp. Parallel Distributed Processing. IEEE Computer Society Press (1995) 25

Automatic Detection of PVM Program Performance Problems[1]

A. Espinosa, T. Margalef, E. Luque.

Computer Science Department
Universitat Autònoma de Barcelona.
08193 Bellaterra, Barcelona, SPAIN.
e-mail: {a.espinosa, t.margalef, iinfd}@cc.uab.es

Abstract. Actual behaviour of parallel programs is of capital importance for the development of an application. Programs will be considered matured applications when their performance is over acceptable limits. Traditional parallel programming forces the programmer to understand the enormous amount of performance information obtained from the execution of a program. In this paper, we propose an automatic analysis tool that lets the programmers of applications avoid this difficult task. This automatic performance analysis tool main objective is to find poor designed structures in the application. It considers the trace file obtained from the execution of the application in order to locate the most important behaviour problems of the application. Then, the tool relates them with the corresponding application code and scans the code looking for any design decision which could be changed to improve the behaviour.

1. Introduction

The performance of a parallel program is one of the main reasons for designing and building a parallel program [1]. When facing the problem of analysing the performance of a parallel program, programmers, designers or occasional parallel systems users must acquire the necessary knowledge to become performance analysis experts.

Traditional parallel program performance analysis has been based on the visualization of several execution graphical views [2, 3, 4, 5]. These high level graphical views represent an abstract description of the execution data obtained from many possible sources and even different executions of the same program [6].

The amount of data to be visualized and analyzed, together with the huge number of sources of information (parallel processors and interconnecting network states, messages between processes, etc.) make this task of becoming a performance expert difficult. Programmers need a high level of experience to be able to derive any

---

[1] This work has been supported by the CICYT under contract number 95-0868

conclusions about the program behaviour using these visualisation tools. Moreover, they also need to have a deep knowledge of the parallel system because the analysis of many performance features must consider architectural aspects like the topology of the system and the interconnection network.

In this paper we describe a Knowledge-based Automatic Parallel Program Analyser for Performance Improvement (KAPPA-PI tool) that eases the performance analysis of a parallel program under the PVM [7] programming model. Analysis experts look for special configurations of the graphical representations of the execution which refer to problems at the execution of the application. Our purpose is to substitute the expert with an automatic analysis tool which, based on a certain knowledge of what the most important performance problems of the parallel applications are, detects the critical execution problems of the application and shows them to the application programmer, together with source code references of the problem found, and indications on how to overcome the problem.

We can find other automatic performance analysis tools which also propose an automatic analysis of the execution of a parallel program in [8, 9, 10]

Performance of a program can also be measured by a pre-compiler, like Fortran approaches (P3T [11]). However, this approach is not applicable to all parallel programs, especially those where the programmer expresses dynamic unstructured behaviour.

In section 2, we describe the analysis methodology briefly, explaining the basis of its operations and the processing steps to detect a performance problem. Finally, section 3 exposes the conclusions and future work on the tool development.

2. Automatic analysis overview

The objective of the automatic performance analysis of parallel programs is to provide information regarding the behaviour of the user's application code.

This information may be obtained analysing statically the code of the parallel program. However, due to the dynamic behaviour of the processes that compose the program and the parallel system features, this static analysis may not be sufficient. Then, execution information is needed to effectively draw any conclusion about the behaviour of the program. This execution information can be collected in a trace file that includes all the events related to the execution of the parallel program. However, the information included in the trace file is not significant to the user who is mainly concerned with the code of the application.

The automatic performance analysis tool concentrates on analysing the behaviour of the parallel application expressed in the trace file in order to detect the most important performance problems. Nonetheless, the analysis process can not stop there and must relate the problems found with the actual code of the application. In this way, user receives meaningful information about the application behaviour.

In figure 1, we represent the basic analysis cycle followed by the tool to analyse the behaviour of a parallel application.

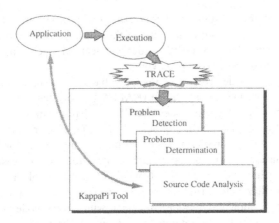

Fig. 1. Schema of the analysis of a parallel application.

The analysis first considers the study of the trace file in order to locate the most important performance problems occurring at the execution. Once those problematic execution intervals have been found, they are studied individually to determinate the type of performance problem for each execution interval.

When the problem is classified under a specific category, the analysis tool scans the segment of application source code related to the execution data previously studied. This analysis of the code brings out any design problem that may have produced the performance problem. Finally, the analysis tool produces an explanation of the problems found at this application design level and recommends what should be changed in the application code to improve its execution behaviour.

In the following points, the operations performed by the analysis tool are explained in detail.

2.1. Problem Detection

The first part of the analysis is the study of the trace file obtained from the execution of the application. In this phase, the analysis tool scans the trace file, obtained with the use of TapePVM [12], with the purpose of following the evolution of the efficiency of the application. The application efficiency is basically found by measuring the number of processors that are not idle during a certain time.

The analysis tool collects those execution time intervals when the efficiency is minimum. These intervals represent those situations where the application is not using all the capabilities of the parallel machine. In order to analyse these intervals further, the analysis tool selects those intervals that affect the most number of processors for the longest time.

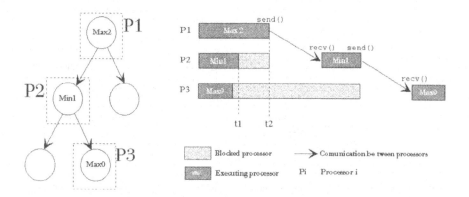

Fig. 2. Application trace file space-time diagram. The analysis tool finds an interval of low efficiency when processors P2 and P3 are idle due to the blocking of the processes "Min1" and "Max0". Then, the execution interval (t1,t2) is considered for further study.

For each problem, only those minimum efficiency situations that are found to be present all along the execution (accumulating up to a certain percentage of the execution time) are considered to be important for further study.

2.2. Problem Determination

Once the most important inefficiencies are found, the analysis tool proceeds to classify the performance with the help of a "knowledge base" of performance problems. This classification is implemented in the form of a problem tree, as seen in figure 3. Each inefficiency problem is exhaustively studied in order to find which branches in the tree describe the problem in a more accurate way.

In the previous example, the analysis tool tries to classify this problem found under one of the categories. To do so, it studies the number of ready-to-execute processes in the interval. As there are no ready processes, it classifies the problem as "lack of ready processes". The analysis tool also finds that the processors are not just idle, but waiting for a message to arrive, so the problem is classified as a communication related.

Then, the analysis tool must find out what the appropriate communication problem is. It starts analyzing the last process (Max0) which is waiting for a message from Min1 process. When the tool tries to study what the Min1 process was doing at that time, it finds that Min1 was already waiting for a message from Max2, so the analysis tool classifies this problem as a blocked sender problem, sorting the process sequence: Max2 sends a message to Min1 and Min1 sends a message to Max0.

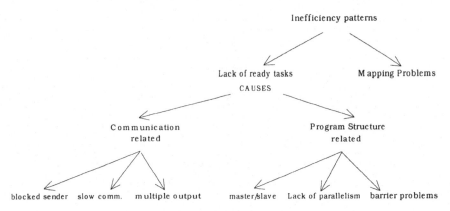

Fig. 3. Classification of the performance problems of an application

2.3. Application of the source code analysis

At this stage of the program evaluation, the analysis tool has found a performance problem in the execution trace file and has classified it under one category.

The aim of the analysis tool at this point is to point out any relationship between the application structure and the performance problem found. This detailed analysis differ from one performance problem to another, but basically consists of the application of several techniques of pattern recognition to the code of the application.

First of all, the analysis tool must select those portions of source code of the application that generated the performance problem when executed.

With the help of the trace file, the tool is able to relate the execution events of certain operations, like sending or receiving a message, to a certain line number in the program code. Therefore, the analysis tool is able to find which instructions in the source code generated a certain behaviour at execution time. Each pattern-matching technique tries to test a certain condition of the source code related to the problem found. For each of the matches obtained in this phase, the analysis tool will generate some explanations of the problem found, the bounds of the problem and what possible alternatives there are to alleviate the problem.

A complete list of performance problems, as well as their implications of the source code of the application can be found at [13].

Following the application of the example in this phase of the analysis, the tool wants to analyse the data dependencies between the messages sent by processes Max2, Min1 and Max0 (see figure 1).

The analysis tool opens the source code file of process Min1 and scans it looking for the send and the receive operations performed. From there, it collects the name of the variables which are actually used to send and receive the messages. This part of the code is expressed on figure 4.

```
1    pvm_recv(-1,-1);
2    pvm_upkfl(&calc,1,1);
3    calc1 = min(calc,1);
4    for(i=0;i<sons;i++)
5    {
6        pvm_initsend(PvmDataDefault);
7        pvm_pkfl(&calc1,1,1);
8        pvm_send(tid_son[i],1);
9    }
```

Fig. 4. "Min1.c" relevant portion of source code.

When the variables are found ("calc" and "calc1" at the example) , the analysis tool starts searching the source code of process "Min1" to find all possible relationships between both variables. As these variables define the communication dependence of the processes, the results of these tests will describe the designed relationship between the processes.

In this example, the dependency test is found true due to the instruction found at line 5, which relates "calc1" with the value of "calc". This dependency means that the message sent to process "Max0" depends on the message received from process "Max2".

The recommendation produced to the user explains this situation of dependency found. The analysis tool suggests the modification of the design of the parallel application in order to distribute part of the code of process "Min1" (the instructions that modify the variable to send) to process "Max0", and then send the same message to "Min1" and to "Max0". This message shown to the user is expressed in figure 5.

```
Analysing  MaxMin....
A Blocked Sender situation has been found in the execution.
Processes involved are:
Max0, Min1, Max2
Recommendation: A dependency between Max2 and Max0 found.
The design of the application should be revised.
Line 5 of Min1 process should be distributed to Max0.
```

Fig. 5. Output of the analysis tool.

This line 5 should be executed in the process Max2, so variable "calc" must be sent to Max2 to solve the expression. Then, the codes of the processes may be changed as follows in figure 6.

In the new processes code, the dependencies between Min1 and Max2 processes have been eliminated. From the execution of these processes we obtain a new trace file, shown in figure 7. In the figure, the process Max2 does not have to wait so long until the message arrives. As a consequence, the execution time of this part of the application has been reduced.

```
 . . .
pvm_recv(-1,-1);
pvm_upkfl(&calc,1,1);
calc1 = min(calc,1);
 . . .
```

Process Min1

```
 . . .
pvm_recv(-1,-1);
pvm_upkfl(&calc,1,1);
calc1 = min(calc,1);
 . . .
```

Process Max0

```
calc = min(old,myvalue);
pvm_initsend(PvmDataDefault);
pvm_pkfl(&calc,1,1);
pvm_send(tid_Min1,1);
pvm_send(tid_Max0,1);
 . . .
```

Process Max2

Fig. 6. New process code

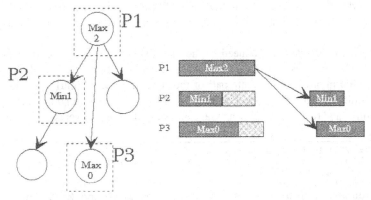

Fig. 7. Space-state diagram of the new execution of the application

3. Conclusions

Programmers must be aware of the behaviour side-effects of introducing changes in the applications when following the suggestion provided by the tool. Hence, once the application code is rebuilt, new analysis should be considered.

Moreover, some problems may be produced by more than one cause. Sometimes it is difficult to separate the different causes of the problems and propose the most adequate solution. This process of progressive analysis of problems with multiple causes is one of the future fields of tool development.

Future work on the tool will consider the increment and refinement of the causes of performance problems, the "knowledge base". The programming model of the analysed applications must also be extended from the currently used (PVM) to other parallel programming paradigms.

But far greater efforts must be focused on the optimisation of the search phases of the program. The search for problems in the trace file and the analysis of causes for a certain problem must be optimised to operate on very large trace files. The computational cost of analysing the trace file to derive these results is not irrelevant, although the tool is built not to generate much more overhead than the operations needed for visual processing of a trace file.

References

1. Pancake, C. M., Simmons, L. M., Yan, J. C.: Performance Evaluation Tools for Parallel and Distributed Systems. IEEE Computer, November 1995, vol. 28, p. 16-19.
2. Heath, M. T., Etheridge, J. A.: Visualizing the performance of parallel programs. IEEE Computer, November 1995, vol. 28, p. 21-28 .
3. Kohl, J.A. and Geist, G.A.: XPVM Users Guide. Tech. Report. Oak Ridge National Laboratory, 1995.
4. Reed, D. A., Aydt, R. A., Noe, R. J., Roth, P. C., Shields, K. A., Schwartz, B. W. and Tavera, L. F.: Scalable Performance Analysis: The Pablo Performance Analysis Environment. Proceedings of Scalable Parallel Libraries Conference. IEEE Computer Society, 1993.
5. Reed, D. A., Giles, R. C., Catlett, C. E.. Distributed Data and Immersive Collaboration. Communications of the ACM. November 1997. Vol. 40, No 11. p. 39-48.
6. Karavanic, K. L. and Miller, B. P.: Experiment Management Support for Performance Tuning. International Conference on Supercomputing, San José, CA, USA, November 1997.
7. Geist, A., Beguelin, A., Dongarra, J. , Jiang, W., Manchek, R. and Sunderam, V.: PVM: Parallel Virtual Machine, A User's Guide and Tutorial for Network Parallel Computing. MIT Press, Cambridge, MA, 1994.
8. Hollingsworth, J. K. and Miller, B. P.: Dynamic Control of Performance Monitoring on Large Scale Parallel Systems. International Conference on Supercomputing , Tokyo, July 1993.
9. Yan, J. C., Sarukhai, S R.: Analyzing parallel program performance using normalized performance indices and trace transformation techniques. Parallel Computing 22 (1996) 1215-1237.
10. Crovella, M. E. and LeBlanc, T. J.: The search for Lost Cycles: A New approach to parallel performance evaluation. TR479. The University of Rochester, Computer Science Department, Rochester, New York, December 1994.
11. Fahringer, T.: Automatic Performance Prediction of Parallel Programs. Kluwer Academic Publishers. 1996
12. Maillet, E.: TAPE/PVM an efficient performance monitor for PVM applications-user guide, LMC-IMAG Grenoble, France. June 1995.
13. Espinosa, A., Margalef, T. and Luque, E.: Automatic Performance Evaluation of Parallel Programs. Proc. of the 6th EUROMICRO Workshop on Parallel and Distributed Processing, pp. 43-49. IEEE CS. 1998.

Evaluating and Modeling Communication Overhead of MPI Primitives on the Meiko CS-2

Gianluigi Folino, Giandomenico Spezzano and Domenico Talia

ISI-CNR, c/o DEIS, UNICAL, 87036 Rende (CS), Italy
Phone: +39 984 839047, Fax: +39 984 839054
Email:{spezzano, talia}@si.deis.unical.it

Abstract. The MPI (Message Passing Interface) is a standard communication library implemented on a large number of parallel computers. It is used for the development of portable parallel software. This paper presents, evaluates and compares the performance of the point-to-point and broadcast communication primitives of the MPI standard library on the Meiko CS-2 parallel machine. Furthermore, the paper proposes a benchmark model of MPI communications based on the size of messages exchanged and the number of involved processors. Finally, the MPI performance results on the CS-2 are compared with the performance of the Meiko Elan Widget library and the IBM SP2.

1 Introduction

Message passing systems simplify the concurrent software development on parallel computers by separating the hardware architecture from the software configuration of processes. Next generation parallel computers will be multi-user general-purpose machines. To achieve this goal, efficient high-level message passing systems are needed. These systems represent a critical aspect in the design and practical use of parallel machines based on message passing. In fact, inter-process communication is the main source of overhead in parallel programs. On the other hand, the use of a general-purpose communication system allows a programmer to develop parallel programs without worrying about the details of the hardware configuration. This approach increases code portability and reusability. For these reasons it is very important that parallel computers provide message passing systems that are efficient and offer a user high-level communication mechanisms to design complex communication patterns.

In the past decade, several communication systems for multicomputers have been implemented. Some of them have been developed for a particular architecture whereas others are more general. Examples of these systems are Express, P4 [2], PARMACS and ZipCode. The need of portable communication facilities for a very large set of parallel architectures leaded to the definition of the MPI (*Message Passing Interface*) standard library [8], which embodies the main features of those earlier systems.

This paper presents, evaluates and compares the performance of the point-to-point and broadcast communication primitives of the MPI standard library on the Meiko CS-2 parallel machine. Furthermore, the paper proposes a benchmark model of MPI communications based on the size of messages exchanged and the number of involved processors. Finally, the MPI performance results on the CS-2 are compared with the performance of the Meiko Elan Widget library and the IBM SP2.

2 CS-2 Overview

The CS-2 (Computing Surface 2) is a distributed memory MIMD parallel computer. It consists of Sparc based processing nodes running the Solaris operating system on each node, so it resembles a cluster of workstations connected by a fast network. Each computing node is composed of one or more Sparc processors, a communication co-processor, the Elan processor, that connects each node to a fat tree network built from Meiko 8x8 crosspoint switches [1][6]. For maximum floating point performance, each node can be optionally equipped with a vector unit. The CS-2 network provides a bi-sectional bandwidth that scales linearly in the number of nodes. Each link in the network is byte wide and clocked at 70 MHz. This gives, after protocol overheads, a user level bandwidth of around 50 Mbytes/link/direction. Our machine is a 12 processors CS-2 based on 200 MHz HyperSparc processors running Solaris 2.5.1.

3 Performance Evaluation and Modeling

In this section, we describe the experimental results obtained running a collection of benchmark programs on a CS-2 to measure the overhead of the main communication primitives of the MPI library. Furthermore, a comparison with the results obtained for the low-level Elan Widget library and those provided by Miguel et al. [7] for the IBM SP2 is presented.

3.1 Benchmarks

The measurements obtained from each experiment concern the minimum, maximum and average values of latency and throughput. The results obtained for the minimum and average values are very close in many cases. The maximum values are considered to show the influence of the operating system. The MPI library is the public version 1.0.13 of *MPICH*. Here we shortly describe the main features of the test programs.

Ping-pong test. This test is based on the code provided by Dongarra and Dunigam [3] and measures the communication times of point-to-point primitives.

Broadcast test. The broadcast test has been executed sending a broadcast message from processor 0, that is the *root* processor, to all the 10 processors used (including itself).

Reduction test. This test is like the previous one, but uses the *MPI_Reduce* instead of *MPI_Bcast*.

Random-2 sets test. The random test has been executed allocating one process per processor and partitioning the available processors in two groups: those with even rank and those with odd. An even process sends data to any one of odd processes, randomly chosen, which responds immediately.

3.2 Experimental Measurements

Figure 1 shows the measured values of the MPI point-to-point communication latency.

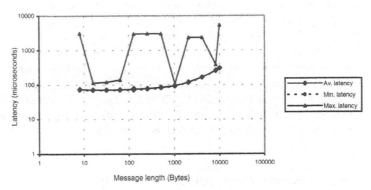

Fig. 1. MPI point-to-point communication latency.

How we can see in figure 1, the average values of the latency are very close to the

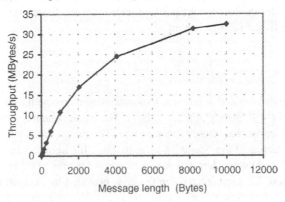

Fig. 2. Point-to-point communication throughput.

minimum values. This demonstrates that the MPI point-to-point communications on the CS-2 have a regular behavior. The measured maximum values are due to the way the operating system schedules the execution of the test processes. Although maximum latency shows in some points very high values, these are rare and have not much impact on the calculus of average values.

Figure 2 shows the measured throughput of MPI point-to-point communications. The trend is that awaited and it tends to the throughput value of 50 Mbytes/s in each direction provided by the manufacturer.

Figure 3 summarizes the results of the average latency of collective communications. While for small messages *MPI_Bcast* and *MPI_Reduce* have quite similar costs, for large messages (>3000 bytes) the cost measured for *MPI_Reduce* is greater than *MPI_Bcast* cost because the reduce operation requires a further phase of communication to return the results to the root process.

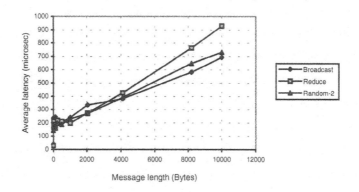

Fig. 3. Average latency of broadcast, reduce e random-2 operations.

3.3 Models of Point-to-point and Collective Communications

In this section, we present the models to characterize the communication times for MPI point-to-point and broadcast communications on a CS-2. These models have been validated using the experimental data previously presented. They represent an efficacy way to accurately estimate the costs of the MPI primitives on the CS-2.

Point-to-point communications. The Hockney's model is one of the most meaningful model to describe the point-to-point communication on parallel machines with distributed memory [5]. According to this model, the communication latency can be expressed as:

$$t = t_0 + \frac{m}{r_\infty} \tag{1}$$

where t_0 is the *startup* time (in microseconds), which is the time needed to send a 0-byte message, m is the message length (bytes) and r_∞ is the asymptotic bandwidth in Mbytes per second, which is the maximal bandwidth achievable when the length approaches infinity. m / r_∞ represents the transmission delay in passing an m-byte message through a network with an asymptotic bandwidth of r_∞ Mbytes/s.

To apply the Hockney's model we calculated the values of t_0 and r_∞. The best fitting between the straight lines obtained by the equation 1 and the experimental curve has been performed by Matlab. The values obtained are $t_0 = 71.17$ and $r_\infty = 42.19$ Mbytes/s, therefore $1/ r_\infty = 0.0237$, so the formula 1 is equal to:

$$t = 71.17 + 0.0237m \qquad (2)$$

The equation 2 gives a careful description of the trend of the point-to-point communication costs as shown in figure 4 where the latency predicted from the model is compared with the experimental average latency.

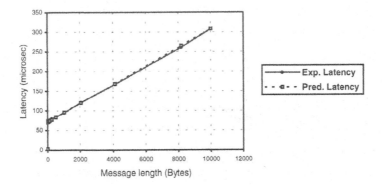

Fig. 4. Comparison of predicted and experimental point-to-point latency.

Collective communications. The Hockney's model applies only to point-to-point communications and therefore it does not allow to model collective communications. Xu and Hwang have defined a simple model that extends the Hockney's model. The Xu and Hwang's model [9] defines the collective communication latency as

$$t = t_0(n) + \frac{m}{r_\infty(n)} \qquad (3)$$

where n is the number of nodes involved in a communication and the other quantities are the same of those above defined. As in the Hockney's model, the latency is a linear function of the message length (m). However, the startup time and the asymptotic bandwidth are both functions, not necessarily linear, of the number of nodes. Although, the formula 3 applies to all the collective communication forms we have used it to model the broadcast operation that is the most used among the collective communication forms. In this case, after the experimental measurements, data have been interpolated and we obtained the following functions for the startup $t_0 = 55.94 \; logn$ and for the asymptotic bandwidth $1/ r_\infty(n) = 0.0167 \; logn$. Substituting these functions in 3 we obtain the equation of the latency for the MPI broadcast communication on the CS-2

$$t = 55.94 \log n + (0.0167 \log n) m \qquad (4)$$

The equation 4 gives a description very close to the experimental data of the latency of broadcast communications as shown in figure 5 where the predicted data are compared with the experimental data of the average latency obtained on 10 nodes of a CS-2.

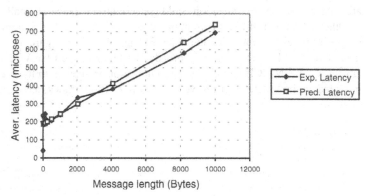

Fig. 5. Comparison of predicted and experimental broadcast latency.

3.4 MPI and Widget Elan Library

Figure 6 compares MPI and Widget Elan Library communications. The main goal of these measurements and comparisons is to evaluate the effectiveness of the MPICH implementation on the CS-2 and identify the bottlenecks to be removed to obtain an optimized version of MPI for the CS-2.

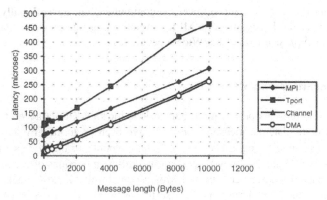

Fig. 6. Comparison of MPI and Elan Widget point-to-point latency.

The tests executed using the Elan Widget library are based on the programs (*cping, dping, tping, gping*) provided by the manufacturer and concern the three main communication forms provided by Elan Widget library (*DMA,Channel and Tport*). The performance of the MPI functions is comparable with those of Elan Widget

Channel and DMA, but it is better than those of the *Tport* type. In particular, the DMA and Channel functions are more efficient for message sizes smaller than 4 Kbytes, while for messages longer than 4 Kbytes, the MPI functions have a lower latency. From these data, we might deduce that the MPICH point-to-point primitives are efficient and any optimization could concern the exchange of small messages.

Other than point-to-point communication, we measured the communication times of the broadcast operation of the Elan Widget library. In figure 7 we compare the latency of the MPI broadcast with broadcast latency of the Elan Widget library. The latency of the MPICH broadcast communication is meaningfully greater than that provided by the low-level primitives of the CS-2. This demonstrates that MPICH does

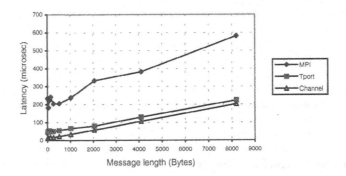

Fig. 7. Comparison of MPI and Elan Widget broadcast latency.

not exploit the collective communication features provided by the CS-2. An optimized version of MPICH could improve the implementation of the collective communications if we want to lower the communication times. Finally, we can note that the irregular behavior of the MPI communication for small messages (up to 256 bytes) is not present in the Elan Widget primitives.

3.5 Comparison with SP2

This section presents performance comparison for the MPI library on CS-2 and IBM SP2. In particular, the measures on SP2 have been performed by Miguel et al. [7] using the same test programs on two different versions of the SP2 (we indicate these versions as SP2 and SP2-new) based on two different versions of the interconnection switch that provide respectively 40 Mbytes/s and 160 Mbytes/s peak bandwidth in each direction. Both these versions use the operating system AIX v4 and a native version of MPI developed by IBM.

Figure 8 we shows that point-to-point communications with small messages (up to 512 bytes) on SP2-new are the most efficient. This is a behavior expected because SP2-new use a faster switch and an optimized version of MPI.

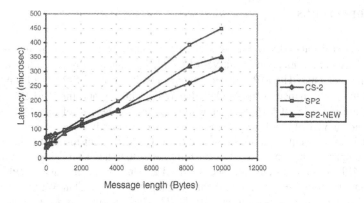

Fig. 8. Comparison of MPI point-to–point latency on the CS-2 and SP2.

For message size comprised between 512 and 4 Kbytes, the CS-2 times are similar to those of the SP2-new, while they are better than the SP2 ones. This positive trend for the CS-2 is more evident for message longer than 4 Kbytes, where the CS-2 is the most efficient, although it uses a communication system with lower hardware bandwidth and a non-native MPI implementation.

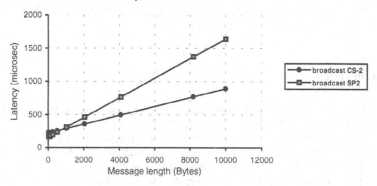

Fig. 9. Comparison of MPI predicted latency on the CS-2 and SP2.

Figure 9 compares the broadcast communication latency on the CS-2 and SP2. The results for the SP2 machine have been achieved using 16 nodes while those for the CS-2 machine have been achieved on 10 nodes. To homogenize the results we compared theoretical data, computed with the performance models, assuming the same number of processors for the two parallel machines. In figure 9 we can see that for small messages (up to 1024 bytes) the latency for the two machines is similar, while for longer message the latency of MPI on the CS-2 is lower in comparison with the latency on the SP2.

4 Conclusions

This paper discussed and evaluated the performance results of the point-to-point and broadcast communication primitives of the MPI-1 standard library on the Meiko CS-2 parallel machine. The MPICH performance results on the CS-2 have been compared with the performance of the Meiko Elan Widget library and the IBM SP2. Finally, a benchmark model of MPI communications based on the size of messages exchanged and the number of involved processors has been proposed.

The experimental results show that the CS-2 MPI point-to-point communications are comparable and in some cases perform better than the Elan Widget primitives and the MPI communications on the IBM SP2. On the other hand, MPI collective communications are not so efficient in comparison with Elan Widget whereas are more efficient in comparison with IBM SP2. These results are positive for the CS-2, although they could be improved by providing a new version of the MPI collective communications on the CS-2 that can be implemented by using the efficient collective communication facilities of the Elan Widget library.

Acknowledgements

This research has been carried out under a contract with QSW in the framework of the PQE1 project funded by ENEA/QSW.

References

1. E. Barton, J. Cownie, and M. McLaren, "Message Passing on the Meiko CS-2", *Parallel Computing*, , North-Holland, vol. 20, pp. 497-507, 1994.
2. R. Butler and E. Lusk, "Monitors, Messages, and Clusters: The P4 Parallel Programming System", *Parallel Computing*, North-Holland, vol. 20, pp. 547-564, 1994.
3. J.J. Dongarra and T. Dunigan, "Message Passing Performance on Varius Computers", Tech. Report UT/CS-95-229, Computer Science Dept., University of Tennessee, Knoxville, 1995. Available at http://www.cs.utk.edu/~library/1995.html.
4. W. Gropp, E. Lusk, N. Doss, and A. Skjellum, "A High-Performance, Portable Implementation of the MPI Message Passing Interface Standard", *Parallel Computing*, North-Holland, vol. 22, pp. 789-828, 1996.
5. R.W. Hockney, "The Communication Challenge for MPP: Intel Paragon and Meiko CS-2", *Parallel Computing*, North-Holland, vol. 20, pp. 389-398, 1994.
6. C.E. Leiserson, "Fat-trees: Universal Networks for Hardware-Efficient Supercomputing", *IEEE Transactions on Computers*, vol. C-34, no. 10, pp. 892-901, 1985.
7. J.Miguel, A. Arruabarrena, R. Beivide, and J.A. Gregorio, "Assessing the Performance of the New IBM SP2 Communication Subsystem", *IEEE Parallel and Distributed Technology*, pp. 12-22, Winter 1996.
8. M. Snir, S. W. Otto, S. Huss-Lederman, D. W. Walker, and J. Dongarra, *MPI: The Complete Reference*, The MIT Press, 1996.
9. Z. Xu and K. Hwang, "Modeling Communication Overhead: MPI and MPL Performance on the IBM SP2", *IEEE Parallel and Distributed Technology*, pp. 9-23, Spring 1996.

A Parallel I/O Test Suite

D. Lancaster[1], C. Addison[2], and T. Oliver[2]

[1] University of Southampton, Southampton, U.K.
[2] Fujitsu European Centre for Information Technology, Uxbridge, U.K.
addison@fecit.co.uk,
WWW page: http://www.fecit.co.uk

Abstract. Amongst its many features, MPI-2 offers the first standard high-performance I/O interface. While this enables a parallel and I/O intensive code to run on multiple platforms, achieving consistent performance levels will be more difficult than many users imagine. To better understand the I/O performance issues in MPI-2, *fecit* and Southampton have developed a parallel I/O test suite for Fujitsu Japan. The design of this test suite is presented, along with a discussion concerning the need for a validation suite for MPI-2 as a whole.

1 Introduction

There are few who will dispute the significant benefit that MPI has brought to those developing software for distributed memory parallel systems. Part of the reason for the success of MPI was the presence of high quality, free distributions, such as MPICH [1], that worked well on a range of architectures.

As with any successful software product, there were features that were intentionally omitted. These included:

- support for parallel I/O operations,
- single-sided communications,
- dynamic processes.

The MPI-2 standard [2] was developed to address these "omissions" and several other important issues, such as language bindings for C++ and Fortran 90.

It is the provision of support for parallel I/O, through the set of routines collectively called MPI-I/O, that is the most exciting of MPI-2's new features. I/O has long been a largely underdeveloped field of computing. This is particularly true in parallel computing, where users were obliged to use vendor specific I/O models that did not always address the major difficulties. MPI-I/O offers the first standard high-performance I/O interface. That deserves considerable credit, but it must also be viewed as just the start of the process.

Coping with I/O is a non-trivial task and MPI-I/O has a rich feature set. A degree of experimentation is required to understand how the different MPI-I/O routines function together. Fortunately, there are portable implementations of MPI-I/O freely available, so that users can experiment with these to gain some of this understanding. This process is aided by the availability of the MPI-I/O test codes developed at Lawrence Livermore National Laboratory [3].

Performance tuning, both from the point of view of using MPI-I/O and from the point of view of supporting MPI-I/O, requires an additional set of tools. *fecit* and the University of Southampton have developed an I/O test suite for Fujitsu Japan to address part of this need.

2 Design principles of the I/O test suite

The Parallel I/O Test Suite is a timely tool to investigate new developments in parallel I/O. In order to best address this goal, tools rather than benchmarks are emphasised, so the suite is directly under the control of the user, and thus implicitly less "automatic". The analysis requirements are greater than for a simple benchmark so the data gathering is separated from analysis to simplify the tests themselves, yet allow analysis of varying degrees of sophistication. Past benchmarking offerings have been criticised as being too complicated for most users, so simplicity has been required of both the tests themselves and of the run procedure.

Notable features of the Test Suite are:

- The tests are organised into low-level and kernel classes.
- Tools rather than benchmarks are emphasised.
- The tests are simple and the timings have clear significance.
- Data gathering is separated from analysis.
- No model for the behaviour of the data is assumed.
- Curves of data are generated rather than single numbers.
- The tests are not intended to comprise a validation suite for MPI-I/O and do not exercise all the advanced features of MPI-I/O.

These features are discussed in detail below along with some of the design criteria for the analysis stage. Some of the design choices arise from evaluation of serial I/O tests (for example [4]) and MPI-1 benchmark suites [5, 6].

2.1 Lessons from serial I/O testing

Some common issues in I/O testing that have had a bearing on the whole suite of tests have become clear in the context of serial I/O testing [4]. The most important issue that must be faced relates to the effect of the hierarchy of intermediate cache levels between the CPU and the final output device. Even when a write request has completed, one cannot be sure that the information resides on disk instead of in some cache. One strategy to ensure that the limiting bandwidth is measured and that the information is on disk, is to write sufficiently large files that fill up and overwhelm the cache. This strategy is not very efficient, since it requires considerable time to write the large files required. It can also be regarded as artificial to bypass the cache because it is an intrinsic part of the I/O system. A partial resolution to this issue is to measure a curve of bandwidths for different filesizes.

When mixing writing and reading, the same cache effects found in the write tests can be seen when reading data that was recently written and that still resides on the cache. This pattern of many reads and writes naturally occurs in the low-level tests because of the need for self checking. A useful feature of MPI is the MPI_file_sync call which flushes the cache to the storage device, and can be used between write and read calls. This call alone does not remove the possibility that a copy of the written data is still in cache. A further point is that compilers are sometimes capable of optimising code so as not to actually perform a read if the data is not used, this means that the data read must always be "touched" in some way.

Another relevant issue that arises in serial I/O testing is the fluctuations in repeated measurements. This is present in all modern systems, even on a dedicated system. This will be discussed at greater length below in section 2.8.

2.2 Low-level and kernel classes

The tests are classified as either Low-Level or Kernel along the lines of PARK-BENCH [6], with the intention of testing the system at different levels.

Lowlevel: Measures fundamental parameters and checks essential features of the implementation. Allows performance bottlenecks to be identified in conjunction with expected performance levels. The tests in this class are:
 - single measures the bandwidth of a single process to write and read a disk file.
 - multiple tests multiple processes operating on a disk file.
 - singleI is the baseline for asynchronous I/O where I/O is interleaved with computation.
 - multipleI is the multi-process equivalent to singleI.
 - sinunix is similar to single except Fortran I/O calls are made rather than MPI-I/O.

Kernel: Tests the MPI implementation at a more advanced level with a wider range more characteristic of real applications. Allows comparisons between implementations. The tests in this class are:
 - matrix2D and matrix3D measure I/O on regular multidimensional arrays. Motivating applications include simulations of 2 or 3 dimensional physical systems, for example computational fluid dynamics, seismic data processing and electronic structure calculations.
 - nonseq measures non-sequential I/O such as arises in database applications, medical image management and the recovery of partial mapping images.
 - gatherscat2D tests Gather/Scatter combined with I/O. This series of steps is often employed when running applications on parallel machines with limited I/O capability. It is interesting to compare multidimensional array I/O rates using this method with fully parallel output.

- **sharedfp** tests I/O using a shared filepointer. This is frequently necessary when writing a log file or when checkpointing.
- **transpose** measures I/O when performing an out-of-core transpose operation on large arrays. Transpose operations are frequently used when performing multidimensional Fourier transforms.

Attention has focussed on tests that address fundamental issues. These are the low-level class of tests and the matrix tests in the kernel class.

2.3 Performance tools

The requirements for a detailed investigation and analysis of the parallel I/O system are not compatible with an automated style of benchmark which supplies a single number characterising performance at the push of a button. We anticipate that the tests will be employed by someone who already has a reasonable knowledge of the system under test and who can estimate the range of parameter values that are of interest. The tests therefore do not self-scale over the huge ranges potentially possible and the user is fully in control of selecting parameter values. As his or her understanding of the system evolves, the user will be able to use more of the tests to concentrate attention on the parameter space of greatest interest.

2.4 Simplicity of tests and their usage

It is important to build upon past work in similar areas. For example, PARK-BENCH has been criticised on the basis of relevancy, expense and ease of use [7]. We insist upon well-defined goals that justify the run time required and in addition we require simplicity of the tests, which must be:

- Easy to understand
- Easy to use
- Have a low overhead (and therefore execute quickly)
- Small (in terms of size of code)

A primary reason for simple code is to clearly expose the precise significance of the timing measurements. The best way to fully understand the meaning of the timings is to look in the code at the location of the timer calls and this is most easily achieved when the code is simple.

The suite interface is designed to be convenient to use and the choice of which tests to run along with the parameters to use is made with a system of keywords in an input file. This system allows many tests, or one test with several parameters, to be submitted together.

In the Low-Level class, simplicity of the tests themselves is particularly important. One might imagine that low-level codes would inevitably be small, easy and quick to run and that difficulty would only arise later when the same simplicity requirements are imposed on more complicated codes. In fact, because of the large quantities of data that must be written to test the system in a genuine manner and the wide range of parameter values that must be checked, even these low-level tests can be very time consuming.

2.5   Separate data gathering from analysis

The running of the tests is separated from the analysis of the data they provide. This approach helps keep the test suite simple yet allows the analysis to be performed at whatever level of complexity is desired. This is necessary because the suite is emphatically for testing rather than benchmarking, so it requires a wider variety and more flexible and sophisticated possibilities of analysis than a benchmark would.

2.6   No data fitting assumptions

Because the suite is intended to provide genuine tests, no model for the behaviour of the data is assumed. For example, PARKBENCH has been criticised because it forces the data to fit a particular model which was not always valid. Only by looking at the raw data can one test whether a particular assumption is valid.

The analysis therefore consists of several stages starting with an exploration of the raw data produced by the simplest low-level tests. The data can provide empirical feedback to analytic models of individual I/O functions. Provided the behaviour can be understood within the context of a target model, one can then proceed with more complicated tests and more sophisticated levels of analysis. The validity of any analytic model must be checked at each new level.

2.7   Curves not single numbers

Although there is little freedom in the basic form of a low-level class I/O test, the choice of parameters, such as the block and file sizes, are of great significance. From experience with serial I/O tests it is clear that a single number describing the bandwidth is not sufficient and that at least one, and probably several, curves are needed to characterise the behaviour of the system. For example, a curve may represent bandwidth as a function of block size, with a different curve plotted for each of several different file sizes. Although we do not adopt any particular data model, we strongly recommend that a full analysis of this type is performed.

Notwithstanding the limitations of a single number, the bandwidth that can be measured by overwhelming any cache mechanism using sufficiently large filesizes is still an important reference. This bandwidth may indeed be relevant to a variety of applications where the cache mechanism is unable to operate effectively but more significantly it acts as a fixed (in the sense that it does not change as the filesize is further increased) reference for the curves which describe the full behaviour of the system.

Another issue is the accuracy of the measurements. An estimate of the accuracy should be calculated and reported as error bars on the curves.

2.8   Data from low-Level tests

For the low-level tests, considerable depth of analysis is possible and the data collected is more than just a single number per filesize and blocksize. Preliminary work has suggested that it is important to measure the time of each write command rather than simply take an implicit average by measuring the time for the full loop. This helps compensate for the fact that modern operating systems can cause large fluctuations in the time taken for successive writes, even on a quiescent machine. Although a single number describing the bandwidth at that blocksize can be derived, the additional data gathered provides interesting information about the system. For example one can check that the machine is as dedicated as expected. The data also provides information about startup effects and this data can be used to produce error bars on the curves. The quantity and potential complexity of data gathered in this way allows for different levels of analysis in the low-level class.

3 Status of the test library

The Parallel I/O Test Suite has only been extensively tested on a prototype MPI-2 implementation on a 4 processor vector system. Preliminary results suggest that most of the test suite works with publically available implementations of MPI-I/O on the Ultra-SPARC based E10000 (from Sun Microsystems) and the AP3000 (from Fujitsu).

Comprehensive tests on these systems using more processors (allowing a 2-D process grid) and larger problem sizes are planned. Such tests will help quantify limitations of the test suite, for instance, with gatherscat2D, memory will become a problem with large matrices.

4 Validating MPI-2 implementations

The emphasis of the project has been to develop a suitable test suite for MPI-I/O programs. There have been many occasions when it would have been useful to have had access to a suite that checked whether part of MPI-2 was supported correctly in an implementation.

To address the different needs of users, a multi-layered validation suite would be needed, with layers such as:

– Baseline level: functional tests to validate correct behaviour of routines used in correct programs. Test sub-classes within this class are necessary. For instance, simple tests would concentrate on a single feature set (such as MPI-I/O or single sided communications) while complex tests might also test for the correct interworking between functionalities (such as MPI-I/O and single sided communications used together). Similar test sets should be developed for each language binding and some tests should involve mixed language programs.

– Robust level: tests to assess whether "sensible" actions are taken (reporting mechanisms etc.) when errors are detected. Tests at the robust level would also determine critical resource limitations and attempt to determine what happens when these limits are exceeded. MPI-I/O contains a large amount of state information (partly because files are involved). Some of the robust tests should determine the correctness of this information and whether the same state information is returned on successive MPI calls.

– Performance level: tests here would not be a full test of all of MPI-2 features. A layered approach is again required, with low-level routines providing users with an understanding of the salient components of performance on a system and more sophisticated tests providing detailed data to better understand some of the subtle performance implications.

The Parallel I/O test suite described here can serve as a model for the latter category. It also addresses the needs for a performance I/O test suite.

There are MPI-1.1 test suites (such as the one available from Intel, [8]) that are quite comprehensive with both C and Fortran 77 interfaces. Since MPI-1.2 is a relatively simple enhancement of MPI-1.1, such existing suites can be improved to cover it relatively cheaply. The test programs from LLNL for MPI-I/O, [3], while not comprehensive, are also a start in the right direction.

So much for the good news. MPI-1.2 defines 129 interfaces while MPI-2 defines a further 188 interfaces and extends another 28. Therefore, assuming that each routine is equally difficult to test, covering the new features of MPI-2 would take about 1.5 times the effort to produce an MPI-1.2 test suite.

In addition, there are C++ bindings to take into account. Some benefits should transfer from producing a validation suite in C to C++, but it would not be trivial. Furthermore, there are a range of quality questions associated with the C++ (and to a lesser extent Fortran 90) bindings that would not be relevant for the C / Fortran 77 bindings. There are also questions relating to heterogeneous environments, particularly in terms of data formats and performance that would be interesting to answer.

Clearly, if some form of validation suite is to be produced in a reasonable time frame, a cooperative venture is required. This not only means pooling resources, but also means building a pool of shared common experience to better target effort on those areas that appear to be most relevant. This is perhaps a lesson that can be learned from the HPF-1 effort. While the HPF-1 standard defined cyclic block distributions and dynamic redistribution, most early versions of HPF either did not support these features or did not support them well. Are there similar features in MPI-2? If so, they could be omitted from early validation suites (this is from a vendor's perspective, an end user who wants to use such features would want them tested).

A comprehensive validation suite provides vendors with a way to provide quality assurance to end users. Being able to buy a validated MPI-2 implementation would be attractive. However, a truly comprehensive suite, with robust tests is more than most organizations are willing to fund. There is also the fact that the specification is not perfect and that different groups might interpret parts of the MPI-2 standard differently. A plan for an evolving suite that started with those features that are of immmediate interest, such as asynchronous I/O, and that grew as the standard was clarified and demand increased would better serve the MPI-2 community.

References

1. W. Gropp, E. Lusk, N. Doss and A. Skjellum, *A High-Performance, Portable Implementation of the MPI Message Passing Interface Standard*,Preprint MCS-P567-0296, July 1996. HTML available at: http://www-c.mcs.anl.gov/mpi/mpich/.
2. The MPI-2 standard is available at: http://www.mpi-forum.org/.
3. The latest version of the Lawrence Livermore National Laboratory is available at: http://www.llnl.gov/sccd/lc/piop/.
4. P.M. Chen and D.A. Patterson, *A New Approach to I/O Performance Evaluation - Self-Scaling I/O Benchmarks, Predicted I/O Performance*, Proc 1993 ACM SIGMETRICS Conference on Measurement and Modeling of Computer Systems, Santa Clara, California, pp. 1-12, May 1993.
5. PALLAS MPI benchmarks. Available from PALLAS at: http://www.pallas.de/.
6. R. Hockney and M. Berry (Eds.). *Public International Benchmarks for Parallel Computers*, Parkbench Committee Report No. 1, Scientific Programming, 3, pp. 101-146, 1994.
7. Private comments by Charles Grassi (13/5/97).
8. The latest version of the Intel MPI V1.1 Validation Suite is available at http://www.ssd.intel.com/mpi.html.

Improving the PVM Daemon Network Performance by Direct Network Access

Ron Lavi and Amnon Barak

Institute of Computer Science
The Hebrew University of Jerusalem
Jerusalem 91904, Israel
tron@cs.huji.ac.il

Abstract. One approach to reduce the multi-layer overhead of TCP/IP is to bypass it, accessing the LAN directly from user level. Most existing implementations of such a shortcut rely on a polling mechanism, they either support a single-user environment, or do not coexist with TCP/IP. In order to improve the PVM daemon network performance, we developed a new Direct Network Access (DNA) library for PVM and the Myrinet LAN, that bypasses and coexists with TCP/IP. The DNA includes a non-polling receive mechanism, an efficient mutual exclusion mechanism and a shared buffer management scheme, thus enabling operation in a time sharing environment. The paper describes the DNA and its integration in the PVM daemon, and presents performance results, which amount to a latency reduction of 18% for PVM tasks.

1 Introduction

Latency and throughput are key parameters for the performance of distributed and parallel programs due to their basic design blocks, which include message passing mechanisms and synchronization primitives. Although the performance of LANs has improved significantly in the past few years, the performance of the TCP/IP protocol has not improved so dramatically. This performance gap is inherited by higher level communication libraries which rely on TCP/IP, including the PVM software system [2].

Studies of the TCP/IP protocol [3] suggest that the main reason for this gap is the overhead caused by several memory copy operations performed by TCP/IP. One way to reduce this overhead is to bypass the TCP/IP layered structure, by accessing the network interface card directly from user level. The Myrinet LAN architecture [1] technically supports this access method using special API.

In the past few years, several research groups adopted this approach, introducing various implementations for a direct network access software libraries, mainly U-net [9], Fast Messages (FM) [7], Active Messages [5] and PM [8]. One common property of all these designs is the complete bypass of the kernel, performing all network operations in user space. This property enables reaching very low latency values of several microseconds. The FM library was integrated into the MPI library [4], achieving 0-byte latency of 19 microseconds to the MPI user. This implementation is restricted to one MPI process on each host due to the FM properties (e.g. lack of concurrency).

The direct network access approach used by these implementations do not integrate well with the PVM daemon (PVMD) because the daemon:

- Performs non-polling receive on several I/O devices, i.e. network and task connections. Busy polling in this case is very inefficient.
- Uses TCP/IP for remote execution, requiring the direct network access to coexist with it.
- Operates in a multi-user environment, requiring concurrent network access.

This paper presents the design and implementation of the Direct Network Access (DNA) library, which supports these properties, and its integration in the PVMD. The DNA is a compromise between a bypass of the kernel and the traditional protocol hierarchy, i.e. bypassing the kernel whenever possible, but still relying on some necessary kernel services. The DNA allows UDP style messaging between processes on the same Myrinet LAN. In order to operate in a general purpose, time sharing environment and to support the above PVM requirements, the DNA extends the native Myrinet API to include:

- Non-polling receive with the *select()* mechanism and the Myrinet driver.
- Efficient mutual exclusion primitives using semaphores on shared memory, avoiding kernel intervention unless a contention situation is encountered.
- Shared buffer management tools, allowing concurrent DMA buffer access.
- Simple user interface that integrates the above with the Myrinet API.

The DNA is implemented as user library routines and includes modifications to the Myrinet driver. Evaluating the DNA performance between two Pentium-Pro 200 MHz machines shows a significant improvement over UDP: latency is reduced by 25% and throughput is increased by 60%.

The DNA library was integrated into the PVMD, replacing its existing UDP communication method, in order to improve its network performance. Some minor PVM design modifications were made in order to fully exploit the capabilities of the DNA library, including startup procedure modifications to distribute the relevant DNA parameters and new memory allocation considerations, reducing memory related overhead. Performance of the improved PVMD shows a reduction of 18% in its latency and an improvement of 10% in its throughput (measured from a task point of view). We note that better latency and throughput between PVM tasks are achieved by using the 'PvmDirectRoute' mechanism, which uses a direct TCP session between tasks. In spite of that we note that the communication between the daemons is an important part of the PVM system, e.g. for control messages between tasks. In addition, UNIX resource limitations (regarding *fds*) may force tasks to route messages through the daemon.

The remaining of this paper is organized as follows. The DNA design is described in section 2. Section 3 details the integration of the DNA library in the PVMD. In section 4 performance results and analysis of the basic DNA library and the improved PVMD are presented. Section 5 summarizes this work.

2 The Direct Network Access Design

This section gives an overview of the Myrinet architecture followed by a description of the DNA design.

2.1 The Myrinet Software Design

Myrinet [1] is a switched based LAN, implementing the physical and data link layers, that operates at 1.28 Gb/s. The Myrinet architecture consists of host interfaces and network switches. The interface control program, called MCP, uses a DMA engine for data transfers, and hardware interrupts to enable a non-polling asynchronous receive for the Myrinet driver. User programs may communicate directly with the MCP using the DMA engine and a special API set. This access method coexists with TCP/IP using logical channels. These cannot be related to specific user programs because of their limited number. The API requires mutual exclusion for channel sharing and DMA buffer access. This API is unsuitable for integration in the PVMD due to several reasons:

- The need to share channels complicates user logic.
- The use of polling is inefficient in the PVMD, as mentioned above.
- DMA buffer management method must be implemented by user programs.
- Using UNIX semaphores for mutual exclusion implies two kernel entrances in every critical section, which is inefficient.

2.2 The DNA Design

The DNA design extends the Myrinet user API to include new functionalities, detailed below. It is implemented in part as a user library. The necessary kernel services are implemented by the Myrinet driver, which is modular to the kernel and accessible from user space via standard OS mechanisms. We note that the current implementation is for the BSD OS [6].

Non-Polling Receive The standard OS non-polling receive mechanism is used. Hardware interrupts are delivered to the Myrinet driver, which multiplexes them to the user level. User programs may use the BSD *select()* system call to wait for messages, thus waiting simultaneously on several I/O devices, viewing Myrinet as a regular device. The MCP was altered to generate an interrupt upon receiving user-destined messages, and an inquiring interface about the channel origin of a received interrupt was added. The Myrinet driver was altered to cooperate with the *select()* mechanism, notifying user processes about received messages.

Efficient Mutual Exclusion Standard UNIX semaphores are relatively inefficient because several kernel entrances are performed. Furthermore, synchronizing between user programs and the Myrinet driver (that share the DMA buffer) complicates the mutual exclusion needed. To reduce kernel entrances, semaphores are implemented on shared memory. Upon contention, non-busy blocking is done by the Myrinet driver, accessed from the user level. This scheme is used in several DNA primitives, including Myrinet channel access and DMA buffer access, enabling direct network access in a time sharing environment. The Myrinet driver synchronizes with user programs using a lock indication, determining whether to extract a message from the MCP, or to delay until a 'release' indication from the lock-holder.

DMA Buffer Management The DMA buffer holds the data blocks and the management tables, and is accessed by both the user processes and the Myrinet driver. The complexity of the DMA access results from mutual exclusion handling and from the access method itself. Those are encapsulated in three simple DMA access primitives: allocate, receive and free, which the DNA implements.

The DNA Design and the Socket Interface We note two design differences between the DNA interface and the regular socket interface:

- Buffer handling: The DNA interface prevents post-access to a sent buffer and pre-access to a receive buffer due to the asynchronous operation of the DMA engine and to the use of shared buffers. The socket interface does not restrict buffer access due to the use of private buffers.
- Destination specification: The TCP/IP protocol suite contains mechanisms for logical naming, e.g. host name and service name, whereas the DNA interface requires more physical dependent destination parameters.

3 Integrating the DNA Library in the PVM Daemon

The integration of the DNA in the PVMD is interesting due to the functional differences mentioned above. This section first summarizes some related PVM design basics and then presents the integration method.

3.1 Related PVM Design Basics

PVM uses several communication methods. The PVMDs communicate among themselves using UDP, with a private higher level reliable protocol. The more natural TCP mechanism is not exploited due to OS resource limitations. Each PVMD communicates with its tasks using stream (reliable) UNIX domain sockets. Tasks may communicate with each other by routing messages through their daemons, or directly using a TCP session.

The PVMD startup method consists of several phases. The first PVMD, named master PVMD, initializes the PVM system. The other PVMDs ,called slaves, are started on their destination machine by the master PVMD, using the remote execution TCP/IP mechanism. The master PVMD maintains a distributed host table, updating it on every new PVMD startup after receiving its basic configuration. Thus, all PVMDs maintain knowledge of each other's properties.

3.2 The Integration Method

Our integration method uses the following basic implementation guidelines:

- The PVMDs prefer to communicate using the DNA library, allowing UDP communication as a fallback method.
- Each PVMD should reduce buffer copies to and from the network under allocation space considerations.

PVMD Startup Method Modifications In order to distribute the PVMDs' DNA parameters, these are included in the basic configuration sent to the master at startup. Host table entries are expanded to hold these parameters, and they are distributed to all PVMDs in the regular host table update process.

Buffer Allocation Considerations The DNA may reduce the buffer allocation and the data copy overhead of the network send and receive operations. This overhead is reduced in the PVMD network receive by temporarily keeping the data on the DMA buffer. Buffer congestion will not occur as the PVMD consumes the data immediately. Because send-packets are not always sent immediately, this congestion may occur in the PVMD send operation if it would allocate these packets directly on the DMA buffer. Therefore, this method is used only for packets from task connections, because these packets are likely to be larger than locally originated packets, and in order to reduce code modifications (this is probably the largest single origin of packets in the PVMD).

Normal Flow Modifications The DNA integrates easily to the main I/O multiplexing loop, as it uses the *select()* mechanism. UDP communication is used if one of the session partners cannot use DNA, thus aiming for performance improvement but enabling regular communication without manual intervention.

4 Performance

This section presents performance results and analysis of the DNA library and the improved PVMD.

4.1 Basic DNA Performance

The basic DNA performance tests were conducted on two different hardware sets, two Pentium 166 MHz machines and two Pentium-Pro 200 MHz machines, examining the relevance of hardware to the DNA library and the direct access approach. Latency was measured by the sender, using an echoing receiver. Throughput was measured by the receiver. A non polling synchronous receive using the *select()* system call is used in all tests.

The latency results, shown in figure 1, indicate that the DNA library improves the latency, compared to UDP, by an average of 25% on Pentium-Pro 200 MHz,

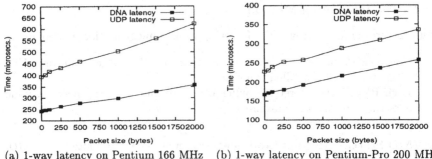

(a) 1-way latency on Pentium 166 MHz   (b) 1-way latency on Pentium-Pro 200 MHz

Fig. 1. Latency results

and by an average of 40% on Pentium 166 MHz. On Pentium-Pro 200 MHz, the 100-byte one way latency of the DNA library is 180 microseconds while the same UDP latency is 240 microseconds.

The throughput results, shown in figure 2, indicate that when using the DNA library instead of UDP, throughput is improved by 60% between two Pentium-Pro 200 MHz and by 300% between two Pentium 166 MHz. On Pentium-Pro 200 MHz, the UDP throughput, using 8KB packet size, is 25MB/s vs. 40MB/s throughput when using the DNA library.

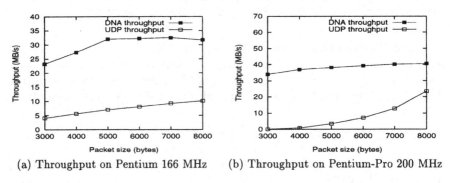

(a) Throughput on Pentium 166 MHz   (b) Throughput on Pentium-Pro 200 MHz

Fig. 2. Throughput results

Because the DNA improves only host related operations, lower relative performance improvement is achieved when improving the host hardware (the latter reduces the host related operations part of the total performance).

Performance Analysis The time costs of the packet flow components are discussed next. These were measured by inserting time samples to the latency test described above, on Pentium 166 MHz. The DNA packet flow is composed of three main groups. The Myrinet related operations (the network time and the

MCP API's time) account for 55% of the total latency time. The OS context switch mechanism accounts for 30% of the total latency time, and the DNA library adds an overhead of 15%. In comparison, host related operations of the UDP protocol account for 65% of the total latency, as shown above.

Focusing on host related operations, we examine the context switch mechanism, which is composed of the Myrinet driver, that wakeup the appropriate process, and the *select()* mechanism. The latter's cost is more significant, accounting for 80% of the total time cost, due to its unique polling scheme. Its overhead was estimated using a fundamental non blocking receive mechanism implemented for this evaluation, showing that the *select()* mechanism doubles the time cost of the context switch operation, depending in the number of I/O devices polled, realizing the tradeoff in a time sharing environment. Note that this mechanism is essential to the PVMD, as detailed above.

4.2 PVM Performance

Evaluating the performance of the improved PVMD was done using latency and throughput tests implementing the above detailed logic using PVM tasks, routing messages through the daemon. The tests were conducted on Pentium-Pro200 MHz machines. The results shown in figure 3 indicate that the latency of the improved PVMD is reduced by 18%. Tests on Pentium 166 MHz show the same relative improvement, because UNIX domain sockets counter balance DNA regarding host related operations. The throughput tests show 10% improvement. The low relative throughput improvement is explained by the integration method, aiming mostly to reduce latency, allocating task packets directly on the DMA buffer as detailed above, causing DMA buffer congestion in overloaded situations like a throughput test. Recall that the PVMD routes packets through UDP in such cases, enabling regular work. In our tests, only 4% of the messages (200 out of 5000) were sent using the DNA mechanism due to insufficient DMA buffer space. Further work is needed here to determine the tradeoff between reduced send overhead and congested DMA buffer.

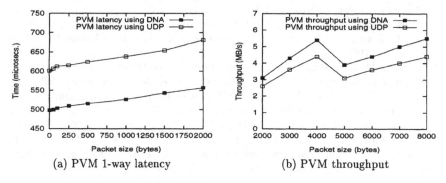

(a) PVM 1-way latency   (b) PVM throughput

Fig. 3. PVM performance results

5 Summary

This paper presents the integration of a Direct Network Access (DNA) mechanism in the PVM daemon (PVMD), in order to improve its network performance. The DNA design addresses the requirements of PVM in a general purpose, time sharing environment. DNA is designed to support a non-receive polling of the network and other I/O devices and it coexists with TCP/IP. Evaluation of the performance improvement of the DNA library shows a reduction of 25% in the latency on Pentium-Pro 200 MHz machines. The latency between PVM tasks, using the PVMD, is reduced by 18%.

As a final remark, we indicate that a natural direction to extend this work is the improvement of the direct communication among PVM tasks, extending the DNA design to allow a reliable TCP-style messaging.

Acknowledgments

We are indebted to Oren Laadan and to Ilia Gilderman for their helpfull suggestions and assistance. This work was supported in part by the MOD.

References

1. N.J. Boden, D. Cohen, R.E. Felderman, A.K. Kulawik, C.L. Seitz, J.N.Seizovic, and W-K. Su. Myrinet: A Gigabit-per-Second Local Area Network. *IEEE Micro*, 15(1):29–36, February 1995.
2. A. Geist, A Beguelin, J. Dongarra, W Jiang, R. Manchek, and V. Sunderam. *PVM: Parallel Virtual Machine, A Users' Guide and Tutorial for Networked Parallel Computing.* The MIT Press, 1994.
3. I. Gilderman. Performance of the Communication Layers in Gigabit LANs. Master's thesis, Institute of Computer Science, The Hebrew University of Jerusalem, 1997.
4. M. Lauria and A. Chien. MPI-FM: High Performance MPI on Workstation Clusters. *Journal of Parallel and Distributed Computing*, 40(1):4–18, January 1997.
5. A. M. Mainwaring and D. E. Culler. Active Message Applications Programming Interface and Communication Subsystem Organization. Technical Report CSD-96-918, U. C. Berkeley, October 1996.
6. M. K. McKusick, K. Bostic, M. J. Karels, and J. S. Quarterman. *The Design and Implementation of the 4.4BSD Operating System.* Addison-Wesley Publishing Company, 1996.
7. S. Pakin, M. Lauria, and A. Chien. High Performance Messaging on Workstations: Illinois Fast Messages (FM) for Myrinet. In *Supercomputing*, December 1995.
8. H. Tezuka, A. Hori, and Y. Ishikawa. PM: A High-Performance Communication Library for Multi-user Paralllel Environments. Technical Report TR-96-015, Tsukuba Research Center, Real World Computing Partnership, November 1996.
9. T. von Eicken, A. Basu, V. Buch, and W. Vogels. U-Net: A User-Level Network Interface for Parallel and Distributed Computing. In *Proc. of the 15th ACM Symposium on Operating Systems principles*, December 1995.

SKaMPI: A Detailed, Accurate MPI Benchmark

Ralf Reussner[1], Peter Sanders[2], Lutz Prechelt[1], and Matthias Müller[1]

[1] University of Karlsruhe, D-76128 Karlsruhe
[2] Max-Planck Institute for Computer Science, D-66123 Saarbrücken
skampi@ira.uka.de

Abstract. *SKaMPI* is a benchmark for MPI implementations. Its purpose is the detailed analysis of the runtime of individual MPI operations and comparison of these for different implementations of MPI. *SKaMPI* can be configured and tuned in many ways: operations, measurement precision, communication modes, packet sizes, number of processors used etc. The technically most interesting feature of *SKaMPI* are measurement mechanisms which combine accuracy, efficiency and robustness. Postprocessors support graphical presentation and comparisons of different sets of results which are collected in a public web-site. We describe the *SKaMPI* design and implementation and illustrate its main aspects with actual measurements.

1 The Role of Benchmarking in Parallel Programming

The primary purpose of parallel (as opposed to sequential) programming is achieving high processing speed. There are two basic approaches to parallel programming. The high-level approach tries to maintain ease of programming as much as possible and is exemplified in languages such as HPF [3]. The low-level approach attempts to achieve maximum speed: the programmer devises all distribution of data and processing explicitly and manually optimizes the program for the idiosyncratic behavior of a particular target machine. This approach is exemplified by message passing programming.

Historically, message passing programs were very machine-specific and hardly portable; libraries such as PVM and MPI overcome this deficiency. However, one must not assume that functional portability also means *performance portability*: Often what works on one machine will still work on another, but be (relatively) much slower. Worse yet, the same may also happen when switching from one MPI implementation to another on the same machine.

Significant investments into performance evaluation tools have been made which can help to identify optimization possibilities. However, these tools have a number of limitations. They require all target configurations to be available for development which is often not the case if a program has to perform well on several platforms or if production runs involve more processors than available for development. Also, these tools can only be applied in late development when the performance-critical parts of the program are already working. Finally, the measurement process itself can distort the results, in particular for the most challenging applications which use many processors and fine-grained communication.

Therefore, we consider a benchmark suite covering all important communication functions to be essential for developing efficient MPI-programs. It must be easy to use and produce detailed, accurate, and reliable results in a reasonable amount of time. If standardized measurements for a wide spectrum of platforms are collected in a publicly available data-base, such a benchmark makes it possible to plan for portable efficiency already in the design stage, thus leading to higher performance at lower development cost. At the same time, the benchmark must be flexible enough to be adapted to special needs and expandable, e.g., to incorporate the functionality of MPI-2.

The *SKaMPI* benchmark was designed with these goals in mind. As a side effect, it can be used to compare different machines and MPI-implementations. Section 2 provides an overview of the benchmark architecture. The specific capabilities of *SKaMPI* and mechanisms for measurements are disussed in Section 3. Section 4 illustrates some of the techniques with actual measurement results.

Related work

Benchmarking has always played an important role in high performance computing, but most benchmarks have different goals or are less sophisticated than *SKaMPI*. Benchmarking of applications or application kernels is a good way of evaluating machines (e.g. [1,4]) but can only indirectly guide the development of efficient programs. A widely used MPI benchmark is the one shipped with the mpich[1] implementation of MPI; it measures nearly all MPI operations. Its primary goal is to validate mpich on the given machine; hence it is less flexible than *SKaMPI*, has less refined measurement mechanisms and is not designed for portability beyond mpich.

The low level part of the *PARKBENCH* benchmarks [4] measure communication performance and have a managed result database[2] but do not give much information about the performance of individual MPI operations.

P. J. Mucci's[3] *mpbench* pursues similar goals as *SKaMPI* but it covers less functions and makes only rather rough measurements assuming a "dead quite" machine.

The *Pallas MPI Benchmark (PMB)*[4] is easy to use and has a simple well defined measurement procedure but has no graphical evaluation yet and only covers relatively few functions.

Many studies measure a few functions in more detail [2,5,6,8] but these codes are usually not publicly available, not user configurable, and are not designed for ease of use, portability, and robust measurements.

---

[1] http://www.mcs.anl.gov/Projects/mpi/mpich/

[2] http://netlib2.cs.utk.edu/performance/html/PDStop.html

[3] http://www.cs.utk.edu/~mucci/mpbench/

[4] http://www.pallas.de/pages/pmbd.htm

2   Overview of *SKaMPI*

The *SKaMPI* benchmark package consists of three parts: (a) the benchmarking program itself, (b) a postprocessing program and (c) a report generation tool. For ease of portability the benchmarking and postprocessing program are both ANSI-C programs, installed by just a single call of the compiler. The report generator is a Perl script which calls gnuplot and LaTeX.

The .skampi run-time parameter file describes all measurements with specific parameters. For a default run, only NODE, NETWORK and USER need to be specified by the user in order to identify the measurement configuration, but very many other customizations are also possible without changing the source code.

The benchmark program produces an ASCII text file skampi.out in a documented format [7]; it can be further processed for various purposes.

The postprocessing program is only needed when the benchmark is run several times, refer to Section 3.3 for details.

The report generator reads the output file and generates a postscript file containing a graphical representation of the results. This includes comparisons of selected measurements. The report generator is also adjustable through a parameter file.

Reports (actually: output files) are collected in the *SKaMPI* result database in Karlsruhe[5] where they are fed through the report generator and latex2html.

2.1   Structuring measurements

Since we investigate parallel operations, we have to coordinate several processes. Measurements with similar coordination structure are grouped into a *pattern*. Thus, when extending the benchmark to a new MPI function one only has to add a small core function; the measurement infrastructure is automatically reused. We now give an overview of the four patterns used by *SKaMPI*: ping-pong, collective, master-worker, and simple.

The *ping-pong pattern* benchmarks point-to-point communication between a pair of processors. For good reasons, MPI provides many variants, so we currently measure nine cases including MPI_Send, MPI_Ssend, MPI_Isend, MPI_Bsend, MPI_Sendrecv and MPI_Sendrecv_replace. The ping-pong pattern uses two processors with maximum ping-pong latency in order to avoid misleading results on clusters of SMP machines.

The *collective pattern* measures functions such as MPI_Bcast, MPI_Barrier, MPI_Reduce, MPI_Alltoall, MPI_Scan, or MPI_Comm_split, in which a subset of the processes works together. We synchronize the processors using MPI_Barrier, measure the time on process 0, and subtract the running time of the barrier synchronization.

Ping-pong cannot model performance-relevant aspects such as the contention arising when one processor communicates with several others at once. Some MPI functions like MPI_Waitsome are specifically designed for such situations. We

---
[5] http://wwwipd.ira.uka.de/~skampi/

measure this using the *master-worker-pattern* which models the following frequent situation: A master process partitions a problem into smaller pieces and dispatches them to several worker processes. These workers send their results back to the master which assembles them into a complete solution. We currently measure nine different implementations focusing either on contention for receiving results or the capability to send out work using different MPI functions.

Finally, we have a *simple pattern*, which measures MPI-operations called on just a single node such as `MPI_Wtime`, `MPI_Comm_rank`, and unsuccessful `MPI_Iprobe`.

3 Measurement Mechanisms

We now describe *SKaMPI*'s approach to efficiently measuring execution times to a given relative accuracy ϵ. The same methods are also useful for other benchmarking purposes.

3.1 A Single Parameter Setting

Each *SKaMPI* result is eventually derived from multiple measurements of single calls to a particular communication pattern, e.g., a ping-pong exchange of two messages of a given length. For each measurement, the number n of repetitions is determined individually to achieve the minimum effort required for the accuracy requested. We need to control both the *systematic* and the *statistical error*.

Systematic error occurs due to the measurement overhead including the call of `MPI_Wtime`. It is usually small and can be corrected by subtracting the time for an empty measurement. Additionally, we warm-up the cache by a dummy call of the measurement routine before actually starting to measure.

Individual measurements are repeated in order to control three sources of *statistical error*: finite clock resolution, execution time fluctuations from various sources, and outliers.

The total time for all repetitions must be at least `MPI_WTick`$/\epsilon$ in order to adapt to the *finite resolution* of the clock.

Execution time fluctuations are controlled by monitoring the standard error $\sigma_{\bar{x}} := \sigma/\sqrt{n}$ where n is the number of measurements, $\sigma = \sqrt{\sum_{i=1}^{n}(x_i - \bar{x})^2/n}$ is the measured standard deviation, and $\bar{x} = \sum_{i=1}^{n} x_i/n$ is the average execution time. The repetition is stopped as soon as $\sigma_{\bar{x}}/\bar{x} < \epsilon$. Additionally, we impose an upper and a lower bound on the number of repetitions.

Under some operating conditions one will observe huge *outliers* due to external delays such as operating system interrupts or other jobs. These can render $\bar{x}$ highly inaccurate. Therefore, we ignore the 25% slowest and the 25% fastest run times for computing the average. Note that we cannot just use the median because its accuracy is limited by the resolution of the clock.

3.2 Adaptive Parameter Refinement

In general, we would like to know the behavior of some communication routine over a range of possible values for the message length m and the number P of processors involved. *SKaMPI* varies only one of these parameters at a time; two-dimensional measurements are written as an explicit sequence of one-dimensional measurements.

Let us focus on the case were we want to find the execution time $t_P(m)$ for a fixed P and message lengths in $[m_{min}, m_{max}]$.

First, we measure at m_{max} and at $m_{min}\gamma^k$ for all k such that $m_{min}\gamma^k < m_{max}$, with $\gamma > 1$. On a logarithmic scale these values are equidistant.

Now the idea is to adaptively subdivide those segments where a linear interpolation would be most inaccurate. Since nonlinear behavior of $t_P(m)$ between two measurements can be overlooked, the initial stepwidth γ should not be too large ($\gamma = \sqrt{2}$ or $\gamma = 2$ are typical values). Fig. 1 shows a line segment between measured points (m_b, t_b) and (m_c, t_c) and its two surrounding segments. Either of the surrounding segments can be extrapolated to "predict" the opposite point of the middle segment.

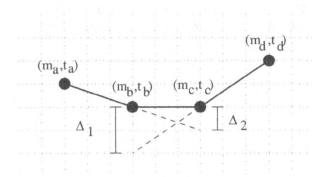

Fig. 1. Deciding about refining a segment $(m_b, t_b) - (m_c, t_c)$.

Let Δ_1 and Δ_2 denote the prediction errors. We use $\min(|\Delta_1|/t_b, |\Delta_2|/t_c, (m_c - m_b)/m_b)$ as an estimate for the error incurred by not subdividing the middle segment.[6] We keep all segments in a priority queue. If m_b and m_c are the abscissae of the segment with largest error, we subdivide it at $\sqrt{m_b m_c}$. We stop when the maximum error drops below ϵ or a bound on the number of measurements is exceeded. In the latter case, the

---

[6] We also considered using the maximum of $|\Delta_1|/t_b$ and $|\Delta_2|/t_c$ but this leads to many superfluous measurements near jumps or sharp bends which occur due to changes of communication mechanisms for different message lengths.

priority queue will ensure that the maximum error is minimized given the available computational resources.

3.3 Multiple Runs

If a measurement run crashed, the user can simply start the benchmark again. *SKaMPI* will identify the measurement which caused the crash, try all functions not measured yet, and will only finally retry the function which led to the crash. This process can be repeated.

If no crash occurred, all measurements are repeated yielding another output file. Multiple output files can be fed to a postprocessor which generates an output file containing the medians of the individual measurements. In this way the remaining outliers can be filtered out which may have been caused by jobs competing for resources or system interrupts taking exceptionally long.

4 Example Measurements

Naturally, it is difficult to demonstrate the entire range of functions measured by *SKaMPI*. We therefore refer to http://wwwipd.ira.uka.de/~skampi for details and concentrate on two condensed examples of particularly interesting measurements.

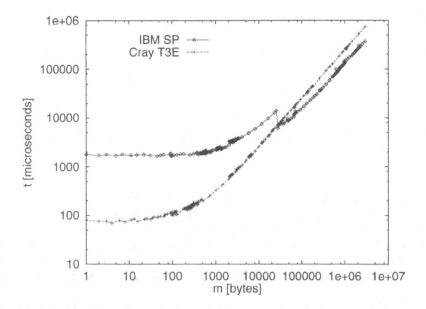

Fig. 2. MPI_Reduce execution time by message length on the IBM SP and Cray T3E.

Fig. 2 shows the execution time of MPI_Reduce on 32 processors of an IBM SP (120 MHz POWER-2 processors) and a Cray T3E with 450 MHz processors. While the Cray achieves an order of magnitude lower latency for small messages, the IBM has higher bandwidth for long messages. Apparently, at message lengths of about 24KByte, it switches to a pipelined implementation. The measurement shows that for this machine configuration, the switch should happen earlier. Similar effects can be observed for MPI_Bcast and MPI_Alltoall. In an application where vector-valued collective operations dominate communication costs (which are not uncommon) fine-tuning for the IBM-SP might therefore require to artificially inflate certain vectors.

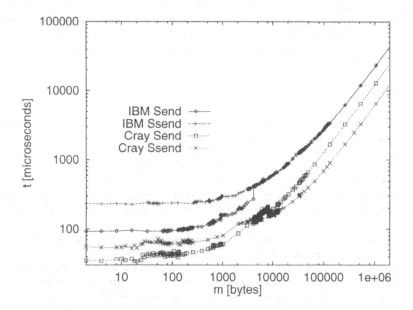

Fig. 3. Point-to-point communication on the IBM SP and Cray T3E.

Fig. 3 compares MPI_Send and MPI_Ssend on an IBM SP and on a Cray T3E. MPI_Ssend has twice as much peak bandwidth than MPI_Send on the Cray while the latter incurs a lower startup overhead. Hence, for optimal performance one needs to have an idea about the message size going to be used in order to select the right function. The IBM apparently switches to MPI_Ssend automatically.

5   Conclusions and Future Work

The *SKaMPI* benchmark infrastructure provides fast and accurate individual measurements, adaptive argument refinement, and a publicly accessible database of detailed MPI measurements on a number of platforms. This makes *SKaMPI* a unique tool for the design of performance-portable MPI programs. The data can also be used to evaluate machines and MPI implementations or to build quantitative performance models of parallel programs.

Nevertheless, many things remain to be done. We are continuing to refine the measurement mechanisms. These are also useful for other applications so that it might make sense to factor them out as a reusable library. *SKaMPI* should eventually encompass an even more complete set of measurements including MPI-2 and more complicated communication patterns including the communication aspects of common application kernels. The current report generator is only a first step in evaluating the results. More compact evaluations including comparisons of different machines could be generated automatically and we even might derive piecewise closed form expressions for the cost of the functions which could then be used in sophisticated adaptive programs which automatically choose the most efficient algorithm depending on problem size and machine configuration.

References

1. D. Bailey, E. Barszcz, J. Barton, D. Browning, and R. Carter. The NAS parallel benchmarks. Technical Report RNR-94-007, RNR, 1994.
2. Vladimir Getov, Emilio Hernandez, and Tony Hey. Message–Passing Performance on Parallel Computers. In C. Lengauer, M. Griebl, and S. Gorlatch, editors, *Euro–Par '97*, pages 1009–1016, New York, 1997. Springer. LNCS 1300.
3. Charles H. Koelbel, David B. Loveman, Robert S. Schreiber, Guy L. Steele, and Mary E. Zosel. *The High Performance Fortran Handbook*. MIT Press, Cambridge, MA, 1994.
4. Parkbench Committee. Public International Benchmarks for Parallel Computers. *Scientific Programming*, 3(2):101–146, 1994. Report 1.
5. J. Piernas, A. Flores, and J. M. Garcia. Analyzing the performance of MPI in a cluster of workstations based on fast ethernet. In *Fourth European PVM/MPI User's Group Meeting*, pages 17–24, New York, November 1997. Springer. LNCS 1332.
6. M. Resch, H. Berger, and T. Boenisch. A comparison of MPI performance in different MPPs. In *Fourth European PVM/MPI User's Group Meeting*, pages 17–24, New York, November 1997. Springer. LNCS 1332.
7. R. Reussner. Portable Leistungsmessung des Message Passing Interfaces. Diplomarbeit, Universität Karlsruhe, Germany, 1997.
8. C.O. Wahl. Evaluierung von Implementationen des Message Passing Interface (MPI)-Standards auf heterogenen Workstation-clustern. Diplomarbeit, RWTH Aachen, Germany, 1996.

Part 2
Extensions and Improvements

MPI on NT: The Current Status and Performance of the Available Environments

Mark Baker

Dept. of Computer Science and Mathematics
University of Portsmouth, UK
http://www.sis.port.ac.uk/~mab
mab@sis.port.ac.uk

Abstract. This paper is a follow up to a previous paper[1] that investigated the functionality and performance of the MPI environments available for NT. In this paper we aim to report on the current status and performance of these environments. We discuss further tests carried out on WinMPICH[2] from the Engineering Research Center at Mississippi State University, WMPI[3] from the Instituto Supererior de Engenharia de Coimbra, Portugal and FM-MPI[4] from the Dept. of Computer Science at the University of Illinois at Urbana-Champaign. In addition, we report on our initial experiences with PaTENT WMPI[5] from Genias Software and MPI/PRO[6] from MPI Software Technology, Inc.

In the first part of the paper we discuss our motivation and briefly discribe each of the environments investigated. In the second part of the paper we describe and then report on the results of a set of communication benchmarks. Finally, we summarise our findings and discuss the changes and progress that has been made since the original investigation was undertaken.

1. Introduction

Using Clusters of Workstations (COW) to prototype, debug and run parallel applications is becoming an increasingly popular alternative to using specialised parallel computing platforms such as the Cray T3E or the IBM SP2. An important factor that has made the usage of workstations a practical proposition is the standardisation of many of the tools and utilities used by parallel applications. Examples of these standards are the Message Passing Interface (MPI[7]) and HPF[8]. This standardisation has allowed applications to be developed, tested and even run on COW and then at a later stage be ported, with little modification, onto dedicated parallel platforms where CPU-time is accounted and charged for.

In the past in science and industry a workstation has inferred some sort of UNIX platform and typically PCs were used for administrative tasks such as word processing. There has, however, been a rapid convergence in processor performance and kernel-level functionality of UNIX workstations and PC-based machines in the last three years - this can be associated with the introduction of Pentium-based machines and the Window NT operating system.

This convergence has led to an increased interest in using PC-based systems as some form of computational resource for parallel computing. This factor, coupled with the their widespread availability in both academia and industry as well as their comparatively low cost has helped initiate a number of software projects whose primary aim is to harness these resources in some collaborative way.

2. MPI Overview

The MPI standard[9] is the amalgamation of what was considered the best aspects of the most popular message-passing systems at the time of its conception. The standard only defines a message passing library and leaves, amongst other things, process initialisation and control to individual developers to define. MPI is available on a wide range of platforms and is fast becoming the *de facto* standard for message passing.

MPI is a portable message-passing standard that facilitates the development of parallel applications and libraries. The design goals of the MPI were portability, efficiency and functionality. Commercial and public domain implementations of MPI exist. These run on a range of systems from tightly coupled, massively-parallel machines, through to COW. MPI has a range of features including: point-to-point, with synchronous and asynchronous communication modes; and collective communication (barrier, broadcast, reduce).

MPICH[10,11], developed by Argonne National Laboratory and Mississippi State University, is probably the most popular of the current, free, implementations of MPI. MPICH is a version of MPI built on top of Chameleon[12]. MPICH and its variants are available for most commonly used distributed and parallel platforms.

3. MPI NT Environments

3. 1 WinMPICH

WinMPICH[13,14] from the Engineering Research Center at Mississippi State University is a port of MPICH for Microsoft Windows NT platforms. WinMPICH allows processes to communicate with each other via either shared memory or over a network. The WinMPICH libraries were originally written to explore threads in the device layer for communication, TCP/IP support was added later. The WinMPICH release consists of source and binaries for a set of libraries and servers configured to be compiled and linked using Microsoft Visual C++ 4.51.

Mississippi State University no longer supports WinMPIch. The technical expertise from the project has been transferred to start-up company, MPI Software Technology Inc.[6], who recently announced a commercial product MPI/PRO[15].

3.2 WMPI

WMPI[3] from the Instituto Supererior de Engenharia de Coimbra, Portugal, is a full implementation of MPI for Microsoft Win32 platforms. WMPI is based on MPICH and includes a P4[16] device standard. P4 provides the communication internals and a startup mechanism (that are not specified in the MPI standard). For this reason WMPI also supports the P4 API.

The WMPI package is a set of libraries (for Borland C++, Microsoft Visual C++ and Microsoft Visual FORTRAN). The release of WMPI provides libraries, header files, examples and daemons for remote starting.

The University of Coimbra continues to support WMPI. In addition a commercial variant of WMPI, know as PaTENT WMPI is being offered by Genias as part of a European project know as WinPar[17].

3.3 Illinois Fast Messages (FM)

FM-MPI[18,19] is from the Dept. of Computer Science at the University of Illinois at Urbana-Champaign. FM-MPI is a version of MPICH built on top of Fast Messages. FM, unlike other messaging layers, is not the surface API, but the underlying semantics. FM contains functions for sending long and short messages and for extracting messages from the network.

FM has a low-level software interface that delivers hardware communication performance; however, higher-level layers interface offers greater functionality, application portability and ease of use. FM has a number of high-level interfaces developed on top of FM: these include MPI, SHMEM and Global Arrays. To run MPI on FM, the MPICH's ADI was adapted to communicate with FM calls. FM-MPI was first developed in October 1995 and was designed to run via Myrinet-connected systems. Recently, a variant of FM-MPI that runs on top of WinSock-2 was released as part of the High-Performance Virtual Machines (HPVM) project[20,21].

FM-MPI and the HPVM environment are supported and developed by the University of Chicago. However, according to the developers the WinSock-based MPI interface is of secondary importance compared to the Myrinet interfaces.

3.4 PaTENT WMPI 4.0

PaTENT WMPI 4.0 is the commercial version of WMPI funded by the EU project WINPAR. PaTENT differs from WMPI in a number of small ways which includes; a sanitised release, easier installation, better documentation and user support via email or telephone. PaTENT is available for Microsoft Visual C++ and Digital Visual Fortran and consists of libraries, include files, examples and daemons for remote starting. It also includes ROMIO, ANL's implementation of MPI-IO configured for UFS. PaTENT uses the Installshield software mechanisms for installation and configuration.

3.5 MPI/PRO for Windows NT

MPI/PRO is a commercial environment recently released by MPI Software Technology, Inc. It is believed by the author that MPI/PRO is based on a WinMPIch, but has been significantly redesigned. In particular the communications performance bottleneck has been removed. In addition MPI/PRO uses installshield for installation and set up of the service daemon. MPI/PRO supports both Intel and Alpha processors and is released to be used with Microsoft Visual C++ and Digital Visual Fortran.

4. Performance Tests

The aim of these tests is restricted to gathering data that helps indicate the expected communications performance (peak bandwidth and message latency) of MPI on NT. The benchmark environment consisted of two NT 4 workstations (SP3) connected by Ethernet (10bT).

4.1 Multi-processor Benchmark - PingPong

In this program increasing sized messages are sent back and forth between processes - this is commonly called PingPong. This benchmark is based on standard blocking `MPI_Send`/`MPI_Recv`. PingPong provides information about latency of `MPI_Send`/`MPI_Recv` and uni-directional bandwidth. To ensure that anomalies in message timings do not occur the PingPong is repeated for all message lengths. Three versions of the PingPong program were developed, C and Fortran 77 with MPI as well as a C version using WinSock[22].

5. Results

5.1 Introduction

For each environment the PingPing benchmark was run in: shared memory mode - here the two processes ran on one machine, and in distributed memory mode – here each process resideded on a different machine connected by Ethernet. The results from the these benchmarks runs are shown in Figures 1 to 4. It should be noted that results from PaTENT and MPI/PRO will be presented at the EuroPVM/MPI98[23] workshop.

5.2 Shared Memory Mode

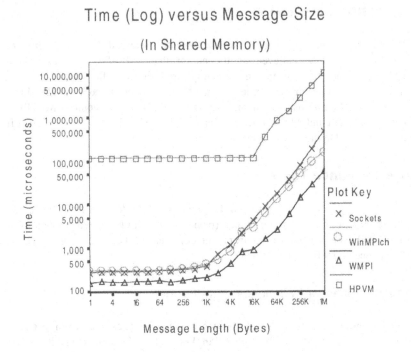

Time (Log) versus Message Size

(In Shared Memory)

Figure 1 – PingPong between two processes on a single processor

5.2.1 Time (Figure 1)

WMPI has the lowest start-up latency of 157 usecs, followed by WinSock (290 usecs) and WinMPIch (306 usecs). There is an approximately constant difference between WMPI and WinSock/WinMPIch up to 1K Byte messages. Thereafter, as the message length increases the times diverge. WMPI and WinMPIch show better performance than WinSock. HPVM has a start up latency of 122 usecs and the time to send 1 Byte or 16 K Bytes is aproximately constant.

5.2.2 Bandwith (Figure 2)

The bandwidth results show that WMPI performs better than WinSock, WinMPIch and HPVM over message lengths tested. The performance of WinMPIch and WinSock are very similar up to 1K Bytes, thereafter WinSock bandwidth is constant and then dips, whereas WinMPIch continues to increase. WMPI peak bandwidth is 24.5 Mbytes/s, WinMPIch is 5.1 Mbytes/s and WinSock is 3.6

MBytes/s. HPVM reaches a peak bandwidth of 0.13 Mbytes/s and then displays a constant bandwith of approximately 0.1 Mbytes/s.

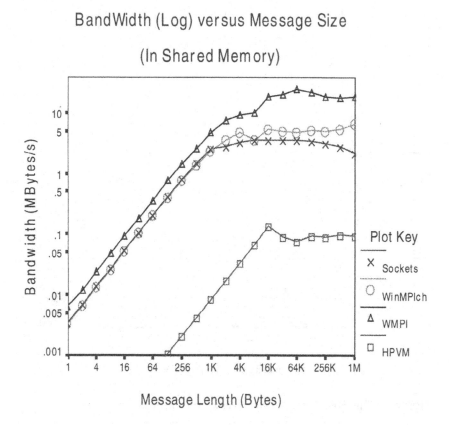

Figure 2 – PingPong between two processes on a single processor

5.3 Distributed Memory Mode

5.3.1 Time (Figure 3)

WinSock has the lowest start-up latency of 0.7 msecs, followed by WMPI (2 msecs), HPVM (29 msecs) and last WinMPIch (8.6 msecs). There is an approximately constant difference between WMPI and HPVM up to 256 Byte messages. WinSock performs best over the range measured. Both WMPI and HPVM exhibit a performance anomoly between 128 and 2 K Byte message length. From 2K onwards WMPI, HPVM and WinSock show an almost identical performance. There is an approximately constant performance difference bewteen

WinMPIch and the others up to 256 Bytes length, thereafter the diference increases rapidly.

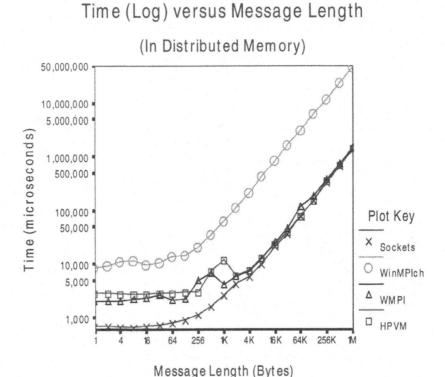

Figure 3 – PingPong between two processes via a network.

5.3.2 Bandthwidth (Figure 4)

The bandwidth results show that WinSock performs better than WMPI, WinMPIch and HPVM. The performance of WMPI and HPVM, again both show a performance anomoly between 128 Bytes and 2K Bytes. WMPI has a marginaly better overall performance than HPVM. The bandwidth of WinMPIch is much poorer than any of the others tested, its bandwidth steadily increases up to 256 Bytes, thereafter it remains fairly constant. WinSock peak bandwidth is 0.86 Mbytes/s, WMPI is 0.72 Mbytes/s, HPVM is 0.84 Mbytes/s and WinMPIch is 0.02 Mbytes/s.

BandWidth (Log) versus Message Size

(In Distributed Memory)

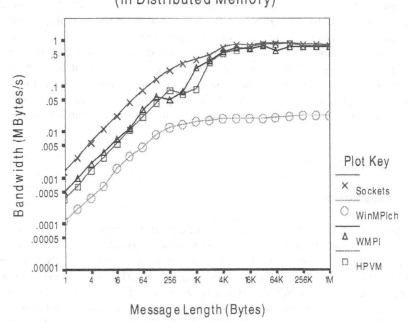

Figure 4 – PingPong between two processes via a network

5.4 Performance Discussion

The reason for producing a WinSock version of the PingPong benchmark was to provide some base measurement with which to compare the performance of the three MPI environments. It should be noted that the WinSock PingPong was not optimised and uses TCP as its communications protocol.

In shared memory mode (Figures 1 and 2) WMPI clearly has the best overall performance. Even though WMPI is built on top of the WinSock protocol it has a much better performance that the WinSock PingPong. It is assumed that this is due to various optimisations and the use of UDP as the internal communications protocol. It can be seen that although WinMPIch uses shared memory semantics internaly its performance is not much better than the WinSock PingPong. It is assumed that the reason for this is because WinMPIch was an early version and had not been fully optimised. The reasons for the poor performance of HPVM is not fully understood by the author and no satisfactory reason has been put forward by the developers either.

In distributed memory mode (Figures 3 and 4) it can be seen that the WinSock PingPong has the best overall performance. This is expected as all the other environments are built on top of the WinSock protocol stack. The performance difference between WinSock and WMPI/HPVM is the overhead of layering a high-level protocol (MPI) on top of WinSock. This overhead is negligible once message sizes are greater that 2 Kbytes. The poor performance of WinMPIch can be wholly explained by the use of a proxy TCP deamons that are used in this mode. Mesasages sent between processes are copied to the local proxy before being sent to the proxy of the destination process where they are copied to the destination process. According to the developers of WinMPIch, the original environment was used to explore threads and the distributed ability was added later.

6. Conclusions

6.1 Introduction

Within this paper we have discussed our latest exeriences with a number of public domain and commercial MPI environments for NT. It should be noted that due to timescales the author has been unable to include any results for PaTENT or MPI/PRO as well as Fortran. The performance of PaTENT is expected to be exactly the same as WMPI. Whereas, even though MPI/PRO is based-on WinMPIch, it is a new environment and its performance is expected to be similar to WMPI. The performance of PaTENT and MPI/PRO will be shown and discused in the talk given at EuroPVM/MPI98[23] and will also be found on the authors Web site[24].

6.2 Performance

In shared memory mode both WinMPIch and WMPI provide fully functional, fast and reliable MPI environments. WMPI is faster than WinMPIch by approximately a factor of two up to 4K and then by a factor of four. WMPI and WinMPIch both out perform the WinSock version of PingPong, however, WinMPIch is not significantly better as would be expected. The performance of HPVM is very poor throughout and difficult to explain.

In distributed memory the performance of WMPI and HPVM is fairly similar throughout the range of message lengths used. The start-up latency of HPVM is approximately 30% greater than WMPI. This difference is nearly constant up until 128 Bytes, thereafter the times and bandwidths are almost the same. Both WMPI and HPVM reach the peak bandwidth of about 0.8 Mbytes/s. The start-up latency of between 2 and 3 msec is similar to that which would be expected between UNIX workstations.

The performance of WinMPIch is poor compared to WMPI and HPVM. The start-up latency of 8.6 msec is at least double that which would normally be expected. In addition, even though the communications bandwidth increases steadily, a peak of around 20 KBytes/s is 400% down on the expect peak rate achievable.

6.3 Overall Conclusions

In terms of functionality and performance WMPI is clearly the best environment of the three investigated for running MPI jobs. The functionality of WinMPIch is good and its performance almost matches that of WMPI in shared memory. However, in distributed memory, WinMPIch has problems with reliability, functionality and performance The problems encountered with non-blocking send/receive (Isend/Irecv) is an area of concern. There is an obvious structural problem - the existence of the proxy daemon highlights this fact. The current structure has a large performance impact (many additional memory copies are needed) and is probably the cause of of the start-up problem encountered.

The HPVM environment has been designed around Myrinet networks and Fast-Message protocols. The availability of several high-level interfaces (MPI, SHMEM and Global-Arrays) makes it a very desirable environment. However, WinSock is not a target interface originally chosen by the developers and consequently can only be considered an early prototype. In shared memory HPVM performs poorly wheras in distributed memory it exhibits performance very close to WMPI.

Finally, it is clear that an MPI implementation should be inter-operable over a heterogeneous computing environment. Only WMPI has such a capability. HPVM requires that the Connection Manager to be ported to each environment and then is only capable of providing heterogeneous support if the byte-ordering is the same on all machine. WinMPIch currently only available on Windows platforms.

6.4 Future Work

The author intends to continue investigating the MPI for NT and will in the near future take a broader look at the performance of MPI on NT against other MPI environments - such as UNIX/Linux clusters. In the longer term a study of alternative technologies, such as Java and Corba, will be undertaken.

Acknowledgments

The author wishes to thank the developers of WinMPIch, WMPI, HPVM, GENIAS Software GmbH, and MPI Software Technology, Inc., for their help with this project. The author also acknowledges the support of the UK TOPIC project and Geoffrey Fox at Syracuse University.

7. References

[1] M.A. Baker and G.C. Fox, *MPI on NT: A Preliminary Evaluation of the Available Environments*, 12th IPPS & 9th SPDP Conference, Orlando, USA. Lecture Notes in Computer Science, Jose Rolim (Ed.), Parallel and Distributed Computing, Springer Verlag, Heidelberg, Germany, 1998. ISBN 3-540 64359-1.

[2] *WinMPICh* - http://www.erc.msstate.edu/mpi/mpiNT.html

[3] *WMPI* - http://alentejo.dei.uc.pt/w32mpi/

[4] *FM-MPI* - http://www-csag.cs.uiuc.edu/projects/comm/mpi-fm.html

[5] PaTENT WMPI - http://www.genias.de/products/patent/

[6] MPI Software Technology, Inc. – http://www.mpi-softtech.com/

[7] Snir, Otto, Huss-Lederman, D. Walker, and J. Dongarra, *MPI The Complete Reference,* MIT Press; 1996.

[8] C. Koelbel, D. Loveman, R. Schreiber, G. Steele Jr., and M. Zosel, *The High Performance Fortran Handbook*, The MIT Press, 1994.

[9] Message Passing Interface Forum, *MPI: A Message-Passing Interface Standard*, May 5, 1994, University of Tennessee, Knoxville, Report No. CS-94-230

[10] *MPICH* - http://www.mcs.anl.gov/mpi/mpich/

[11] W. Gropp, et. al., *A high-performance, portable implementation of the MPI message passing interface standard* - http://www-c.mcs.anl.gov/mpi/mpicharticle/paper.html

[12] W. Gropp and B. Smith, *Chameleon parallel programming tools users manual.* Technical Report ANL-93/23, Argonne National Laboratory, March 1993.

[13] *WinMPICh* - http://www.erc.msstate.edu/mpi/mpiNT.html

[14] Protopopov, B., *MPI Implementation for NT*, Mississippi State University, May 1996 - http://www.erc.msstate.edu/mpi/NTfiles/winMPICHpresent.ps

[15] MPI/PRO - http://www.mpi-softtech.com/products/mpi/mpipro/PDS-MPIProNT-Feb1998-1.html

[16] R. Buttler and E. Lusk, *User's Guide to the p4 Parallel Programming System.* ANL-92/17, Argonne National Laboratory, October 1992.

[17] WINdows based PARallel computing - http://www.genias.de/genias_welcome.html

[18] *FM-MPI* - http://www-csag.cs.uiuc.edu/projects/comm/mpi-fm.html

[19] S. Parkin, V. Karamcheti and A. Chien, *Fast-Message (FM): Efficient, Portable Communication for Workstation Clusters and Massively-Parallel Processors*, IEEE Microprocessor Operating Systems, April - June, 1997, pp 60 -73.

[20] *HPVM* - http://www-csag.cs.uiuc.edu/projects/clusters.html

[21] S. Parkin, M. Lauria, A. Chien, et. al, *High Performance Virtual Machines (HPVM): Clusters with Supercomputing APIs and Performance.* Eighth SIAM Conference on Parallel Processing for Scientific Computing (PP97); March, 1997.

[22] TOPIC – http://www.sis.port.ac.uk/~mab/TOPIC

[23] EuroPVM/MPI98 – http://www.csc.liv.ac.uk/~pvmmpi98

[24] Recent Talks - http://www.sis.port.ac.uk/~mab/Talks/

Harness: The Next Generation Beyond PVM

G. A. Geist *

Oak Ridge National Laboratory, USA

Abstract. Harness is the next generation heterogeneous distributed computing package being developed by the PVM team at Oak Ridge National Laboratory, University of Tennessee, and Emory University. This paper describes the changing trends in cluster computing and how Harness is being designed to address the future needs of PVM and MPI application developers. Harness (which will support both PVM and MPI) will allow users to dynamically customize, adapt, and extend a virtual machine's features to more closely match the needs of their application and to optimize for the underlying computer resources. This paper will describe the architecture and core services of this new virtual machine paradigm, our progress on this project, and our experiences with early prototypes of Harness.

1 Introduction

Distributed computing has been popularized by the availability of powerful PCs and software to cluster them together. The growth of the Web is also raising the awareness of people to the concepts of distributed information and computing. While originally focused on problems in academia and scientific research, distributed computing is now expanding into the fields of business, collaboration, commerce, medicine, entertainment and education. Yet the capabilities of distributed computing have not kept up with the demands of users and application developers. Although distributed computing frameworks such as PVM [2] continue to be expanded and improved, the growing need in terms of functionality, paradigms, and performance quite simply increases faster than the pace of these improvements.

Numerous factors contribute to this situation. One crucial aspect is the lag between development and deployment times for innovative concepts. Because systems and frameworks tend to be constructed in monolithic fashion, technology and application requirements have often changed by the time a system's infrastructure is developed and implemented. Further, incremental changes to subsystems often cannot be made without affecting other parts of the framework. Plug-ins offer one solution to this problem. Plug-ins are code modules that literally plug into a computing framework to add capabilities that previously did not exist. This concept has become popularized by Web browsers. For

* This work was supported in part by the Applied Mathematical Sciences subprogram of the Office of Energy Research, U.S. Department of Energy, under Contract DE-AC05-96OR22464 with Lockheed Martin Energy Research Corporation

example, there are Netscape plug-ins for playing live audio files, displaying PDF files, VRML and movies. The central theme of Harness is to adapt this plug-in concept and extend it into the realm of parallel distributed computing.

By developing a distributed computing framework that supports plug-ins, it will be possible to extend or modify the capabilities available to parallel applications without requiring immediate changes in the standards, or endless iterations of ever-larger software packages. For example, a distributed virtual machine could plug in modules for distributed shared memory programming support along with message passing support, allowing two legacy applications, each written in their own paradigm, to interoperate in the same virtual machine. Virtual machine plug-ins enable many capabilities, such as adapting to new advanced communication protocols or networks, programming models, resource management algorithms, encryption or compression methods, and auxiliary tools, without the need for extensive re-engineering of the computing framework. In addition, Harness plug-ins will be dynamic in nature, or "hot-pluggable". Certain features or functionality will plug in temporarily, only while needed by an application, and then unplug to free up system resources. Distributed application developers no longer will need to adjust their applications to fit the capabilities of the distributed computing environment. The environment will be able to dynamically adapt to the needs of the application on-the-fly.

In Harness we have broadened this concept of pluggability to encompass the merging and splitting of multiple virtual machines that was pioneered in IceT [5], as well as the attachment of tools and applications [6]. Being able to temporarily merge two virtual machines allows collaborating groups at different sites to work together without feeling like they have to place their resources into some larger pool that anyone might use.

Looking at the new capabilities of Harness from the software and application's viewpoint, analysis tools will be able to plug into applications on-the-fly to collect information or steer computations. In addition, peer applications will be able to "dock" with each other to exchange intermediate results or even active objects (e.g. Java bytecode) thereby facilitating collaborative computing at the software level.

From the hardware perspective, as more and more high-performance commodity processors find their way into scientific computing, there is a need for distributed applications to interact between Window and UNIX systems. All of our Harness research is being done within a heterogeneous environment that can include a mixture of Unix and NT hosts; in fact, the plug-in methodology will permit greater flexibility and adaptability in this regard.

The rest of this paper describes the work of the Harness team, which includes researchers at Emory University, Oak Ridge National Laboratory, and the University of Tennessee. The work leverages heavily on other distributed computing projects the team is concurrently working on, particularly Snipe [1] and IceT [5]. In the next section we describe the basic architecture, then follow with a description of the design of the Harness daemon. In section 4, we describe the core services that are provided by the Harness library upon which the Harness daemon is built. Finally, we present the latest results and future development plans.

2 Harness Architecture

The Harness architecture is built on the concept of a distributed set of daemons making up a single distributed virtual machine (DVM). The high level architectural view is similar to the very successful PVM model where there is one daemon per IP address within a given DVM. Where Harness deviates sharply from PVM is in the composition of the daemon and the control structure.

The Harness daemon is composed of a minimal kernel, which understands little more than how to plug-in other modules, and a required set of plug-in modules, which supply the basic virtual machine features. The required modules are: communication, process control, and resource management. The design also allows the user to extend the feature set of their DVM by plugging in additional modules written by the user community.

Figure 1 shows how the plug-ins and daemons fit into the overall Harness architecture.

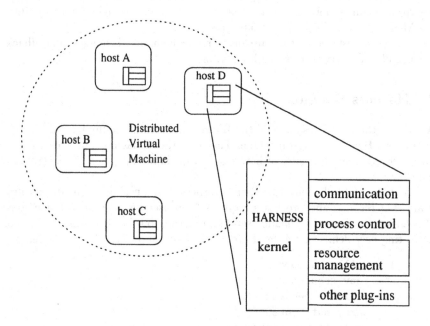

Fig. 1. Distributed Virtual machine is composed of daemons running on each computer and each daemon is composed of 3 required modules (plus possibly others)

2.1 Distributed Control

One goal of Harness is to be much more adaptable and robust than PVM. One weakness in PVM is that it has a single point of failure. When PVM first starts up it selects one daemon to be the "master daemon" responsible for arbitrating conflicting requests and race conditions. All other hosts and daemons in PVM can come and go dynamically, but if contact with the master daemon ever fails the entire DVM gracefully shuts down. We have designed Harness without a single or even multiple point of failure short of all the Harness daemons failing at the same time. This flexibility is not just a nice new feature, but is necessary when you consider the dynamic plug-in environment with constantly changing available resources that Harness is designed to work in.

Two distributed control designs are being investigated for the Harness project. The first is based on multicast and the dynamic reconstruction of the DVM state from remaining daemons in the case of failure. This design is described in [7]. The second design is based on all daemons being peers with full knowledge of the DVM state. The second design is described in detail in [4].

Both designs meet the following requirements that we have specified for the Harness control structure.

- Changes to the DVM state are seen in the same order by all members.
- All members can inject change requests at the same time.
- No daemon is more important than any other i.e. no single point of failure.
- Members can be added or deleted fast.
- Failure of host does not negate any partially committed changes, no rollback.
- Parallel recovery from multi-host failure.

3 Harness Daemon

As seen in the above description, the Harness daemon is the fundamental structure of the Harness virtual machine. The cooperating daemons provide the services needed to use a cluster of heterogeneous computers as a single distributed memory machine.

At its most fundamental level the Harness daemon is an event driven program that receives and processes requests from user tasks or remote daemons. Processing a request may include sending requests to other Harness daemons or activating user defined plug-ins. Here is the outer loop of the Harness daemon.

```
loop till shutdown
    recv request
    validate request
    carry out request
    reply to the requester
endloop
```

The first step after a request is received is to check that the requester is authorized to execute this service on the specified resource. Since PVM was a single user environment this was an unnecessary step, but since Harness allows multiple DVMs to merge, there can be multiple users sharing a DVM. Harness must provide some measure of authorization and protection in its heterogeneous distributed environment, just as an operating system supplies in a multiple user parallel computer. The act of registering with a DVM will return a certificate that will be used to specify the scope of permissions given to a user.

There are three classes of requests that the daemon understands. The first class of request is to perform a local service. The daemon checks its table of available services which includes the core services such as "load a new plug-in", required plug-in services such as spawn a task, and user plug-in services such as balance the load. If available, and the user is authorized, the requested service is executed. Otherwise an error message is returned to the requester. The second class of request is to handle distributed control updates. There are steady pulses of information constantly being exchanged between daemons so that changes to the state of the DVM are consistently made. Each daemon's contribution to the arbitration of state changes is passed around in the form of requests. For example, a request may come in that says, "daemon-X wants to add host-Y to the DVM." The local daemon can pass it on as a way of saying, "OK" or the daemon may know that host-Z needs to be added to the DVM state first and reacts accordingly. (Exactly how it reacts depends on which of the two distributed control methods is being used.) The third class of request is to forward a request to a remote daemon. For example, a local task may send a request to the local daemon to spawn a new task on a remote host. The local daemon could forward the request to the daemon on this host rather than try to invoke a remote procedure call.

4 Core Services

A key realization is that the set of daemons can be thought of as just another parallel application, not unlike a user's parallel application. The daemons need to send information back and forth, they need to be able to coordinate, and to keep track of the state of the virtual machine. These are the same kinds of needs every parallel program has. Therefore the Harness approach is to design a library of functions required to build the daemons and to make this library available to application developers. This library is called the core services and can be divided into four areas: plug-in/run interface, data transfer, global storage, and user registration.

4.1 Plug-in/Run Interface

The basic concept behind Harness is that pluggability exists at every level. At the lowest level, a Harness daemon or a user application can plug-in a new feature, library, or method. At the middle level, two parallel applications can plug-in to one another and form a larger multiphase application. At the highest level, two virtual machines can merge (plug-in) to each other to share computational resources.

Since Harness is object oriented in its design, the plug-in function can be generalized to accept a wide range of components from low level modules to entire DVM. For symmetry there is also an unplug function that reverses the plug-in operation for a given component.

There are times when it is convenient to load and run a plug-in in a single step. A common example is the spawning of a parallel application. There are other times when it is more efficient to preload plug-ins and run them only when necessary. For this reason the core plug-in service presently allows three different instantiation options. The first option is "load only". This is for plug-ins such as libraries that are not runable, for preloading runable processes, and for joining two already running components together. The second option is "load and run". This provides a convenient means to add new hosts to the DVM by starting a remote daemon and also for spawning parallel applications. The third option is "load, run, and wait till completion". This option provides the same model as Remote Procedure Call (RPC) in Unix and has the same utility. As users get more experience with Harness, other options may be added depending on the application needs.

From a practical point of view it may make sense to consider plugging in a single component in a single location separately from plugging in components across many (possibly heterogeneous) locations. In the latter case there are situations, such as spawning a parallel application, where no coordination is required, and other situations, such as loading a new communication plug-in, where strict coordination is required. The latter case also requires the specification of a set of locations as well as a vector of return codes to specify the success or failure of each of the components. For these reasons there are separate functions for these two cases.

Here are the four functions being considered for the plug-in/run interface.

```
object = plugin( component, args, options )
         run( object, args )
         stop( object )
         unplug( component )
```

4.2   Global Storage

The Harness virtual machine needs to store its state information in a robust, fault tolerant database that is accessible to any daemon in the DVM. User applications also need to have a robust information storage and retrieval. For Harness we propose to use the persistent message interface that was developed for the final version of PVM.

In a typical message passing system, messages are transitive and the focus is on making their existence as brief as possible by decreasing latency and increasing bandwidth. But there are a growing number of situations in distributed applications in which programming would be much easier if there was a way to have persistent messages. This was the purpose of the *Message Box* feature in PVM 3.4 [3]. The Message Box is an internal tuple space in the virtual machine. The six functions that make up the Message Box in Harness are:

```
index = putinfo( name, msgbuf, flag )
        recvinfo( name, index, flag )
        delinfo( name, index, flag )
        searchmbox( pattern, matching_names, info )
        subscribe_for_notification()
        cancel_subscription()
```

Tasks can use the Harness data transfer routines to create an arbitrary message, and then use putinfo() to place this message into the Message Box with an associated name. Copies of this message can be retrieved by any Harness task that knows the name. And if the name is unknown or changing dynamically, then searchmbox() can be used to find the list of names active in the Message Box. The flag parameter defines the properties of the stored message, such as, who is allowed to delete this message, does this name allow multiple instances of messages, does a *put* to the same name overwrite the message? The flag also allows extension of this interface as users give us feedback on how they use the features of Message Box.

The recvinfo() function generates a request to the local daemon to find the message associated with the specified name in the global storage and to send it to the reqesting task. The task receives and decodes the message using the Harness data transfer routines.

Here are a few of the many uses for the Message Box feature. A visualization tool can be started that queries the message box for the existence and instructions on how to attach to a large distributed simulation. A performance monitor can leave its findings in the Message Box for other tools to use. A multipart, multiphase application can use the Message Box as a means to keep track of the different parts of the application as they move to the best available resources.

The capability to have persistent messages in a distributed computing environment opens up many new application possibilities, not only in high performance computing but also in collaborative technologies.

4.3 Data Transfer

Because the daemons need to be able to send and receive requests, the core services need to provide a means to transfer data between two components in a DVM. Experience with PVM has shown that message-passing is the most portable and heterogeneous of the possible paradigms, so this is what is provided in Harness as the basic data transfer mechanism.

The core services provide the blocking and nonblocking send and receive routines that users have grown accustomed to in MPI [8] and PVM. The core services also provide the test, wait, and cancel operations required with the nonblocking sends and receives.

The following nine functions are considered core data transfer operations in Harness, while higher level operations like reduce and gather/scatter are expected to be supplied by a collective communication plug-in.

```
  send - blocking send
  recv - blocking receive
 mcast - send to a set of destinations
 nrecv - nonblocking receive as defined in PVM
 isend - nonblocking send
 irecv - post a nonblocking receive as defined in MPI
  test - test for completion of isend or irecv
  wait - block till completion of isend or irecv
cancel - cancel an isend or irecv
```

4.4 User Registration

Unlike PVM or MPI, Harness is a multi-user environment, which requires some form of authorization and protection between the different users. For example, is one user authorized to kill another users application? The Harness daemons constantly get requests to perform services within the DVM. They must have a way to validate each request and check if the requester is authorized to receive the service. For this reason a user registration function is provided as a core service. The initial prototype of this function provides a simple interface to register with the Harness virtual machine and also a means for entering a password if the requested service needs authentication.

```
VMcontext = registerUser( arg-list)
```

A virtual machine context is returned (VMcontext)). VMcontext specifies a user's authorizations and his communication contextt within a given virtual machine. (Note that there can be multiple DVM in Harness.) The VMcontext combines the concept of a certificate and an MPI communicator into a single identifier in the Harness environment.

5 Sumary and Future Plans

With emerging concepts like mobile networks and roaming applications it is apparent that existing virtual machine environments like PVM are inadequate for the new classes of applications that will be built upon these concepts. The PVM development team has begun design of a new virtual machine model, called Harness. The central theme of Harness is to adapt the concept of a plug-in and extend it into the realm of parallel distributed computing. By building an environment that allows users to write plug-ins for distributed virtual machines, innovative new features and high performance communication can quickly be integrated and made available to the entire Harness community.

The architecture and basic design of Harness have been completed, based on successful proof-of-concept experiments performed over the past year. A prototype implementation of Harness written entirely in Java and based on the first of two distributed control schemes is now running [7]. Another prototype implementation written in C++ and based on the second distributed control scheme should be running by the Fall of 1998.

A publicly available version of Harness is planned for the Fall of 1999.

Acknowledgements

The ideas expressed in this paper are the product of the entire Harness development team with includes: Micah Beck, Jack Dongarra, Graham Fagg, Al Geist, Paul Gray, James Kohl, Mauro Migliardi, Keith Moore, Terry Moore, Philip Papadopoulos, Stephen Scott, and Vaidy Sunderam. It is a collaborative effort between Oak Ridge National Laboratory, Emory University, and the University of Tennessee.

References

1. G. Fagg, K. Moore, J. Dongarra, and A. Geist, Scalable Networked Information Processing Environment (SNIPE), In *Proc. SC97*, November 1997.
2. A. Geist, A. Beguelin, J. Dongarra, W. Jiang, B. Manchek, and V. Sunderam. *PVM: Parallel Virtual Machine A User's Guide and Tutorial for Networked Parallel Computing*. MIT Press, Cambridge, MA, 1994.
3. A. Geist, J. Kohl, R. Manchek, and P. Papadopoulos. New features of PVM 3.4 and beyond. In Dongarra, Gengler, Tourancheau, and Vigouroux, editors, *EuroPVM'95*, pages 1–10. Hermes Press, Paris, 1995.
4. A. Geist, and P. Papadopoulos. Symmetric Distributed Control in Network-based Parallel Computing Journal of Computer Communications, 1998. (http://www.epm.ornl.gov/harness/dc2.ps).
5. P. Gray and V. Sunderam. *The IceT Project: An Environment for Cooperative Distributed Computing*, 1997. (http://www.mathcs.emory.edu/~gray/IceT.ps).
6. T. Ludwig, R. Wismuller, V. Sunderam, and A. Bode. Omis – on-line monitoring interface specification. Technical Report TUM-19609, Technische Universität München, February 1996.
7. M. Migliard, J. Dongarra, A. Geist, and V. Sunderam. *Dynamic Reconfiguration and Virtual Machine Management in the Harness Metacomputing System*, ISCOPE 1998. (http://www.epm.ornl.gov/harness/om.ps).
8. M. Snir, S. Otto, S. Huss-Lederman, D. Walker, and J. Dongarra. *MPI: The Complete Reference*. MIT Press, Cambridge, MA, 1996.

Advances in Heterogeneous Network Computing

Paul Gray, Alan Krantz, Soeren Olesen, Vaidy Sunderam *

Department of Math and Computer Science
Emory University, Atlanta, GA 30322, USA
{gray,atk,olesen,vss}@mathcs.emory.edu

Abstract. Frameworks that facilitate network computing have proven viable for high performance applications as well as for traditional distributed computing. Performance and functionality that such methodologies can provide, as well as their limitations and potential, have become reasonably well understood. In this paper, we discuss some selected aspects of heterogeneous computing in the context of the PVM system, and describe evolutionary enhancements to the system. Our experiences with PVM and experiments with optimization, light-weight processes, and client-server computing, have suggested useful directions that the next generation of heterogeneous systems might follow. A prototype design of such a next-generation heterogeneous computing framework is presented in the second half of this paper.

1 Introduction

Parallel computing methodologies using clusters of heterogeneous systems have demonstrated their viability in the past several years, both for high-performance scientific computing as well as for more "general purpose" applications. The most common methodology for realizing such a mode of computing is exemplified by PVM (Parallel Virtual Machine) – a software framework that emulates a generalized distributed memory multiprocessor in heterogeneous networked environments. For a number of reasons, including portability, support for heterogeneity, robustness, and a simple but complete programming interface, the PVM system has gained widespread acceptance in the high-performance concurrent computing community.

In the course of experiences with PVM, both by the developers and by the numerous external users, substantial knowledge has been gained about the limitations, potential, and pitfalls of heterogeneous network concurrent computing. One of the most important factors concerns delivered performance for scientific supercomputing applications or their compute intensive mathematical kernels. Another concerns the programming model supported; for several classes of applications, an alternative computing model would be desirable. The above issues have emerged and have been addressed by different methods with varying degrees of success. Recently however, there have been two important shifts in focus.

* Research supported by U. S. DoE, MICS grant DE-FG05-91ER25105, and NSF awards ASC-9527186, and CCR-9523544.

Heterogeneous computing on a wide area basis is receiving renewed attention, with various forms of national or global virtual computing frameworks. Second, the coupling of parallel and concurrent computing to the World Wide Web, and/or its underlying technologies, is being investigated. Several projects based on one or both of the above are currently in progress, e.g. NetSolve [1], Globus [6], Ninf[9], Fafner [7], and Legion [2]. In this paper, we present a complementary approach – one that evolves incrementally from the existing PVM infrastructure and addresses issues concerning future heterogeneous computing systems.

2 PVM Experiences and Extensions

The PVM software system is an integrated set of software tools and libraries that emulates a general purpose, flexible, heterogeneous concurrent computing framework on interconnected computers of varied architecture. Detailed descriptions and discussions of the concepts, logistics, and methodologies involved in this network-based computing process may be found in [3, 4]; briefly, the principles upon which PVM is based include: (a) explicit message passing model and partitioning, process-based computation and scheduling; (b) user configured host pool with dynamic reconfiguration ability, and translucent access to hardware; (c) heterogeneity support for machines and message, portability across multiple platforms; and (d) computing entities decoupled in space, and loosely coupled in time.

2.1 PVM Performance

Since performance is a critical issue, we include herein some recent results of using PVM to execute the NAS computational fluid dynamics parallel benchmarks from NASA. These benchmarks are designed to substantially exercise the processor, memory, and communication systems of current generation parallel computers. The five NPB (NAS parallel benchmark) kernels, with the exception of the embarrassingly parallel application, are all highly communication intensive when parallelized for message passing systems. As such, they form a rigorous suite of quasi-real applications that heavily exercise system facilities and also provide insights into bottlenecks and hot-spots for specific distributed memory architectures. In order to investigate the viability of clusters and heterogeneous concurrent systems for such applications, the NPB kernels were ported to execute on the PVM system. Detailed discussions and analyses are presented in [5]; here we present summary results of representative experiments on Ethernet and ATM networks with the following configurations:

Workstations on Ethernet. This environment consists of 16 Sun Sparc Ultra 1 Model 140 workstations, each with one 143Mhz UltraSparc processor, 256Mbytes memory, and 2.1 Gbyte fast SCSI-2 disk. These machines are connected by 10Mbps Ethernet.

Workstations on ATM. This environment consists of 12 Sun Ultra2 Model 2170 workstations, each with two 167 UltraSparc-1 processors, 256 Mbytes memory, and two 2.1 Gbyte fast/wide SCSI-2 disks. These machines are connected by 155Mbps ATM.

Results - NPB Kernel Benchmarks: The results in table 1 and table 2 summarizes the performance measurements from running the problem size A NPB kernels on the two test environments. The reference benchmark, kernel EP, scales linearly with the number of processors as expected for both environments. Kernel MG also displays nearly linear speed-up and spends relatively little time in communication. Kernel CG has the major drawback that communication time dominates the total execution time and that in some cases communication time increases with the number of processors; therefore, adding more processors in the Ethernet environment causes increased total benchmark time, and in the ATM environment produces insignificant improvement. For kernel IS communication also takes up the majority of the total execution time; however, the communication volume does not grow excessively and some scalability is obtained. Kernel FT has the largest demand on communication volume; however, the communication volume is constant in the number of processors and communication consists of few large messages. Therefore, kernel FT obtains high utilization of network bandwidth and exhibits good scalability. Generally, the performance trends for the two computation environments are similar, with the 12 Ultra2/ATM testbed obtaining the best overall performance. This is as expected. In some cases, e.g. kernel CG, the excessive communication causes the Ultra1/Ethernet testbed to perform very poorly compared to the Ultra2/ATM testbed.

| | 4 SSU1 | | | 8 SSU1 | | | 16 SSU1 | | |
| | Time | Vol. | Comm. | Time | Vol. | Comm. | Time | Vol. | Comm. |
Benchmark	(s)	(MB)	time (s)	(s)	(MB)	time (s)	(s)	(MB)	time (s)
EP	597	NA	NA	324	NA	NA	152	NA	NA
MG	135	95	21	73	191	21	46	382	23
CG	68	125	28	93	375	83	56	375	47
IS	98	480	81	70	560	63	53	600	49
FT	377	1736	249	203	1736	131	116	1736	77

Table 1. Problem size A NPB Kernels on SS Ultra1, ethernet

2.2   Client-Server Computing with PVM

The message passing model supported by PVM is powerful and well suited to SPMD and some MPMD applications, especially in scientific computing. However, providing only a message-passing interface has restricted PVM application categories significantly. Furthermore, the message-passing model requires a number of potentially complex tasks to be programmed explicitly by the user, including process identification and table maintenance; message preparation,

Benchmark	4 SSU2			8 SSU2			12 SSU2		
	Time (s)	Vol. (MB)	Comm. time (s)	Time (s)	Vol. (MB)	Comm. time (s)	Time (s)	Vol. (MB)	Comm. time (s)
EP	505	NA	NA	253	NA	NA	126	NA	NA
MG	113	95	14	59	191	14	38	382	18
CG	54	125	22	51	375	41	49	375	41
IS	66	480	52	44	560	37	41	560	37
FT	198	1736	146	128	1736	98	82	1736	62

Table 2. Problem size A NPB Kernels on SS Ultra2, ATM

transmission/reception, ordering, and discrimination; and task synchronization. In contrast, traditional distributed computing is based on the "client-server" model. In this paradigm, entities known as servers provide services that may be invoked by clients. Implicit in this abstract definition is the potential for varying levels of implementation semantics. To support client-server applications in a more natural manner, we have developed an RPC system for the PVM framework [8]. PVM-RPC is loosely based on the RPC model in which references to remote services mimic a procedure call. The service provider designs and implements a server which may export one or more services. These services can then be accessed by a client via an invocation that looks and behaves like a procedure call.

An Overview of PVM RPC: PVM-RPC is loosely based on the well-known RPC model in which references to remote services mimic a procedure call. The service provider designs and implements a server which may export one or more services. These services can then be accessed by a client via an invocation that looks and behaves like a procedure call. However, there are a number of issues which arise since the procedure call invokes a non-local service. These issues include name binding, parameter passing, asynchronous processing, and redundancy as it applies to fault tolerance and load balancing. Some of these issues are facilitated by the PVM system, while others are implemented in the PVM-RPC subsystem.

PVM-RPC has four major components, the pvm daemon (PVMD), the service broker (SB), the servers, and the clients. The SB maps service names, as known to clients, to a tuple consisting of a server and service id recognizable to the server. In order to ensure that PVM-RPC is at least as reliable as PVM, with respect to hardware failure, the SB runs on the same machine as the master PVMD. While there are various ways that the SB can start, any server that is trying to register a service will start the SB if it is not already running.

When a server starts, it first locates the SB from the PVMD using the table facility (or starts one if necessary). The server then registers its services with the SB and no further communication between the server and the SB is required. Similarly, when a client wishes to use a service, it first locates the SB from the PVMD and then gets a list of available services from the SB. In the client's case, a request for a list of registered services results in a complete list of all known services and addresses, which the client caches locally to eliminate unnecessary communication between the client and SB. While the list of servers and services may change during the client's execution, this is not an issue unless the client requires a service whose address is not cached, or there is a problem with a known provider of a service (due either to server failure or congestion). In either of these cases, the client can update its list of known services. If more than one server is available for a particular service, the client will, by default, interleave requests among available servers.

Details regarding the programming API as well as experiences with the use of PVM-RPC and some experimental results may be found in [8]. The current version of PVM-RPC has given us some insight into the benefits and drawbacks of the system design, functionality, and performance. Although efficiency and performance are satisfactory, the API, tolerance to failures, and the load balancing mechanism can be improved. We are addressing these issues and have begun to implement our proposed solutions. We are also conducting more extensive tests on a number of other classes of applications, to ensure that the RPC paradigm is indeed suitable in a variety of circumstances. We expect that successful completion of these investigations will make PVM-RPC a viable and valuable platform for parallel distributed computation.

3 Agents, Scripts, and Heterogeneous Computing

Our experiments with client-server computing, and other novel models including multithreaded computing [10] and coordination [13], all within the context of a traditional, process-oriented message passing system, have demonstrated the potential for the unification of paradigms from distributed computing and parallel processing. The thread-based concurrent computing infrastructure was found to be very valuable in permitting finer granularity, hiding latency, and exploiting multi-CPU workstations. The client-server and coordination models showed that even for traditional applications, there are several benefits of using a request-response paradigm especially with regard to expressiveness and ease of use. Considering that there is little or no performance degradation, this is very valuable; especially given the enhanced potential for transparent fault tolerance and load balancing that can be built into RPC servers.

Building further on the idea of a service-oriented computing framework, with well-encapsulated multithreaded computing entities, a natural progression is to move towards agent-based computing. When imposing the constraints or requirements of portability and heterogeneous computing, scripting languages appear to be promising. In order to investigate the potential for these ideas, we propose the IceT heterogeneous network computing framework.

3.1 The IceT Model

The IceT project proposes an approach to metacomputing that is based on a few unique concepts, i.e. collaborative virtual machines, mobile computational units, and dynamism in the infrastructure via replaceable system modules. In the past year or so, we have conducted ad-hoc experiments with some of these ideas; our experiences have demonstrated that a framework integrating these concepts is viable and likely to be very effective.

IceT Overview: The IceT system creates a flexible and generalized concurrent computing framework upon collections of internetworked computer systems, as most other metacomputing systems do. The IceT model extends the notion of traditional metacomputing by providing a more flexible confluence of *computational resources* (software and hardware), *data* (input, output, and dynamic, including output *visualizations*), and invoking *users* and *processes*. Consider the entities *resources, processes, data,* and *users* as they relate to distributed computations. The users and the computational resources are physical quantities while the data and processes are dynamic representations which may be created, modified or otherwise manipulated within the computational environment. While that might be an obvious observation, it does give a basis for the realization that the most general genre of distributed computing is to allow processes and data to flow freely between the fixed, physical quantities of users and computational resources. In pragmatic terms, IceT aims to provide an infrastructure on which heterogeneous resources may be aggregated, upon these resources data and IceT processes may be passed freely, receiving interaction and being visualized by multiple users.

IceT views metacomputing as a collaborative activity, both in terms of resources brought to the pool by different users and in the controlled exchange of processes and data among them. The model is based on several users who each contribute some resources to the IceT VM, which they then share in a controlled manner, and eventually withdraw from the host pool. Since this is dynamic, VM's may merge and split as computations proceed, with appropriate handling of executing processes. Users may contribute resources with differing levels of access, thus prioritizing usage by ownership, pool share, and other parameters, and enabling security and other restrictions under owner control. When a VM is configured and operational as outlined above, computational entities may be launched. For concurrent and distributed applications, the native programming model is one based on strongly-typed message passing, but as we will describe later, IceT can be extended by users to support other programming environments. In the standard case, multiple processes are spawned at various locations on the VM and cooperate by exchanging messages. The base programming language is Java, and spawning in IceT may include uploading and soft installation of bytecode; IceT also supports the transport, dynamic linking, and execution of relocatable object modules written in C or Fortran. Processes may be serialized and moved when necessary; the runtime system maps identifiers to facilitate continued interaction among peers transparently.

IceT Virtual Machines: An IceT virtual machine or environment consists of one or more "sub-machines", each of which is comprised of a collection of host computers related either administratively, by a subnet, or some other common factor. It is assumed that an individual user or group of users has control over a sub-machine; they may contribute part or all of their sub-machine to the IceT VM, imposing appropriate restrictions on each host. As mentioned, our assumption is that typical VM's will be comprised of small numbers of sub-machines, consistent with working within an enterprise or across collaborative teams. Each VM is uniquely identifiable within naming domains selected by users. The default naming scheme that IceT assumes is nameserver based; a simple http-based nameserver is identified by a URL. Nameservers maintain information about past and current IceT virtual machines, including VM composition, control and status data. Multiple nameservers may exist, perhaps based on administrative or collaborative domains. Nameserver providers establish one of several possible policies for entering VM names into directories, and may also choose to impose authentication and access control for looking up VM information. Users, either via an IceT console or from within application programs, utilize IceT methods to interact with the environment. Programs enroll in the environment by calling the "IceT()" method, following which characteristics of the local environment may be obtained by calling the "queryLocalResources" method.

Since collaborative computing is central to IceT, programs (or interactive users via a graphical tool) wishing to access external resources might probe nameservers for other IceT configurations. Alternatively, additional resources might be desired for a distributed computation. For this latter case, the program might be written to access and merge with additional resources using IceT. When merging resources, a request for additional resources from the local white pages server returns the IDs for additional resources, which may be merged together with the local environment. When a spawn request is issued, the "Slave.class" file and its dependencies are located within the combined environment, soft-installed if necessary on each resource, and instantiated as separate threads of execution under the security conditions imposed by the owner(s) of the respective resources. Upon termination of the slave processes on the remote resource, the soft-installed versions of the process are garbage collected, which means that the soft-installation of the slave processes can be accomplished without ever accessing the filesystem(s) on the remote hosts.

This scenario shows one of the modes of concurrent computing in IceT, viz. based on traditional process spawning and message based communication. In this mode, all tasks registered within the collection of resources may interact and use resources within the allowed constraints. While this simple API appears straightforward, we face several challenges in the runtime system. One of the most important is security and usage restrictions, since IceT gives overarching priority to the restrictions imposed by resource owners while encouraging collaborative resource sharing. The collection of IceT kernels executing upon all machines in the pool interact and present the IceT VM to users and to application programs. The example above has already hinted at the kind of facilities that the IceT machine offers as well as the method invocation paradigm used to access these facilities.

Computation in IceT: The base programming model in IceT is concurrent and distributed computing via explicit message passing. On an operational VM, IceT kernels or daemons interact with each other using a reliable multi-way communication fabric; this facility is also exported to user level processes via an enhanced API. In addition, IceT provides a graphical user interface to facilitate control of the virtual machine, start applications, interact with other users in a collaboration, and other cooperative activities.

The IceT environment provides message-based communication, synchronization and coordination facilities between processes. We intend that upon this base model, advanced and specialized environments will be constructed, either by extending native IceT methods or by developing independent modules. The default IceT communication framework provides standard, strongly typed, message construction, passing and routing of these messages amongst processes, and mechanisms which allow processes to read in and interpret message contents.

In addition to primitive data types, the Java programming language allows packing and distribution of much more complex forms. The `Serializable` interface of Java allows any object which implements this interface to be packed into a message using mechanisms similar to the manner in which one would "serialize" an object to disk. The IceT API leverages this ability by providing the programmer appropriate methods in the API. IceT leverages the basic functionality of the Java Serializable interface by providing direct methods to support not only standard cross-platform migration of executable Serializable objects, but also the supplanting of hooks into system-dependent methods (native codes). For example, consider a Serializable IceT thread whose task is to solve large linear systems. For speed considerations, this thread makes use of the basic linear algebra subroutines (BLAS) `saxpy`, `daxpy`, etc. by making native method calls to a relocatable object module which contains a wrapped, system-dependent blas library. In Java, a serializable object cannot be "serialized" if it has any non-null references to objects such as files, sockets, input streams, or, generally speaking, any type of file descriptor. Serializable objects are intended to be portable across systems, and such references restrict serializability since they refer to specific characteristics relevant only to the local environment. Loosely speaking, dependence on native methods also violates the "serializability" of the object. Thus, for similar reasons, references to classes which contain native methods must be nullified prior to an object's serialization.

The above outline description of IceT is intended to serve as a brief introduction to the next generation of heterogeneous computing research that we are pursuing, by building upon our experiences and experiments with PVM. Our preliminary work indicates that this is a promising direction and that IceT builds upon the abstract concepts of PVM and extends them significantly in an appropriate direction for the next generation of network computing frameworks.

Performance Comparisons: Table 3 gives some indication of how the IceT programming environment compares with PVM implementations of equivalent problems. The results depicted in Table 3 are based upon a simple block-decomposed *matrix-matrix* multiplication problem. A full characterization of the Java-binding of the IceT implementation, including program listings, is given in [11].

# processes (Master + Slaves)	Java-based Processes IceT Substrate	C-based Processes IceT Substrate	C-based Processes PVM3.3 Substrate
1	291.796	41.480	37.134
2	161.589	45.116	24.608
4	87.044	28.920	16.575
8	50.695	21.287	16.272

Table 3. *Benchmarks (in seconds) for computation of multiplying two 400x400 matrices on a cluster of Sun Sparc20 workstations.*

The first column of times represent times required for the distributed multiplication of two 400x400 matrices using Java-based Master and Slave programs supported by the IceT substrate. The next column shows the performance when the same IceT substrate is used for task creation and communication but the actual computations are performed using C-based Master and Slave programs. This second column requires some additional comment. One of the avenues in which IceT is evolving in is in a utility capacity. IceT is able to serve as a conduit over which system-*dependent* code is ported, meaning that computationally-intense parallel processes already written in C or FORTRAN (to obtain significant performance gains over Java, as seen when comparing the first two columns of times above) could be ported amongst appropriate architectures within the extended IceT environment. The last column represents times for the equivalent C-based Master and Slave programs executed under PVM 3.3. These results show that IceT mixed with system-dependent computational components performs quite competitively with PVM.

4   Conclusions

Heterogeneous concurrent computing on networks of independent computer systems is a technology that has evolved during the last decade or so. It has been extremely valuable as an effective and ubiquitous high-performance computing platform, and has permitted parallel computing without hardware investment. At the same time, the limitations of network computing have also become evident – some of which have been overcome by novel approaches, tools, and implementations. These experiences, in conjunction with complementary advances and developments, such as the MBone and the World Wide Web, have prompted the quest for the next generation of heterogeneous network-based concurrent computing systems. In this paper, we have outlined an incremental and evolutionary approach towards this goal.

References

1. H. Casanova and J. Dongarra, "NetSolve: A Network Server for Solving Computational Science Problems", *Proc. Supercomputing '96*, November 1996 (to appear).
2. A. Grimshaw, et. al., "A Synopsis of the Legion Project", *University of Virginia Technical Report CS-94-20*, June 8, 1994.
3. V. S. Sunderam, "PVM : A Framework for Parallel Distributed Computing", *Journal of Concurrency: Practice and Experience*, **2**(4), pp. 315-339, December 1990.
4. V. S. Sunderam, G. A. Geist, J. J. Dongarra, and R. Manchek, "The PVM Concurrent Computing System: Evolution, Experiences, and Trends", *Journal of Parallel Computing*, **20**(4), pp. 531-546, March 1994.
5. A. Alund, S. White, and V. S. Sunderam, "Performance of the NAS Parallel Benchmarks on PVM Based Networks", *Journal of Parallel and Distributed Computing*, Vol. 26, No. 1, pp. 61-71, April 1995.
6. I. Foster, S. Tuecke, "Enabling Technologies for Web-Based Ubiquitous Supercomputing", *Proc. 5th IEEE Symp. on High Performance Distributed Computing*, Syracuse, August 1996.
7. G. Fox, W. Furmanski, "Web Based High Performance Computing and Communications", *Proc. 5th IEEE Symp. on High Performance Distributed Computing*, Syracuse, August 1996.
8. A. Zadroga, A. Krantz, S. Chodrow, V. Sunderam, "An RPC Facility for PVM", *Proceedings – High-Performance Computing and Networking '96*, Brussels, Belgium, Springer-Verlag, pp. 798-805, April 1996.
9. S. Sekiguchi, M. Sato, H. Nakada, S. Matsuoka and U. Nagashima, "Ninf : Network based Information Library for Globally High Performance Computing", *Proc. of Parallel Object-Oriented Methods and Applications (POOMA)*, Santa Fe, Feb., 1996.
10. A. Ferrari and V. S. Sunderam, "TPVM: Distributed Concurrent Computing with Lightweight Processes", *Proceedings – 4th High-Performance Distributed Computing Symposium*, Washington, DC, pp. 211-218, August, 1995.
11. Gray, P., and Sunderam, V., IceT: Distributed Computing and Java. *Concurrency, Practice and Experience 9*, 11 (Nov. 1997), 1161–1168.
12. Gray, P., and Sunderam, V., Native Language-Based Distributed Computing Across Network and Filesystem Boundaries. *Concurrency, Practice and Experience* (1998). To Appear.
13. O. Krone, M. Aguilar, B. Hirsbrunner, V. Sunderam, "Integrating Coordination Features in PVM", *Proceedings – First International Conference on Coordination Models and Languages*, Cesena, Italy, Springer-Verlag, pp. 432-435, April 1996.

MPI_Connect Managing Heterogeneous MPI Applications Interoperation and Process Control
Extended Abstract

Graham E. Fagg[1], Kevin S. London[1] and Jack J. Dongarra[1,2]

[1] Department of Computer Science, University of Tennessee, Knoxville, TN
37996-1301
[2] Mathematical Sciences Section, Oak Ridge National Laboratory, Oak Ridge, TN
37831-6367

Abstract. Presently, different vendors' MPI implementations cannot interoperate directly with each other. As a result, performance of distributed computing across different vendors' machines requires use of a single MPI implementation, such as MPICH. This solution may be sub-optimal since it can not utilize the vendors' own optimized MPI implementations. *MPI_Connect*, a software package currently under development at the University of Tennessee, provides the needed interoperability between different vendors' optimized MPI implementations. This project grew out of the *PVMPI* project that utilized *PVM* to provide inter-platform communication and process control, and was upgraded to use the new MetaComputing SNIPE system which has proven more flexible and less restrictive than *PVM* when operating upon certain MPPs. *MPI_Connect* provides two distrinct programming models to its users. The first is a single MPI_COMM_WORLD model similar to that provided by the contempary PACX project. Where inter-communication is completely transparent to MPI applications thus requiring no source level modification of applications. The second is that of uniquely identified process groups that inter-communicate via MPI point-to-point calls. Both systems use the MPI profiling interface to maitain portability between MPI implementations. A unique feature of this system is its ability to allow MPI-2 dynamic process control and inter-operation between MPI implementations. Currently supported implementation include MPICH, LAM 6, IBM MPIF and SGI MPI.

1 Introduction

The past several years have seen numerous efforts to address the deficiencies of the different message passing systems and to introduce a single standard for such systems. These efforts culminated in the first Message Passing Interface (MPI) standard, introduced in June 1994 [8]. Within a year, various implementations of MPI were available, including both commercial and public domain systems.

One of MPI's prime goals was to produce a system that would allow manufacturers of high-performance massively parallel processing (MPPs) computers to provide highly optimized and efficient implementations. In contrast, systems such as PVM [1] were designed for clusters of computers, with the primary goals of portability, and ease-of-use.

The aim of *MPI_Connect* is to interface the flexible process and virtual machine control from Metacomputer systems with several optimized MPI communication systems thus allowing MPI applications the ability to interoperate transparently across multiple heterogeneous hosts.

2 MPI Communicators

Processes in MPI are arranged in rank order, from 0 to N-1, where N is the number of processes in a group. These process groups define the scope for all collective operations within that group. Communicators consist of a process group, context, topology information and local attribute caching. All MPI communications can only occur within a communicator.

Once all the expected MPI processes have started a common communicator is created by the system for them called MPI_COMM_WORLD. Communications between processes within the same communicator or group are referred to as *intra-communicator communications*. Communications between disjoint groups are *inter-communicator communications.* The formation of an inter-communicator requires two separate (non overlapping) groups and a common communicator between the leaders of each group.

The MPI-1 standard does not provide a way to create an inter-communicator between two separately initiated MPI applications since no global communicator exists between them. The scope of each application is limited by its own MPI_COMM_WORLD which by its nature is distinct from any other applications' MPI_COMM_WORLD. Since all internal details are hidden from the user and MPI communicators have relevance only within a particular run-time instance, MPI-1 implementations cannot inter-operate.

Under the proposed MPI-2 specification MPI applications are able to expand their ability to address processes outside of their original MPI_COMM_WORLD. They can perform this via either *spawning* (starting) new processes or by building connections to separately initiated application by using a well known port address or external third party naming service. Currently only LAM 6.X provides MPI-2 dynamic process control symantics, although it does not make allowances for possible inter-operation with other implementations.

3 PVMPI, PACX and PLUS

Although several MPI implementations are built upon other established message-passing libraries such as Chameleon-based MPICH [5], LAM [3] and Unify [4], none allow true inter-operation between separate MPI applications across different MPI implementations.

There are three projects known to the authors that attempts to directly interconnect MPI applications:

1. *PVMPI* [6] from the University of Tennessee at Knoxville, discussed below.
2. *PACX* [2] from the Rechenzentrum Universitaet in Stuttgart. This project uses TCP/IP sockets between additional MPI process relay tasks, to allow pairs of Cray T3E machines to run a *single* MPI applications.
3. *PLUS* [9] from the Paderborn Center for Parallel Computing, Germany. This system uses separate *PLUS* daemons to handle external communications between processes, using their own UDP based communications protocol. This system also supports PVM and PARIX application APIs.

4 From *PVMPI* to *MPI_Connect* System

The *PVMPI* system was a prototype used to study the issues in interconnecting MPI applications using flexible process management from PVM. Three separate areas were addressed by this system:

1. mapping identifiers and managing multiple MPI and PVM IDs
2. transparent MPI message passing
3. start-up facilities and process management

Once a method was found for address resolution bwteen MPI application tasks that was globaly scopable, interconnecting became a matter of address and data translation. Hiding this complexity from user applications became an API decision that was simplified by hiding all complexity other than the neccassary additional naming and resolution calls behind the normal MPI API by utilizing the MPI profiling interface.

Under *PVMPI*, MPI application tasks are identified by a tuple pair that maps from {global name, rank} to each internal MPI representation of {process group, rank} or {communicator, rank}. These mappings were originally stored in PVMs group server *pvmgs*. Three additional calls were added to the API to allow global names to be added, looked up and then removed.

When a separate application looked up a global name, it would be returned an MPI intercommunicator, which it could then use with the normal MPI point-to-point communications, thus maintaining the look and feel of the original MPI API.

One of the main draw backs with *PVMPI* was that it relied upon the PVM system to be avialable. (This was also one of its strengths as PVM provided process control and syncronous notification of failures and data type conversion). Reliance on PVM was a problem with MPPs such as the IBM SP series. The PVM version required was the workstation version (*RS6K*). Under runtime systems such as PBS-POE it was found to be impossible to make the virtual machine and then start MPI over the top on the same nodes, without PBS killing the PVM daemons. I.e. no additional pre-existing processes allowed. Slightly different conditions exhibited concurrent PVM and MPI use on the Intel Paragon, and no public domain PVM version of PVM was available for the Cray T3E.

The solution taken was to restructure the code to use relay processes much like PACX to perform external communication, with the added restriction that they should be able to communicate without the need for additional processes/daemons on the same nodes.

We chose to use the new MetaComputing system *SNIPE* [7] to provide our communication, data conversion and name resolution services. Modularity of the original code aided our migration from *PVM* based *PVMPI* to *SNIPE* based *MPI_Connect*.

Restructuring allowed us to alter the programming model offered to provide users the ability to run a single application transpartently across multiple machines instead of having to code separate applications that explicitly communicate.

5 The full paper

The full paper will detail the internals of the *MPI_Connect* system and its performance for several test applications including the NAS Shallow Water Parallel Benchmark, as well as the impact of compression and security encryption between hosts.

Details will also be given of a new collabrotive project between the developers of PVMPI and PACX that is currently under discussion.

References

1. A. L. Beguelin, J. J. Dongarra, A. Geist, R. J. Manchek, and V. S. Sunderam. Heterogeneous Network Computing. *Sixth SIAM Conference on Parallel Processing*, 1993.
2. Thomas Beisel. "Ein effizientes Message-Passing-Interface (MPI) fuer HiPPI", Diploma thesis, University of Stuttgart, 1996.
3. Greg Burns, Raja Daoud and James Vaigl. LAM: An Open Cluster Environment for MPI. Technical report, Ohio Supercomputer Center, Columbus, Ohio, 1994.
4. Fei-Chen Cheng. Unifying the MPI and PVM 3 Systems. Technical report, Department of Computer Science, Mississippi State University, May 1994.
5. Nathan Doss, William Gropp, Ewing Lusk and Anthony Skjellum. A model implementation of MPI. Technical report MCS-P393-1193, Mathematics and Computer Science Division, Argonne National Laboratory, Argonne, IL 60439, 1993.
6. Graham E. Fagg, Jack J. Dongarra and Al Geist, PVMPI provides Interoperability between MPI Implementations Proceedings of Eight SIAM conference on Parallel Processing March 1997
7. Graham E Fagg, Keith Moore, Jack Dongarra and Al Geist. "Scalable Networked Information Processing Environment (SNIPE)" Proc. of SuperComputing 97, San Jose, November 1997.
8. Message Passing Interface Forum. MPI: A Message-Passing Interface Standard. *International Journal of Supercomputer Applications*, 8(3/4), 1994. Special issue on MPI.
9. Alexander Reinfeld, Jorn Gehring and Matthias Brune, Communicating Across Parallel Message-Passing Environments Journal of Systems Architecture, Special Issue on Cluster Computing, 1997.

An Active Layer Extension to MPI*

Malolan Chetlur, Girindra D. Sharma, Nael Abu-Ghazaleh,
Umesh Kumar V. Rajasekaran and Philip A. Wilsey

Computer Architecture Design Laboratory
Dept. of ECECS, PO Box 210030
University of Cincinnati, Cincinnati, OH 45221–0030
(513) 556–4779 (voice)   (513) 556–7326 (fax)   phil.wilsey@uc.edu

Abstract. Communication costs represent a significant portion of the execution time of most distributed applications. Thus, it is important to optimize the communication behavior of the algorithm to match the capabilities of the underlying communication fabric. Traditionally, optimizations to the communication behavior have been carried out statically and at the application level (optimizing partitioning, using the most appropriate communication protocols, etc). This paper introduces a new class of optimizations to communication: active run-time matching between the application communication behavior and the communication layer. We propose an *active layer* extension to the Message Passing Interface (MPI) that dynamically reduces the average communication overhead associated with message sends and receives. The active layer uses *dynamic message aggregation* to reduce the send overheads and *infrequent polling* to reduce the receive overhead of messages. The performance of the active layer is evaluated using a number of applications.

1   Introduction

The performance of a distributed application is greatly influenced by its communication behavior. Communication operations are expensive because of: (i) the large software overheads involved in sending and receiving messages; and (ii) the propagation delay of the messages through the physical network. The evolution of network architectures has resulted in networks with low propagation delays and high throughput [6]. Unfortunately, reducing the message propagation delay does not affect the large software overheads associated with communication operations. These overheads are due to the gap between the capabilities supported by the network and the user communication requirements [12].

The software overhead can be addressed directly at the *protocol* level. More precisely, rather than using a standardized set of communication primitives that are necessarily general, the most efficient communication primitives for the application are synthesized at compile time (*protocol-compilation*) [1, 8]. However, the distributed processing community has moved towards using standardized

---

* Support for this work was provided in part by the Advanced Research Projects Agency under contract numbers DABT63–96–C–0055 and J–FBI–93–116.

communication libraries that are portable and easy to use [11,18]. Considerable effort has been expended into making these libraries flexible and efficient [10]. When writing a distributed application, the communication needs of the application must be optimized with respect to the capabilities of the underlying communication layer as represented by the communication library. Algorithms that minimize the number of messages must be chosen and the most efficient communication primitives used [5]. In addition, it is important to find an efficient partitioning of the tasks and data to minimize communication [2,3,13,17].

Application-level optimizations are carried out statically at or before compile time. At that time, it is difficult to account for several factors that are only known at run-time. For example, system load and network traffic and congestion can only be known at run-time. In addition, for some applications the communication patterns are dynamic and unpredictable. Often the application is written to be portable to multiple platforms, and cannot be directly optimized for all of them. Dynamic partitioning and process migration also complicate static optimization. Thus, static optimizations are necessarily limited because some critical information is available only at run-time.

In this paper we propose the use of dynamic run-time matching to optimize the communication behavior of distributed applications. Run-time matching is supported using an active communication layer that executes concurrently with the application. Communication operations requested by the application are delivered to the communication layer. In turn, the communication layer decides how and when to implement these operations for optimal performance with respect to the underlying communication fabric and the current machine state. Thus, the active layer is a bridge between the requirements of the user and the facilities provided by the physical network. The active layer is implemented as a transparent extension of the Message Passing Interface (MPI) communication library; we call the extended version of MPI, MPI-A. The application is compiled and linked with the MPI-A library instead of standard MPI. The performance of the MPI-A is studied using a number of distributed applications.

The remainder of this paper is organized as follows. Section 2 describes the cost components of communication operations in message passing environments. Section 3 presents the active layer abstraction, and discusses implementation alternatives for it. Section 4 describes the optimizations incorporated in MPI-A. In Section 5, the performance of the MPI-A is investigated using a number of distributed applications. Finally, Section 6 presents some concluding remarks.

2 MPI and Communication Cost

MPI is the *de facto* standard for message passing on distributed environments. It provides a uniform high level interface to the underlying hardware, allowing programmers to write portable programs without compromising efficiency and functionality. The performance of MPI has been studied for different MPI implementations, and on different platforms [7,21]. These studies demonstrated that the cost of communication in a message passing environment is divided into two components: (i) an overhead that is independent of the message size (s), and (ii) a cost that varies with the size of the message ($n \cdot r$, where n is the size of the message, and r is the variable cost for a unit size message) [10, 15, 16].

The static overhead component s is almost completely a software overhead incurred in the various levels of preparing the message and delivering it according to the required protocol. More precisely, when the application requests a message send, the following sequence of events occurs. First, a context switch to the kernel is triggered, and the send request is passed to the kernel. The kernel allocates buffer space for the message and copies it from user space. The message is propagated through the different network layers; each layer is responsible for implementing a subset of the functions guaranteed by the communication layer (routing, reliability, FIFO delivery, deadlock-detection and avoidance, etc.). At the receive side, dual sets of operations are necessary to unpackage the message and perform security and reliability checks. These overheads are incurred for each message, regardless of the size of the message.

3 Run-Time Communication Matching — Active MPI

This paper explores the use of run-time matching between the application communication behavior and the capabilities of the underlying hardware. Run-time matching has the potential of outperforming traditional static optimizations because it reacts to run-time phenomena that is generally not predictable a priori. In addition, run-time optimization can exploit information specific to the environment; such information is typically unaccounted for in applications that are portable across platforms, The run-time matching is implemented as an active entity that resides conceptually between the application and the communication network. It can be implemented at three different levels:

- As a component of the application. At this level, a run-time matching module is implemented as a "communication manager" in the application. This implementation has the advantage of having access to application specific information. For example, if the application is idle, the communication manager learns that no new message sends are likely to arrive soon and takes a decision accordingly. The drawback is the effort required for building and customizing a manager for each application.
- As an extension to the communication library. In this approach, the communication library is replaced with an active library that automatically includes a generic communication manager with the application. The active library intercepts communication requests from the application (by overriding the MPI methods); only the communication manager generates physical communication requests. No changes to the application are necessary, but the communication manager is not customized to the application.
- As an extension to the network protocol. At this level, the communication manager receives all the communication messages generated by all the applications executing on the processor. Thus, it can optimize the communication behavior for all the applications simultaneously.

In this paper, we investigate and report experiences with the second approach — matching as an extension to the communication library. Ultimately, we would like to move to the third approach (extension to the network protocol) because it offers system-level matching. The next section describes the optimizations currently implemented in the layer.

4 Matching Strategies and Optimizations

Currently, the active layer extension to MPI (called *MPI-A*) implements a small number of optimizations as a proof of the general methodology. In this section, we present and motivate the primary optimizations implemented in the layer.

Dynamic Message Aggregation : In message passing environments, there is a large overhead for message sends that is independent of the message size. Therefore, it is more efficient to communicate many data items in a single physical message than to send them as separate messages. Aggregation also has the side effect of reducing the total physical message size since the header information is shared across all application messages. The active layer identifies messages that occur in close temporal proximity and are targeted towards the same destination, and groups them as a single physical message. By aggregating two messages of size n_1 and n_2, we reduce the communication cost from $2s + r(n_1 + n_2)$ to $s + r(n_1 + n_2)$ for a gain of s. Note that static aggregation has been used successfully to optimize applications [10]; however, dynamic aggregation can identify a larger pool of messages to aggregate because it is carried out at run time.

The reduction in communication overhead is proportional to the number of messages that are aggregated. However, this reasoning ignores the effect of delaying messages (in hope of receiving other messages for aggregation). If the receiver needs the delayed message, its computation is impeded. For example, if the application consists of two processes that communicate synchronously, delaying messages at the send side is harmful because no further messages are sent until the current message is acknowledged. On the other hand, asynchronous applications are much less sensitive to delays in message delivery. In either case, aggregation must be controlled to prevent deadlocks. In our implementation, a timeout mechanism ensures that messages are not delayed indefinitely.

The aggregation heuristic used is based on a fixed buffer size. More precisely, messages are aggregated until the size of the aggregate reaches the predefined aggregation buffer size (or the timeout occurs). The optimal buffer size is a function of the application and the system that can be approximated using adaptive schemes. Consider the case where the application enters a bursty communication region, the size of the buffer can be temporarily increased to take advantage of this region; however, it has to be reduced again once the message arrival rate drops in order to ensure that messages are not delayed excessively.

Infrequent Polling : Asynchronous distributed applications check for arrival of new messages and, if none are present, resume the computation with their available information. Optimistically synchronized applications are an instance of this type of application [9]. In addition, many distributed algorithms execute concurrently and asynchronously with the main computation. Polling is necessary because the message arrival rates are not predictable using local information. The optimal polling frequency varies with the characteristics of the system and the application; in a study of the polling behavior in our Time-Warp simulator, we discovered that 97% of all message probes were unsuccessful. Based on this observation an infrequent polling mechanism that attempts to converge to the optimal polling frequency has been incorporated in MPI-A. The layer tracks the arrival rate of messages and polls the communication layer based on this rate (and not for every request from the application).

Other Optimizations : The dynamic layer bridges the "protocol gap" as defined by Felten [8]. Features that are available in other communication libraries can be supported through the layer. Features like up-calls found in communication libraries based on active messages can be incorporated in this layer [20] (when the active layer discovers that a message has arrived, it signals the application thread). Support of "true zero copy" can be incorporated in the active layer [19]. The layer can adapt the communication behavior to account for the processor specifications and system load. We are currently investigating these and similar optimizations that can be incorporated within the active layer framework.

5 Analysis

The initial implementation of the active layer was built on top of the MPI. We used the following three distributed applications to evaluate its performance: (i) WARPED [14]: an optimistic parallel discrete event simulator synchronized using the Time-Warp paradigm [9]; (ii) LU benchmark (part of the NAS parallel benchmark suite [4]); and (iii) a ping-pong application. The parallel simulator's communication behavior is asynchronous, dynamic and highly unpredictable. In contrast, the LU benchmark is a high-granularity, synchronous application with periodic communication patterns; it proceeds in iterations that are alternately bursty and sparsely-communicating. Finally, the ping-pong variant we use is unsynchronized (there are no dependencies between messages sent and those received). Thus, there is no harm from delaying messages indefinitely (either at the send or receive side). This benchmark is useful in establishing the upper-bound on performance that can be obtained using the layer.

The performance of the three applications was studied as a function of the aggregation buffer size. Figure 1 shows the performance of the WARPED simulator simulating a RAID parallel disk array model. As the size of the buffer was increased, improved performance was achieved (more messages were aggregated). An optimal performance is reached with a buffer size of approximately 1K. With aggregates bigger than 1K, messages are delayed excessively and the benefit from aggregation is outweighed by the delay caused to the receiving processor. Figure 2 shows the performance of the LU decomposition algorithm. This algorithm is highly synchronous and alternates between bursty and lazy communication modes. At low buffer sizes, not enough messages could be aggregated

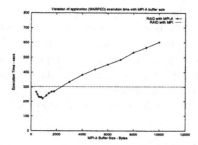

Fig. 1. The performance of Warped as a function of the aggregate buffer size

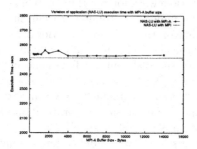

Fig. 2. The performance of Warped as a function of the aggregate buffer size

to achieve faster performance. At higher buffer sizes, the penalty suffered in the synchronous regions of the application outweighed the advantages obtained from aggregation. Although the application was unable to benefit from dynamic aggregation, the execution time remained close to the native MPI implementation.

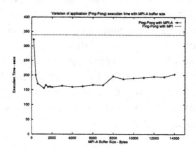

Fig. 3. The performance of the Ping-Pong model as a function of the aggregate buffer size

Figure 3 plots the performance of the ping-pong model as a function of the aggregate buffer size. Recall that the ping-pong version used is unsynchronized; there is no adverse effect from delaying messages indefinitely. As the aggregate size is increased, the performance of the application improved. After a certain aggregate size, the performance flattens out. Possible explanations are that the large aggregate size exceeds the network bandwidth causing a drop in the performance. The ping-pong performance results represent an upper limit on the improvement obtained from aggregation (there is no negative effect from delaying messages); these results demonstrate that there is significant room for reducing the communication overhead for similar applications.

6 Concluding Remarks

This paper presented a framework for run-time matching of application communication behavior to the underlying communication hardware. The aim of the framework is to capitalize on the run-time behavior of the application to reduce the communication overhead — whereas static communication optimizations at the application level are successful in yielding some improvement in the performance of the application, such optimizations do not have access to run-time information that can assist the communication optimizations. Consider the case of message aggregation: if the message generation rate is dynamic or unpredictable, little aggregation is possible statically.

We identified three distinct levels (application, communication library, and network protocol) where the framework can be implemented and discussed the advantages and drawbacks of each level. An initial implementation of the framework at the communication library level was chosen. More specifically, an active layer extension (MPI-A) to the MPI communication library was presented. MPI-A implements a small number of optimizations including dynamic message aggregation and infrequent polling for message arrival. The performance of MPI-A was reported on three different applications. While MPI-A demonstrated considerable improvement in performance on the asynchronous applications, it was not able to optimize the performance of the highly synchronous LU application. This suggests the need for allowing the application to provide hints to the active layer about the types of messages being communicated: if a message is part of a synchronous protocol, it can be sent immediately.

We are in the process identifying other optimizations that can be beneficial in the active layer framework. Finally, we are pursuing the implementation of the framework at the network protocol level; such an implementation promises to yield higher performance because it draws on multiple sources to obtain a large pool of application messages.

References

1. AMARASINGHE, S., AND LAM, M. Communication optimization and code generation for distributed memory machines. In *SIGPLAN '93 Conference on Programming Language Design and Implementation* (1991), pp. 126–138.
2. BAILEY, M. L., JR., J. V. B., AND CHAMBERLAIN, R. D. Parallel logic simulation of VLSI systems. *ACM Computing Surveys 26*, 3 (September 1994), 255–294.

3. BRINER, JR., J. V. *Parallel Mixed-Level Simulation of Digital Circuits using Virtual Time*. PhD thesis, Duke University, Durham, North Carolina, 1990.

4. CENTER, N. A. R. NAS parallel benchmarks home page. `http://science.nas.nasa.gov/Software/NPB/`.

5. CHANDRASEKARAN, S., AND VENKATESAN, S. A message optimal algorithm for distributed termination detection. *Journal Of Parallel and Distributed Computing 8* (1990), 245–252.

6. CHILD, J. Bus wars the sequel: Vme shoots back. *Computer Design* (March 1997).

7. DILLON, E., SANOTS, C. G. D., AND GUYARD, J. Homogenous and heterogenous network of workstations: Message passing overhead. In *MPI Developers Conference* (June 1995).

8. FELTEN, E. W. Protocol compilation: High-performance communication for parallel programs. Tech. rep., University of Washington — Dept. of Computer Science, 1993.

9. FUJIMOTO, R. Parallel discrete event simulation. *Communications of the ACM 33*, 10 (October 1990), 30–53.

10. GROPP, W., AND LUSK, E. Tuning MPI programs for peak performance. `http://www.mcs.anl.gov/mpi/`.

11. GROPP, W., LUSK, E., AND SKJELLUM, A. *Using MPI: Portable Parallel Programming with the Message-Passing Interface*. MIT Press, Cambridge, MA, 1994.

12. KARAMCHETI, V., AND CHIEN, A. Software overhead in messaging layers: Where does the time go? In *Proceedings of ASPLOS - VI, SanJose, California* (March 1994).

13. LEVENDEL, Y. H., MENON, P. R., AND PATEL, S. H. Special purpose computer for logic simulation using distributed processing. *Bell Syst. Tech. J. 61, 10,2873 2909* (1982).

14. MARTIN, D. E., McBRAYER, T. J., AND WILSEY, P. A. WARPED: A time warp simulation kernel for analysis and application development. In *29th Hawaii International Conference on System Sciences (HICSS-29)* (Jan. 1996), H. El-Rewini and B. D. Shriver, Eds., vol. Volume I, pp. 383–386.

15. NEVIN., N. The performance of LAM 6.0 and MPICH 1.0.12 on a workstation cluster. Tech. Rep. OSC-TR-1996-4, Ohio Supercomputer Center Technical Report Columbus, OhioTech., 1996.

16. NUPAIROJ, N., AND NI., L. Performance evaluation of some MPI implementations. Tech. Rep. Tech. Rept. MSU-CPS-ACS-94, Dept. of Computer Science, Michigan State University, Sept. 1994.

17. SMITH, S. P., UNDERWOOD, B., AND MERCER, M. R. An analysis of several approaches to circuit partitioning for parallel logic simulation. In *In Proceedings of the 1987 International Conference on Computer Design.* (1987), IEEE, NewYork, pp. 664–667.

18. SUNDERRAM, V. PVM: A framework for parallel and distributed computing. *Concurrency : Practice and Experience* (December 1990), 315–339.

19. VON EICKEN, T., BASU, A., BUCH, V., AND VOGELS, W. U-net: A user-level network interface for parallel and distributes computing. In *Proceedings of the 15th ACM Symposium on Operating Sysytem Principles* (December 1995).

20. VON EICKEN, T., CULLER, D., GOLDSTEIN, S., AND SCHASUER, K. Active messages: A mechanism for integrated communication and computation. In *Proceedings of the 19th International Symposium on Computer Architecture* (May 1992).

21. XU, ZHIWEI. HWANG, K. Modeling communication overhead: MPI and MPL performance on the IBM SP. *IEEE Parallel & Distributed Technology. 4*, 1 (Spring 1996), 9–23.

Interconnecting PVM and MPI Applications

Pedro D. Medeiros, José C. Cunha

Departamento de Informática – Universidade Nova de Lisboa – Portugal *

Abstract. It should be possible to build an entire application environment through the composition of independently developed application components and tools (e.g. computational intensive, data and performance visualizers, and user interaction components). Such composition should require small modifications to each individual component.

In this paper we describe our approach to the above problem, based on a interconnection model called PHIS. The PHIS model is based on a specialized form of process group which supports multicast, asynchronous message delivery and collective synchronization mechanisms. Such characteristics make the model suitable to support several forms of component interaction. PHIS prototypes support communication between applications which were written using different parallel programming models, for example a PVM-based component and a MPI-based component. In order to evaluate the functionalities provided by the PHIS model, as well as its flexibility, we describe one experiment where we have used PHIS to interconnect two already existent parallel genetic algorithm simulators, one written in PVM an the other in MPI.

1 Introduction

In order to exploit the large diversity of parallel application components that have been developed in recent years, it is necessary to address the heterogeneity issue, not only at the architecture and operating system levels, but also at the computational level. In order to provide flexibility and the ability of reusing pre-existing components, one must support the integration of the different computational models that are possibly used by each application component.

To allow the exchange of information and synchronization between processes of different components we could use some common interprocess communication mechanism. (eg. TCP/IP sockets). However, this requires the use of a new programming model and the interconnection code cannot be reused. Alternatives are the use of standard message–passing systems (PVM or MPI) and the development of a separated system dedicated to the interconnection of separately developed components.

In MPI-1 there are no mechanisms to allow interprocess communication between independently started applications. In MPI–2 [For96] the concept of *port*

---

* This work was partly supported by the CIENCIA and PRAXIS XXI (projects PRO-LOPPE and SETNA-ParComp) Portuguese Research programmes, the EC Copernicus programme and DEC EERP PADIPRO project.

(which has similarities to connection-oriented sockets) has been introduced to allow the interoperation of several independently-started MPI applications. The limitations of the MPI-2 port concept are that only MPI-based components can be interconnected and that it only supports point-to-point connections.

PVM [GBD+95] can be used to support communication between components. This has the advantage of not introducing a new programming model, but it imposes a unique programming model for each component. A rewriting of PVM code may be required in order to eliminate possible message tag conflicts. The introduction of contexts and message handlers in PVM 3.4 eases the construction of interconnection facilities.

Schooner [Hom94], CAVEComm [DPPS96], Legion [Har95] and PLUS are examples of systems dedicated to component interconnection. We briefly discuss the PLUS system, as a representative example of this class of systems.

PLUS [BGR97] supports the component interconnection by addressing processes in other components as communication endpoints of the internal communication layer, eg. PVM task tids for a PVM component. At runtime, PLUS tests the validity of the address of such endpoint and invokes PLUS if the address corresponds to an external process. This has the advantage of allowing an easy rewriting of the interconnection parts in each component, but has the drawback of making it difficult to support interactions between processes in different components.

In brief, we can say that none of above systems offer a satisfactory approach to the problem of interconnecting components concerning communication model expressiveness, architecture and operating system dependence, and performance.

As an alternative approach we propose PHIS (Parallel Heterogeneous Interconnection System), PHIS uses group-based abstractions to model the structuring of heterogeneous applications. A distributed application is organized into separate components that perform distinct tasks such as computationally intensive simulations, monitoring, visualization, or control tasks. Each component can rely on a specific sequential or a parallel computation model. In order to model the interactions between components we need an interconnection model that is neutral regarding the internal model used by individual components. In our approach all such interactions must occur regarding well-defined groups, that allow point-to-point and multicast communication.

The delivery of messages inside each component depends on its internal model so it is up to its internal processes to declare their interest in joining a group, and receive message notifications from the other group members. This aspect makes the model very generic and independent of each application component.

Organization of the paper In section 2 we describe the PHIS model. After presenting its implementation and comparing its performance with PVM and MPI in section 3, we describe an application of PHIS in section 4.

2 A group-oriented approach for component interconnection

In PHIS an application is built by interconnecting several *components*. Each component is a sequential or parallel program that runs on a virtual machine, that can be supported on top of a heterogeneous network of workstations, a distributed-memory or shared-memory multiprocessor. For example, using PHIS, a PVM-based simulation component can be connected to a X-Windows data visualization component that can be based on a event-driven computational model.

After having studied the interaction patterns between components in several applications, we identified the following requirements:

- A process in a given component must be able to address processes in another component. All processes in a component can be addressed as a single entity or individually.
- Synchronization operations involving processes in distinct components must be supported, including the coordinated startup of the application components.

This led us to propose a group-oriented approach to the problem of component interconnection, with the following characteristics:

Semi-static model of interconnection There is a semi-static model for component interconnection, i.e., the number of components is fixed, but the number of interacting processes can change during the execution.

Group-based communication The communication between components is supported by *interconnection or PHIS messages* (simply called messages in the following) which are completely independent from the communication mechanisms used internally to each application component. Processes in different components can cooperate by organizing themselves in *process groups*. These groups are *open*, *dynamic* and automatically created by the first joining process.

Group-based synchronization Groups are also used for intercomponent synchronization with barrier-like operations.

Asynchronous sending of messages The sending of messages to groups is asynchronous, allowing the sending process to proceed with its normal activity. The destination process is identified by a pair *(group name, index in the group)*, where *index* is returned when the process joins the group. The pair *(group name, ALL)* allows to address all current group members. All processes inside a component implicitly belong to a group with the same name as the component. Regarding the semantics of message delivery, the PHIS model supports the specification of the desired semantics (atomic, causal or with no guarantees) [BJKS89].

Asynchronous delivery and message reception A default handler routine is responsible for enqueuing each incoming message. When joining a group, each process can define a user handler for immediate processing of the message, otherwise a default handler is used. Message reception is supported by a blocking primitive and by a non-blocking primitive to test the availability of pending messages in the mentioned queue. This characteristic guarantee that the sending and receiving of interconnection messages do not interfere with the communication that occurs inside the component.

To integrate an already existent component in an application one must have access to its source code. The most important step is to define which processes within the component will interact with other components. Figure 1 shows an example of the modifications that must be made to a program in order to use PHIS:

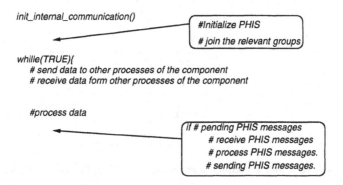

Fig. 1. Example of modifications made to a program, due to PHIS use

3   Implementation of PHIS

The implementation of the PHIS library is supported in three layers:

L0: non-reliable datagram service This layer is the only one that is architecture dependent, and implements a non reliable-datagram service over the native communication system.

L1: reliable datagram service The role of this layer is to provide a reliable datagram service over L0. L0 and L1 layers use parts of the CID system [Nik95].

L2: support of incompletely-interconnected configurations This layer supports the communication between all processes of the components even if some of the components cannot communicate directly.

The communication between all the processes is supported by a software bus that uses the UDP protocol. Regarding the direct accessibility of processes to the UDP protocol we can have two situations, which are illustrated in figure 2.

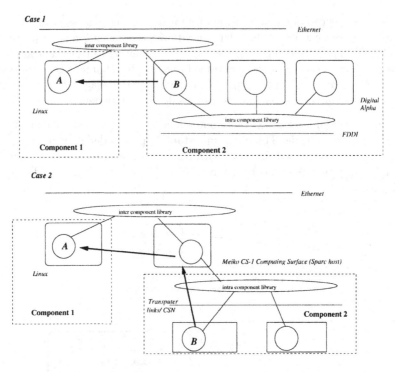

Fig. 2. Processes A and B communicating using direct and indirect communication

Case 1: Processes have direct access to the UDP protocol: in this case, two processes of different components can communicate directly using UDP sockets. A prototype was built that allows a parallel component running on a FDDI-connected cluster of OSF/1 Alpha processors to interact with components running in UNIX workstations.

Case 2: One (or both) processes don't have access to UDP protocols: in this case, the processes must communicate through bridge processes. A prototype was built that allowed a parallel component running on a Transputer-based multicomputer (Meiko CS-1) and using the native message-passing system (CSTools) to communicate with components running in UNIX workstations.

These prototypes have convinced us of the ease of porting PHIS to different architectures.

Fig 3 shows the performance of PHIS communication primitives compared with PVM 3.3.11 and MPICH 1.1.0 in the same hardware (LINUX PCs and SparcStations connected by 10 Mbps-Ethernet) The benchmark used is the ping-pong program.

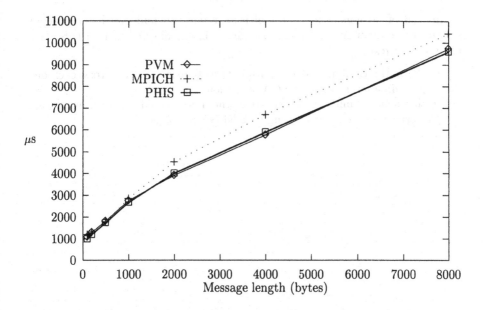

Fig. 3. Message transit time for PHIS, PVM and MPICH

The performance results that we have measured with the current prototype are encouraging, as they give a good indication about the low overhead associated with the interconnection mechanism.

4 A PHIS application

Genetic algorithms (GA) are widely used in many optimization problems. In particular GA are used in the area of parallel processing namely in processor scheduling and load balancing. The use of parallel processing in the area of GA is very attractive as its structure makes them an easy target for parallelization. One of the most known efforts in the area of the parallelization of GA is the package PGAPack [Lev96] of Argonne National Laboratory. We have separately developed two prototypes of parallel GA simulators using PVM and MPI [DD96].

They are both based on the *island model* where multiple instances of a initial population are allowed to evolve autonomously. In the PVM-based prototype (see figure 4) each population is evaluated by a sequential GA simulator running as a PVM task. A monitor process is responsible for the distribution of populations to the PVM tasks. Periodically the best individuals in each population are allowed to migrate (using PVM communication) to adjacent islands. This is supported by the satellite PVM tasks which form a ring. From the GA field it is know that migration can greatly improve the overall convergence of the solution.

Instead of an homogeneous set of islands one can build an heterogeneous system where different GA simulators can be interconnected using PHIS. This has several advantages:

- It allows the combination of multiple already existing simulators, each one using a different strategy for GA execution.
- It allows each simulator to execute in the most suitable hardware/software platform, i.e. to exploit existing parallel GA packages.

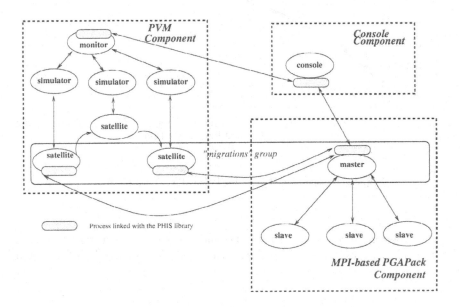

Fig. 4. Interconnecting a MPI-based GA simulator with a PVM-based simulator

This is shown in figure 4, where the above mentioned PVM prototype is combined with another island based on the PGAPack simulator. PGAPack can run on a specific multiprocessor platform and it uses a different strategy for GA execution, where multiple slices of the initial population are distributed to multiple slave processes, by a master.

In this application we have three components: the 'console' component (that is used to make the initial distribution of the populations and to gather the results), the 'PGAPack' component and the 'PVM component'. Message exchange is as follows:

- the console process sends the initial population as a PHIS message to the initial processes of each component, namely the monitor in the PVM component ("PVM", 0) and the master in the PGAPack component ("PGAPack", 0);

- the results are sent back to the console ("Console",0) by the monitor and master process.
- PHIS messages are also used to exchange the migrating individuals as shown in figure 4, where the involved processes have previously joined the "migrations" group.

5 Conclusions and ongoing work

In this paper we have first reviewed the PHIS model. Its distinctive feature is the use of group-oriented abstractions to model the interactions between heterogeneous components. Existing PVM-based and MPI-based applications and tools can be interconnected with small effort. This has been confirmed by our experience and was illustrated in the described application of PHIS for the implementation of a heterogeneous genetic algorithm execution environment.

In ongoing work, we are using PHIS to support the development of a heterogeneous problem–solving environment that can be adapted to specific application domains.

References

[BGR97]   M. Brune, J. Gehring, and A. Reinefeldn. A lightweight communication interface between parallel programming environments. In *Proceedings of HPCN'97 High Performance Computing and Networking*, pages 17–31. Spinger Verlag, 1997.

[BJKS89]   K. Birman, T. Joseph, K. Kane, and F. Schmuck. Isis system manual (version 1.2). Technical report, Cornell University, 1989.

[DD96]   Lus Duarte and Jlio Duarte. Genetic algorithms and parallel processing. Technical report, Dep. de Informtica, Univ. Nova de Lisboa, 1996. in Portuguese.

[DPPS96]   T.L. Disz, M.E. Papka, M. Pellegrino, and M. Szymanski. CAVEComm users manual. Technical Report ANL/MCS-TM-218, Argonne National Laboratory, September 1996.

[For96]   Message Passing Interface Forum. MPI-2: Extensions to the message-passing interface. Technical report, University of Tennessee, November 1996.

[GBD+95]   G. Geist, A. Beguelin, J. Dongarra, W. Cheng, R. Manchek, and V. Sunderam. *Parallel Virtual Machine: A User's Guide and Tutorial for Network Parallel Computing*. MIT Press, 1995.

[Har95]   R.R. Harper. Interoperability of parallel systems: Running PVM in the Legion environment. Technical Report CS-95-23, Dept. of Computer Science, University of Virginia, May 1995.

[Hom94]   Patrick T. Homer. *Constructing scientific applications from heterogeneous resources*. PhD thesis, University of Arizona, December 1994.

[Lev96]   David Levine. Users guide to the PGAPack parallel genetic algorithm library. Technical Report ANL-95/18, Argonne National Laboratory, January 1996.

[Nik95]   R.S. Nikhil. User's guide for the CID system, version 0.981. Technical report, DEC Cambridge Research Laboratory, June 1995.

WMPI
Message Passing Interface for Win32 Clusters

José Marinho[1] and João Gabriel Silva[2]

[1]Instituto Superior de Engenharia de Coimbra, Portugal
fafe@isec.pt
[2]Departamento de Engenharia Informática, Universidade de Coimbra, Portugal
jgabriel@dei.uc.pt

Abstract. This paper describes WMPI[1], the first full implementation of the Message Passing Interface standard (MPI) for clusters of Microsoft's Windows platforms (Win32). Its internal architecture and user interface, and some performance test results (for release v1.1), that evaluates how much of the total underlying system capacity for communication is delivered to the MPI based parallel applications, are presented. WMPI is based on MPICH, a portable implementation of the MPI standard for UNIX® machines from the Argonne National Laboratory and, even when performance requisites cannot be satisfied, it is a useful tool for application developing, teaching and training. WMPI processes are also compatible with MPICH processes running on Unix workstations.

1. Introduction

Parallel platforms based on heterogeneous networked environments are widely accepted. This kind of architecture is particularly appropriate to the message-passing paradigm that has been made official by the Message Passing Interface standard (MPI) [1]. Some relevant advantages over massively parallel machines are availability and excellent competitive performance/cost ratios, and the main disadvantage relies on the underlying networks and communication subsystems that are not optimised for message exchange performance but reliability and low cost.

Most of the communities presently interested in parallel programming (and probably in the future) may not have access to massively parallel computers but do have networks of both PC and UNIX machines that are able to communicate with each other. MPI libraries were first available for clusters of UNIX workstations with the same or even lower capabilities than personal computers (PCs) running the Microsoft Win32 operating systems (Win32 platforms). Being these PCs almost

---
[1] This work was partially supported by the Portuguese Ministério da Ciência e Tecnologia, the European Union through the R&D Unit 326/94 (CISUC), the project ESPRIT IV 23516 (WINPAR) and the project PRAXIS XXI 2/2.1/TIT/1625/95 (PARQUANTUM)

everywhere and having reached competitive levels of computational power [2,3], there was no reason to keep them out of the world of parallel programming. Additionally, since many local area networks (LAN's) consist of a mix of PC and UNIX workstations, protocol compatibility between UNIX and Win32 MPI systems is an important feature. These considerations lead to the development of the WMPI package, the first MPI implementation for clusters of Win32 machines, first released on April 1996. WMPI provides the ability to run MPI programs on heterogeneous environments of Win32 (Windows 95 and NT) and UNIX architectures. The wide availability of Win32 platforms makes WMPI a good learning and application development tool for the MPI standard.

Section 2 introduces the bases of the WMPI package development. Then, section 3 shortly describes how to use WMPI for developing and running parallel applications. In section 4 some internal details are explained and, finally, the performance of WMPI is evaluated in section 5 with clusters based on Win32 platforms.

2. Design Philosophy

MPICH [4,5], a message passing implementation from Argonne National Laboratory/Mississippi State University, is fully available for general-purpose UNIX workstations and it enables heterogeneous UNIX platforms to cooperate using the message-passing computational model. Therefore, an MPICH compatible WMPI implementation was considered to be the most appropriate and time-effective solution for the integration of Win32 and UNIX platforms into the same virtual parallel machine.

MPICH has a layered implementation. The upper layer implements all the MPI functions, is independent of the underlying architecture and relies on an Abstract Device Interface (ADI) that is implemented to match a specific hardware dependent communication subsystem [6,7]. Depending on the environment, the latter can be a native subsystem or another message passing system like p4 or pvm.

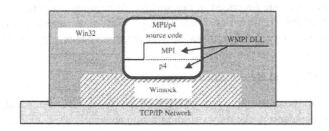

Fig. 1. WMPI and Wp4 process structure

For the sake of compatibility with UNIX workstations and to shorten development time, p4 [8], an earlier portable message passing system from the Argonne National Laboratory/Mississippi State University, was chosen because it is the communication subsystem that is used by MPICH for TCP/IP networked UNIX workstations (MPICH/ch_p4). Most of the porting work is just concerned with p4, being this layer the only that directly works on top of the operating system.

3. User Interface

WMPI consists of dynamic link libraries, for console and GUI Win32 applications, that offer all the MPI and p4 application programming interfaces (API) with C/C++ and Fortran 77 bindings, and a daemon that runs in each Win32 machine for automated remote starting. MPI and p4 programs written for UNIX require almost no changes except for UNIX specific system calls (e.g., fork()'s), which are not very frequent in this type of applications anyway.

3.1. Startup of the Virtual Parallel Machine

WMPI and Wp4 application's startup and configuration are similar to the original p4 communication system, being every process of a parallel application statically defined in a well-known process group file.

3.2. Remote Starting

For remote starting, the original MPICH and p4 UNIX systems try to contact two specific daemons on target machines - the p4 secure server and the p4 old server. A compatible implementation of the p4 old server daemon is available for WMPI as an application and as an NT service. If this server is not available, WMPI tries to contact a remote shell daemon in the remote machine.

4. Internal Architecture

Some internal details are described in this section. As mentioned earlier, the p4 layer handles most of the platform dependent features. Hence, the major concern of the following discussion is related to this communication subsystem.

4.1. Compatibility and Heterogeneity Issues

For the sake of compatibility with MPICH/ch_p4 for UNIX, the same message structures and protocols are kept for communication between distinct clusters.

Communication can be established between a pair of nodes with different internal data representations. To deal with this situation appropriate data conversions must be performed on message contents to match the destination format. As with the original systems, WMPI and Wp4 processes are aware of data representation for the other processes and handle it in a transparent way to the users. Data conversion only occurs when strictly necessary and a subset of the standard XDR protocol has been implemented for that purpose, although the MPI layer just uses simple byte swapping whenever it is possible.

4.2. Local Communication

Messages that are sent between WMPI processes in the same cluster (set of processes running in the same machine) are internally exchanged via shared memory, with each process having a message queue. For that purpose, each cluster has a private large contiguous shared memory block that is dynamically managed (global shared memory) using the monitor paradigm. The Win32 API provides some efficient and simple mechanisms to allow the sharing of resources between processes despite of distinct virtual address spaces and contexts [9].

4.3. Remote Communication

Communication between distinct clusters is achieved through the standard TCP protocol that provides a simple and fast reliable delivery service. To access the TCP protocol a variation of BSD sockets called Windows sockets or simply Winsock, which was approved as a standard for TCP/IP communication under MS Windows, is used.

For every process, a dedicated thread (network receiving thread) receives all the TCP incoming messages and puts them into the corresponding message queue. As a result, MPI receive calls just test the message queues for the presence of messages.

4.4. Performance Tuning

WMPI is designed to avoid any kind of active waiting. Any thread that starts waiting for some event to occur stops competing for the CPU immediately and does not use its entire quantum. As an example, when its message queue is empty, a process that makes a blocking receive call stops waiting for a semaphore that is in a non-signaled state (counter equal to zero). Then, just after adding a message to the empty queue, the network receiving thread or a local process turn the semaphore into a signaled state, then enabling the waiting process.

5. Performance Evaluation

The main goal of this section is to quantify the efficiency of WMPI (release v1.1) for delivering the underlying communication capacity of a system to the applications. Also, results obtained with single and dual Pentium boxes are compared.

5.1. Testbed

All the machines involved in the experiments (Table 1) are hooked together by dedicated 10 Base T or 100 Base T Ethernet hubs. These are the maximum theoretical limits. Also, some sources of significant overhead (software and hardware) already exist between the transmission physical medium and the Winsock interface that is used by WMPI. To quantify the real overhead that the WMPI layer is responsible for, some of the experiments are repeated directly on top of the Winsock (TCP/IP) interface. Every socket is configured with the TCP_NODELAY option, as in the Wp4 layer, in order to avoid small messages to be delayed by the TCP protocol (default behaviour).

Table 1. Machines used for the experiment

CPU	OS	RAM	#
Dual Pentium Pro 200Mhz	NT Server	128 MB	1
Dual Pentium Pro 200Mhz	NT Workstation	128 MB	1
Single Pentium Pro 200Mhz	NT Workstation	64 MB	4

5.2. MPI Benchmark Tests

Message passing overhead is the main bottleneck for speedup. Some results that have been obtained with the Pallas MPI benchmarks (PMB) [10] are reported here.

Table 2. Pallas MPI benchmark tests

PingPong	Two messages are passed back and forth between two processes (MPI_Send/ MPI_Recv).
PingPing	Two messages are exchanged simultaneously between two processes (MPI_Sendrecv).
Xover	Two messages are sent and received in reverse order (MPI_Isend/ MPI_Recv).
Cshift	A cyclic shift of data along a one-dimensional torus of four processes (MPI_Sendrecv).
Exchange	In one-dimensional torus of four processes, each process sends a message to its right neighbour and then to the left one (MPI_Isend). Then, it receives a message from its left neighbour and then from the right one.

Every test is repeated with messages of variable length. For each message length, ranging from 0 bytes to 4 Mbytes, tests are repeated several times[2] to smooth characteristic random effects and latency is half (for PingPong, PingPing and Cshift) or a quarter (for Xover and Exchange) the measured average time to complete.

5.3. Remote Communication

Tables 3 and 4 depict some results of the Ping-Pong test with processes running on distinct machines. A pair of Dual Pentium machines and another of Single Pentium machines are separately used. For this latter, an equivalent Ping-Pong test that is directly implemented on top of the Winsock interface is also executed. The overhead columns of these tables represent the percentage of the available bandwidth at the Winsock interface (the Winsock columns) that, because of its internal operation, the WMPI layer cannot deliver to end-users.

---

[2] For message lengths up to 256 Kbytes: 100 times. For message lengths equal to 512 Kbytes, 1 Mbyte, 2 Mbytes and 4 Mbytes: 80, 40, 20 and 10 times respectively.

Table 3. Bandwidth with a 10 Base T hub

Size	Dual Pentium	Single Pentium		
(bytes)	WMPI (Mbps)	WMPI (Mbps)	Winsock (Mbps)	Overhead (%)
1	0.01	0.01	0.04	63.6
4	0.06	0.06	0.16	63.6
16	0.23	0.23	0.64	63.6
64	0.73	0.93	2.05	54.5
256	2.40	2.93	5.12	42.9
1024	5.81	6.07	7.80	22.2
4096	7.49	7.98	8.84	9.7
8192	7.99	8.49	8.97	5.2
32768	8.30	8.75	8.95	2.2
65536	8.34	8.81	8.93	1.3
131072	8.28	8.81	8.94	1.5
262144	8.27	8.79	8.94	1.7
1048576	8.27	8.77	8.94	1.9
4194304	8.18	8.74	8.93	2.2

Table 4. Bandwidth with a 100 Base T hub

Size	Dual Pentium	Single Pentium		
(bytes)	WMPI (Mbps)	WMPI (Mbps)	Winsock (Mbps)	Overhead (%)
1	0.02	0.02	0.05	66.7
4	0.05	0.07	0.21	66.7
16	0.26	0.28	0.85	66.7
64	0.94	1.14	3.41	66.7
256	2.71	4.50	13.65	67.0
1024	14.89	16.38	32.77	50.0
4096	34.86	36.41	59.58	38.9
8192	39.60	48.37	68.62	29.5
32768	51.35	68.89	71.72	3.9
65536	50.83	68.85	74.79	7.9
131072	49.53	69.10	85.11	18.8
262144	51.92	70.05	86.71	19.2
1048576	49.48	71.14	87.94	19.1
4194304	45.50	63.88	87.48	27.0

As expected, WMPI is less performing than the Winsock interface. For small messages the message size independent overhead of WMPI (e.g., constant-size header fields) gives rise to overhead values over 50% in tables 3 and 4. For large messages, the copying of data bytes between WMPI internal buffers and the application allocated buffers is one of the main contributions for the overhead. It doesn't depend on the available bandwidth because only internal processing is included. Thus, the overhead of WMPI for large messages is much higher with the 100 Base T connection. For larger messages, performance starts decreasing because memory management (e.g., copying) gets less efficient for larger blocks.

The Dual Pentium boxes always perform worst than the single ones. A possible reason may be that some data has to be exchanged between processes (e.g., between a WMPI process and the TCP service provider) that are, possibly, running on different processors. Thus, data that has to be exchanged between distinct processes is not found in the data cache of the destination processor.

As a conclusion and despite of some significant overhead, it can be concluded that WMPI is able to give a significant portion of the underlying available bandwidth to the applications. Encouraging maximum values of 8.8 Mbps and 71.14 Mbps are obtained with 10 Base T and 100 Base T connections, respectively.

5.4. More Communication Patterns

Other PMB benchmarks (PingPing, Xover, Cshift and Exchange) have been also executed with four single Pentium Pro machines and a 100 Base T hub (table 5).

Table 5. Bandwidth (Mbps) with a 100 Base T hub and 4 single Pentium Pro machines

Size (bytes)	PingPong (2 proc.)	PingPing (2 proc.)	Xover (2 proc.)	Cshift (4 proc.)	Exchange (4 proc.)
1	0.02	0.02	0.02	0.02	0.02
4	0.07	0.09	0.08	0.06	0.10
16	0.28	0.37	0.32	0.32	0.39
64	1.14	1.26	1.36	1.28	1.46
256	4.50	5.12	5.12	4.95	5.74
1024	16.38	18.20	20.35	18.20	20.74
4096	36.41	46.81	42.28	32.73	32.71
16384	60.82	65.37	60.89	36.36	35.13
65536	68.85	74.26	66.07	33.24	38.55
262144	70.05	76.71	64.19	34.73	35.68
524288	70.54	77.38	65.34	38.26	36.79
1048576	71.14	77.03	65.80	39.82	40.51
2097152	69.44	75.21	63.97	40.10	39.81
4194304	63.88	69.66	60.02	39.78	39.17

When compared to the Ping-Pong test results, only Cshift and Exchange experience a significant difference for messages up from 4 Kbytes. Being Cshift and Exchange the only tests that make the four processes access the network bus simultaneously to send messages, the increased number of collisions is the main reason for that performance loss.

5.5. Local Communication

Table 6. Bandwidth (Mbps) for local communication

Size (bytes)	Dual Pentium PingPong	Single Pentium		
		PingPong	PingPing	Xover
1	0.05	0.16	0.16	0.10
4	0.40	0.64	0.64	0.43
16	1.60	2.56	2.56	1.71
32	1.65	5.12	2.56	3.41
128	13.65	20.48	10.24	13.65
512	26.43	81.92	40.96	54.61
2048	105.70	163.84	163.84	163.84
8192	168.04	327.68	327.68	262.14
16384	278.88	524.29	524.29	403.30
32768	280.37	655.36	582.54	386.93
131072	150.77	282.64	265.13	173.75
262144	150.82	238.04	233.93	177.50
1048576	147.07	227.87	222.58	174.29
4194304	145.10	220.46	215.44	173.16

Table 6 depicts some results with two processes running on the same machine. As expected, communication between two processes running on the same machine is much more efficient than remote communication because it is achieved through shared memory. It is also visible that the already noticed performance discrepancy between Dual and Single Pentium boxes and performance decreasing is greatly enhanced. With just a single processor the probability of a receiving process to get a message, or part of it, from its local data cache is very high because local communication between two WMPI processes is exclusively based on shared data.

6. Conclusions

WMPI fulfills the goals outlined at the beginning of this document, i.e., an MPI support for widely available Win32 platforms that widespread this accepted programming model and makes powerful low cost Win32 machines co-operate with each other and with UNIX ones to offer accessible parallel processing. Additionally, the download of WMPI (http://dsg.dei.uc.pt/w32mpi) by more than 1700 different institutions (until March 98) since its first release (April 96) demonstrates how real is the interest for MPI based parallel processing under Win32 clusters and how valuable and useful has been the development of WMPI.

Presently there are a few other available implementations of MPI for Windows, but WMPI is still the most efficient and easy to use MPI package for Win32 based clusters [11]. More complex communication patterns of some real applications can result in higher communication overheads. Nevertheless, the expected performance is promising due to a positive evolution of the interconnection technologies and of the individual computational power for Win32 platforms.

References

1. Message Passing Interface Forum, "MPI: A Message-passing Interface Standard", Technical report CS-94-230, Computer Science Dept., University of Tennessee, Knoxville, TN, 1994
2. Tom R. Halfhill, "UNIX vs WINDOWS NT", Byte magazine, pp. 42-52, May 1996
3. Selinda Chiquoine and Dave Rowell, "Pentium Pro Makes NT Fly", Byte magazine, pp. 155-162, February 1996
4. William Gropp, "Porting the MPICH MPI implementation to the sun4 system", January 12, 1996
5. P. Bridges, et. Al., "User's Guide to MPICH, a Portable Implementation of MPI", November 1994
6. William Gropp, Ewing Lusk, "MPICH Working Note: Creating a new MPICH device using the Channel interface - DRAFT", ANL/MCS-TM-000, Argonne National Laboratory, Mathematics and Computer Science Division
7. William Gropp, Ewing Lusk, "MPICH ADI Implementation Reference Manual - DRAFT", ANL-000, Argonne National Laboratory, August 23, 1995
8. Ralph Butler, Ewing Lusk, "User's Guide to the p4 Parallel Programming System", Argonne National Laboratory, Technical Report TM-ANL-92/17, October 1992, Revised April 1994
9. Jeffrey Richter , "ADVANCED WINDOWS, The Developer's Guide to the Win32 API for Wondows NT 3.5 and Windows 95", Microsoft Press, Redmond, Washington, 1995
10.Elke Krausse-Brandt, Hans-Christian Hoppe, Hans-Joachim Plum and Gero Ritzenhöfer, "PALLAS MPI Benchmarks – PMB", Revision 1.0, 1997
11.Mark Baker and Geoffrey Fox, "MPI on NT: A Preliminary Evaluation of the Available Environments", "http://www.sis.port.ac.uk/~mab/Papers/ PC-NOW/", November 1997

A Java Interface for WMPI

Paulo Martins, Luís M. Silva, João Gabriel Silva

Departamento Engenharia Informática
Universidade de Coimbra - POLO II
Vila Franca - 3030 Coimbra
PORTUGAL
Email: {pmartins,luis}@dsg.dei.uc.pt

Abstract. Traditionally, parallel programs have been developed in Fortran and C. However, the extraordinary success of the Java language has raised an impressive hype among the community of software programmers, in such a way that it seems quite promising that parallel programmers could also use Java in their applications.

In this paper, we describe the implementation of Java interface for WMPI, a Windows-based implementations of MPI that have been developed and supported by our group. We show some details about the implementation and we present some experimental results that compare the performance of Java WMPI, Java WPVM and the C programs counterparts.

1. Introduction

PVM and MPI have become widely accepted in the high-performance community and there are several implementations of PVM and MPI for UNIX Workstations, supercomputers and parallel machines [1][2]. Both libraries provide a C, C++ and a Fortran interface.

We have ported the PVM and MPI libraries to Microsoft Win32 platforms. The PVM port is called WPVM [3] (Windows Parallel Virtual Machine) and the MPI port is called WMPI [4]. WPVM and WMPI already include interfaces for C and Fortran, but with the increasing number of Java programmers it seems quite promising that those communication libraries should also provide a Java interface.

According to [5] the current number of Java programmers varies between 250.000 and 2.5000.000. The same author predicts that in 2001 year there would be at least 5.000.000 Java programmers and Java will be the dominant language. Java was developed as a language for the Internet but it is not restricted for the development of Web-pages with animated applets. In the recent past we have seen that the language is also being used for other class of applications, like client/server computing, office applications, embedded systems, programs that use databases and GUI-based interfaces and business applications [6]. The nice features provided by Java, like portability, robustness and flexibility can also be of much use for the development of scientific and parallel applications. In fact there is already a Java Grande Forum that was created to develop some consensus among the HPC community for the establishment of Java for parallel and scientific computing [7].

In this line it is meaningful to provide Java bindings for the existing standards, like MPI, and other libraries that have been widely used, like PVM. The idea is not to replace all the software written in traditional languages with new Java programs. By the contrary, the access to standard libraries is essential not only for performance reasons, but also for software engineering considerations: it would allow existing Fortran and C code to be reused at virtually no extra cost when writing new applications in Java.

With all these goals in mind we have ported the JavaPVM interface [8] for the Windows version of PVM (WPVM) and we develop from scratch a similar Java interface for WMPI. JavaWPVM and JavaWMPI extend the capabilities of WPVM/WMPI to the new, exciting world of Java. These bindings allow Java applications and existing C/C++ applications to communicate with one another using the PVM/MPI API.

In this paper we only describe the implementation of the JavaWMPI interface. The rest of the paper is organized as follows: the next section presents a brief overview of WPVM and WMPI libraries. Section 3 describes the features of our Java to WMPI interface, while section 4 presents some performance results. The related work is described in section 5, while section 6 concludes the paper.

2. WPVM and WMPI

Both WPVM and WMPI are full ports of the standard specifications of PVM and MPI, thereby ensuring that parallel applications developed on top of PVM and MPI can be executed in the MS Windows operating system. Both ports can run together in a heterogeneous cluster of Windows 95/NT and Unix machines.

WPVM[1] (Windows Parallel Virtual Machine) is an implementation of the PVM message passing environment as defined in release 3.3 of the original PVM package from the Oak Ridge National Laboratory. WPVM includes libraries for Borland C++ 4.51, Microsoft VisualC++ 2.0, Watcom 10.5 and Microsoft Fortran PowerStation. On the other hand, WMPI[2] is an implementation of the Message Passing Interface standard for Microsoft Win32 platforms. It is based on MPICH 1.0.13 with the ch_p4 device from Argonne National Laboratory/Mississippi State University (ANL). WMPI includes libraries for Borland C++ 5.0, Microsoft Visual C++ 4.51 and Microsoft Fortran PowerStation.

---

[1] WPVM is available at: http://dsg.dei.uc.pt/wpvm/
[2] WMPI is available at: http://dsg.dei.uc.pt/w32mpi/

3. A Java Binding for WMPI

To develop a Java binding we need a programming interface for native methods. The JDK release from Sun provides a Java-to-native programming interface, called JNI. It allows Java code that runs inside a Java Virtual Machine to inter-operate with applications and libraries written in other programming languages, such as C and C++.

3.1 Overview

All JavaWMPI classes, constants, and methods are declared within the scope of a wmpi package. Thus, by importing the wmpi package or using the wmpi.xxx prefix, we can reference the WMPI Java wrapper.

In the development of this package we tried to provide the user with MPI-like API. Someone that is used to program with MPI will not find any difficulty with using JavaWMPI. To achieve this similarity, all the methods corresponding to WMPI functions are defined in class JavaWMPI and have exactly the same name and number of parameters. The user just needs to extend the JavaWMPI class.

3.2 Opaque objects used by WMPI

Opaque objects are system objects that are accessed through some handler. The user knows the handle to the object but does not know what is inside. Since the MPI does not specify the internal structure of these objects, there is no way to reconstruct them in Java. So, the best thing to do is to keep the handle to the object. To do this, we have implemented one Java class for each opaque object used by WMPI.

These Java classes hide inside them the handle to the real WMPI opaque objects. The programmer only has to create new instances of these objects and use them as arguments to JavaWMPI methods. In order to fit into some system that has 64 bits pointers, we use a Java long to store the WMPI object handle.

3.3 Java Datatypes

The following table lists all the Java basic types and their corresponding C/C++ and MPI datatypes.

Table 1. JavaWMPI datatypes.

Java datatype	C/C++ Datatype	MPI datatype	JavaWMPI datatype
byte	signed char	MPI_CHAR	MPI_BYTE
char	unsigned short int	MPI_UNSIGNED_SHORT	MPI_CHAR
short	signed short int	MPI_SHORT	MPI_SHORT
boolean	unsigned char	MPI_UNSIGNED_CHAR	MPI_BOOLEAN
int	signed long int	MPI_LONG	MPI_INT
long	signed long long int	MPI_LONG_LONG_INT	MPI_LONG
float	float	MPI_FLOAT	MPI_FLOAT
double	double	MPI_DOUBLE	MPI_DOUBLE

Because Java is platform independent, the size of simple types will be the same in all platforms. We have defined JavaWMPI datatypes that map directly to the Java datatypes. As a consequence, the user does not need to worry about the mapping between Java datatypes and MPI datatypes.

Beside these datatypes, JavaWMPI also provides the `MPI_PACKED` datatype that is used with packed messages, the `MPI_LB` pseudo-datatype that can be used to mark the lower bound of a datatype and `MPI_UB` that is used to mark the upper bound of a datatype.

3.4 Problems due to strong typing and the absence of pointers

All MPI functions with choice arguments associate actual arguments of different datatypes with the same dummy argument. Java does not allow this since it has no pointers and the associated casting.

When we have methods with different arguments we would have to use method overloading as shown in Figure 1.

```
public static native MPI_Send (int[], ...);
public static native MPI_Send (long[], ...);
```
Fig. 1. Example of methods with different argument datatypes.

However, there are many MPI communication functions, e.g. `MPI_Send`, `MPI_Bsend`, `MPI_Ssend`, `MPI_Rsend`, etc. If we used this approach, we would have tons of native methods for each function and datatype. To overcome this problem we introduce a set of native methods, called *SetData*, that performs the polymorphism between different Java datatypes.

These native methods return the starting memory address of the array as a Java long variable that can be used in the MPI routines. For example, in Figure 2 we can see the original WMPI call to `MPI_Send` in C/C++, followed by the equivalent Java call using our Java to WMPI interface.

```
MPI_Send(array, 10, MPI_DOUBLE, 0, TAG, MPI_COMM_WORLD);
MPI_Send(SetData(array), 10, MPI_DOUBLE, 0, TAG, MPI_COMM_WORLD);
```
Fig. 2. Equivalent C/C++ and Java calls to MPI_Send.

Another variant of these methods was implemented. This variant has one additional argument that specifies an index into the array. Figure 3 shows an example of this use.

```
MPI_Send(&array[5], 10, MPI_DOUBLE, 0, TAG, MPI_COMM_WORLD);
MPI_Send(SetData(array,5), 10, MPI_DOUBLE, 0, TAG, MPI_COMM_WORLD);
```
Fig. 3. Equivalent C/C++ and Java calls to MPI_Send using an index.

3.5 Mapping between WMPI and JavaWMPI arguments

The next Table presents the mapping between WMPI and JavaWMPI arguments.

Table 2. Mapping between WMPI and JavaWMPI arguments.

WMPI argument	JavaWMPI argument
int	int
int*	java.lang.Integer
int[]	int[]
void[]	SetData(type[])
MPI_Aint	long
MPI_Aint*	java.lang.Long
MPI_Aint[]	long[]
MPI_Status (or *)	MPI_Status
MPI_Datatype (or *)	MPI_Datatype
MPI_Comm (or *)	MPI_Comm
MPI_Group (or *)	MPI_Group
MPI_Request (or *)	MPI_Request
MPI_Op (or *)	MPI_Op
MPI_Errhandler (or *)	MPI_Errhandler

When we use int* we refer to a pointer to a int variable and when we use int[] we refer to an array of int variables.

There are some exceptions to the mapping scheme presented in Table 2. The methods MPI_Pack, MPI_Unpack, MPI_Attach_buffer and MPI_Dettach_buffer use a byte array instead of the value returned by the method SetData. This is due to the particular behaviour of these routines. When we are packing and unpacking data or declaring a memory zone to be attached to WMPI is more efficient to use an array of bytes.

4. Performance Results

In this section we present some performance results of the two Java bindings that we have implemented. All the measurements were taken with the NQueens benchmark with 14 queens in a cluster of Pentiums 200MHz running Windows NT 4.0, which are connected through a non-dedicated 10 Mbit/sec Ethernet.

The next Table presents the legend to some versions of the NQueens application that we have implemented in our study. This legend will be used in the Figures that are presented in the rest of the section.

Table 3. Different versions of the NQueens benchmark.

Versions of Nqueens Benchmark	
Legend	**Description**
CWMPI	C version using WMPI.
JWMPI	Java interface using WMPI.
JWMPI (Native)	Java interface but the real computation is done by a call to a native method written in C.

In the first experiment, presented in Figure 4, we compare the performance of the Java version of the NQueens benchmark with the C version, both using WMPI and WPVM libraries to communicate. The Java processes are executing with a Just-in-Time compiler by using the Symantec JIT that is distributed with JDK1.1.4. It uses our Java bindings to access the WMPI/WPVM routines.

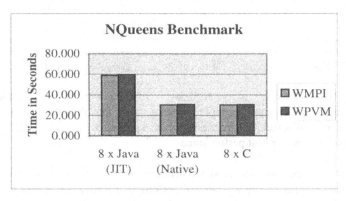

Fig. 4. The performance of Java versus C.

As can be seen in Figure 4, Just-in-Time compilation cannot achieve the performance of C compiled code, but when compared with interpreted Java it presents a drastic increase in performance. Interpreted Java run approximately 10 times slower when compared with Just-In-Time compilation and near 20 times slower when compared with C compiled code. We believe that with the evolution of JIT compilers and the appearance of new technologies that make use of dynamic compilation techniques, like the new HotSpot VM of Sun [9], the Java language will run as fast even or faster than compiled code.

Figure 4 also presents a Java version of the NQueens benchmark that uses a native method written in C to compute the kernel of the algorithm. The results obtained with this Java (Native) version allow us to conclude that practically no overhead is introduced by our Java bindings.

In Figure 5 we present several different combinations of heterogeneous clusters of processes using WMPI library. As can be seen we combined in an effective way programs that use Java and C processes in the same computation. These experiments are quite interesting since they prove that with the help provided by our Java bindings, we can achieve real heterogeneous computations.

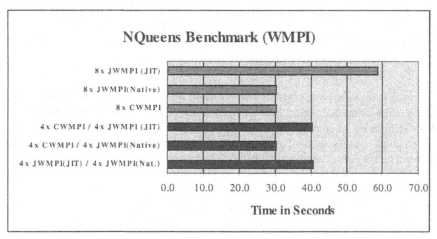

Fig. 5. Heterogeneous clusters of processes using the WMPI library.

In our implementations of the NQueens Benchmark the jobs are delivered on demand, allowing the faster workers to compute more jobs than the slower ones. All the computations that include C processes or Java processes that use the native version of the kernel present the best performance.

Until the Java compiler technology reaches maturity, the use of native code in Java programs is certainly a way to improve performance. Providing access to standard libraries often used in high-performance and scientific programming seems imperative in order to allow the reuse of existing code that was developed with MPI and PVM.

6. Related Work

The idea of providing access to standard libraries written in other languages is very attractive and there are several similar on going projects.

JavaMPI is a Java binding for MPI that was developed in Syracuse University [10]. In this binding only a few routines of MPI were implemented. JavaMPI does not use JNI; it uses instead the old native programming interface provided by JDK1.0.2 that is no longer supported in future releases of JDK.

JavaPVM is a Java to PVM interface [8]. Like our binding JavaPVM also made use of JNI and we have ported this binding to our Windows version of PVM.

A very interesting idea was presented in [11] and [12]. They developed a tool, called JCI, that can be used for automatically binding existing native C libraries to Java. They used the JCI tool to bind MPI, PBLAS and ScaLAPACK to Java.

The JPVM library presented in [13] provides a Java-based tool for PVM programming. Unlike JavaPVM, JPVM is a real implementation of PVM in Java and it presents a serious drawback: the lack of compatibility with PVM.

JavaNOW is another Java-based parallel programming tool presented in [14]. This system implemented the Linda programming model in Java and is not directly related with PVM and MPI. Finally, in [15] was presented another Java binding, but this one is oriented to the Nexus system.

7. Conclusions

In this paper, we have described the implementation of a Java interface for WMPI and we compared the performance of a parallel benchmark when using the Java interface in WMPI, WPVM and the C versions counterparts. The first results are quite promising and show that it is possible to program an application in Java that makes use of WPVM and WMPI. Some other results were taken in a mixed configuration where some of the processes were executing in Java and others in C. Those experiments show that it is possible to achieve really heterogeneous computations with some of the parts running in different languages.

References

1. Parallel Virtual Machine, http://www.epm.ornl.gov/pvm/
2. Message Passing Interface, http://www.mcs.anl.gov/mpi/
3. A.Alves, L.M.Silva, J.Carreira, J.G.Silva, *"WPVM: Parallel Computing for the People"*, Proc. of HPCN'95, High Performance Computing and Networking Europe, May 1995, Milano, Italy, Lecture Notes in Computer Science 918, pp. 582-587
4. Windows Message Passing Interface, http://dsg.dei.uc.pt/wmpi/
5. W.Blundon, *"Predictions for the Millennium"*, Java World Magazine, February 1998, http://www.javaworld.com/javaworld/jw-02-1998/jw-02-blundon.html/
6. A. van Hoff, *"Java: Getting Down to Business"*, Dr Dobbs Journal, pp. 20-24, January 1998
7. First Meeting of the Java Grande Forum, http://jhpc.org/grande/meeting.htm/
8. JavaPVM Homepage, http://homer.isye.gatech.edu/chmsr/JavaPVM/
9. Eric Armstrong, *"HotSpot: A new breed of virtual machine"*, JavaWorld, March 1998, http://www.javaworld.com/javaworld/jw-03-1998/jw-03-hotspot.html
10. MPI Java Wrapper Implementation, by Yuh-Jye Chang, B. Carpenter, G. Fox, http://www.npac.syr.edu/users/yjchang/mpi/mpi.html
11. S. Mintchev, V. Getov, *"Automatic Binding of Native Scientific Libraries to Java"*, Proceedings of ISCOPE'97, Springer LNCS, September 5, 1997
12. V. Getov, S. Flynn-Hummel, S. Mintchev, *"High-Performance Parallel Programming in Java: Exploiting Native Libraries"*, Proc. of ACM 1998 Workshop on Java for High-Performance Network Computing, February 1998, Palo Alto, California
13. A.J. Ferrari, *"JPVM: Network Parallel Computing in Java"*, Proc. of ACM 1998 Workshop on Java for High-Performance Network Computing, February 1998, Palo Alto, California
14. JavaNOW Project, http://www.mcs.anl.gov/george/projects.htm
15. I.Foster, G.K.Thiruvathukal, S.Tuecke. *"Technologies for Ubiquitous Supercomputing: A Java Interface to the Nexus Communication System"*, Syracuse NY, August 1996.

Part 3
Implementation Issues

Porting CHAOS Library to MPI

Marian Bubak[1,2], Piotr Luszczek[1], Agnieszka Wierzbowska[1]

[1] Institute of Computer Science, AGH, al. Mickiewicza 30, 30-059 Kraków, Poland
[2] Academic Computer Centre - CYFRONET, Nawojki 11, 30-950 Kraków, Poland
email: bubak@uci.agh.edu.pl
phone: (+48 12) 617 39 64, *fax:* (+48 12) 633 80 54

Abstract. CHAOS is a very flexible library for runtime support of irregular problems, yet unfortunately, its original implementation is not applicable to parallel programs which are running under MPI. This paper presents details of porting CHAOS to MPI. The most important feature of the new improved version consists in separate MPI communicators: for internal CHAOS use and for an application program. The code of the library was carefully revised and now it is ANSI C compliant. Porting CHAOS to MPI allows for a much wider usability of this library as now it may be applied on virtually every parallel computer.

1 Introduction

Recently, parallelization of so called irregular problems is becoming increasingly important direction in the development of large scale computations. The major feature of irregular problems is that access patterns to data are unknown until the runtime and their data structures are accessed through one or more levels of indirections. Therefore, these problems are extremely difficult to parallelize manually and, moreover, it is hard to develop parallelizing compilers which generate an efficient parallel code. That is why preprocessing and analysis should be done to define efficient communication schedules [1].

CHAOS, a runtime support library for parallelisation of irregular problems was developed in University of Maryland in 1994 [2, 3]. It was succesfully used to parallelize many applications – unstructured scientific problems including explicit multigrid unstructured computational fluid dynamic solvers, molecular dynamics codes, diagonal or polynomial preconditioned iterative linear solvers, direct Monte Carlo simulation codes and particle-in-cell codes [4, 5]. The extensions of CHAOS were also used by experimental parallelizing compilers.

CHAOS is a very flexible and powerful tool, so it may be an appropriate basis for further development of programming tools for more complex problems like runtime support for out-of-core problems. Many large scientific computer programs require large datasets, and, consequently, their execution times are determined by the time spent in input/output operations [6, 7].

Although from the very begining CHAOS was meant to be portable, unfortunately, it was not developed to co-operate with MPI standard. It is a real drawback, especially taking into account the new features of MPI-2, namely parallel I/O [8]. This motivated our efforts to port CHAOS to MPI, as we are interested in development of the programming environment supporting irregular out-of-core applications. Our intention was

- to create a stable, portable, extendable, well documented, tested and highly efficient tool,
- to offer CHAOS for future advanced unstructured applications as well as parallelizing compilers,
- to support parallel I/O in MPI-2 and relatively easy application of CHAOS functions in the field of out-of-core parallel programming.

2 Short overview of CHAOS

CHAOS was built on top of the PARTI library [9] which supported programming according to so called *inspector-executor* model. CHAOS may be useful in parallelization of different types of irregular problems:

- static problems where access patterns to data arrays are not known until runtime, and they do not change in the course of computation,
- partially adaptive (or multiphase) problems which consist of multiple phases, while in each phase access patterns do not change significantly,
- adaptive problems which consist of several phases whereas the access patterns change a lot from phase to phase.

The library enables

- dynamic partition and redistribution of data and work during runtime using communication schedules,
- automatic generation of send and receive messages,
- efficient translation from global to local indices,
- runtime optimization to achieve good load balancing and to reduce communication overheads.

3 CHAOS under MPI

Although CHAOS was designed as a portable library it was first implemented on Paragon parallel computer and this, in turn, resulted in a relatively strong dependence on the specific features of this architecture and NX message passing system. For this reason, the porting consisted not only in changing the communication layer but, first of all, in careful reviewing of the code. It is worth mentioning that there are about 300 functions and 20000 lines of code in original version of CHAOS [3].

The most important change we have introduced is a new relation between parallel program, CHAOS library, and MPI message-passing environment as presented in Fig. 1: we have separated the MPI communicator for internal CHAOS use from the application one. This results in additional flexibility and safety.

Another important feature is that now the number of computing nodes is not restricted any more to powers of 2, and it is possible to organize computations in such a way that only a part of computing nodes available to an application are used by CHAOS.

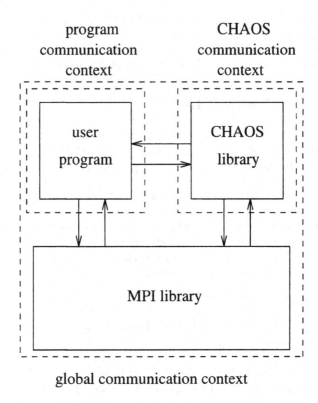

Fig. 1. Relations between application, CHAOS and MPI

As original version of CHAOS code was written according to Kernighan and Ritchie fashion of programming, we have restructured it to be compliant with the ANSI C standard and now one may compile the CHAOS source code without any warnings. The whole C code is ANSI C conformant, i.e.: all functions have been supplied with typed prototypes and all constants are typed. The internal structure of the library have become more clear, relevant comments have been added, the source code was organized according to its logical structure and the internal data types has been described. All the internal definitions, functions and types are now hidden from the user and now there is only one library file build up from the sources.

New types have been defined to support MPI opaque types, and explicit output functions are reprogrammed so they are portable to most of parallel platforms. In the original code, there were no name clashes between CHAOS and MPI, so there was no need to change CHAOS function calls in all the applications using previous version of CHAOS.

During the thorough revision of the code the following mistakes have been fixed: a few logical bugs, mistakes in CHAOS manual, as well as missing and duplicate functions.

Fig. 2 illustrates how new CHAOS library may be used together with MPI to develop a parallel program for solving an adaptive irregular problem. First, MPI and CHAOS are independently initiated with their own contexts (see Fig. 1). In the next stage, the code is parallelized by calling CHAOS procedures. CHAOS_schedule_proc is used to build a communication schedule by inspecting indirection array, CHAOS_Xgather gets data from other processors whereas CHAOS_Xscatter sends data to other processors according to established communication schedule.

4 Summary

The new library was successfully tested on Hewlett-Packard Exemplar S2000 under HP MPI 1.4.using C language version of programs (Ising model simulation and graph algorithms) supplied with the original CHAOS [3].

Now we are working on an extension of the library for parallel computations on heterogeneous networks of computers, adding portable Fortran wrappers, and developing the more general data partitioners suitable for any number of computing nodes which may differ from a power of 2. The next step will be development of the procedures which support solving out-of-core problems under MPI using this new version of CHAOS.

Porting CHAOS to MPI allows for a much wider usability of this powerful library as now it may be available on almost all parallel computers. It may interoperate with other libraries without a danger of interference while internal (i.e. CHAOS) messages are separated from user-defined communication in an application. MPI contexts are much more flexible than the use of huge tag numbers in NX message-passing system. Moreover, this enhances portabilty of applications based on CHAOS as well as its extensions for compilers parallelizing irregular codes.

Acknowledgements

We are indebted to Prof. Peter Brezany from Vienna University for introducing us to a very interesting subject of research, his kindness and expertise, and valuable discussions and suggestions. We are also grateful to Prof. Jacek Mościński, Mr. Marek Pogoda, and Mr. Włodzimierz Funika for their comments and suggestions.

This work was partially supported by KBN under grant 8 T11C 006 15.

```
#include <chaos.h>

int main(int argc, char **argv)
{
    ...
    /* Initialize MPI library. */
    MPI_Init( &argc, &argv );
    ...
    /* Initialize CHAOS library --
        all processes go into CHAOS messaging context
        and will perform CHAOS library calls. */
    CHAOS_setup( NULL, 0 );

    /* for each time step */
    for ( i = 0 ; i < N ; i++ )
    {
        /* create communication schedule as fast as possible */
        schedule = CHAOS_schedule_proc( indirection_array );

        /* perform communication */
        /* X = {d,f,i,c} according to type of data transferred */

        CHAOS_Xgather( buffer, data, schedule );

        /* perform computation */

        /* perform communication */
        CHAOS_Xscatter( buffer, data, schedule );

        /* 'schedule' will not be useful anymore */
        CHAOS_free_sched( schedule );

        /* change access pattern */
        for ( i = 0 /* ... */ )
            indirection_array[i] = f( i );
    }
    /* Leave CHAOS library. */
    CHAOS_exit();
    ...
    /* Leave MPI library. */
    MPI_Finalize();
    ...
}
```

Fig. 2. Template of a parallel program using CHAOS for solving an adaptive problem;

References

1. Mukherjee, S., Sharma, S., Hill, M., Larus, J., Rogers, A., and Saltz, J.: Efficient Support for Irregular Applications on Distributed-Memory Machines, Proceedings of the Fifth ACM SIGPLAN Symposium on Principles & Practice of Parallel Programming '95, Santa Barbara, California, July 19-21 (1995) 68-79
2. Hwang, Y.-S., Moon, B., Sharma, S., Ponnusamy, R., Das, R., and Saltz, J.: Runtime and Language Support for Compiling Adaptive Irregular Programs on Distributed Memory Machines, Software: Practice & Experience 25 (6) (1995) 597-621
3. Saltz, J., Ponnusammy, R., Sharma, S., Moon, B., Hwang,Y.-S., Uysal, M., and Das, R.: A Manual for the CHAOS Runtime Library, UMIACS Technical Reports CS-TR-3437 and UMIACS-TR-95-34, University of Maryland: Department of Computer Science, March 1995;
   ftp://hpsl.cs.umd.edu/pub/chaos_distribution
4. Hwang, J.-S., Das, R., Saltz, J., Brooks, B., and Hodoscek, M.: Parallelizing Molecular Dynamics Programs for Distributed Memory Machines: An Application of the CHAOS Runtime Support Library, IEEE Computational Science and Engineering, 2 (1995) 18-29
5. Edjlali, G., Sussman, A., and Saltz, J.: Interoperability of Data Parallel Runtime Libraries, International Parallel Processing Symposium 1997, April 1997
6. Brezany, P., Choudhary, A.: Techniques and Optimization for Developing Irregular Out-of-Core Applications on Distributed-memory Systems, Institute for Software technology and Parallel Systems, University of Vienna, TR 96-4, December 1996
7. Brezany, P.: Input/Output Intensively Parallel Computing, Lecture Notes in Computer Science, Vol. 1220, Springer-Verlag, Berlin Heildelberg New York (1997)
8. Message Passing Interface Forum: MPI-2: Extensions to the Message-Passing Interface, July 18, 1997;
   http://www.mpi-forum.org/docs/mpi-20.ps
9. Berryman, H., Saltz, J., and Scroggs, J.: Execution time support for adaptive scientific algorithms on distributed memory machines, Concurency: Practice and Experience 3 (1991) 159-178

Athapascan: An Experience on Mixing MPI Communications and Threads

Alexandre Carissimi[1,2] and Marcelo Pasin[1,3]

[1] APACHE Project (sponsored by CNRS, IMAG, INRIA and UJF)
Laboratoire de Modélisation et Calcul
B.P. 53, F-38041 Grenoble Cedex 9, France
{alexandre.carissimi, marcelo.pasin}imag.fr
[2] On leave from UFRGS-Informatica, Brazil, CAPES-COFECUB fellow.
[3] On leave from UFSM-DELC, Brazil, CAPES-COFECUB fellow.

Abstract. Current parallel programming models as message passing exploit properly coarse-grain parallelism and suit well for regular applications. However, many applications have irregular behaviour and fine-grain parallelism, in which cases multithreading is more suitable. Multiprocessing and clustering have became cost-effective manner to build distributed-memory parallel machines due to technological progress. This paper discusses Athapascan, a multithreaded, portable, parallel programming runtime system, targeted for irregular applications. It is designed to integrate multithreading and communication, taking profit of both multiprocessing and communicating networks.

1 Introduction

In the recent past years, the message-passing model emerged as a paradigm for parallel programming, exploiting coarse-grain parallelism on regular algorithms. These algorithms usually present good data locality and can be split on small weighted computations with a reasonable knowledge of their communication patterns. However, many applications are irregular, presenting dynamic data locality, unbalanced computations and unpredictable communication patterns. These applications are better suited for multithreading, which allows data transfer by shared memory, load balancing by time-sharing and no communication.

Nevertheless, multithreading is designed to exploit parallelism on shared-memory multiprocessor, or within a single address space. One of the open research problem is how to integrate threads and communication in an efficient way on distributed-memory systems to exploit fine- and coarse-grain parallelism.

In this paper we present some experiences and results obtained with the Athapascan [9] project, designed to deal in an efficient and portable way with the integration of multithreading and communications. This paper is organized as follows: section 2 introduces Athapascan and some of its implementations issues, section 3 presents the main drawbacks found when integrating threads and communications on Athapascan developement. Some results to illustrate Athapascan performance are given on section 4. On section 5 we present related work from other research projects. Finally, we conclude on section 6.

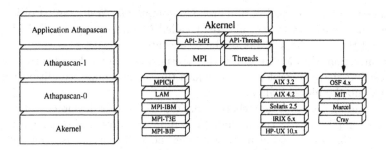

Fig. 1. Athapascan architecture

2 Athapascan

Athapascan is a parallel programming environment designed to be both portable and efficient [9]. It has a multi-layer organization and each layer provides a well-defined interface. It is possible to write applications on top of any of its layers (see figure 1). The upper layer, Athapascan-1, is a high-level data-flow language with explicit parallelism and enabling various scheduling strategies to allow load balancing. The middle layer, Athapascan-0, provides local and remote thread handling and multithreaded communication. The lower layer is called Akernel, short for Athapascan-Kernel. It provides raw thread-to-thread communication over standard MPI and POSIX-threads libraries. This article is focused on the two lower layers, Athapascan-0 and Akernel.

Athapascan-0 establishes at startup time a virtual machine composed by nodes. Each node executes a main thread (function main()) and new threads can be created locally or remotely, on demand base. The thread handling interface of Athapascan-0 is strongly based on POSIX-threads, adding remote creation. Local synchronization facilities as mutexes, semaphores and condition variables are available. Athapascan-0 inherits POSIX-threads' scheduling policies and priorities.

Every communication is based on a **port**, an address used by threads to send and receive messages. The message passing functions of Athapascan-0 are basically point-to-point send and receive. Every Athapascan-0 call involving communication (messages, remote thread creation, remote urgent calls) can be synchronous or asynchronous. They have an associated **request**, which can be used to check their status or wait for their completion.

The lower layer, Akernel, is intended to be the portability layer. It is built on top of standard MPI and threads libraries (POSIX, DCE). It contains a set of macros (thread-API) that gives the to upper layer an homogeneous interface for threads, independent of the threads implementation used. It also provides a thread-safe subset of MPI throught a MPI-API.

Send and receive calls executed by Akernel generate an MPI request, which is stored in a request handler passed by the caller thread. Each request handler has an object (**wait context**) allocated to it which stores a conditional variable used to block the calling thread until its request completion. Wait context objects are stored on a linked list. A special thread, called Akernel daemon, polls MPI every now and then, to check if any of the wait contexts in the list is completed. At the completion of an MPI request, the Akernel daemon marks its corresponding request handler as completed and signals the corresponding condition variable to wake-up the blocked thread.

Depending on the system characteristics, the Akernel daemon can be configured at compile time to run in one of two different ways: poll or timed. On poll mode, the daemon runs indefinitely, polling the MPI requests associated to each wait context, usually yielding the processor only at the end of its time-slice. On timed mode, the daemon periodically sleeps for a certain time and then it polls all the MPI requests on the queue. In either poll or timed mode, the Akernel daemon pauses if a request is completed or if the queue has been completely polled. In poll mode, the pause is done by just yielding the processor while in timed mode the daemon goes to sleep again.

3 MPI and POSIX-threads

One of the Athapascan initial goals was to be able to run transparently on heterogeneous systems. This goal, associated with portability, carried us to use *de facto* standards, like MPI and POSIX-threads, as basic building blocks, nevertheless we found some drawbacks. MPI has emerged as being a well supported standard for communication, providing a rich set of communication primitives, promising portability, heterogeneity and good performance. However some problems arise due to MPI defining an interface and not a protocol. On the other hand, the behavior of MPI implementations when used in presence of multithreaded programs is somewhat awkward. MPI interface was conceived to be thread-safe but nearly all implementations are not. These problems are discussed on the next two sub-sections.

3.1 MPI is an interface, not a protocol

The primitive idea of Athapascan was to define an heterogeneous Athapascan virtual machine to exploit both network and architectures heterogeneities. The first problem found, while doing that, arises from the fact that none of current MPI implementations can use more than one underlying communication library at the same time. As an immediately consequence a single MPI task can not be connected to two differents network interfaces prohibiting heterogeneous networked clusters. One possible solution is to provide at application level some routing facilities. To implement that we must think about a single addressing scheme indepedently of underlying network and ways to define topologies. Until now MPI implementations have inherited as node identifier the same addressing scheme presented by underlying network (IP for TCP/IP, node number to switched machines, etc).

However MPI is an interface not a protocol. It means that MPI standard defines only function interfaces and does not specify any internal structure or message format. Every MPI implementation has a different node identification scheme and a different command line syntax. The different MPI implementors defined their structures according to their needs. Consequently, different MPI implementations do not interact, even using the same network.

Many computer manufacturers deliver their parallel machines with well-tuned versions of MPI to their proprietary networks. Even public domain MPi versions are conceived to exploit efficiently many differents networks. For example, MPICH uses MPL (native communication library of system's high-performance switch) on IBM-SP machines, to obtain low latencies and high bandwidth communication. The same MPICH uses TCP/IP in a general network of Unix workstations. Clustering together IBM-SP and single workstations leads to use MPICH TCP/IP version despite of MPI high performance offered by MPL version. In this case even the internal IBM-SP nodes are obliged to communicate using MPICH TCP/IP implying in worst performances.

By now Athapascan is ported on different hardware platforms, networks, and operating systems, using different MPI implementations. It still remains homogeneous on some aspects, i.e., all nodes use the same MPI implementation and the same network type. It would be helpful if MPI standard comprised a protocol definition, with common launching procedures, unified node identification and some routing facilities.

3.2 MPI: thread-safe, thread-aware, thread-unsafe

In multithreaded programs, functions can be called and resources can be accessed concurrently by several threads. Code written for multithreaded programs must consider these accesses to ensure data consistency and resources integrity. To allow concurrent access, functions must be reentrant: they cannot have any local static data remaining from one call to another, neither can they return pointers to static data.

A thread-safe function is a reentrant function whose shared resources are protected from concurrent access by mutexes, so it can be called by multiple threads without risk of corruption. Thread-safe functions have one important limitation: progress is not guaranteed. If a thread-safe function does a blocking call keeping a locked mutex, it can block all of others threads needing to lock the same mutex, even the entire process.

A function is called thread-aware when it works despite the fact that it is being executed concurrently or sequentially by different threads. A thread-aware function, like thread-safe functions, is reentrant and protects concurrent accesses with mutexes, but it does not block other threads when it executes blocking calls. Similarly, a thread-unsafe function is not thread-aware, not even thread-safe.

MPI standard defines a thread-safe interface. No MPI calls need local static data or have to return pointers to static data. Unfortunately, our experiments showed that most MPI implementations are neither thread-safe nor thread-

Table 1. Latencies and bandwidths

	MPI mode	Ath	MPI	MPI+1	MPI+2
Latency	poll	614	95	598	1790
(μs)	yield	620	106	230	450
0-byte messages	sleep	624	150	820	2410
Bandwidth	poll	12.5	19.5	6	3.1
(Mbyte/s)	yield	12.5	19.5	12.3	7.7
64k-byte messages	sleep	12.5	16.6	5.5	2.9

aware, [1] wich implies in two problems. When a thread does a blocking MPI call, the entire MPI process is blocked waiting for its completion, so all other threads cannot execute. To avoid it, one can think about making only non-blocking calls to MPI. This leads to another problem: data integrity when MPI is called concurrently from different threads. To implement MPI's thread-awareness, Athapascan makes only non-blocking calls to MPI, all protected by a mutex. All Athapascan communication blocking primitives are translated onto a non-blocking call. Blocking behavior is simulated using conditions variables.

4 Some results

In this section we present the overhead introduced by Athapascan layers, if compared to the MPI communication library used, measuring latency and bandwidth when executing a ping-pong benchmark. After, we introduce a parallel ping-pong, allowing several threads to execute simultaneous ping-pongs. We show the effect of communication and computation overlapping. The values presented were obtained doing an average of 1000 samples for each message size. Our test platform is an IBM-SP with 32 nodes running IBM MPI 2.3 over AIX 4.2. Each node is composed by Power-1 processors at 66 MHz and the crossbar high-performance switch technology is TB2.

This Athapascan implementation attracted special interest due to the thread-awareness of IBM MPI 2.3. It has three operating modes which define its behavior when it waits for a request completion: poll, yield and sleep. On poll mode, the calling thread does a busy-wait loop checking for the completion, returning when it's done. The thread only yields the processor in its time slice end. On yield mode, the caller thread polls once and yields the processor, repeating this procedure every time it is rescheduled until the completion. On sleep mode, the caller thread is blocked. Every time a network packet arrives MPI checks all blocked requests and unblocks the completed ones.

We wanted first to evaluate the overhead introduced in the communication by Akernel daemon. The test program is a simple ping-pong using 0- and 64k-byte messages, the first to measure the latency, the last to measure the bandwidth.

---

[1] By our knowledge, only the IBM MPI (version 2.3) is thread-aware.

Table 1 shows the values of latency and bandwidth for Athapascan-0 (Ath column), compared to MPI (MPI column) for all MPI modes. Athapascan has permanently two pending communications, requested by internal daemon threads (remote thread creation and urgent service call). In a ping-pong program, no remote thread is created, no remote urgent call is done, and both daemons stay blocked in message reception. To better compare MPI with Athapascan, we added one and two more threads, just blocked in a receive for the whole execution of the MPI ping-pong program. The columns MPI+1 and MPI+2 of table 1 show the values of latency and bandwidth measured for MPI in those executions.

Athapascan latencies and bandwidths are independent from MPI modes because we defined a different polling policy: Athapascan threads block on condition variables, not inside MPI. Only non-blocking MPI call are used. While in MPI (poll and yield modes) every thread does its own poll, Athapascan has the Akernel daemon to do it for all of them. MPI's sleep mode is slower because the network packet of the TB2 is relatively small and it interrupts MPI too often.

The advantage obtained with the mixture of multithreading and communication is overlapping computing and communication phases. When a thread blocks, waiting for a communication completion, other threads can continue executing, keeping the processor busy. To measure this characteristic, we used a multithreaded ping-pong program. A certain number of threads were created on two nodes, each pair of those threads doing a ping-pong. Figure 2 gives Athapascan bandwidth for a ping-pong thread. If for one ping-pong we have 12.5 Mbyte/s, doing 4 concurrent ping-pongs we have 15.6 Mbyte/sec (3.9 Mbyte/s for each). In other systems we have similar results. For example, on a network of Pentium (@133Mhz), running solaris 2.5, LAM MPI, and an ethernet 100 Mbits network we found the following values: MPI ping-pong version gives a latency of 0.7 ms and a bandwith of 3.4 Mbyte/s, while Athapascan presents a constant latency of 1.2 ms and a bandwith equals to 3.2 Mbyte/s for one ping-pong thread, 3.4 Mbyte/s for 2 threads, and 3.8 Mbyte/s for 4 threads. We noted that Athapascan-0 adds thread-safety to MPI.

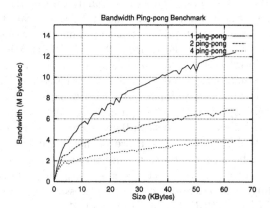

Fig. 2. Athapascan-0 bandwidth on multithreaded ping-pong benchmark

5 Related work

Other research groups proposed runtime systems to integrate communication libraries and multithreading libraries. We discuss some of them below.

Chant [3] is a multithreading package which provides communication using both point-to-point and remote service request primitives. Chant is built using standard multithreading and communication libraries (POSIX-threads [2] and MPI [1]). Communications are provided extending the threads library interface to support two new types of global objects: chanters, and ropes. A chanter is a global thread identifier, a triplet consisting of a processing element id, a process id, and a local thread id. A rope is a group of chanter threads, intended for collective communications.

Nexus [4] is a runtime library integrating threads and communications. Its design is based on two key concepts: global pointers and remote service requests. A global pointer is an object representing an address within a given address space. A remote service request represents an asynchronous event that invokes a handler function pointed by a global pointer. A new thread can be created to execute the handler function.

PM^2 [5] is a portable programming environment which proposes a programming model to exploit fine grain parallelism on irregular applications. PM^2 is implemented on the top of Marcel threads [6] and a communication kernel (PVM, MPI or TCP/IP). Its programming model is based on lightweight remote procedure calls and allows thread migration.

Panda [7] is a parallel virtual machine designed to hide system dependencies on natives operating system and hardware, allowing easy portability to Orca, an object-based distributed shared memory system. Its base building blocks are not standard. This decision was based on performance reasons and by the fact that Panda was first designed to run on the top of Amoeba operating system. Panda implements its own multithreading package (based on POSIX-threads) and exploits efficiently native communications primitives.

Athapascan-0 with respect of Chant gives remote thread creation and a more rich set of communication primitives. Nexus and Athapascan-0 have different philosophies, while Nexus is a target abstract machine to systems programming tools (e.g., compositional C++, Fortran-M, RPC, MPICH) Athapascan-0 gives a more complete interface for program developpment on an abstract machine. PM^2 is similar to Athapascan-0 in many aspects, but loses on portability because Marcel threads are tunned to each platform. Also Athapascan-0 is used as base to Athapascan-1 giving a more robust programming tool based on data-flow concept. Compared with Panda, Athapascan-0 gives more and easier portability because it uses standard building blocks. However this portability sometimes leads to less performance because standards are not tunned to exploit native systems characteristics. We can still cite other systems which integrate communication and multithreading: Athapascan-0a [8] (the predecessor of Athapascan-0, based on PVM), TPVM [10], MPI-F [11], and PORTS [12].

6 Conclusion and Future Work

We have described our experiences on Athapascan runtime system design. The discussion was focused on Athapascan-0 layer whose main goal is to integrate communications and multithreaded programming. We have discussed how Athapascan kernel manages this integration and the main difficulties found during its implementation. Also, we have presented some performance values.

The current and future work on Athapascan runtime system is based on two axes. The first one is trying to reduce polling overheads, changing the interaction algorithm between Athapascan-0 and its lower layers. Special attention is given to multiprocessor architectures. The second aspect is porting Athapascan to use shared-memory facilities on NUMA machines (e.g. SGI Origin2000).

References

1. W. Gropp, E. Lusk, and A. Skjellum, "Using MPI: Portable Parallel Programming with the Message Passing Interface", MIT Press, 1995.
2. IEEE, "IEEE P1003.1c/D10: Draft Standard for Information technology - Portable Operating System Interface (POSIX)", September, 1994.
3. M. Haines, D. Cronk, and P. Mehrotra, "On the Design of Chant: A Talking Threads Package", Supercomputing '94, pp. 350–359, nov, 1994.
4. I. Foster, C. Kesselman and S. Tuecke, "The Nexus Approach to Integrating Multithreading and Communication", Journal of Parallel and Distributed Computing, v.37, 1, pp. 70–82, 25, aug, 1996.
5. R. Namyst, J.F. Mhaut, "PM2: Parallel Multithreaded Machine. A computing environment on top of PVM", 2nd EuroPVM Meeting, pp. 179-184, Lyon 1995.
6. R. Namyst, J.F. Mhaut, "MARCEL: Une bibliotheque de Processus Legers", LIFL, Universite de Lille, 1995.
7. R. Bhoedjang, T. Ruhl, R. Hofman, K. Langendoen, H. Bal, and F. Kaashoek, "Panda: A Portable Platform to Support Parallel Programming Languages", Proceedings of the USENIX Symposium on Experiences with Distributed and Multiprocessor Systems, (SEDMSIV): September 22–23, 1993, San Diego, California.
8. M. Christaller, "Vers un support d'excution portable pour applications paralleles irrgulires : Athapascan-0", Ph.D. thesis, Universit Joseph Fourier, Grenoble, France, 1996.
9. I. Ginzburg, "Athapascan-0b: Integration efficace et portable de multiprogramation legere et de communications", Ph.D. thesis, Institut National Polytechnique de Grenoble, Grenoble, France, 1997.
10. A. Ferrari and V.S. Sunderman, "TPVM: Distributed concurrent computing with lightweight processes", Proc. of IEEE High Performance Computing, IEEE Press, Washington D.C., 1995, pp. 211–218.
11. H. Franke, P. Hochschild, P. Pattnaik, J.P. Prost and M. Snir, "MPI-F: an MPI Prototype Implementation on IBM-SP1." Proc. 2nd workshop on environments and tools for parallel scientific computing, J.Dongarra and B.Tourancheau eds., SIAM, Townsend Tennessee, 1994, pp. 43–55.
12. The PORTS Consortium, "PORTS:POrtable Run Time System", *documents avaiable from:* http://www.cs.uoregon.edu/paracomp/ports, 1996.

Developing Message–Passing Applications on MPICH under Ensemble

Yiannis Cotronis

Dep. of Informatics, Univ. of Athens, Panepistimiopolis, 17184 Athens, Greece
Phone:+301 7275223, Fax:+301 7219561, e–mail:cotronis@di.uoa.gr

Abstract. We present an implementation methodology for message–passing applications, called Ensemble applied to MPI. Applications are implemented by reusable executables having open, scalable interfaces and by scripts specifying process communication graphs, annotated with application execution information. An MPICH procgroup file is generated from scripts and executed my mpirun.

1 Introduction

The design and implementation of message–passing (MP) applications have been recognized as complex tasks. Designing MP applications involves designing the combined behavior of its processes, that is, their individual execution restricted by their communication and synchronization interactions. Implementation of MP applications involves programming of its sequential processes, as well as (latent) management of processes and architecture resources. The emergence of Message Passing Environments (MPE), such as PVM [5] and MPI [7], or more correctly its implementations (e.g. [2,1]), provide abstractions of architectures significantly simplifying process and resource management.

Nevertheless, the step from design to implementation remains, in general, a demanding task, requiring special effort. The main implementation complexity arises from the process management models of MPEs. Each MPE is suited for specific types of process topologies, those being closer to its process management model. For example, PVM and, respectively MPI favor tree and, respectively ring or grid topologies. Topologies not well suited to an MPE may certainly be implemented, but require complex programming. Consequently, the implementation effort does not depend only on the design, but also on the target MPE, each requiring different techniques. More effort is required for implementing scaling of topologies and code reuse.

We have developed an implementation methodology, called Ensemble, alleviating the above problems. Implementations maintain the original design, look similar on different MPEs, are easily maintainable, scalable, reusable and mechanically portable to other MPEs. In section 2, we examine implementation complexities under MPICH; in section 3, we outline Ensemble and tools for MPICH; in 4, we demonstrate the reusability of executables; and in 5, we present our conclusions.

2 Implementation on MPI and MPICH on Clusters

Process management, in general, involves process creation and their identification, and establishment of communication channels. In MPICH, processes are created by the mpirun command. If the implementation is organized in a SPMD style the command mpirun -np<np><progname> runs progname on np processors. If an application is organized in an MPMD style, a procgroup file is needed, which contains a list of executables in the form <hostname> <#procs> <progname>. The command mpirun -p4pg<procgroup><myprog> starts the application, where myprog is started directly. Mpirun has a number of other options, which are beyond the scope of exploring here. In all cases, mpirun manages processes and architecture resources.

Processes in MPI are identified by their rank number. Similarly to other MPEs, channels in MPI are established implicitly by providing the appropriate process identifiers (rank), tagging identifiers (tagid) and context (communicator), as parameters to communication routines. Such implicit channel establishment demands programming and its complexity depends on the topology, as well as on the MPE.

In a regular topology, rank identifiers may be associated to process positions by functions and, consequently, each process may determine its communicating processes from its own rank. Scaling regular topologies is implemented by parameterizing process position functions. Designs of irregular process topologies are much more difficult to implement, as the association of process ranks with their position is not possible, in general. Scaling of irregular topologies is also difficult to implement, as there may only be local, regular sub-topologies. Finally, reusability of executables is limited as they are programmed to operate in a fixed topology.

To alleviate such problems we propose a scheme for establishing channels explicitly, rather than implicitly. We design executables with open communication interfaces, a set of communication ports. Ports in MPI are structures of triplets (rank, tagid, and communicator), which specify communication channels. Communication routines in programs refer to such (open) ports, rather than using triplets directly. Processes get values for their ports upon their creation.

Topology creation and scaling requires the replication of processes and establishing channels, by symmetric and consistent port assignments. For topologies, such as a torus or a ring, it is sufficient to replicate identical processes, each having the same number of ports. However, for other topologies, such as master/slave or client/server, each process may have any number of ports, possibly within a range. We thus permit scaling of interface ports for individual processes. In this scheme (process creation, interface scaling, interface assignments) any topology, regular or irregular, may be easily established and scaled. Furthermore, programs are reusable like library components, as they do not rely on communicating with any specific processes. In the next section we describe the Ensemble tools which support this scheme.

3 MPICH and the Ensemble Methodology and Tools

Ensemble implementations consist of an 'ensemble' of: 1. Scripts specifying annotated Process Communication Graphs (PCG). PCGs depict the process topologies; nodes and arcs of PCGs are annotated with MPICH related information required for process creation on specific architecture and communication. 2. The reusable executables, which are message–passing library components having open scalable interfaces. 3. The Loader, which interprets the annotated PCGs and runs applications. We simply use mpirun on an appropriate procgroup file generated from the annotated PCG.

We demonstrate Ensemble by implementing the application Get Maximum. The requirement is simple: there are Terminal processes, which get an integer parameter and require the maximum of these integers. We design the following solution, called Terminal–Relays–in–Ring: Terminals are connected as client processes to associated Relay processes. Each Terminal sends (via port Out) its integer parameter to its Relay and, eventually, receives (via port In) the required maximum. Relays receive (via their Cin ports) integer values from their client Terminals and find the local maximum. Relays are connected in a ring. They find the global maximum by sending (via Pout port) their current maximum to their next neighbor in the ring, receiving (via Pin port) a value from their previous neighbor, comparing and selecting the maximum of these two values. Relays repeat the send–receive–select cycle M-1 times, where M is the size of the ring. Finally, Relays send (via Cout ports) the global maximum to their client Terminal processes. The topology or process communication graph (PCG) of the design is depicted in Fig. 1. The design is irregular, as Relays are associated with distinct numbers of Terminals.

3.1 The Application Script

The script is directly obtained from the design and abstractly specifies an implementation: the program components; the processes and their interface; the communication channels; the application parameters; the use of architecture resources. The script for Terminal-Relays-in-Ring for three Relays and six Terminals is depicted in the first column of Fig. 1.

The script is structured in three main parts. The first part, headed by PCG, specifies the PCG of the application, which is independent of any MPE or architecture. The PCG part has three sections. In the Components section, we specify abstractions of the components involved in the topology (e.g. Terminal) by their name (e.g. T), their communication interface and their design parameters, explained in the sequel. For components we specify their communication port types and the valid range of ports of each type in brackets. Communication types are depicted on PCGs on the inner circle of process nodes. The actual ports are depicted on the outer circle. The Terminal component, for example, has two synchronous communication types (In and Out), whilst the Relay component has four, two asynchronous (Cin, Cout) and two synchronous (Pin, Pout). Types In and Out of Terminal have exactly one port. A Relay process may have

Application Script		PCG and its Annotation

`APPLICATION Get_Maximum_by_Ring;`
`PCG`
`Components`
`  T:In,Out(Synch)[1..1]`
`  R:Pin,Pout(Asynch)[0..1],`
`    Cin,Cout(Synch)[0..];`
`    design: M;`
`Processes`
`  T[1],T[2],T[3],`
`  T[4],T[5],T[6]#In,Out:1;`
`  R[1]#Cin,Cout:1,Pout,Pin:1;M=3;`
`  R[2]#Cin,Cout:2,Pout,Pin:1;M=3;`
`  R[3]#Cin,Cout:3,Pout,Pin:1;M=3;`
`Channels`
`  T[1].Out[1] -> R[1].Cin[1];`
`  T[2].Out[1] -> R[2].Cin[1];`
`  T[3].Out[1] -> R[2].Cin[2];`
`  T[4].Out[1] -> R[3].Cin[1];`
`  T[5].Out[1] -> R[3].Cin[2];`
`  T[6].Out[1] -> R[3].Cin[3];`
`  T[1].In[1] <- R[1].Cout[1];`
`  T[2].In[1] <- R[2].Cout[1];`
`  T[3].In[1] <- R[2].Cout[2];`
`  T[4].In[1] <- R[3].Cout[1];`
`  T[5].In[1] <- R[3].Cout[2];`
`  T[6].In[1] <- R[3].Cout[3];`
`  R[1].Pout[1] -> R[2].Pin[1];`
`  R[2].Pout[1] -> R[3].Pin[1];`
`  R[3].Pout[1] -> R[1].Pin[1];`
	P
	C
	G
	
	B
	u
	i
	l
	d
	e
	r
		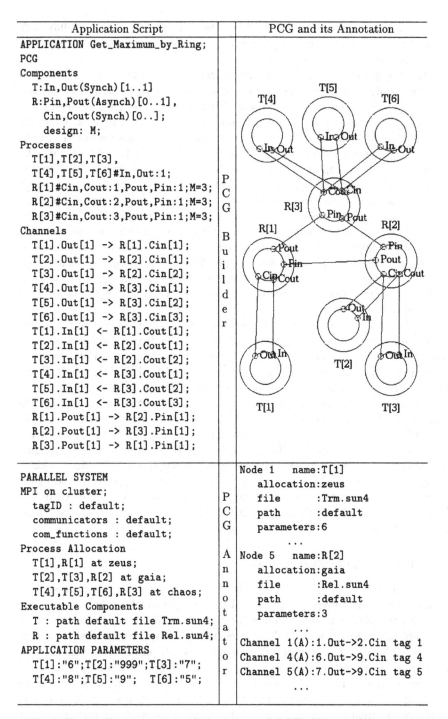

`PARALLEL SYSTEM`
`MPI on cluster;`
`  tagID : default;`
`  communicators : default;`
`  com_functions : default;`
`Process Allocation`
`  T[1],R[1] at zeus;`
`  T[2],T[3],R[2] at gaia;`
`  T[4],T[5],T[6],R[3] at chaos;`
`Executable Components`
`  T : path default file Trm.sun4;`
`  R : path default file Rel.sun4;`
`APPLICATION PARAMETERS`
`  T[1]:"6";T[2]:"999";T[3]:"7";`
`  T[4]:"8";T[5]:"9";  T[6]:"5";`
	P
	C
	G
	
	A
	n
	n
	o
	t
	a
	t
	o
	r
		`Node 1    name:T[1]`
		`  allocation:zeus`
		`  file      :Trm.sun4`
		`  path      :default`
		`  parameters:6`
		`      ...`
		`Node 5    name:R[2]`
		`  allocation:gaia`
		`  file      :Rel.sun4`
		`  path      :default`
		`  parameters:3`
		`      ...`
		`Channel 1(A):1.Out->2.Cin tag 1`
		`Channel 4(A):6.Out->9.Cin tag 4`
		`Channel 5(A):7.Out->9.Cin tag 5`
		`      ...`

Fig. 1. The application script and the annotated PCG of Terminal-Relays-in-Ring

any number of Terminals as its client processes. Types Pin and Pout may have at most one port (there are no ports when there is only one Relay). Types Cin and Cout have any positive number of ports.

We also specify parameters, which are required for the correct behavior of the executables and are related to the designed topology and not to the application requirement. For this reason, they are called design parameters. For example, Relays must repeat the send–receive–select cycle M-1 times. The value M depends on the size of the ring and is crucial for producing the correct result.

The Processes section specifies the nodes of the PCG, naming them by uniquely indexing component names (e.g. T[1],...,T[6] and R[1],R[2],R[3]) setting their number of ports for each communication type and values for their design parameters. All Terminal nodes have exactly one port of each type. Each of the three Relay processes has a distinct number of ports of types Cin (respectively Cout), depending on the number of clients they have, and one port of types Pin (respectively Pout). The design parameter of all Relays is set to 3, the size of the Relays ring. The Channels section specifies point–to–point communication channels, by associating ports. A tool program, the PCG–builder, reads the PCG part and actually generates a representation of the PCG, giving rank identifiers to the nodes.

The second part of the script, headed by PARALLEL SYSTEM, specifies information for processes and channels required by MPICH running on clusters. It specifies for each channel the values for tagid and communicator; In the example script default indicates unique tagid generation and MPI_COMM_WORLD, respectively. The rank is obtained from the rank of the node at the other end of arcs. In addition we may specify the type of communication to be used (blocking, standard, etc.) when using a port. The allocation of processes is also specified, followed by the file names of executables. Finally, the third part of the script, headed by APPLICATION PARAMETERS, specifies process parameters required in the application. In the example script, each Terminal is given an integer parameter. The second and third parts are interpreted by the PCG–annotator, appropriately annotating nodes and arcs of the PCG created by the PCG–builder. In Fig. 1 below the general PCG, the annotation of some of its nodes and channels for MPICH is shown.

3.2   The Reusable Executables

The Ensemble components compute results and do not involve any process management or assume any topology in which they operate. They have open ports for point-to point communication with any compatible port of any process in any application and are reusable as executable library components. A port in MPI is implemented as a structure, which stores a triplet of (rank, tagid, communicator). Ports of the same type form arrays and arrays of all types form the interface of the component. All send and receive operations in processes refer to ports, identified by a communication type and a port index within the type. As processes are created, they get the actual number of ports of each type from their command line parameters. Processes scale their interface by executing a routine, called MakePorts. Processes also get the values for the communication parameters for each port from their command line parameters. Processes set actual values to their interface by executing a routine, called SetInterface. Each MPE demands its own MakePorts and SetInterface routines. A skeleton for program components, which may be seen in Fig. 2 has been developed. In association with wrapper routines Usend and Ureceive, which call MPI routines, all differences are hidden and the appearance of components of any MPE is unified.

```
/* Terminal Code */
void RealMain(Interface,argc,argv)
   struct port_types *Interface;
   int argc; char **argv;
{ int Typecount=2;
  GetParams(V);
  Usend(Out[1],V);
  Ureceive(In[1],Max);}
------------------------------------
/*Common main for all executables*/
void main(argc,argv)
     int argc; char **argc;
{ struct Ps
     {int rank,tag,comm,Ftype;}
  struct Pt
     {int PCount;struct Ps *port;}
  typedef struct Pt InterfaceType;
  extern int TypeCount;
  InterfaceType Interface;

  MakePorts(Interface,TypeCount);
  SetInterface(Interface,TypeCount);
  RealMain(Interface,argc,argv); }
```

```
/* Relay Code */
void RealMain(Interface,argc,argv)
   struct port_types *Interface;
   int argc; char **argv;
{ int Typecount=4;
  GetParam(M);
  LMax=0;
  for(j=1;
       j<=Interface[Cin].PCount;
       j++)
  { Ureceive(Cin[j],V);
    if (V > LMax) Lmax=V;}

  Gmax=Lmax;
  for (i=1;i<=M-1;i++)
  {  Usend(Pout[1],GMax);
     Ureceive(Pin[1],V);
     if(V > GMax)Gmax=V;}

  for(j=1;
       j<=Interface[Cout].PCount;
       j++)
  USend(Cout[j],Gmax);}
```

Fig. 2. Terminal and Relay program components

For each component, we set the number of communication types that it requires (TypeCount), as specified in the design; Terminal has two and Relay four communication types. Processes first call MakePorts to set–up the appropriate number of ports of their Interface, then call SetInteface to set values to ports of Interface and they call their RealMain actions. Using the component skeleton, only RealMain, the actions related to the application, needs to be coded.

3.3 Executing Applications

A pre–loader program visits the PCG nodes and generates the procgroup file of executables and the appropriate parameters, which mpirun uses to create processes. All necessary information annotates the PCG: the process rank, the

associated executable and its host allocation; its design and application parameters and the number of ports and of each type as well as their values.

4 Design and Implementation Variations

In this section, we demonstrate the reusability of executables. We design a variation of Get Maximum, which reuses Terminal and Relay. The application script
and the PCG of the application are depicted in Fig. 3.

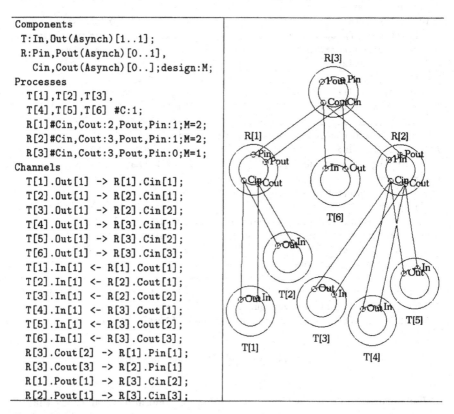

```
Components
 T:In,Out(Asynch)[1..1];
 R:Pin,Pout(Asynch)[0..1],
   Cin,Cout(Asynch)[0..];design:M;
Processes
  T[1],T[2],T[3],
  T[4],T[5],T[6] #C:1;
  R[1]#Cin,Cout:2,Pout,Pin:1;M=2;
  R[2]#Cin,Cout:3,Pout,Pin:1;M=2;
  R[3]#Cin,Cout:3,Pout,Pin:0;M=1;
Channels
  T[1].Out[1] -> R[1].Cin[1];
  T[2].Out[1] -> R[2].Cin[1];
  T[3].Out[1] -> R[2].Cin[2];
  T[4].Out[1] -> R[3].Cin[1];
  T[5].Out[1] -> R[3].Cin[2];
  T[6].Out[1] -> R[3].Cin[3];
  T[1].In[1] <- R[1].Cout[1];
  T[2].In[1] <- R[2].Cout[1];
  T[3].In[1] <- R[2].Cout[2];
  T[4].In[1] <- R[3].Cout[1];
  T[5].In[1] <- R[3].Cout[2];
  T[6].In[1] <- R[3].Cout[3];
  R[3].Cout[2] -> R[1].Pin[1];
  R[3].Cout[3] -> R[2].Pin[1]
  R[1].Pout[1] -> R[3].Cin[2];
  R[2].Pout[1] -> R[3].Cin[3];
```

Fig. 3. The application script and PCG for Get Maximum Selectors and Relays in tree

In this variation, Relay processes are organized in a tree, with R[3] being
the root, which has no Pout and Pin ports. R[1] and R[2] have one Pout and
one Pin ports, which are connected to the Cin and Cout ports, respectively, of
their parent R[3]. R[3] has also T[6] connected as a client process. R[1] has T[1]
and T[2] as its client processes and Server[2] has T[3], T[4] and T[5] as its client
processes.

We have specified that all communication is asynchronous for the ports to be
compatible for communication. R[1] and R[2] receive values from their clients,

find their local maximum and send it to their Pout port, which is connected to a Cin port of R[3]. R[3] finds the global maximum, and as it is not connected in a ring, it directly sends the global maximum to its clients. T[6] gets the global maximum, as well as R[1] and R[2]. R[1] and R[2] "select" the global maximum and send it to their client processes.

5   Conclusions

We have presented Ensemble and its tools applied to MPICH. Ensemble structures implementations into scripts, which specify process topologies, channel specifications and resource allocation, and into program components, which encode application computations. As the elements of the implementations are separated, they may be modified independently of one another, thus simplifying program debugging and maintenance.

Portability does not necessarily imply that the same source runs efficiently on any architecture. For a ported program to run efficiently it usually has to be adapted and fine-tuned. Ensemble permits rapid program variations.

We have applied Ensemble [4] [3] on PVM and on Parix [8], respectively. Although, MPEs differ [6] Ensemble implementations look similar in MPI, PVM and Parix and porting them from one environment to the other is mechanical. Ensemble does not suggest a new MPE, it does not demand any changes to MPEs and its tools are independent of any design, visualization, performance, or any other tools which may be used with an MPE. Future work includes high level parametric topology descriptions in scripts, support for dynamic process creation, tools for porting applications to different MPEs.

References

1. Alasdair, R., Bruce, A., Mills, J.G., Smith, A.G.: CHIMP/MPI User Guide. EPCC, The University of Edinburgh
2. Bridges, P., Doss, N., Gropp, W., Karrels, E., Lusk, E., Skjellum, A.: User's Guide to MPICH, a Portable Implementation of MPI. Argone National Laboratory, 1995.
3. Cotronis, J.Y.: Efficient Program Composition on Parix by the Ensemble Methodology. In: Milligan, P., Kuchcinski, K. (eds), 22nd Euromicro Conference 96, IEEE Computer Society Press, Los Alamitos, 1996, 545–552
4. Cotronis, J.Y.: Message–Passing Program Development by Ensemble. In: Bubak, M., Dongarra, J. (eds.): Recent Advances in PVM and MPI. LNCS Vol. 1332, Springer–Verlag, Berlin Heidelberg New York (1997) 242–249
5. Geist, A. , Beguelin, A. , Dongarra, J. , Jiang, W. , Manchek, R. , Sunderam, V.: PVM 3 User's guide and Reference Manual. ORNL/TM–12187, May 1994
6. Gropp, W., Lusk, E.: Why Are PVM and MPI So Differrent? In: Bubak, M., Dongarra, J. (eds.): Recent Advances in PVM and MPI. LNCS Vol. 1332, Springer–Verlag, Berlin Heidelberg New York (1997) 3–10
7. M.P.I. Forum: MPI: A Message–Passing Interface Standard. International Journal of Supercomputer Applications, 8(3/4),1994
8. Parsytec Computer Gmbh.: Report Parix 1.2 and 1.9 Software Documentation. 1993

The NAG Parallel Library and the PINEAPL Project

Mishi Derakhshan[1] and Arnold Krommer[1]

Numerical Algorithms Group Ltd., Wilkinson House,
Jordan Hill Road, Oxford, OX2 8DR, UK
Email: {mishi, arnoldk}@nag.co.uk
URL: http://www.nag.co.uk/

Abstract. The NAG Parallel Library is a portable library of routines for solving numerical problems, written specifically for use on parallel computing systems, including both dedicated parallel machines such as the IBM SP2, Hitachi SR2201 and SGI Origin 2000 as well as clusters of UNIX and Linux workstations and PCs.

During the last two and half years NAG have been coordinating the European project PINEAPL, an ESPRIT project in the area of High Performance Computing and Networking with the main objective of producing a general-purpose library of parallel numerical library suitable for a wide range of computationally intensive industrial applications.

Results from the PINEAPL Project will be included in the NAG Parallel Library for solving numerical problems on high-performance computers. The close cooperation between end-users and developers in the PINEAPL Project will ensure that the contents of this library will meet the needs of industry as the adoption of parallel computing have increased in past few years.

1 Introduction

This paper describes the design of the NAG Parallel Library [7] and the role that PINEAPL plays in NAG's HPC library activities.

The NAG Parallel Library is a library of parallel numerical routines, designed originally for distributed memory parallel machines. The library uses the message-passing mechanism to achieve parallelism. It is has been implemented for homogeneous networks and clusters of workstations, and for dedicated distributed memory machines such as the IBM SP2, Hitachi SR2201, Fujitsu AP3000, Fujitsu VPP and SMP types machines such as Origin 2000 and DEC Alpha 4100. The library relies on PVM [4] or MPI [5] for its underlying message passing software.

The PINEAPL (Parallel Industrial NumErical Applications and Portable Libraries) Project is an ESPRIT project in the area of High Performance Computing and Networking, with the main objective of producing a general-purpose library of parallel numerical software suitable for a wide range of computationally intensive industrial applications. The project consortium is composed of ten academic, research and industrial organisations from United Kingdom, France, Denmark and Italy[1] (see also [8] for more details)

The scope of the library has been mainly determined by the requirements of several application codes which have been brought into the project by the industrial partners. The following methodology has been adopted in the framework of PINEAPL activities:

1. Analysing the end-users' application code to identify the computational kernel.
2. Defining a set of benchmark for each applications.
3. Utilising the numerical in the participation research organisations to design the relevant numerical software.
4. Parallelizing the application codes using the library.
5. Benchmarking the resulting parallel end-users' codes.

2 The NAG Parallel Library

2.1 Library Design

One of the principal design aims for the NAG Parallel Library was to make the library simple for novice users to understand while retaining the flexibility to be useful to more experienced users. The interfaces to the library routines have been made as similar to the equivalent NAG Fortran 77 Library routines as possible to encourage established users of sequential NAG libraries to experiment with parallelism.

The NAG Parallel Library is divided into chapters, each devoted to a branch of numerical analysis or statistics. Furthermore, a set of utility/support routines to assist the user in parallel programming have been included in the library, mainly to shield the users from the underlying message-passing mechanism. With the facilities provided in the library it is possible to create parallel programs to solve some quite complex problems very quickly.

2.2 Model of Parallelism

The NAG Parallel Library was designed according to the Single Program Multiple Data (SPMD) model of parallelism; this model was chosen for several reasons:

- its simplicity, but with the flexibility to mimic other, more complex models of parallelism;
- its compatibility with PBLAS (Parallel Basic Linear Algebra Subprograms) and ScaLAPACK materials (see [1]);
- its compatibility with the model assumed by HPF (see [6]).

---

[1] BAe (UK), CERFACS (FR), CPS-CNR(IT), DHI (DK), IBM SEMEA (IT), Math-Tech (DK), NAG (UK), Piaggio (IT), Thomson-CSF (FR), University of Manchester (UK)

Each instance of the user program that is executed forms one of the logical processors in a two-dimensional logical processor grid (as used by PBLAS and ScaLAPACK). By using the library utilities, the user can create a parallel program that looks remarkably similar to a conventional sequential program.

2.3 The Message Passing Mechanism

The BLACS [3] were chosen for the message-passing environment due to their ease of use, ready availability and ease of portability between MPI or PVM. The majority of routines in the library make use of the BLACS for communication but, in certain exceptional circumstances, MPI or PVM is used where the BLACS lack the required functionality: it should be emphasized that the BLACS were designed for the regular communications found in most linear algebra algorithms – other algorithms which are based on task farming (e.g., adaptive quadrature) have less predictable communication requirements, hence, explicit usage of MPI or PVM is utilised in these library routines.

A great deal of effort has been put into hiding the details of the use of the underlying communication mechanism . Most of the details of managing the parallel processes can be left to the *support* routines which are provided in the library (see [7]). However, enough flexibility has been built into the support routines to enable users to use MPI or PVM in their application codes.

2.4 Data Distribution

Arguments to NAG Parallel Library routines are categorised in one of two classes for data distribution purposes, local or global. A global input argument must have the same value on all logical processors participating in a calculation on entry to a library routine. Global output arguments will have the same value on all processors participating in a calculation on exit from a library routine. Local arguments may assume different values on different processors, for example the elements of a distributed matrix on input and the *LU* factors of the same distributed matrix on output.

In general, the distribution of data is the responsibility of the user as the numerical routines assume that the data is in-place ensuring no hidden or unnecessary communications for data distribution. However, the correct distribution of data can be an error-prone area for novice users of distributed memory machines. In particular, the '2-d block-cyclic distribution' common to ScaLAPACK routines can be difficult to program correctly, with no easy way of checking and debugging. The NAG Parallel Library contains a number of non-numerical routines which assist users in their data-distribution task. Several routines exist for reading matrices from external files – each processor reads in the whole matrix but only stores its local portion; this means that no more storage space must be allocated than is necessary to hold the local part of the matrix and that each processor reads to the same point in the file (i.e., the end of the matrix data). These input routines have their counterparts which output distributed data to an external file. To prevent write conflicts between processors, a single processor is designated to output to the external file and all other processors communicate their data to the designated output processor in turn.

In addition, where it is possible to code the value of matrix elements as a Fortran expression, library routines are available that accept a user-supplied subroutine that returns the value of specified matrix elements. These library routines calculate which matrix elements are to be stored locally on each processor for a given data distribution and use the user-supplied routine to fill the appropriate local arrays with correctly distributed data.

2.5 Error Trapping

To maintain efficiency, parallel numerical algorithms must minimize the amount of failure checking between processors since it introduces communication (and possibly synchronisation) between processors that does not contribute directly to the computation. Where it is necessary for processors to compare their error condition, it is carried out at a point where there is some other (unavoidable) reason for a synchronisation point in the code.

As far as possible the arguments supplied to any NAG routine are checked for consistency and correctness and this feature is maintained in the NAG Parallel Library with some additional checking. A global argument must have the same value on entry to the library routine on every logical processor. Each library routine compares the values of its global arguments for consistency across the processors and treats any differences it finds as a failure condition. Both global and local arguments are also tested in the conventional manner to see if they have meaningful values. It has to be stressed that this level of efficiency incur some communication cost. In the forthcoming release (Release 3) of the Parallel library a new mechanism has been adopted that allows the user to switch off error checking and thereby by-passing the unnecessary communication overhead in checking these arguments during their production phase.

3   The PINEAPL Project

The application codes in the PINEAPL Project come from a good, representative spectrum of industrial problems that should, in principle, lead to highly useful and reusable numerical software. All of the problems being solved use numerical techniques in different areas of numerical analysis such as Partial Differential Equations (PDEs), fast Fourier Transforms (FFTs), optimisation, linear algebra, etc. All these areas involve very large amounts of data and in all cases, the end-users have existing software at some stage of development (which incorporate some kind of numerical techniques) for solving their problems.

Generally, it is not easy to produce general-purpose software for solving general end-user problems, an example being the solution of PDEs. Fortunately there is much that can be done to supply the end-users with the numerical components that can be used as building-blocks to solve the majority of their problems. On the PDE front, the methods of solving these equations, with large irregular data-sets today almost invariably reduce to the solution of large, sparse systems of equations. Typically, the solution of such systems of equations can consume around 65–85% of the execution time for the whole problem. So the provision of good parallel sparse solvers alone could lead to significant speedups in the end-user applications codes. Most of the remaining execution time is spent in setting up the problem and here too some help could be given to users, in the form of data distribution utilities and mesh-partitioning software.

Since sparse systems of equations occur in most of the application codes, special attention has been given to this area of the library software. Other library material being developed by PINEAPL partners includes optimization, Fast Fourier Transform, and Fast Poisson Solver routines.

In the following sections we give a brief summary of some applications which make extensive use of various numerical areas which emerged within PINEAPL.

3.1 Sparse Linear Algebra

Two-Stroke Engine Simulation: Piaggio engineers use the KIVA-3 application software for numerical simulations of the "scavenging process" in a two–stroke engine configuration. KIVA-3 is the third generation of the KIVA family of codes, developed at Los Alamos National Laboratories and distributed in source form for numerical simulation of chemically reactive flows with sprays in engine applications.

The mathematical model of KIVA–3 is the complete system of unsteady Navier-Stokes equations, coupled with chemical kinetic and spray droplet dynamic models (see [2] for more details). The numerical method of KIVA–3 is based on the implicit Euler temporal finite difference scheme, where the time-step are chosen using accuracy criteria. The resulting systems of equations are both symmetric and unsymmetric (see [2] for more details).

Thermo-electromagentic Application: This application deals with nanometric recording devices, based on a coupled electromagnetic-thermal physical model.

The underlying physical model is the coupling of the three-dimensional harmonic Maxwell equations with the three-dimensional thermal equation. This leads to a fixed-point iteration whose internal steps are:

1. Solve the Maxwell equations to get thermal sources from lossy media.
2. From the thermal sources, compute the temperature.
3. From the temperature, compute the new dielectrics constants from a linear or nonlinear model.

The Maxwell and the thermal equations are solved by the Finite Element method with two well separated representations. The Maxwell equations are solved using Hcurl elements while the thermal equation is discretized using P2 Lagrange elements. Both formulations lead to linear systems $Ax = b$, where the matrix A is complex and non-Hermitian for the Maxwell system and real for the thermal system.

Oil Reservoir Simulation Application: The oil reservoir simulator was originally designed to simulate the flow of different types of oil, gas and water in the chalk under the sea-bed in the North sea. Wells of all orientations from which oil and gas is produced or water is injected can also be simulated. The objective is of course to experiment with different recovery schemes in order to identify the optimal solution.

The basic problem is governed by a system of partial differential equations. These are discretized in space using a finite volume scheme, which transforms the problem to a set of ordinary differential equations. The grid can be either Cartesian, cylindrical or irregular.

The ordinary differential equations are discretized in time using an implicit Euler method. This transforms the problem to a set of nonlinear algebraic equations. The nonlinear equations are linearized with a (usually) few steps of the Newton-Raphson method. In each step of this method, a large sparse system of linear equations must be solved.

Hydrodynamic Application: MIKE 3 is a non-hydrostatic, three-dimensional hydrodynamic modeling system. The application area of MIKE 3 span from estuarine and coastal hydraulics and oceanography to environmental hydraulics and sediment processes modeling.

MIKE 3 consists of a basic hydrodynamic module (HD) and a number of add-on modules, including the environmental modules advection-dispersion (AD), water quality (WQ) and eutrophication (EU) and the sediment processes modules mud transport (MT) and particle tracking (PA).

The HD module is the fundamental engine of the modeling system. This module can be subdivided into a basic flow module, a density module and a turbulence module. In case of stratified flows with variable density, the density module is applied in order to calculate the local density as a function of temperature and/or salinity. In case of turbulent flows the turbulent module is applied in order to calculate the eddy viscosity based on one of three available turbulence models.

The mathematical basis for the new numerical kernel of the HD-module is the time-dependent conservation equations of mass and momentum in three dimensions for an incompressible Boussinesq fluid.

3.2 Optimization

Aerodynamics Application: The design of a wing that provides maximum lift for a minimum drag is an example of multi-objective optimization used in this study.

The process of designing a new wing is highly complex. A large number of design variables need to be processed for the required specification to be met. It is not possible to examine the whole of the problem space in the required detail, due to the computational effort needed. Thus an engineer has to set up a window in the problem space based on his experience, and explore many such windows. However the engineer will not be in a position to either know this or have a method of selecting the most suitable window. In this situation robust optimization routines that can identify features in the problem space, offer a way to reduce the complexity of the design process, and increase the capability of engineers.

Although efforts are nowadays made to analyze wing performance using 3-d codes, the process of designing a new wing can still involve a significant role for 2-d aerofoil design.

The sub-sonic and trans-sonic cases will be independent for the analysis using simple bounds on a number of aerofoil parameters using the quasi-Newton algorithm (subject to simple bounds).

For an optimum design taking into account the sub-sonic and trans-sonic cases a sequential quadratic programming algorithm (subject to general constraints) will be used. This algorithm will allow more general constraints on a number of aerofoil design parameters.

3.3 FFT

Rod Laser Application: The Rod Laser Application code used at Thomson-CSF is concerned with the numerical simulation of the propagation of electromagnetic waves in diodes-pumped rod lasers, coupled with thermal effects. The final goal is to estimate the deformation and the amplification of laser spots, and to find an optimal coupling between laser beams and pumping devices. This simulation plays a central role in the optimization of the design of rod lasers, leading to a reduction of the development time; therefore, the whole design process could benefit from an effective use of high-performance computers, that allows a reduction of the so-called "time-to-market" while giving the possibility of increasing the level of detail in the simulation.

Numerical experiments performed on this application have shown that the most time consuming part of the algorithm is the execution of backward/forward FFTs, which requires at least 70% of the total computation time in some realistic simulations. Nevertheless, the percentage of time required by the FFTs depends strongly on the time spent in the definition of the index profile and it may fall under 50%. Even in such case, the performance of the code is expected to be improved by parallelism, since the parallelization has been done on the entire propagation method.

4 Conclusion

NAG seldom has the opportunity to work intimately with end-users' application codes. This is because NAG has traditionally been a product-based company, relying for most of its business on selling library software of general widespread applicability. NAG endeavors to develop and maintain sufficient contacts with end-users to ensure that its library software does meet their needs as far as possible but those contacts seldom reach the point of intensive examination of any one end-user's specific applications. This type of work usually stems from consultancy, and NAG has undertaken an increasing amount of consultancy work in recent years. Consultancy work can give valuable additional insights into end-users' requirements for library software but there may be technical or commercial constraints which impede an immediate transfer of software from consultancy into NAG's library products.

It is for these reasons that a project like PINEAPL is so important to achieving the aim of producing library software that is relevant to the industrial community. NAG is provided with the detailed technical knowledge of users' needs and the users are given an early start in making use of the numerical software. **Acknowledgment:** Funding support of this project by the European Union, through its Fourth Framework programme for research and technological development in information technology, is gratefully acknowledged. The authors also wish to express their thanks to all the PINEAPL partners for their input.

References

1. Blackford, L. S., Choi, J., Cleary, A., D'Azevedo, E., Demmel, J., Dhillon, I, Dongarra, J., Hammarling, S., Henry, G., Petitet, A., Walker, D., Whaley, R.C.: ScaLAPACK Users' Guide, SIAM, Philadelphia, 1997.
2. D'Ambra, P., Fillipone, S. and Nobile, P.: The Use of a Parallel Library in Industrial Simulations: The Case Study of the Design of a Two-Stroke Engine. In: Proceedings of 'Annual Meeting of Italian Society of Computer Simulation', Naples, Italy, December 1997, and Tech. Rep. n. 97-24, CPS-CNR, December 1997.
3. Dongarra, J.J., Whaley, R.C.: A User's Guide to the BLACS v1.0. Technical Report CS-95-281 (1995), Department of Computer Science, University of Tennessee.
4. Geist, A., Beguelin, A., Dongarra, J.J., Jiang, W., Manchek, R., Sunderam, V.: PVM 3. A User's Guide and Tutorial for Networked Parallel Computing, The MIT Press (1994).
5. Gropp, W., Lusk, E., Skjellum, A.: Using MPI. Portable Parallel Programming with the Message Passing Interface, The MIT Press (1994).
6. Koelbel, C.H., Loveman, D.B., Schreiber, R.S., Steele, G.L., Zosel, M.E.: The High Performance Fortran Handbook, The MIT Press (1994).
7. NAG Parallel Library Manual, Release 2, Numerical Algorithms Group Ltd, Oxford (1997).
8. PINEAPL Second Annual Report: Reference: FP4/PIN/NAG/AR2, Numerical Algorithms Group Ltd, Oxford (1998).

High Performance Fortran: A Status Report
or:
Are We Ready to Give Up MPI?

Mike Delves[1] and Hans Zima[2]

[1] N.A. Software Ltd
delves@nasoftware.co.uk
[2] University of Vienna
zima@par.univie.ac.at

Abstract. High Performance Fortran (HPF) is a data-parallel language designed to provide the user with a high-level interface for programming scientific applications, while delegating to the compiler the task of handling the details of producing parallel code. HPF aims to relegate the role of MPI to that of an assembler language: used only when necessary, and with decreasing frequency as time goes by. In this position paper, we give an overview of the development of HPF, followed by a discussion of the expressivity of the current version of the language and the performance of current compilers. The paper closes with a look forward to future developments and to other approaches to high-level parallel program development.

1 Introduction

The emergence of distributed-memory architectures more than a decade ago brought into sharp focus two issues: the necessity of controlling locality and the complexity of parallel programming. One approach to the control of locality is to use an explicitly parallel approach, e.g., C or Fortran coupled with message passing: the main subject matter of this conference. However, from the viewpoint of an applications programmer, this approach is very low-level: hard to learn, and leading to programs which are expensive to maintain.

It soon became clear that a higher level approach was both desirable and possible. It was impracticable to develop autoparallelising compilers which could extract the parallelism from serial codes without programmer assistance; but one *could* use a high-level "data parallel" language with a single thread of control coupled with user-specified annotations for distribution of data and computation across processors. In effect, the user can then leave all or most of the low-level details to the compiler and runtime system, and need only give broad guidance to the compiler.

High Performance Fortran (HPF) is at the forefront of such languages, and for the first time brings application programmers the ability to program scientific/engineering computations for MIMD architectures, at a high level of abstraction. In this paper we look at the history and development of HPF and its current and future status and utility.

2 Developments Leading to HPF

HPF arose from research into high-level programming support for distributed-memory architectures, conducted in the 1980's at the GMD (Germany) and the California Institute of Technology. This research resulted in the design of the *Single-Program-Multiple-Data (SPMD)* paradigm for distributed-memory machines. *SUPERB* [9], developed at the University of Bonn between 1985 and 1989, was the first compilation system to implement this paradigm and translate Fortran to explicitly parallel code for distributed-memory architectures. Related early compiler work included projects at Cornell and Yale Universities, Applied Parallel Research, IRISA, and ICASE. These systems enable the user to write code using global data references, as for shared memory, but require the specification of a data distribution, which is then used to guide the process of restructuring the code into an explicitly parallel SPMD message passing program for execution on the target machine. The compiler translates global data references into local and non-local references based on the data distributions; non-local references are satisfied by inserting appropriate message-passing statements in the generated code. Finally, the communication is optimized by combining messages and sending data at the earliest possible point in time. In algorithms where data references are made through a level of indirection (such as for unstructured mesh codes and sparse matrix solvers), some of the analysis has to be performed at runtime and the compiler must generate code to perform this analysis and set up the required communication.

The success of these and other projects – which generally used an ad-hoc approach to language issues – paved the way for the development of the first generation of *High Performance Languages* such as Fortran D [6] and Vienna Fortran [2, 10]. These languages provide high-level features for the declaration of abstract processor sets and the specification of data distribution, data alignment, and explicitly parallel loop constructs. The use of these features enables the compiler to produce (potentially) efficient code, while removing the need for the programmer to manipulate the details required by an explicit message passing approach. Without *some* user assistance, albeit at a high level, current (and foreseeable) compiler technology would fail to provide the necessary efficiency for any realistic code.

3 The Genesis of High Performance Fortran

3.1 HPF1

The success of Fortran D and Vienna Fortran led to the formation of the HPF Forum, a group of about 40 researchers, which met at intervals of six weeks starting March 1992, with the aim of producing a standardised proposal for a data parallel language based on Fortran. The ESPRIT PPPE project made a significant contribution to the work of the Forum, in addition to its important role in the design of MPI. The HPFF released the design of Version 1.0 of HPF in May 1993. In November 1994, HPF Version 1.1, mainly incorporating corrections to the language, was produced.

HPF 1.1 provided support for regular applications by offering block and cyclic data distributions, replication, parallel loops and a range of alignment features; first commercial compilers for a language subset appeared on the market in 1995. The ESPRIT PHAROS project (see section 4.2), as well as many other studies in academia and industry, demonstrated the usefulness of HPF 1.1 for regular codes. However, at the same time it became clear [3] that the language could not express advanced applications such as multiblock codes, unstructured meshes, adaptive grid codes, or sparse matrix computations, without incurring significant overheads with respect to memory or execution time.

HPF 2.0 and HPF+

The HPF Forum continued a third round of meetings in 1995 and 1996, with the aim of building upon initial experience with HPF1 to improve the expressivity of the language. This resulted in the release of HPF 2.0 in January 1997. The standards documents produced are available at the HPF Web site at http://www.crpc.rice.edu/HPFF/home.html.

In parallel to the development of HPF 2.0, the ESPRIT project *HPF+* was conducted by a consortium including application developers (ESI, AVL, and ECMWF), academic institutions (Universities of Vienna and Pavia) and NA Software. The project finished in April 1998, producing an enhanced language specification [1] and the Vienna Fortran Compiler (VFC), integrated with the performance analysis tool MEDEA. The language and compiling system were successfully applied to a set of benchmark codes provided by the application partners. Documents can be found at the HPF+ Web site at http://www.par.univie.ac.at/ hpf+.

The language extensions required to eliminate the deficiencies in HPF1.1 for irregular applications include (1) a generalization of the data distribution mechanism, permitting non-standard and irregular distributions, (2) the distribution of data to subsets of processor arrays, (3) the distribution of subobjects of derived types, and (4) a flexible facility to specify work distribution, in particular for parallel loop iterations.

Both the HPF 2.0 as well as the HPF+ language developments took into account these issues. Many of the HPF 2.0 language features were influenced by the preliminary HPF+ proposal [3] and the Vienna Fortran language specification [2, 10]. HPF+ followed the strategy of accepting those features of the HPF 2.0 defacto standard which provided sufficient functionality. However, HPF+ included new features explicitly supporting the efficient execution of irregular programs. This includes in particular language control of communication schedules and the concept of *halos*. The efficacy of these extensions was amply demonstrated by the benchmarks produced within the project.

4 HPF Compilers: Current State

4.1 Vendor Support

Commercial HPF compilers are available from DEC (alpha-based systems) and IBM (PowerPC-based systems) based on in-house developments. Independently developed compilers come from APR and PGI (US) and N.A. Software (NASL) (UK); and the remaining US hardware vendors have products or announced developments using primarily PGI technology. Each major Japanese hardware vendor has an HPF compiler in development, although none has yet reached market status.

The PGI, APR and NASL compilers are available on a range of supercomputers and also on open systems (PC and workstation clusters).

Thus, the language is well supported by vendors.

4.2 Compiler Performance on Regular Problems

So, HPF is a nice language, and widely available. How well does it run? And do the compilers cope with *real* codes as well as toy demonstrators?

Table 1 shows that the overheads introduced by using an HPF compiler (rather than a serial Fortran compiler) can be very low for "regular" applications. It gives times (seconds) to run two standard small benchmark codes, with the Release 2.1 NASL HPF compiler on a PC ethernetted cluster and on the Fujitsu VPP700 system at FECIT. "Serial" times were obtained with the NASL Fortran90 compiler, and the Fujitsu `frt` compiler, respectively.

Table 1: Model Benchmark Times using the NASL HPFPlus Compiler

System	Code	Parameters	Serial	P=1	P=2	P=3	P=4
PC Cluster	Gauss	N=512	40.4	30.8	17.7	13.1	10.2
	Shallow	N=512	13.4	13.3	8.7	5.6	3.0
Fujitsu	Gauss	N=2048	6.3	6.0	3.6	2.8	
	Shallow	N=1536	0.8	1.0	0.55	0.3	

The "*HPF Overheads*" shown vary from -25% to +20%; and the speedups are as good as can be achieved using MPI. The Fujitsu times correspond to around 700MFlops per processor.

The performance achieved on regular industrial codes can be equally good. The PHAROS ESPRIT project brought together European vendors of HPF tools (NASL (HPFPlus compiler); Simulog (FORESYS F77 to F90 translator); and Pallas (VAMPIR performance monitor) together with four applications code vendors. These F77 codes were ported first to Fortran90 and then to HPF, and benchmarked against the original serial F77 version, and against existing (F77 + MPI) versions, on either the Meiko CS2 or the IBM SP2.

Figure 1 shows the results obtained for the debis DBETSY3D code on the SP2, with two industrial datasets; the HPF overheads were again negligible, and both scalability and performance are essentially as good as for MPI.

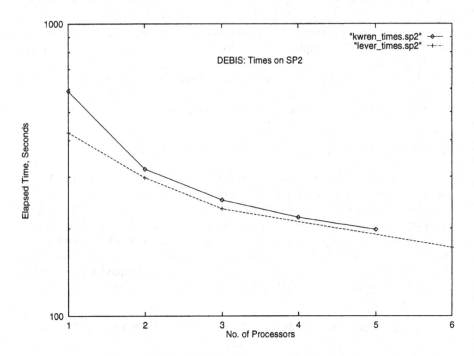

Fig. 1. DBETSY3D Benchmarks on the IBM SP2

However, on the Meiko CS2 the absolute performance achieved fell well below that obtainable with a hand coded MPI version. This is illustrated in Figure 2 which shows times on the CS2 for the SEMCAP/ESI SEM3D electromagnetic response simulation code. Scalability is good; but performance relative to F77/MPI is relatively poor with a factor of over three lost –sufficient to preclude HPF for production use with this code. But *do not* blame HPF for this performance gap; it is wholly attributable to the backend Fortran90 compiler, which on the CS2 performs poorly relative to the highly optimised F77 compiler.

Overall, the PHAROS results show that HPF now provides a viable alternative to MPI, even for porting "old" F77 codes, for problems primarily involving regular grids.

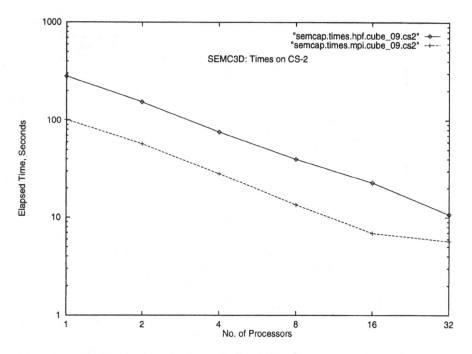

Fig. 2. SEM3D on the Meiko CS2 for HPF and MPI

4.3 Irregular Codes

The codes chosen in PHAROS were "HPF-sympathetic": they describe irregular regions in terms of a set of subregions over which regular grids are placed. This makes the language facilities in HPF1 amply adequate; and places much less strain on an HPF compiler, and on accompanying tools, than does a fully irregular problem (in Fortran terms: a problem dominated by indirect addressing).

Many applications use irregular grids, or depend on indirect addressing for other reasons. Current HPF compilers cannot handle these effectively. The difficulties include:

- HPF1 provides only "regular" distributions for data arrays: BLOCK, CYCLIC. Problems which require a less regular distribution for efficiency or load balancing, are not addressed;
- Even within these distributions, it is very difficult to provide efficient runtime code for irregular array accesses: the communications needed can not be predicted at compile time, and sophisticated runtime techniques are needed which have not been available previously.

It is possible to handle some problems involving irregular array accesses, using HPF1 and current compilers, by arranging that the irregular accesses occur only between data on a single processor, and that the compiler is aware of this. An illustration of the effectiveness of such an approach comes from GMD work

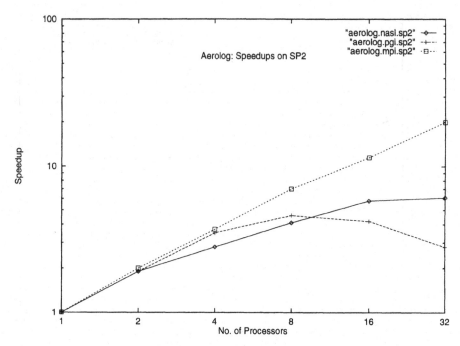

Fig. 3. Speedups for the PHAROS Aerolog code on the IBM SP2

during PHAROS on the Aerolog fluid flow code, for which the irregular nature of the boundary conditions caused problems. Figure 4 shows results for the Aerolog code on the SP2 using the NASL and PGI compilers.

Despite the substantial irregular component in the calculation, both commercial compilers provide reasonable scalability. However, neither compiler matches the (highly tuned) MPI results.

However, there are many problems for which this approach leads to excessive memory use; or partial loss of parallelism; or is plain impossible. These are the "irregular" problems. They *must* be addressed if HPF is to become a full replacement for MPI.

As noted above, the Esprit LTR HPF+ project led by the University of Vienna addressed this major difficulty.

An example of the effectiveness of the language constructs and compilation techniques developed is given by the PAMCRASH kernel studied in HPF+. PAMCRASH is an industrial code developed by ESI which models the deformation of structures such as cars under dynamic loads such as crashes. It uses highly irregular grids very extensively, and the contact terms in particular are difficult to parallelise. The HPF+ kernel encapsulates these difficulties, and current commercial HPF compilers (including the NASL compiler) fail to provide any speedup at all. Figure 3 shows the results obtained with VFC; to demonstrate the importance of schedule re–use, results with and without this feature are given. Results for one processor were obtained using the serial backend compiler (ie no HPF overheads are included).

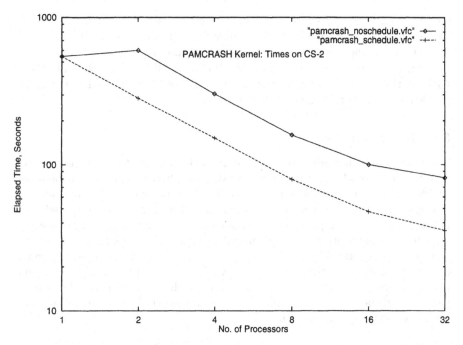

Fig. 4. Times for the PAMCRASH Kernel using VFC with and without schedule re–use

5 Beyond HPF2

HPF was primarily designed to support data parallel programming on architectures for which memory locality is important. Summarising the discussion above: experience with the language has shown that the current version, i.e. HPF2 with Approved Extensions, is substantially more versatile than many sceptics expected three years ago. For example, many standard parallel paradigms which are not usually considered as data parallel, including farms, pipelines, and many problems requiring heterogeneous concurrent tasks, can be expressed readily in HPF2. However, the current language is not necessarily well suited to all classes of applications nor to all kinds of parallel architecture. In this section, we will discuss a few aspects of this issue.

5.1 Difficult Data Parallel Problems

HPF does best on simple, regular problems, such as dense linear algebra and partial differential equations on regular meshes. It is also effective for many irregular problems, if the full scope of the language is used; this has been amply illustrated by the results of the ESPRIT project *HPF+*.

However, there are data parallel applications which currently cannot (so far as has been demonstrated) be handled well in "high level" HPF, even if the advanced features of HPF 2.0 and HPF+ are taken into account. One example of such a method is Discrete Simulation Monte Carlo (DSMC), which tracks the motion of millions of discrete particles in rarefied gases. The complexity of the data structures in this algorithm in combination with an intricate updating and sorting process appears to require the use of explicit message passing, if adequate performance is to be achieved, although this can still be achieved while using HPF as the prime framework, via the use of HPF_LOCAL procedures. Similar problems of expressivity arise with tree codes.

5.2 Task Parallelism

The data parallel paradigm represented by HPF supports the coordinated execution of a set of identical processes working on different segments of the same problem. For some scientific applications, the discipline enforced by this model is too rigid: they need a capability to express parallelism in a less structured way. Examples of such task parallel applications include real-time signal processing, branch and bound problems, and multidisciplinary applications. They can be generally characterized by the fact that tasks may be created dynamically in an unstructured way, different tasks may have different resource requirements and priorities, and that the structure and volume of the communication between a pair of tasks may vary dramatically, from an exchange of boolean signals to data transfers involving millions of numbers.

HPF is currently not designed to deal with such problems adequately: neither the explicit TASK_REGION construct of HPF2, which provides for coarse grain tasking, nor the INDEPENDENT loop construct which essentially provides fine grain tasking, provides for inter–task communication. A number of methods have been proposed to address this issue in the context of the language. There are two ways of incorporating general task parallelism in HPF. One way is to spawn threads within an HPF program, to carry out fine-grain parallel tasks. The other approach is to activate an entire HPF program as a task. This provides coarse-grain parallelism, and within each task one can still express and exploit fine-grain loop or array parallelism. We look in turn at each of these approaches.

Fine Grain Parallelism There has been little work done in introducing fine-grain task parallelism in HPF. The independent loop construct can be considered as a mechanism for the implicit spawning of fine-grain tasks; similarly, a pure procedure can be spawned as an independently executing task. Finally, the TASK_REGION directive provides a simple mechanism for indicating segments of code which can be executed concurrently similar to parallel sections found in other languages.

While these features allow the spawning of tasks, there are no mechanisms for synchronization or communication, although reductions are allowed in independent loops. Thus these constructs suffice for algorithms like divide and conquer, which require no inter-task communication; however, they will not work for branch and bound, and other algorithms where inter-task communication is essential.

The OpenMP [12] standard provides flexible facilities for expressing fine grain parallelism, and a preliminary study [11] shows that these facilities can coexist with those of HPF. Especially given the current importance of SMP clusters (see section 5.3) this is a promising way to extend HPF.

Coarse Grain Parallelism Use of coarse-grain tasks, each comprising an entire HPF program, is relatively easy. One is, in effect, wrapping HPF in a coordination language. Efforts along this line include Fortran M[5], in which coarse-grain tasks communicate via "channels" in a mode very similar to message-passing. Another approach is the language Opus [4]. Opus encapsulates HPF programs as object-oriented modules, passing data between them by accessing *shared abstractions (SDAs)* which are monitor-like constructs. Opus was explicitly designed to support multidisciplinary analysis and design, and related applications with significant coarse-grain parallelism.

However, the choice of coordinating language is of relatively little importance since coordination of the large scale processes is likely to represent only a minor part of the programming effort. A language that has recently gained increasing popularity is *Java*. Java provides an object-oriented paradigm that can be naturally used in a heterogeneous environment such as the WWW. Although current Java is not an adequate language for scientific computing, it could play an important role as a coordination language for high performance applications whether run locally or connected over a network.

5.3 Challenges Posed by New Parallel Architectures

In recent years, a new generation of high performance architectures has become commercially available. Many of these machines are either symmetric shared-memory architectures (SMPs) or clusters of SMPs, where an interconnection network connects a number of nodes, each of which is an SMP. These machines display a hybrid structure integrating shared-memory with distributed-memory parallelism. One of their dominating characteristics is their use of a deep memory hierarchy, often involving multiple levels of cache.

As a consequence, these architectures have not only to deal with the locality problem typical for distributed-memory machines – which is addressed by HPF –, but also with cache locality. A cache miss in a program executing on a cluster of SMPs may be more expensive than a non-local memory access.

HPF and its current generation of compilers are not designed to deal with such issues. Further work on compilers is required to develop modified compilation and runtime systems which take account of this two- or multi–level nonuniformity of memory access. It also seems likely that marrying other models (such as OpenMP) with HPF will prove to be useful.

Another trend in architectures definitely favors HPF: for homogeneous clusters of workstations or PCs HPF provides a natural programming paradigm. An Opus-like extension (or a Java binding) as discussed above would also support heterogeneous networks at least for cooperating large scale processes.

6 Conclusion

The development of HPF and related compilation technology forms an important step towards providing high-level support for high-performance computing, which has already proven its value and practicality and which in the near future seems capable of leading to more cost-effective and reliable development of a wide range of industrial and commercial applications. We expect that in the long run message passing will be replaced by a high-level paradigm along the lines of HPF, similar to the gradual disappearance of assembly language programming with the advent of high-level languages in the 1960s. Today, this is already practicable for a wide range of applications; but not yet for all.

References

1. S.Benkner,E.Laure,H.Zima. HPF+. An Extension of HPF for Advanced Industrial Applications. Deliverable D2.1c, ESPRIT Project *HPF+*, February 1998.
2. B. Chapman, P. Mehrotra, and H. Zima. Programming in Vienna Fortran. *Scientific Programming* 1(1):31-50, Fall 1992.
3. B. Chapman, P. Mehrotra, and H. Zima. Extending HPF for Advanced Data-Parallel Applications. *IEEE Parallel & Distributed Technology* 2(3):59-70, Fall 1994.
4. B. Chapman, M. Haines, P. Mehrotra, J. Van Rosendale, and H. Zima. Opus: A coordination language for multidisciplinary applications. *Scientific Programming (to appear)*, 1997.
5. I. T. Foster and K. M. Chandy. Fortran M: A language for modular parallel programming. Technical Report MCS-P327-0992 Revision 1, Mathematics and Computer Science Division, Argonne National Laboratory, June 1993.
6. G. Fox, S. Hiranandani, K. Kennedy, C. Koelbel, U. Kremer, C. Tseng, and M. Wu. Fortran D language specification. Department of Computer Science Rice COMP TR90079, Rice University, March 1991.
7. High Performance Fortran Forum. High Performance Fortran Language Specification Version 1.0. Technical Report, Rice University, Houston, TX, May 3, 1993. Also available as Scientific Programming 2(1-2):1-170, Spring and Summer 1993.
8. Thinking Machines Corporation. CM Fortran Reference Manual, Version 5.2. Thinking Machines Corporation, Cambridge, MA, September 1989.
9. H. Zima, H. Bast, and M. Gerndt. Superb: A tool for semi-automatic MIMD/SIMD parallelization. *Parallel Computing*, 6:1–18, 1988.
10. H. Zima, P. Brezany, B. Chapman, P. Mehrotra, and A. Schwald. Vienna Fortran – a language specification. Internal Report 21, ICASE, Hampton, VA, March 1992.
11. B. Chapman and P. Mehrotra. OpenMP and HPF: Integrating Two Paradigms University of Vienna Report, 1998
12. OpenMP Consortium. OpenMP Fortran Application Program Interface, Version 1.0, October 1997

On the Implementation of a Portable, Client-Server Based MPI-IO Interface *

Thomas Fuerle, Erich Schikuta, Christoph Loeffelhardt,
Kurt Stockinger, Helmut Wanek

Institute of Applied Computer Science and Information Systems
Department of Data Engineering, University of Vienna,
Rathausstr. 19/4, A-1010 Vienna, Austria
fuerle@vipios.pri.univie.ac.at

Abstract. In this paper we present the MPI-IO Interface kernel in the **Vienna Parallel Input Output System** (ViPIOS), which is a client-server based parallel I/O system. Compared to the already existing parallel I/O systems and libraries the concept of an independent distributed server promises to greatly enhance the usability and acceptance of the I/O system as well as the portability of client applications. The programmer of a client application does not have to deal with details like file layout on disk, sharing of filepointers etc. Instead high level MPI-IO requests may be issued and the server is expected to perform them in a (near) optimal way.
ViPIOS is based on MPI and is targeted (but not restricted) to MPP's using the SPMD paradigm. We describe the current system architecture in general and give a detailed overview of MPI-related design considerations.

Keywords

parallel I/O, server-client, SPMD, ViPIOS, MPI-IO, I/O chapter in MPI-2

1 Introduction

ViPIOS is an I/O runtime system, which provides efficient access to persistent files, by optimizing the data layout on the disks and allowing parallel read/write operations. ViPIOS is targeted as a supporting I/O module for high performance languages (e.g. HPF).

The basic idea to solve the I/O bottleneck in ViPIOS is *de-coupling*. The disk access operations are de-coupled from the application and performed by an independent I/O subsystem, ViPIOS. This leads to the situation that an application just sends disk requests to ViPIOS only, which performs the actual disk accesses in turn. This idea is caught by Figure 1.

---

* This work was carried out as part of the research project "Language, Compiler, and Advanced Data Structure Support for Parallel I/O Operations" supported by the Austrian Science Foundation (FWF Grant P11006-MAT)

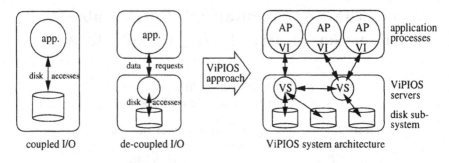

Fig. 1. Disk access decoupling - ViPIOS approach

The ViPIOS system architecture is built upon a set of cooperating server processes, which accomplish the requests of the application client processes. Each application process AP is linked by the ViPIOS interface VI to the ViPIOS servers VS.

The design of ViPIOS followed a data engineering approach characterized by two design principles,

- *Efficiency.* This is achieved by a *Two-Phase Data Administration* method, which aims to minimize the number of disk accesses by both compile time and runtime optimization. It provides a suitable data organization of the stored data on disk to the 'outside world' and organizes the data layout on disks respectively to the static application problem description and the dynamic runtime requirements.
- *Portability.* ViPIOS was designed to run on a large class of computer systems and to allow easy ports. Therefore the system is based on the MPI standard. All systems supported by MPI should provide a platform for ViPIOS.

1.1 The Two-Phase Data Administration method

The management of data by ViPIOS servers is split into two distinct phases, the preparation and the administration phase (see Figure 2).

The *preparation phase* precedes the execution of the application processes (mostly during the startup time). This phase uses the information collected during the application program compilation process in form of *hints* from the compiler. Based on this problem-specific knowledge the physical data layout schemes are defined, the actual ViPIOS server process for each application process and the disks for the stored data are chosen. Further, the data storage areas are prepared, the necessary main memory buffers allocated, and so on.

The following *administration phase* accomplishes the I/O requests of the application processes during their execution, i.e. the physical read/write operations, and performs necessary reorganization of the data layout.

The Two-Phase data administration method aims for putting all the data layout decisions, and data distribution operations into the preparation phase,

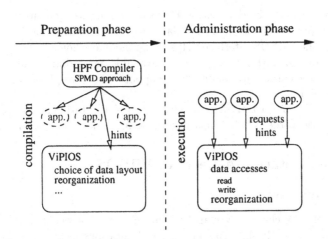

Fig. 2. The Two-phase data administration method

in advance to the actual application execution. Thus the administration phase performs the data accesses and possible data prefetching only.

1.2 System Modes

ViPIOS can be used in 3 different system modes, as

- runtime library,
- dependent system, or
- independent system.

Runtime Library. Application programs can be linked with a ViPIOS runtime module, which performs all disk I/O requests of the program. In this case ViPIOS is not running on independent servers, but as part of the application. The interface is therefore not only calling the requested data action, but also performing it itself. This mode provides only restricted functionality due to the missing independent I/O system. Parallelism can only be expressed by the application (i.e. the programmer).

Dependent System. In this case ViPIOS is running as an independent module in parallel to the application, but is started together with the application. This is inflicted by the MPI-1 specific characteristic that cooperating processes have to be started at the same time. This mode allows smart parallel data administration but objects the Two-Phase-Administration method by a missing preparation phase.

Independent System. In this case ViPIOS is running as a client-server system similar to a parallel file system or a database server waiting for application to connect via the ViPIOS interface. This is the mode of choice to achieve highest possible I/O bandwidth by exploiting all available data administration possibilities, because it is the only mode which supports the Two-phase data administration method.

Therefore we have to strive for an efficient implementation of the independent mode, in other words, ViPIOS has to execute as a client-server system.

2 Implementation Aspects of ViPIOS

2.1 Introduction

Unfortunately the client-server architecture described above can not be implemented directly on all platforms because of limitations in the underlying hard- or software (like no dedicated I/O nodes, no multitasking on processing nodes, no threading, etc.). So in order to support a wide range of different plattforms ViPIOS uses MPI for portability and offers multiple *operation modes* to cope with various restrictions.

2.2 Restrictions in Client-Server Computing with MPI

Independent Mode is not directly supported by MPI-1. MPI-1 restricts client-server computing by imposing that all the communicating processes have to be started at the same time. Thus it is not possible to have the server processes run independently and to start the clients at some later point in time. Also the number of clients can not be changed during execution

Clients and Servers share MPI_COMM_WORLD in MPI-1. With MPI-1 the global communicator MPI_COMM_WORLD is shared by all participating processes. Thus clients using this communicator for collective operations will also block the server processes. Furthermore client and server processes have to share the same range of process ranks. This makes it hard to guarantee that client processes get consecutive numbers starting with zero, especially if the number of client or server processes changes dynamically.

Simple solutions to this problem (like using separate communicators for clients and servers) are offered by some ViPIOS operation modes, but they all require, that an application program has to be specifically adapted in order to use ViPIOS.

Public MPI-Implementations (mpich, lam) are not MT-Safe. Both public implementations mpich and lam are not mt-save, thus non-blocking calls (e.g. MPI_Iread, MPI_Iwrite) are not possible without a workaround. Another drawback without threads is that the servers have to work with busy waits (MPI_Iprobe) to operate on multiple communicators.

2.3 Operation Modes of ViPIOS

ViPIOS can be compiled for the following different operation modes.

Runtime Library Mode behaves basically like ROMIO [7] or PMPIO [4], i.e. ViPIOS is linked as a runtime library to the application.

- *Advantage*
    - ready to run solution with any MPI-implementation (mpich, lam)
- *Disadvantage*
    - nonblocking calls are not supported. Optimization like redistributing in the background or prefetching is not supported
    - preparation phase is not possible, because ViPIOS is statically bound to the clients and started together with them
    - remote file access is not supported, because there is no server waiting to handle remote file access requests, i.e. in static mode the server functions are called directly and no messages are sent

Client Server Modes allow optimizations like file redistribution or prefetching and remote file accesses.

Dependent Mode. In Client-Server mode clients and server start at the same time using application schemes, see mpich.

- *Advantage*
    - ready to run solution (e.g with mpich)
- *Disadvantage*
    - preparation phase is not possible, because the ViPIOS servers must be started together with the clients

Independent Mode. In order to allow an efficient preparation phase the use of independently running servers is absolutely necessary.

This can be achieved by using one of the following strategies:

1. MPI-1 based implementations.
   Starting and stopping processes arbitrarily can be simulated with MPI-1 by using a number of "dummy" client processes which are actually idle and spawn the appropriate client process when needed. This simple workaround limits the number of available client processes to the number of "dummy" processes started.
   This workaround can't be used on systems which do not offer multitasking because the idle "dummy" process will lock a processor completely. Furthermore additional programming effort for waking up the dummy proccesses is needed.
   - Advantage
       - ready to run solution with any MPI-1 implementation

– Disadvantage
  - workaround for spawning the clients necessary, because clients cannot be started dynamically

2. MPI-2 based implementations.
   Supports the connection of independently started MPI-applications with ports. The servers offer a connection through a port, and client groups, which are started independently from the servers, try to establish a connection to the servers using this port. Up to now the servers can only work with one client group at the same time, thus the client groups requesting a connection to the servers are processed in a batch oriented way, i.e. every client group is automatically put into a queue, and as soon as the client group the servers are working with has terminated, it is disconnected from the servers and the servers work with the next client group waiting in the queue.

   – Advantages
     - ready to run solution with any MPI-2 implementation
     - No workaround needed, because client groups can be started dynamically and independently from the server group
     - Once the servers have been started, the user can start as many client applications as he wants without having to take care for the server group
     - No problems with MPI_COMM_WORLD. As the server processes and the client processes belong to two different groups of processes which are started independently, each group has implicitly a separated MPI_COMM_WORLD

   – Disadvantage
     - The current LAM version does not support multi-threading, which would offer the possibiliy of concurrent work on all client groups without busy waits

3. Third party protocol for communication between clients and servers (e.g. PVM).
   This mode behaves like MPI-IO/PIOFS [2] or MPI-IO for HPSS [5], but ViPIOS uses PVM and/or PVMPI (when it is available) for communication between clients and servers. Client-client and server-server communication is still done with MPI.

   – Advantage
     - ready to run solution with any MPI-implementation and PVM
     - Clients can be started easily out of the shell
     - no problems with MPI_COMM_WORLD, because there exist two distinct global communicators

   – Disadvantage
     - PVM and/or PVMPI is additionally needed

2.4 Sharing MPI_COMM_WORLD

So far, the independent mode using PVM(PI) or MPI-2 is the only ones which allows to use ViPIOS in a completely transparent way. For the other modes one of the following methods can be used to simplify or prevent necessary adaptations of applications.

1. Clients and servers share the global communicator MPI_COMM_WORLD. In this mode ViPIOS offers an intra-communicator MPI_COMM_APP for communication of client processes and uses another one (MPI_COMM_SERV) for server processes. This also solves the problem with ranking but the application programmer must use MPI_COMM_APP in every call instead of MPI_COMM_WORLD.
2. Clients can use MPI_COMM_WORLD exclusively. This can be achieved patching the underlying MPI-Implementation and also copes the problem with ranking.

A graphical comparison of this solutions is depicted in Figure 3.

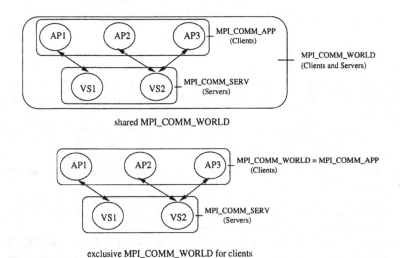

Fig. 3. shared MPI_COMM_WORLD versus exclusive MPI_COMM_WORLD

2.5 Implemented Modes

So far we have implemented the following modes

- runtime library mode with MPI-1 (mpich)
- dependent mode with MPI-1 with threads (mpich and patched mpich)
- independent mode with the usage of PVM and MPI-1 (mpich)
- independent mode with MPI-2 without threads (lam)

3 Conclusion and Future Work

This paper presents a practical application, which shows a deficiency of MPI. MPI-1 does not support the communication between independently started process groups. In the case of our ViPIOS client server architecture this is a strong drawback, which results in poor or non optimal performance. The introduction of ports in MPI-2 copes only to a limiting factor with this situation. Thus we showed some workarounds to handle this problem. Furthermore the public implementations of MPI (e.g. lam, mpich) do not support multithreading. We expect in the near future that new developments will provide us with similar capabilities in the MPI-standard as recognizable by the PVMPI [3] approach and that public implementations of MPI will be MT-Safe.

However in the near future the first running implementation of ViPIOS offering all presented operation modes will be finished. Currently we aim for the VFC compiler [1] (support for other HPF compilers is planned).

We also intend to add optimizations like prefetching and caching, and a port to a threaded (partly already implemented) version is on the way.

For preliminary performance results of ViPIOS refer to [6].

References

1. S. Benkner, K. Sanjari, V. Sipkova, and B. Velkov. Parallelizing irregular applications with the vienna hpf+ compiler vfc. In *Proceedings HPCN'98*. Springer Verlag, April 1998.
2. Peter F. Corbett, Dror G. Feitelson, Jean-Pierre Prost, George S. Almasi, Sandra Johnson Baylor, Anthony S. Bolmarcich, Yarsun Hsu, Julian Satran, Marc Snir, Robert Colao, Brian Herr, Joseph Kavaky, Thomas R. Morgan, and Anthony Zlotek. Parallel file systems for the IBM SP computers. *IBM Systems Journal*, 34(2):222–248, January 1995.
3. G. Fagg, J. Dongarra, and A. Geist. Heterogeneous mpi application interoperation and process management under pvmpi. Technical report, University of Tennessee Computer Science Department, June 1997.
4. Samuel A. Fineberg, Parkson Wong, Bill Nitzberg, and Chris Kuszmaul. PMPIO—a portable implementation of MPI-IO. In *Proceedings of the Sixth Symposium on the Frontiers of Massively Parallel Computation*, pages 188–195. IEEE Computer Society Press, October 1996.
5. Terry Jones, Richard Mark, Jeanne Martin, John May, Elsie Pierce, and Linda Stanberry. An MPI-IO interface to HPSS. In *Proceedings of the Fifth NASA Goddard conference on Mass Storage Systems*, pages I:37–50, September 1996.
6. E. Schikuta, T. Fuerle, C. Loeffelhardt, K. Stockinger, and H. Wanek. On the performance and scalability of client-server based disk i/o. Technical Report TR98201, Institute for Applied Computer Science and Information Systems, Juli 1998.
7. Rajeev Thakur, Ewing Lusk, and William Gropp. Users guide for ROMIO: A high-performance, portable MPI-IO implementation. Technical Report ANL/MCS-TM-234, Mathematics and Computer Science Division, Argonne National Laboratory, October 1997.

Distributed Computing in a Heterogeneous Computing Environment

Edgar Gabriel, Michael Resch, Thomas Beisel and Rainer Keller

High Performance Computing Center Stuttgart
Parallel Computing Department
Allmandring 30
D-70550 Stuttgart, Germany
gabriel@hlrs.de
resch@hlrs.de

Abstract. Distributed computing is a means to overcome the limitations of single computing systems. In this paper we describe how clusters of heterogeneous supercomputers can be used to run a single application or a set of applications. We concentrate on the communication problem in such a configuration and present a software library called PACX-MPI that was developed to allow a single system image from the point of view of an MPI programmer. We describe the concepts that have been implemented for heterogeneous clusters of this type and give a description of real applications using this library.

1 Introduction

The simulation of very large systems often requires computational capabilities which cannot be satisfied by a single massively parallel processing system (MPP) or a parallel vector processor (PVP). A possible way to solve this problem is to couple different computational resources distributed all over the world. Although there are different definitions of metacomputing, this is how in the following we use this term.

The coupling of MPPs and/or PVPs requires a reliable and - if possible - dedicated network connection between the machines, a software which enables interoperability but also algorithms which allow to exploit the underlying power of such a metacomputer. Loosely coupled applications and applications with a clear break in the communication pattern seem to be optimal for metacomputing [1, 2]. However, it was shown, that even closely coupled applications can be adapted for metacomputing [3].

Since MPI as the message-passing standard provides no interoperability, one has to use special software to make an application run on a metacomputer. Several libraries are available that give support in this field. MPICH [4] provides a kind of interoperability, but all communication has to be done via TCP/IP. The number of TCP connections e.g. for the coupling of two Cray T3Es may be as high as 512*512. PVMPI [5] is a library that enables the coupling of already running MPI applications using PVM for the communication. This concept has two major disadvantages: firstly the user has to change his sources for that and secondly he may only use point-to-point communication after having created an inter-communicator between the different machines. A similar library - developed at the PC^2 - is PLUS [6]. It enables the coupling of different message-passing libraries such as MPI, PVM or PARMACS. Again the user has to add some non-standard calls to the code; and again only point-to-point communication is possible.

We have recently presented a library to couple different MPPs called PACX-MPI (PArallel Computer eXtension) [7]. The major advantage of this library is that the user does not need to change his code; he may simply develop the program on a smaller test case using a single MPP and then couple different supercomputers by only linking the PACX-MPI library to his application.

In chapter two of this paper we will briefly present the concepts of PACX-MPI focussing on the major improvements and experiences during the last year. Chapter three presents some applications using PACX-MPI and the results we have achieved. Finally we give a brief outlook of the developments in the project and of ongoing metacomputing activities.

2   Concept of PACX-MPI

PACX-MPI is a library that enables the clustering of two (Version 2.0) or more (Version 3.0) MPPs into one single resource. This allows to use a metacomputer just like an ordinary MPP. The main goals of the PACX-MPI project have already been described in [7] and are only summarised here:

- No changes in the source code
- The programmer should have a single system image
- Use of the vendor implemented fast MPI for internal communication
- Use of a standard protocol for external communication.

2.1   Usage concept of PACX-MPI

To use PACX-MPI for an application, one has to compile and link the application with the PACX-MPI library. The main difference for the user is the start-up of the application. First he has to provide two additional nodes on each machine, which handle the external communication. An application that needs 1024 nodes on a T3E thus takes 514 if running on two separate T3Es. Then he has to configure a hostfile, which has to be identical on each machine. The hostfile contains the name of the machines, the number of application nodes, the used protocol for the communication with this machine and optionally the start-up command, if one wants to make use of the automatic start-up facility of PACX-MPI 3.0. Such a hostfile may look like this:

```
#machine nodes protocol  start-up command
host1    100   tcp
host2    100   tcp       (rsh host2 mpirun -np 102 ./exename)
host3    100   tcp       (rsh host3 mpirun -np 102 ./exename)
host4    100   tcp       (rsh host4 mpirun -np 102 ./exename)
```

2.2 Technical concept of PACX-MPI

To enable metacomputing, PACX-MPI redirects the MPI-calls to its own PACX-MPI library calls. For applications written in C this is done by using a macro-directive. Fortran applications first have to link with the PACX-MPI library before linking with the original MPI-library. Thus PACX-MPI is a kind of additional layer between the application and MPI.

The creation of a distributed global MPI_COMM_WORLD requires two numberings for each node; a local number for the MPI_COMM_WORLD locally established and a global one. In figure 1 the local numbers are in the lower part of the boxes and the global numbers in the upper one. The external communication is handled by two additional communication nodes, which are not considered in the global numbering. Since for the application only the global numbering is relevant these communication nodes are completely transparent. To explain their role in PACX-MPI, we describe the sequence of a point-to-point communication between global node two and global node seven. The sending node will check

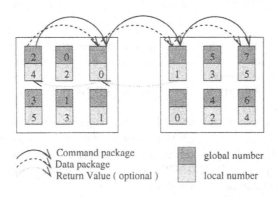

Command package
Data package
Return Value (optional)

global number

local number

Fig. 1. Point to point communication for a metacomputer consisting of two machines

first, whether the receiver is on the same MPP or not. If it is on the same machine, it will do a normal MPI_Send. If it is not, it creates a command-package, which has the same function as the message-envelope in MPI, and transfers this command-package and the data to one of the communication nodes, the so-called MPI-server. The MPI-server compresses the data and transfers them via TCP/IP to the destination machine. There the command-package and the data are received by the so-called PACX-server, the second communication node. Data are decompressed and passed on to the destination node seven. This is done by mapping the global node number to the local one and using native vendor MPI.

Buffering concept of PACX-MPI In previous PACX-MPI versions the receiver only checked whether the sending node is on the same machine or not. This is no problem for the coupling of two machines but may lead to race conditions if more than two machines are involved or if one process belongs to more than one communicator. To avoid this, message buffering on the receiving side is done. The decision was to buffer messages without matching MPI_Recv at the destination node rather than at the PACX-server. This allows to distribute both memory requirements and working time. In a point-to-point communication the receiving node first checks whether the message is an internal one. In case it is, it is received by directly using MPI. If it is not an internal message, the receiving node has to check whether the expected message is already in the buffer. Only if this is not the case, the message is received from the PACX-server directly.

Data conversion in PACX-MPI To support heterogeneous metacomputing, the new version of PACX-MPI has to do data conversion. Initially we thought of having the two communication nodes handle all data conversion. However, for the MPI_Packed datatype the receiver has to know exactly what the content of the message is. Therefore we decided to design the data conversion concept as follows:

- The sending node does a data conversion into an XDR-data format, if it prepares a message for another machine. For internal communication, no additional work accrues.
- The receiver converts the data from the XDR-format into its own data representation.
- For the data-type MPI_PACKED a data conversion to XDR-format will be done while executing MPI_PACK, even for internal communication.
- Because of the high overhead, data conversion can be enabled and disabled by a compiler option of PACX-MPI. This allows the optimisation of applications for homogeneous metacomputing.

2.3 Global Communication in PACX-MPI

In the PACX-MPI Version 2.0, some parts of the global communication were executed by the communication nodes [7]. As there are situations in which this can lead to a blocking of the application, the communication nodes are no longer involved in global operations in the current version. The sequence of a broadcast operation of node 2 to MPI_COMM_WORLD is shown in fig. 2. At first the root-node of the broadcast sends a command-package and a data-package to the

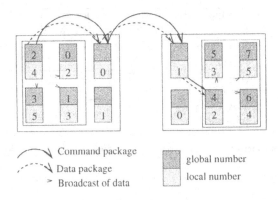

Command package
Data package
Broadcast of data

global number
local number

Fig. 2. A broadcast operation in PACX-MPI 3.0

MPI-server. Then a local MPI_Bcast is executed. Both the command-package and the data-package are transferred to the other machines. There PACX-server transfers the command and the data-package to the node with the smallest local number. This node does the local broadcast. This means that global operations are handled locally by nodes from the application part now rather than by one of the servers.

3   Results

Up to now, PACX-MPI is used by a small number of applications [1]. There are two applications that are developed at Stuttgart which we would like to describe here briefly.

The first metacomputer consisted of the Cray T3E 512 of the Stuttgart University and the Cray T3E 512 of the Pittsburgh Supercomputing Center. For the tests we had a dedicated network connection with a bandwidth of 2Mbits/second and a physical latency of about 70ms. Using PACX-MPI we achieved a sustained bandwidth of about 1 Mbit/s and a latency of about 75ms.

URANUS The first application is a Navier-Stokes Solver called URANUS (Upwind Relaxation Algorithm for Nonequilibrum flows of the University of Stuttgart), which is used to simulate the non-equilibrium flows around the re-entry vehicle in a wide altitude-velocity range [3]. The code is based on a regular grid decomposition, which leads to a very good load balancing and a simple communication pattern. URANUS was chosen for our metacomputing experiments because the simulation of re-entry vehicles requires an amount of memory that can not be provided by a single machine.

In the following we give the overall time it takes to simulate a medium size problem with 880.000 grid cells. For the tests we simulated 10 Iterations. We compared a single machine with 128 nodes and two machines with 2 times 64

Method	128 nodes using MPI	2*64 nodes using PACX-MPI
URANUS unchanged	102.4	156.7
URANUS modified	91.2	150.5
URANUS pipelined	-	116.7

Table 1. Comparison of timing results (sec) in metacomputing for URANUS

nodes. Obviously the unchanged code is much slower on two machines. However, the overhead of 50% is relatively small with respect to the slow network. Modification of the pre-processing does not improve the situation much. A lot more can be gained by fully asynchronous message-passing. Using so called "Message Pipelining" [3] messages are only received if available. The receiving node may continue the iteration process without having the most recent data in that case. This helped to reduce the computing time significantly. Tests for one single machine were not run because results are no longer comparable with respect to numerical convergence. Based on this final version, however, a full space vehicle configuration using more than 1 million cells was run on 760 nodes successfully during SC'97.

However, this requires a minor change in the code which shows that for closely coupled applications metacomputing can not be exploited easily without modifying the algorithm. Still the advantage for the user with PACX-MPI is, that the code remains portable.

P3T-DSMC The second application is P3T-DSMC. This is an object-oriented Direct Simulation Monte Carlo Code which was developed at the Institute for Computer Applications (ICA I) of Stuttgart University for general particle tracking problems [8].

Since Monte Carlo Methods are well suited for metacomputing, this application gives a very good performance on the transatlantic connection. For small number of particles the metacomputing shows some overhead. But up to 125.000 particles timings for one time step are identical. This excellent behaviour is due to two basic features of the code. First, the computation to communication ratio is becoming better if more particles are simulated per process. Second, latency can be hidden more easily if the number of particles increases.

During SC'97 this application was able to set a new world record for molecular dynamics simulating a crystal with 1.4 billion particles on two T3E's using 1024 processors. This gives hope that metacomputing can be a tool to further push the frontiers of scientific research.

In a joint effort with the Forschungszentrum Jülich GmbH at the beginning of May the new PACX-MPI Version successfully coupled three Cray T3E's for one application; the Cray T3E/900-512 at Stuttgart, a Cray T3E/900-256 and a Cray

Particles/CPU	60 nodes using MPI	2*30 nodes using PACX-MPI
1935	0.05	0.28
3906	0.1	0.31
7812	0.2	0.31
15625	0.4	0.4
31250	0.81	0.81
125000	3.27	3.3
500000	13.04	13.4

Table 2. Comparison of timing results (sec) in metacomputing for P3T-DSMC

T3E/600-512 at Jülich. The main difference between this metacomputer and the one used during SC'97 is that for this one Internet was used for coupling and therefore neither reliable bandwidth nor a constant latency could be achieved.

The latency between Stuttgart and Jülich was between 13 ms and 35ms with an average value of about 29 ms. Bandwidth was about 0.27 MB/second. The latency between the two T3E's of Jülich was about 7ms and the bandwidth was about 14 MB/second.

The application used was a version of P3T-DSMC which has to communicate a lot more than the previous test case does. That is why the results for this test were not as good as the previous ones. For a smaller test-suite using 34 nodes on three machines we show in the following table the overall time for a simulation:

Simulation on a single T3E	126.6 sec
Metacomputer with data-compression	163.2 sec
Metacomputer without data-compression	220.8 sec

Table 3. Simulation times for a P3T-DSMC test case with 3 MPP's

The table points out, that one really benefits from using the data-compression of PACX-MPI here. This behaviour was not seen when dedicated networks were used.

4 Outlook

We have presented new results of a library, that enables MPI-based metacomputing. Although the application test cases exhibit some overhead for metacomputing, it was shown that based on PACX-MPI we can solve problems that cannot be solved otherwise. However, metacomputing should not be understood as an alternative to very big MPPs. It is mainly suitable for problems that cannot be solved because of lacking performance and resources such as main memory at one site.

The development of PACX-MPI will be forced in the near future, as there are requests from users for such a library. Therefore the first advancement of PACX-MPI will be to enlarge the number of supported functions, according to our application needs.

Another main direction will be the support of some parts of the MPI-2 functionality, especially support for dynamic process start. But here we will have to wait until first vendor implementations of the new standard are available.

As a protocol for external communication, only TCP/IP is supported at the moment. For long distance connections, there actually seems to be no alternative with respect to reliability. But for local networks it would be reasonable to support other network protocols like HiPPI or ATM.

References

1. Th. Eickermann, J. Heinrichs, M. Resch, R. Stoy, R. Völpel, 'Metacomputing in Gigabit Environments: Networks, Tools and Appplications' to appear in Parallel Computing (1998).
2. Toshiya Kimura, Hiroshi Takemiya, 'Local Area Metacomputing for Multidisciplinary Problems: A Case Study for Fluid/Structure Coupled Simulation', 12th ACM International Conference on Supercomputing, Melbourne, July 13-17 (1998).
3. Thomas Bönisch and Roland Rühle, 'Adapting a CFD code for metacomputing', 10th International Conference on Parallel CFD, Hsinchu/Taiwan, May 11-14, (1998).
4. W. Gropp, E. Lusk, N. Doss, A. Skjellum, 'A high-performance, portable implementation of the MPI message-passing interface standard', Parallel Computing, 22 (1996).
5. Graham E. Fagg, Jack J. Dongarra and Al Geist, 'Heterogeneous MPI Application Interoperation and Process management under PVMPI', in: Marian Bubak, Jack Dongarra, Jerzy Wasniewski (Eds.), 'Recent Advances in Parallel Virtual Machine and Message Passing Interface', 91–98, Springer (1997).
6. Matthias Brune, Jörn Gehring and Alexander Reinefeld, 'Heterogeneous Message Passing and a Link to Resource Management', Journal of Supercomputing, Vol. 11, 1–17 (1997).
7. Thomas Beisel, Edgar Gabriel, Michael Resch , 'An Extension to MPI for Distributed Computing on MPPs' in: Marian Bubak, Jack Dongarra, Jerzy Wasniewski (Eds.) 'Recent Advances in Parallel Virtual Machine and Message Passing Interface', Lecture Notes in Computer Science, 75–83, Springer (1997).
8. Matthias Müller and Hans J. Herrmann, 'DSMC - a stochastic algorithm for granular matter', in: Hans J. Herrmann and J.-P. Hovi and Stefan Luding (Eds.) 'Physics of dry granular media', Kluwer Academic Publisher (1998).

Acknowledgements

The authors gratefully acknowledge support from PSC, KFA Jülich and the High Performance Computing Center Stuttgart.
This article was processed using the LATEX macro package with LLNCS style

Rank Reordering Strategy for MPI Topology Creation Functions [*]

Takao Hatazaki

NKK Corporation, 1-1-2 Marunouchi, Chiyoda-ku, Tokyo 100-8202, Japan
email: hatazaki@nkknet.or.jp

Abstract. A large fraction of all parallel applications use process topologies. Mapping of those topologies onto hardware architecture has been studied for long time. Meanwhile, many current multiprocessor systems are implemented in modular architecture. This paper presents a new mapping strategy that takes advantage of this modularity. The idea was implemented in MPI's topology creation functions and found to be very effective.

1 Introduction

A large fraction of all parallel applications use process topologies such as ring, torus, and hypercube. Meanwhile, there are many variations for the hardware architecture and configuration of runtime environment. For portable applications to be independent from the runtime environment, MPI [8] provides the concept of "virtual topology", on which the application can be implemented.

Mapping of the virtual topology onto hardware architecture has been studied for long time. The virtual topology is represented in a graph in which each vertex represents a process and edges represent communication paths. The hardware topology is also represented in a graph in which each vertex represents a processor and edges are weighted in terms of communication capacity between processors. The objective is to minimize the overall communication cost between processes mapped on the hardware topology graph. This problem is known to be NP-complete [1, 2].

The major focus has been on developing heuristics for particular interconnection topologies of processors in homogeneous systems. However, many current parallel systems implement multiple levels of interconnection architecture. Typically, Symmetric Multi-Processor (SMP) architecture or its variant is used to connect a small number of processors on shared memory and a high speed network is used to connect those SMP nodes. The latter connection is interconnection network on high-end large servers, or commodity network that is becoming popular for low-cost cluster systems.

This modularity of architecture is expected to become more complex as larger number of processors are connected and more communication capability between

---

[*] This work was done as part of MPI development project at Hewlett-Packard Company

processors is required [1]. The modularity of the system often determines characteristics of communication performance [6]. It is likely that processors in the same finest level of module have the shortest distance and ones between coarsest level of modules have the longest distance in terms of communication capacity.

A new heuristic algorithm was developed for the mapping problem by considering this modularity of processors and implemented in MPI's virtual topology creation functions.

In the following section, the objective is illustrated with a simple example. In Sect. 3, the algorithm is introduced, followed by another section that describes the implementation. In Sect. 5, performance results with a benchmark program are analyzed. Finally the conclusion is given in Sect. 6. Throughout this paper the term *processes* is used distinctively for virtual topology and *processors* is used for hardware topology.

2 Objective

Suppose that the application is written using the virtual topology depicted in Fig. 1(a) and the hardware platform is a cluster of SMP's as depicted in Fig. 1(b). Each of processes A, B, C, and D communicates to its neighbor(s). There are three edges, i.e. communication paths, in the virtual topology. Assume that A, B, C, and D are assigned to processor $P1$, $P3$, $P2$, and $P4$, respectively. In this case, all of three communication paths are across SMP's. If A, B, C, and D are assigned to $P1$, $P2$, $P3$, and $P4$, respectively, then two paths are within the same SMP. Most MPI systems use shared memory for communications within an SMP, which is usually much faster than network. Therefore, the latter process-to-processor mapping likely yields better performance than the former one. Our objective is to find a sufficiently good mapping in a given configuration.

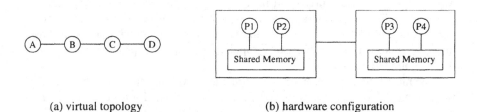

(a) virtual topology   (b) hardware configuration

Fig. 1. Example of mapping problem

Traditionally, the hardware configuration shown in Fig. 1(b) is represented in a graph as shown in Fig. 2(a), in which vertices represent processors and edges are underlying communication links weighted in terms of their capacity. Mapping of the graph Fig. 1(a) onto Fig. 2(a) is called a *graph embedding problem*.

A semi-formal description of our problem is as follows. A virtual topology is given by a graph $V = (X, E)$ where X is a set of processes and E is the

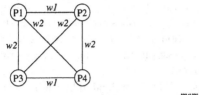
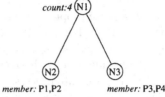

w1: cost of shared memory communication
w2: cost of network communication

(a) connection graph   (b) module tree

Fig. 2. Hardware topology

communication paths between processes. Edges E are not weighted, that is, it is assumed that the virtual topology does balance communications. The hardware configuration is given by a graph $N = (P, C)$ where P is a set of processors and C is weight of the edges. N is a perfectly connected network. $C_{u \cdot v}$ is the weight of an edge $u \leftrightarrow v$ $(u, v \in P)$. Note that the weight denotes the communication distance between processors at endpoints of the edge. $|P| \geq |X|$ is assumed. Given that the virtual topology already partitions the compute task properly, the assumptions are reasonable.

The overall communication cost for V mapped onto N is given by:

$$C_z = \sum_{e \in E} C_{\pi(x_1) \cdot \pi(x_2)} \tag{1}$$

Note that x_1 and x_2 are endpoints of the edge e. The objective is to find a mapping $\pi : V \to N$ that produces sufficiently small C_z.

3 Algorithm

While many good heuristics have been developed for the problem [11], those algorithms are expensive. Our approach takes advantage of modularity of processors in the system with assuming that processors in the same module have more communication capacity than ones in different modules. Figure 2(b) is a graph representation of the hardware configuration in the context of modularity. Each vertex represents a module that may contain submodules. Modules that do not have submodules are terminal vertices. Since each module has at most one super-module, the graph is a tree. It is called a *module tree*.

Leaf nodes, i.e. terminal vertices, are annotated with *member* property which is a list of processors in the module. Inner nodes are annotated with *count* property that is a total number of the members in its rooting subtree. Edges do not have properties. There are only two levels of modularity in the example, however, there can be more.

The goal is to minimize the communication between modules. The multilevel partitioning is applied as the following. At first, all processes are assigned to the root node in the module tree. Then they are partitioned onto sibling nodes accordingly to the *count* properties so that few edges connect processes between nodes. By recursively applying the partitioning with the module tree in breadth-first manner, the mapping between processes in the virtual topology graph and leaf nodes in the module tree is obtained.

Processes are mapped onto processors that are indicated by the *member* property in the leaf node. The exact mapping between those processes and processors is not explicit. This is implied from the assumption that the communication costs between processors in a module are the same. This cost attribute, which is the edge weight in the processor network (Fig. 2(a)), is abstracted into the modularity.

Graph partitioning problem is a special case of the graph embedding problem, primarily defined as a bipartitioning problem. While many advanced heuristic algorithms have been developed for large graphs containing tens of thousand of vertices [9], the size of the virtual topology graph is small. The steepest descent, Kernighan-Lin heuristic algorithm [3, 5], is adopted for our implementation. It is known to be high quality and still being widely used even for post-refining of those advanced heuristics. N-way partitioning can be accomplished by recursively applying the bipartitioning [5].

So far it is assumed that $|X|$, the number of processes in virtual topology, is equal to $|P|$, the number of available processors. In the case of $|X| < |P|$, the *network affinity* $A_i = (\sum_{j=1}^{|P|} C_{i,j})^{-1}$ is computed for each processor, then $|X|$ processors that have larger affinity than the rest are selected. The module tree is composed with those selected processors.

4 Implementation

The MPI system assigns a sequential number, called the *rank*, to each process. MPI_Cart_create() and MPI_Graph_create() take a virtual topology description of ranks. A process can query the MPI system, for example, its neighboring rank after calling these functions. More interestingly, these functions take the "reorder" flag as a parameter, which allows the MPI system to reorder ranks on processes. A process's neighboring rank may be on a different process from unreordered case. The mapping strategy is implemented for this reordering in these functions. The implementation is independent from the hardware platform or operating system, except for the composition of the module tree.

The HP Exemplar X-class server has three levels of modularity. As shown in Fig. 3, each module use a different medium for communication if viewed as a message passing machine. Processors in a hypernode communicate via hypernode-private shared memory, ones in different hypernodes (but in the same subcomplex) communicate via global shared memory, and ones in different subcomplexes communicate via tcp/ip network [4]. Figure 4 shows performance figures with the ping-pong benchmark program bundled in HP MPI. $C_{u \cdot v}$, the communication cost between processor u and v, can roughly be parameterized as 1 ($u, v \in$

hypernode), 10 ($u, v \in$ subcomplex), or 100 (u and v are in different subcomplexes). If an application runs on a cluster of two or more systems connected in network, there will be one more level of modularity.

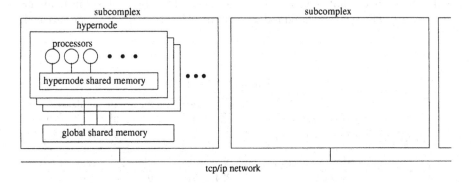

Fig. 3. HP Exemplar X-class architecture

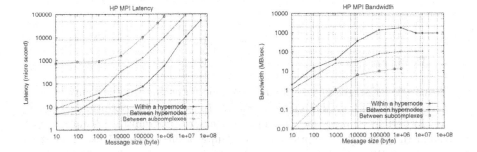

Fig. 4. Ping-pong communication performance

At first, an off-line utility is developed in order to estimate the effectiveness of the reordering by the algorithm. Table 1 compares the number of communication paths in the initial rank ordering, that is in block assign order with respect to the modularity, and those in reordered mapping for some particular cases. The sample configuration consists of 8 hosts, each consists of 2 subcomplexes containing 4 hypernodes. Each hypernode contains 16 processors. Therefore, the system consists of $8 \times (2 \times (4 \times 16)) = 1024$ processors. Embedding virtual topology for case 1 is a 32×32 grid torus. If we assume $C_{u \cdot v} = 150$ for processors between hosts, the cost function defined by Formula (1) is reduced 38% by the reordering. Case 2 is with embedding an $8 \times 8 \times 16$ hypercube. The cost function is reduced 41% by the reordering. Cases 3 and 4 are the configuration used for performance tests described in the next section. It consists of 8 hypernodes, each of which contains 16 processors. There are only two levels of modularity, which are the whole system and the hypernode. Case 3 is embedding a 4 × 32 grid torus. Case 4 is embedding an 8 × 16 grid torus. The reordering reduced the cost function 63% and 41%, respectively. Cases 5 and 6 are a duplication of cases 3 and 4, respectively, but the configuration consists of 8 subcomplexes instead of 8 hypernodes. Those obtain good reductions, too. The objective has been satisfied.

Table 1. Solution by the algorithm

		case 1	case 2	case 3	case 4	case 5	case 6
Unreordered	between hosts	256	1024	0	0	0	0
	between subcomplexes	256	256	0	0	136	128
	between hypernodes	576	768	136	128	0	0
	within a hypernode	960	1024	120	128	120	128
Reordered	between hosts	224	512	0	0	0	0
	between subcomplexes	64	256	0	0	32	64
	between hypernodes	256	768	32	64	0	0
	within a hypernode	1504	1536	224	192	224	192
Reduction in cost function (%)		37.7	40.6	63.2	40.9	75.0	49.0

5 Performance

The cost function given in Formula (1) is good for evaluating the solution, but it is too simplistic for predicting performance. To measure the performance gain by the reordering, we developed a simple benchmark program that mimics the Jacobi method for a Poisson problem solver [10]. It at first calls MPI_Cart_create() to set up MPI environment with regard to the virtual topology. Then all processes collectively execute:

for each dimension **begin**
    send data to upward neighbor, receive data from downward neighbor
    send data to downward neighbor, receive data from upward neighbor
end

The program does no computations, just communications. Elapsed time for some iterations of this communication pattern was measured. Since elapsed time was found to be proportional to the iteration count, that axis was removed.

The benchmark test was conducted on the same configuration as described for simulations cases 3 through 6 in Table 1. Figure 5 shows the reduction rate in elapsed time. Note, for example, that a 90% reduction rate means that elapsed time with reordered mapping is 10% of that with unreordered mapping.

The plot on the left, which depicts the performance on 8-hypernode system, shows that the effectiveness of the reordering depends on size of the message. In

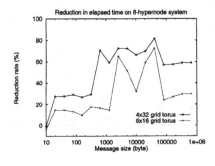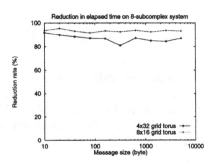

Fig. 5. Benchmark test on 128-processor system

this configuration, processes communicate via either hypernode-private or global shared memory. The ratio of communication capacity between those medium is approximately 1:10. With 10 byte message size, the reordering did not get a reduction. With latency bound communication, optimal mappings contribute little to performance because the slowest path likely dominates the elapsed time. However, with larger message sizes, the reordering yielded good reductions. As expected from cases 3 and 4 in Table 1, the 4×32 grid torus benefited more by the reordering than the 8×16 grid torus did.

The right plot in Fig. 5 compares reductions with the configuration that involves hypernode shared memory and tcp/ip network. The ratio of communication capacity between those medium is approximately 1:100. The effect of reordering is apparent.

6 Conclusion

The technique was applied to a production MPI application that uses MPI_Cart_create(), and it obtained the performance improvement that was expected from the benchmark test. This particular application has been known to be sensitive to the process placement on HP Exemplar X-class server, which is a non-uniform message-passing system, as well as a non-uniform memory architecture system.

An automatic optimal process placement requires information about system's uniformity and application's communication pattern. Because the non-uniformity is derived from system's modular architecture, we composed the module tree to concisely represent the information. MPI's topology creation functions give information about application's communication pattern with the virtual topology. One way to combine those information to get near-optimal process placement was presented.

The latter information can be given differently than via a description of the virtual topology. If the communication pattern is fixed regardless of input data, the communication profile data can be used to compose the communication topology graph. In such a graph representation, edges need to be weighted, and the multilevel partitioning is still possible. However, the cost function in the processor connection graph will need to be refined.

7 Acknowledgment

The author would like to thank the MPI development group at Hewlett-Packard Company for providing the opportunity, resources, and valuable comments on this matter.

References

1. V. David, Ch. Fraboul, JY. Rousselot, and P. Siron: *Partitioning and mapping communication graphs on a modular reconfigurable parallel architecture.* Parallel Processing: CONPAR92-VAPPV, 2nd Joint International Conference on Vector and Parallel Processing. Lyon, France Sep. 1992
2. F. Ercal, J. Ramanujam, and P. Sadayappan: *Task Allocation onto a Hypercube by Recursive Mincut Bipartitioning.* Journal of Parallel and Distributed Computing **10** (1990) 35–44
3. C. M. Fiduccia and R. M. Mattheyses: *A linear-time heuristic for improving network partitions.* Proceedings of the 19th Design Automation Conference, pp. 175–181 (1982)
4. Hewlett-Packard Company: *HP MPI User's Guide.* HP Press (1997)
5. B. W. Kernighan and S. Lin: *An Efficient Heuristic Procedure for Partitioning Graphs.* The Bell System Technical Journal vol. 49, pp. 291–307 (1970)
6. Steven S. Lumetta, Alan M. Mainwaring, and David E. Culler: *Multi-Protocol Active Messages on a Cluster of SMP's.* Proceedings of Super Computing Conference '97 (1997)
7. O. Kramer and H. Muhlenbein: *Mapping strategies in message-based multiprocessor systems.* Parallel Computing **9** (1989) 213–225
8. Message-Passing Forum: *MPI: Message-Passing Interface Standard.* June 1995
9. Alex Pothen: *Graph Partitioning Algorithms with Applications to Scientific Computing.* Old Dominion Univ. Technical Report (1997)
10. W. Gropp, E. Lusk, and A. Skjellum: *USING MPI: Portable Parallel Programming with the Message-Passing Interface.* The MIT Press (1994)
11. John E. Savege and Markus G. Wloka: *Parallel Graph-Embedding and the Mob Heuristic.* Brown University Department of Computer Science, Technical Report No. CS-91-07 (1991)

Scalable and Adaptive Resource Sharing in PVM

Michael Kemelmakher and Orly Kremien

Department of Mathematics and Computer Science,
Bar Ilan University,
Ramat Gan,529000,Israel
{kemelma,orly,dsg}@macs.biu.ac.il
http://www.cs.biu.ac.il:8080/~ dsg/

Abstract. PVM uses round-robin as its default policy for process allocation to processors. The main drawbacks of this policy are the fact that PVM ignores load variations among different nodes and also the inability of PVM to distinguish between machines of different speeds. To redress this deficiency a Resource Manager (RM) is implemented which replaces round-robin with a scalable and adaptive algorithm for resource sharing [11] providing a High Performance Computing Cluster (HPCC). In this paper an implementation of a Resource Manager is proposed. The RM can be transparently plugged into PVM to offer improved performance to its users. The design of a resource manager to extend PVM is described. A prototype implementation in PVM is then measured to illustrate the utility of the approach. Finally, performance results favorably comparing the enhanced version to the original PVM are presented ...

1   Introduction

High capacity clusters of workstations are becoming an appealing vehicle for parallel computing. A parallel system may be viewed as a collection of services. There are workstations which seek services and those available which provide services. Much of the computing power is frequently idle. Resource sharing in complex network systems aims at achieving maximal system performance by utilizing the available system resources efficiently.

The PVM (Parallel Virtual Machine) system, used worldwide, enables a collection of heterogeneous computers connected by dissimilar networks to be used as a coherent and flexible concurrent computational resource. The concept of PVM pluggability is introduced in [7]. It describes a Resource Manger (RM) which can be transparently plugged into PVM offering improved process allocation. The default policy employed by PVM for resource allocation is round-robin. The main drawbacks of this policy are the fact that PVM ignores the load variations among the different nodes and also PVM is unable to distinguish between machines of different speeds. To redress this deficiency a tool that manipulates and administers system resources must replace round-robin allocation. Such a resource management system is described in this paper. It provides a replacement for the round-robin policy with a scalable and adaptive algorithm for resource sharing [11] .

Section 2 of this paper describes PVM and its process control. In section 3 adaptive resource sharing algorithms are briefly described. Section 4 presents the PVM Resource Management (RM) system. In Section 5 an implementation of a RM which replaces the default round-robin assignment is described followed by prototype implementation measurements. Finally, conclusions derived from this study and directions recommended for future research are given in section 6.

2 PVM

PVM is composed of two parts - the library of PVM interface routines, called *"pvmlib"*, and the support software system. The latter is executed on all the computers, that make up the virtual machine, called *"daemon"* - pvmd. These pvmds are interconnected with each other by a network. Each daemon is responsible for all the application component processes executing on its host. There is a master daemon which controls the physical configuration and acts as a name server. Otherwise, the control of the virtual machine is completely distributed. Process control is addressed in the following paragraphs.

PVM process control includes the policies and means by which PVM manages the assignment of tasks (processes in the PVM system) to processors and controls their execution. The computational resources may be accessed by tasks using the following policies: *default (transparent)* policy, *architecture dependent* policy, *machine specific* or a policy *defined by the user* to substitute the default (round-robin) PVM process control.

In the case of default/transparent, when a task initiation request pvm_spawn() is invoked, the local daemon determines a candidate pool of target nodes. The next node is then selected from this pool in a round-robin manner. The main drawbacks of such policy are the fact that PVM ignores the load variations among the different nodes and also PVM is incapable of distinguishing between machines of different speeds. Adaptive resource sharing algorithms respond to state changes. Such algorithms are briefly discussed below.

3 Adaptive Resource Sharing

The problem of resource sharing was extensively studied by DS (Distributed Systems) and DAI (Distributed Artificial Intelligence) researchers, particularly in relation to the load-sharing problem in such systems. Matching algorithms efficiently couple together nodes sharing a common interest. The performance of location policies with different complexity levels of load sharing algorithms was compared in [6]. Three location policies were studied: random policy (which is not adaptive), threshold policy, and shortest policy.

The random policy yields a dramatic performance improvement. Still, a lot of excessive overhead is required for the remote execution attempts, many of which may prove to be fruitless. Threshold policy probes up to a small number of nodes before actually sending a task for remote execution at the first one probed which is of mutual interest. In this manner, the amount of data, carried by the communication network, is decreased. This policy significantly improves performance. However, the performance of the shortest policy that tries to find the best choice from the set of probed nodes, is not much better than that of the threshold policy. The complexity of an algorithm should be weighed against its relative benefit, in order to evaluate its real usefulness.

All three algorithms mentioned above have the disadvantage of the necessity to initiate negotiation with remote nodes upon request. This may result in a lengthy operation. In [2],[15] state information is maintained locally and periodically updated. A node often deletes information regarding resource holders which are still of interest. In order to better support similar and repeated resource access requests, cache entries of mutual interest should be retained as long as they are of interest.

In the flexible load sharing algorithm FLS [11] biased random selection is used to retain entries of mutual interest and select others to replace discarded entries. The algorithm supports mutual inclusion and exclusion, and is further rendered fail-safe by treating cached data as hints. Nodes sharing mutual interests are retained, thus premature deletion is prevented. Also, state information is updated on a regular basis, rather than waiting for the need to perform the matching to actually arise, in order to start gathering the relevant information. This policy shortens the time period that passes between issuing the request for matching and actually finding a partner having a mutual interest. In [10] an extension to FLS is proposed to further limit negotiation with remote nodes experiencing lengthy resource access delays. It is shown that handling proximity significantly improves and further stabilizes performance.

Also, the calculation of local loads at each single processor is a prerequisite for successful load balancing [2]. In a configuration with processors of different speeds, local load value must be divided by the relative speed of the processor, defined as the ratio between the speed of the specific processor and the speed of the processors with maximal possible speed. This normalization provides a common basis by which the local loads of different speed processors can be compared. For example, if the system has two processors, one with maximal speed and one with half that speed, then the load of the latter will be twice as high as the load of the first processor when running the same set of processes.

Preservation of mutual interests enables coping with dynamic and drastic changes to system configuration. Such changes characterize mobile and wireless systems. The algorithm for preserving mutual interests is general, being applicable to other applications requiring scalability and possessing some criteria for node mutual interest (e.g. dynamic parking assignment, recharging electronic cars, e-commerce).

Integration of an adaptive resource sharing algorithm based on preservation of mutual interests in PVM is discussed in the following section.

4 PVM Resource Manager

The concept of PVM pluggability is introduced in [7], and described at three levels: low level messaging, mid-level resource and analysis tools, and high-level control of the virtual machine. The level of interest to us is the mid-level tool that manipulates and administers system resources. To optimize PVM performance and enable its customization we decided to develop our resource management (RM) system. Our RM implements the scalable and adaptive algorithm for initial allocation [11].

A Resource Manager (RM) interface was introduced in the version 3.3 of PVM [2,4]. A RM is a PVM task. Once installed in the virtual machine, it is equivalent to a complete "take-over" of all scheduling policies. This includes host addition and deletion procedures, various event notifications, task information and spawning placement.

A RM is a completely transparent facility (layer) from the point of view of both PVM users and applications. The number of RMs registered can vary from a single one for the entire virtual machine to one per pvmd. The RM running on the master host manages all slave pvmds that do not have their own RM.

A task connecting anonymously to a virtual machine is assigned the default RM of the pvmd to which it connects. A task spawned from within the system inherits the RM of its parent task. If a task has a RM assigned to it, all PVM system service requests (pvm_spawn, pvm_addhosts, pvm_delhosts, etc.) from the task to its pvmd are routed to the RM instead.

We use RM to provide an alternative spawn service in PVM, which is completely transparent to the user. In our case when a PVM user uses pvm_spawn() function, the SM_SPAWN message is then sent to RM instead of TM_SPAWN message which pvmlib sends to the pvmd by default.

Assuming that the user lets PVM decide where to execute new tasks a PVM event sequence occurs as described below (see Fig. 1):

1. PVM task releases an execution request by calling pvm_spawn() function and suspending until execution is performed;
2. Message TM_SPAWN is sent to the local pvmd;
3. The local pvmd chooses the next available host from the pool in a round robin manner;
4. Local pvmd sends DM_EXEC to the remote pvmd running on the selected host;
5. The remote pvmd spawns a new task and sends DM_EXECACK to the requested pvmd;
6. The local pvmd receives DM_EXECACK and composes a reply containing new tasks ids or error codes to the calling task.

In the situation described above PVM uses a simple round-robin scheduling policy. Such a policy may be efficient in a few specific cases. As an example, we can look at the execution platform of a NOW (Network of Workstations), which consists of identical workstations. The system is idle (without any background

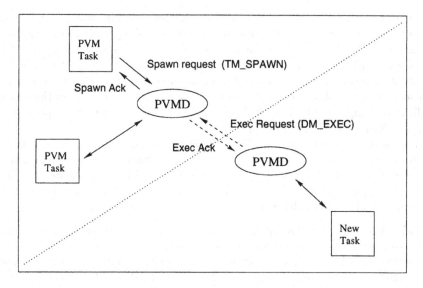

Fig. 1. Generic PVM spawn service mechanism.

load). PVM performs well, in case we have identical processes, and the number of processes is less than or proportional to the size of NOW. If the number of processes is bigger than or not proportional to the size of a cluster, PVM overhead may grow. Also if there is background load or the workstations are not identical (differ in the amount of memory or CPU speeds) round-robin policy is less efficient. In such cases, PVM requires changes in the scheduling policies it uses to achieve performance gains. For these purposes RM and an external system that execute a load-sharing algorithm and give placement decisions were designed and developed.

RM operates transparently for a pvm-user. For several reasons we decided to develop a layer of RMs in PVM rather than a single RM. The first and main reason for such a decision was that, as the system grows one RM per the entire machine might become a bottleneck and also a single point of failure.

5 The design and implementation of RM

The essence of a resource manager in PVM is the defined protocol for both sides, meaning RM and pvmd. The protocol for RM defines its syntax, i.e. message structure, types of requests that it may receive and also its semantics, i.e. behavior upon receipt of such a message. The protocol for pvmd defines types of requests it can receive from RM. The RM developer should then decide how the design of RM would be defined within this framework. We decided to implement RM and an external system (naming it PMI - Preservation of Mutual Interests system) using the object oriented paradigm and C++ language. If a system is designed carefully by separating design and implementation concerns and generalizing the handling of similar operations, then it is straightforward to exchange one implementation detail for another. If an object has a well-defined interface and encapsulates its internal state and operations, then a new object, with a compatible interface but a different internal implementation, can be inserted in place of the first object without disturbing the overall functioning of the system [4]. In our implementation of RM, we tried to make it as general as possible to enable future code reuse and upgrade.

As was mentioned above a RM should handle several system services. In our implementation each system service, which RM should handle, is represented as a separate class/object. There is also a main object that registers services objects and also handles request arrivals on the initial stages. The current implementation is briefly described:

Main Reactor: initial setup, registration of service objects, request receipt and assignment to corresponding service objects.

Hoster: RMs layer management, initial startup of remote RMs, machine configuration information dissemination, RMs shutdown, holds the information about hosts in a virtual machine, handles host management requests (pvm_addhosts, pvm_delhosts) and information requests (pvm_config). Hoster in each RM holds a replication of the configuration information and acts independently.

Spawner: spawn request handling, communication with PMI.

This implementation covers basic system services that should be implemented to provide the possibility to check different scheduling policies. There are additional services, like notification facility (pvm_notify), which are not present in the current implementation.

5.1 External PMI System

The prototype of the algorithm preserving mutual interests is used for providing a load sharing service. In this case an overloaded node is of mutual interest to an underloaded one and vice versa where each may be used by the other for performance improvement. Distributed programming environments running on a network of workstations may use this service. Such environments perform component assignment to nodes of the physical system, i.e. hosts. Some systems [3][4] apply rudimentary scheduling techniques for component allocation. The performance of these systems may be improved by considering computation and communication loads in the system. This is done by PMI (Preservation of Mutual Interests).

The PMI prototype is named Mutual Interests Daemon (*mid*). As an example of a typical use of the load sharing service consider the PVM task spawning. The system may be viewed as a collection of PVM daemons (*pvmds*) and the mutual interests daemons (*mids*). The mids provide a load-sharing framework for the system, while the pvmds create an execution environment for distributed applications.

A particular application of PMI is determined by the state definition, thus all the specific functionality may be localized in the state implementation. The object-oriented paradigm facilitates our design approach. Encapsulation allows a node state to be defined in a separate class. The PMI algorithm is implemented as a template class the parameter of which is the node state class. New applications may be achieved by redefinition of the node state and reuse of the same methods. Thus implementation of PMI may be used as a basis for new application software. The design described above is flexible, general, and reusable.

5.2 Spawn service implementation

Spawn service implementation consists of two parts. The first is the Spawner object, which is part of RM. The second is PMI - which is the external system. PMI is completely independent of PVM (not being a PVM task). Spawner communicates with PMI via its interface library. Spawner supports all default scheduling facilities provided by PVM (round robin, architecture dependent, and machine dependent). Also Spawner can set its own scheduling decisions, transparently for pvm applications. In this case the task execution scenario will be as follows (see Fig. 2):

1. PVM task releases execution request by calling pvm_spawn() function and suspending until execution is performed;
2. Message SM_SPAWN is sent by pvmlib to local RM instead of local pvmd;
3. The local RM requests placement decision from local PMI daemon. This request is not a time consuming operation, since the PMI system executes independently and makes load information caching;
4. The local RM sends the spawn request to the remote RM at "hostname" (the "hostname" is received from local PMI daemon);
5. The remote RM commands pvmd on its host. Pvmd spawns a new task and by SM_EXECACK gives the information to the RM assigned to it;
6. The remote RM sends spawn information to the requested RM;
7. The local RM composes a reply containing new tasks ids or error codes to the calling task.

The placement decision which uses the external PMI system is implemented as a separate method of the Spawner object. Since the implementation language is C++, the design of Spawner allows overloading of this method by other implementations, which may use different load sharing algorithms, in the future.

We implemented the RM in PVM version 3.3. This version enabled the implementation of the RM, but there were many obstacles. Since the RM is a special pvm task, it deals with system level requests. However, to be platform independent, the RM should be written using only user level primitives of PVM. In many cases user level primitives of PVM 3.3 do not fit the demands of a complex distributed system.

For example, a spawn request can not be served immediately and requires the sequence of actions shown in Fig. 2. In the case of multiple spawn requests the

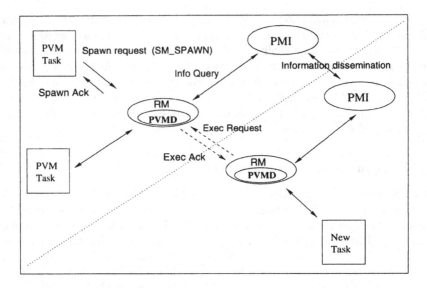

Fig. 2. PVM spawn service mechanism extended by RM and PMI systems.

only solution is to work asynchronously. For such purposes an additional message identification information is required in addition to a message tag, a message source and a task id of a sender provided by PVM 3.3. While PVM 3.3 provides pvm_setmwid() and pvm_getmwid() functions, it is not sufficient to enable the implementation of a powerful pvm-task which deals with the system work. PVM 3.4 introduces message boxes, message handlers, and communicational contexts [7][8]. This will extend our capability to implement RM and will be used in future implementations.

One common question may arise: why not use a high-level library on top of pvmlib (the library of PVM interface routines) rather than a RM facility. Each one of these solutions has its merits and shortcomings. The high-level library may be an acceptable technical solution for substitution of spawn service in PVM. Such a solution may result in less significant overhead than a layer of RMs, as described above. On the other hand, a library on top of pvmlib will not be transparent to the program code in FORTRAN or C languages (C++ provides the "function overloading" facility). The RM system on the contrary is completely transparent to the pvm programmer in any language.

5.3 Performance Measurement

The aim of this measurement study is to show the utility of approach rather than to produce statistically valid results. The execution platform for benchmarks is a NOW configuration composed of identical, Pentium Pro 200 based workstations that were connected by an Ethernet100 LAN. The operating system used UNIX BSDI 3.1 and PVM 3.3. We impose on our system an average load between 80%

- 90%. We compare PVM performance to that of our enhanced PVM system. The load is generated on each node (workstation) with the sequence of execution requests with random arrivals and exponentially distributed CPU demand. System average response time is then measured. An example of such measurement is shown in the tables below :

Table 1. Benchmark on system composed of 5 nodes. Each node produces 100 processes

Load (%)	CPU demand	PVM RT	Extended PVM RT	Speedup
80%	12.52 sec.	45.68 sec.	23.59 sec.	48.70%
85%	13.16 sec.	53.12 sec.	28.49 sec.	46.37%
90%	13.70 sec.	76.54 sec.	36.89 sec.	51.80%

Table 2. Benchmark on system composed of 9 nodes. Each node produces 100 processes

Load (%)	CPU demand	PVM RT	Extended PVM RT	Speedup
80%	12.42 sec.	32.76 sec.	23.66 sec.	32.04%
85%	13.20 sec.	60.88 sec.	29.75 sec.	51.13%
90%	13.96 sec.	80.62 sec.	36.04 sec.	55.30%

6 Conclusions and Future Study

This paper presented a PVM-based implementation of a scalable and adaptive resource sharing facility. Our system is based on commodity hardware (PCs and networking) and software (PVM) offering a low cost solution as an alternative to mainframes and MPP's. Such a system adapts to state changes which are unpredictable in a complex network environment. Simulation and prototype implementation results demonstrate the utility of an algorithm preserving mutual interests to such environments. We are encouraged by the relative ease of PMI implementation and the results it provides.

Our current implementation supports scalable and adaptive initial placement. It will be complemented by migration after start-up [2] to support a general purpose PVM-based high performance computation (HPC) server. We are working on adaptation of this cluster computation server to the Internet environment and its technologies (like JAVA, CORBA). Initial results demonstrate PMI generality and usefulness to support load sharing and also the dynamic parking assignment problem. We are currently working on its customization to e-commerce.

Process control is currently implemented via a Resource Manager (RM). We will also try the other alternative which will provide this support via an extension of pvmlib.

Further work is necessary to gain experience with the current algorithms and others for selecting cache members. We are working on schemes for prolonging the time state information is retained, consistent with [12].

Acknowledgments We gratefully acknowledge the Ministry of Science grant no. 8500 for its financial support. We extend our thanks to Peggy Weinreich for her valuable editorial work.

References

1. A.Barak, A. Braverman, I.Gilderman, O. Laadan, "Performance of PVM and the MOSIX Preemptive Process migration Scheme", Proc. 7th Israeli Conf. on Computer Systems and Software Engineering, IEEE Computer Society Press 1996.
2. A. Barak, S. Guday and R.G. Wheeler. "The MOSIX Distributed Operating System, Load Balancing for UNIX", Lecture Notes in Computer Science, Vol. 672, Springer-Verlag, 1993.
3. A. Beguelin, J. Dongarra, G.A. Geist, W. Jiang, R. Manchek, V. Sunderam, "PVM: Parallel Virtual Mchine, a Users Guide and Tutorial for Networked Parallel Computing, MIT Press, Cambridge, MA, 1994.
4. S. Crane, K. Twidle, "Constructing Distributed Unix Utilities in Regis", Proceedings of the Second International Workshop on Configurable Distributed Systems, March 1994.
5. A. Dupuy, J. Schwartz, "Nest: Network Simulation Tool", Technical Report, Communications of the ACM, October, No. 10, 1990, Vol. 33.
6. Eager D. L., E. D. Lazowska, J. Zahorjan, "Adaptive Load Sharing in Homogeneous Distributed Systems", IEEE Trans. on Software Eng., 12(5), pp. 662-675, May 1986.
7. G.A. Geist, J.A.Kohl, P.M. Papadopoulos, S.L. Scott "Beyond PVM 3.4: What we have Learned , Whats Next, and Why ", Oak ridge National Laboratory, Computer Science and Mathematics Division, Oak Ridge, URL: http://www.epm.ornl.gov/pvm/context.ps, 1997
8. G.A. Geist, J.A. Kohl, R. Manchek, P. M. Papadopoulus, "New Features of PVM 3.4", 1995 EuroPVM Users Group Meeting, Lyon, France, September 1995.
9. G.A. Geist, J.A. Kohl, P. M. Papadopoulus, "CUMULVS": Providing Fault Tolerance, Visualization and Steering of Parallel Applications", SIAM, August 1996.
10. M. Kapelevich, O. Kremien, "Scalable Resource Scheduling : Design , Assessment, Prototyping", Proc. 8th Israeli Conf. on Computer Systems and Software Engineering, IEEE Computer Society Press 1997.
11. O. Kremien, J. Kramer, J. Magee, "Scalable, Adaptive Load Sharing Algorithms", IEEE Parallel and Distributed Technology, August 1993, 62-70.
12. F. Krueger, N. Shivaratri, "Adaptive Location Policies for Global Scheduling", IEEE Transactions on Software Engineering, June, No. 6,1994, Vol. 20, 432-444
13. M. Satyanarayanan, "Scale and Performance in Distributed File System", IEEE Transactions on Software Engineering, January, No. 1, 1992, Vol. 18, 1-8.
14. Shivaratri N., P. Krueger, M. Singhal, "Load Distributing for Locally Distributed Systems", Computer, 33-44, December 1992.
15. S. Zhou, "A Trace-Driven Simulation Study of Dynamic Load Balancing", IEEE Transactions on Software Engineering, September, No. 9, 1988, Vol. 14, 1327-1341.

Load Balancing for Network Based Multi-threaded Applications

Oliver Krone[‡], Martin Raab[¶][*], Béat Hirsbrunner[‡]
[‡]Institut d'Informatique, Université de Fribourg, Switzerland
[¶]Institut für Informatik, Technische Universität München, Germany

Abstract. In this paper we present LBS, a load-management-system for network based concurrent computing. The system is built on PT-PVM, a library based on the PVM system. PT-PVM provides message passing and process management facilities at thread and process level for a cluster of workstations running the UNIX operating system.

The presented system is realized as an open library which can be easily used to implement new load-balancing algorithms. In addition to that, the unit of load which has to be distributed (either data or lightweight processes) can be transparently adapted to application needs. Therefore the system serves as an ideal test-bed for comparing different load-balancing methods.

1 Introduction

With the increasing computing power of dedicated workstations and the observation that an enormous potential of CPU cycles is merely unused because workstations tend to be idle most of the time, network-based concurrent computing (also commonly referred to as NOWs, networks of workstations) has recently become a major research topic. Other motivating aspects include heterogeneity, excellent price/performance characteristics and powerful development tools [11] for these machines.

The "usual" unit of parallelism for network based concurrent computing is a heavy-weight UNIX process, however in the past years a new type of process, called light-weight process or "thread" has emerged which has a couple of advantages compared to heavy-weight UNIX processes. Applications using this process type are commonly referred to as multi-threaded applications.

The notion of "thread" has been introduced as early as 1965 by Dijkstra [3] as a sequential flow of control, and is defined as *a sequence of instructions executed within the context of a process* [9]. It has its own program counter, register set and stack, but shares a common address space and operating system resources with other threads in a process. Multi-threaded applications provide many advantages for example) such as: small context switching time, fast thread to thread communication, increased application responsiveness due to overlapping of computation and communication [12].

The rest of this paper is organized as follows: in Section 2 we summarize some characteristics of load-management schemes in general and for NOWs in

---

[*] partly supported by the German Science Foundation (DFG), grant Ma 870/5-1

particular, Section 3 is devoted to a detailed description of our system, Section 4 shows some preliminary performance results, and Section 5 concludes this paper and gives an outlook on future work.

2   Classification of Load Management Systems

A distributed application can be modeled by an *application graph* $H = (U, F)$ The nodes represent the application processes and their computational requests and the edges represent the communications and their intensity.

A distributed computer can also be modeled by a *hardware graph* $G = (V, E)$ where V is the set of processors and the edges represent the communication links between the processors. In this model, the load-management-problem can be stated as graph-embedding problem: we are looking for a function $\pi : U \to V$ which minimizes a given cost function.

Depending on the application graph used, one can distinguish the following two cases: (1) The application graph does not change over time. In this case π can be determined at application set up time and the load balancing functionality is reduced to an *embedding problem* or *mapping problem* depending whether a cost function is taken under consideration or not. (2) The application graph changes, which means that the mapping of load onto the available resources is done at runtime, and is adapted according to dynamic properties of the actual configuration, such as the load of a CPU, available network bandwidth and the like. In the sequel we will concentrate on this case, also known as the *dynamic load-balancing problem*.

A Model for Load Management Systems on NOWs A heterogeneous network of workstations is modeled by a vertex-weighted graph $G = (V, E; \alpha)$ where $\alpha : V \to [0, 1]$ is the normalized performance of a processor: Let t_{v_0} be the time needed by processor v_0 to execute a sequential process, and t_v the time needed on processor v, then $\alpha_v := t_{v_0}/t_v$ is the *performance* of v with respect to v_0. The *average load* $\overline{w_V}$ of a set V of processors, with w_v as the load of a processor $v \in V$, is defined by $\overline{w_V} := \dfrac{\sum_{v \in V} w_v}{\sum_{v \in V} \alpha_v}$, and the *optimal load* of a processor v is given by $w_v^* = \alpha_v \overline{w_V}$. The *speedup* is defined as usual as: $S(V) := t_{v_0}/t_V$ where t_V is the time needed by the processors in V, but now depends on the chosen reference machine v_0. In order to get a meaningful notion of *efficiency* one slightly changes the normal definition of efficiency: instead of dividing the speedup by the number of processors, one divides it by the total performance α_V of the network, where $\alpha_V := \sum_{v \in V} \alpha_v$. Note that the efficiency is independent of the machine of reference.

A similar model applies for *non-dedicated environments* where the available processor-performance may change due to other applications running on the same processor. The load induced by the processing of other applications can only be controlled by load-management systems working at operating-system level. Application-integrated load-management systems cannot influence the workload distribution of other applications. This load is thus referred to as *external load*, see for example [7] for an relationship of load average to program execution time on networks of workstations. *Internal load* is the load generated by the application and thus the load which can be manipulated by the load-management system.

A load-management scheme must now determine the load itself (both external and internal), specify how it can be measured, and when and where it is created. There are several approaches for this in the literature, for example the gradient model [5] uses a threshold method to describe the load (low, middle, high), in [13] a quantitative approach is used, and in [2] a qualitative method is proposed.

Load-Balancing on Heterogeneous, Non-dedicated NOWs. After having studied several factors which influence the efficiency of load balancing systems (for a general overview see [6]), we identified the following important properties for load balancing schemes on heterogeneous, non-dedicated NOWs:

- Due to the heterogeneity at different levels (hard-and software), a load balancing scheme for NOWs should be *application integrated*. It seems impossible to adapt all the different machines used in NOWs for load balancing purposes at operating system level;
- Heterogeneity at hardware level implies that the performance with respect to a reference machine must be taken into consideration. Because these machines are typically used by other users (non-dedicated), their *external load* should influence the load balancing system;
- Communication on a LAN is a relatively expensive operation, compared to the high performance networks of "real" parallel computers, therefore the migration space of the load to be transferred is limited, that is, *locality aspects* like the neighborhood of a CPU should be considered;
- Node *information* (actual load and the like) may already be obsolete or *outdated* when the information arrives at another node, a load balancing system for NOWs should consider this;
- NOWs are typically connected via a bus and do not use a special topology, such as a grid for example. Since many load balancing methods in the literature assume that the CPUs are connected in a regular topology, a load balancing system for NOWs must provide means to arrange the workstations in a (virtual) *topology*;
- Load balancing schemes for NOWs are *asynchronous*, a synchronous variant would introduce too much administrative overhead.

3   LBS: Load Balancing System

This Section introduces LBS *(Load Balancing System)* [8]. The main goal was to combine the advantages of operating-system integrated load-balancing tools (*i.e.* application independence, ease of use, etc.) with those of application-integrated load-balancing libraries (*i.e.* performance) and to provide an easily extensible load-management tool which may serve as a testbed for different load-balancing algorithms. In order to achieve this, LBS was built in a modular way, such that new load-balancing algorithms may be easily integrated into an existing system without changing the application program.

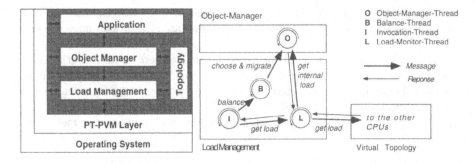

Fig. 1: Basic Structure of Lʙs.　　　**Fig. 2:** Internal Structure of Lʙs.

Basic Structure of Lʙs. From the operating-system's point of view, Lʙs is a part of the application program because the load-balancing is done at application-level, whereas from the application programmer's point of view, Lʙs is simply a library which is linked to the application.

Lʙs is built on Pᴛ-Pᴠᴍ [4] which provides a Pᴠᴍ [10] like programming model at thread-level. All the communication between the application threads on the different machines is done using Pᴛ-Pᴠᴍ. Fig. 1 illustrates the interplay between the different software components of Lʙs.

Lʙs does not know the type of the load objects. Therefore the interface between Lʙs and the application program must be implemented by a component called **Object Manager**. The rest of the Lʙs system communicates with the **Object Manager** via well-defined functions which allow to evaluate the current load and to move load-objects between neighborhood machines.

The **Load Management** comprehends the functionality of a control feedback control system and is described in detail in the following Section.

Most of the load-balancing algorithms try to achieve system-wide load-balance by local load movements. Thus we need a notion of "locality", *i.e.* a library which implements a topology. This is done by the (virtual) **Topology** component in Lʙs.

Internal Structure of Lʙs. The internal structure is illustrated in Fig. 2. The structure is influenced by the following approach: In order to emphasize the load balancing process in time, one models the load-balancing problem as a feedback control system and splits it up into three phases:

- During the *load* capture phase, the load-balancing system collects load-information of the neighbor machines and activates, if necessary, the decision-phase, otherwise the load capture component falls asleep for a time determined by the load-balancing algorithm and then starts over again.
- In the *decision*-phase the load-balancing system decides *whether* load-balancing has to be done at all and if so, determines *how much* load has to be moved and determines the *sender* and *receiver*. Depending on the type of the load, the system also has to determine *which* load-objects have to be moved.

```
void farmer(FARMER_PARAM prm) {          typedef struct { ... } TASK;
  TASK task; RESULT res, size_t size;    typedef struct { ... } RESULT;
  forall tasks                           void worker(WK_PARAM prm,
    distribute_task(prm, &task, sizeof(task));   void *task, size_t size) {
  forall results                           RESULT res;
    get_result(prm, &res, &size);          res = compute_result();
  compute_final_result();                  return_result(prm, &res, sizeof(res));
}                                        }
```

Fig. 3: TFLBS application skeleton.

– During the *load-migration* phase the actual migration takes place.

These three phases have a strong influence on the design of most load-balancing systems and lead to a modular structure of the system. In the case of LBS, the different phases are implemented by PT-PVM threads:

– The `load_monitor_thread` implements the load capture component. This thread is responsible for getting the internal and external load and for getting the load of the neighbors. Because the type of the load-objects is not known to LBS, this is done by communicating with the `object_manager_thread`. The external load is evaluated by calling operating system services.

– The `invocation_thread` implements the invocation policy. Depending on the chosen policy, the `load_monitor_thread` is queried for the current load, and if necessary load-balancing is activated by sending a request to the `balance_thread`.

– The `balance_thread` does the actual load-balancing. When receiving a load-balancing request, the load-movements are computed and the object-manager is invoked to move the load in the appropriate directions.

TFLBS— **Load-balancing for Task-Farming.** Many problems may be formulated using the *task-farming* paradigm: A task-farming program consists of a number of independent subproblems, which may be solved independently on any processor. Data dependencies between tasks can be handled by creating the tasks only when all the tasks from whom information is needed have already been solved.

The TFLBS library provides a simple interface for task-farming programs and handles the interaction with the LBS system. It is thus an instance of an object-manager. TFLBS application programs consist of a main-function called `farmer()` which creates the tasks (by calling `distribute_task()`) and collects the results (`get_result()`) at the end of the computation.

The tasks are computed by a `worker()`-function. `worker()` gets a parameter of the type WK_PARAM which is application-dependent and allows the programmer to identify the tasks. During the execution of a task, new tasks may be created and at the end the result is sent to the farmer by calling `return_result()`. The outline of a typical TFLBS application is sketched in Fig. 3.

The actual implementation of TFLBS is as follows: on each machine in the LBS system an `object_manager` is installed which handles the list of tasks assigned to that machine. Another thread called `worker_thread` fetches waiting tasks from the task-queue, processes them and sends the results back to the farmer. The load-balancing is done in the background by moving tasks from longer queues to empty queues.

The implementation of the `object_manager` is thus quite simple: the `object_manager` thread must handle the queue of tasks assigned to a machine. The queue management supports the following operations:

- Returning the length of the queue in order to estimate the internal load of the machine;
- Inserting new tasks into the queue;
- Removing a task from the queue: the `object_manager` supports two ways of removing tasks from the queue: the *synchronous* remove and the *asynchronous* remove. When the `worker_thread` asks the `object_manager` for a new task, and the queue is empty, the `worker_thread` has to block until some new tasks arrive, whereas it is possible that LBS might want to reallocate more tasks from one machine to another than there are currently available — in this case LBS must not block, it is sufficient to inform LBS that there are no more tasks on the machine.

The other crucial part of TFLBS is the `distribute_task()` function. It is the function that assigns the first tasks to the machines. The more efficiently this is done, the less load-balancing is needed. One possible approach is to assign the new tasks always to the neighbor with the least load. Another possibility is to assign the tasks to a randomly chosen machine, hoping that this leads to a more or less balanced load situation — it has been shown that the maximal load can be reduced exponentially by randomly choosing two processors and assigning the new task to the least loaded [1].

4 Performance Results

We have tested LBS with a simple program that computes the Mandelbrot set. This program is based on the TFLBS library. The Mandelbrot program splits the area for which the Mandelbrot-set is computed into $M \times N$ rectangles each containing $m \times n$ points. Each of the rectangles is computed by a different task. The running-time distribution is thus given by the number of points contained in each rectangle and by the "depth" of the computation, *i.e.* the number of iterations considered when determining the convergence.

For this experiment we implemented the Local Pre-computation-based Load Balancing Algorithm (LPLB), a variant of the PLB-algorithm [2], in LBS and used a load-sharing calling strategy, *i.e.* every time a PE[1] runs out of work, the load will be locally re-balanced. Fig. 4 and 5 show the distribution of load on 6 Sparc stations 5 running Solaris 2.5, PVM 3.3.9 and PT-PVM 1.13 with and without LBS, respectively.

---

[1] Process Environment, a UNIX process which may host one or more PT-PVM threads.

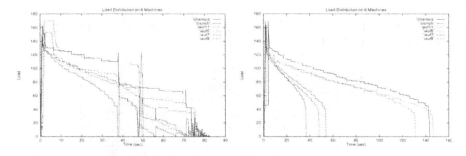

Fig. 4: Distribution of Load using LBS.   **Fig. 5:** Distribution of Load without LBS.

Table 1 shows the average execution time in seconds for several test sets and different configurations of LBS. The test sets consist all of $M \times M$ tasks, each containing $m \times m$ points. The "depth" of the computation was the same for all test sets. For "lb" the LPLB load-balancing-algorithm and the load-sharing calling strategy is used. In "lb_noex" the same algorithm is used, but the external load is not considered, "lb_noex_ABKU" uses the mapping-algorithm described in [1]. In "no_lb" and "nolb_noex_ABKU" no load-balancing is done at all. The results show that LBS significantly reduces the the running time for NOWs that consist of more than 2 PEs, whereas if only two PEs are used, the overhead due to LBS dominates. One also sees, that the ABKU-mapping algorithm doesn't behave well in our case, which is due to the fact that all the load is created at the same time.

5 Conclusion

This paper described LBS, a system for load balancing for network based multi-threaded applications. Starting from a classification of design issues for load-management systems, we identified significant properties for load-management systems to be used for NOWs. These recommendations have been realized in our system, LBS, which is implemented on top of PT-PVM, a software package based on the PVM system which provides message passing and process management facilities at thread and process level for a cluster of workstations running the UNIX operating system. LBS's distinct features include a modular multi-threaded software structure, its object-, load-, topology-, management is implemented as separate PT-PVM threads. By implementing a special object manager in the form of the TFLBS library, we showed how the efficiency of a well known parallel programming model (task-farming) can be increased if used in combination with a load-management system for concurrent network based computing.

Future work include a dynamic virtual topology management (for the moment the topology is fixed at application startup), and an improved mechanism to determine the external load of a workstation.

In addition to that, we are currently implementing new object managers, for example object managers which change the topology dynamically according to the actual load in the system, and started some promising experiments with threads as load objects.

# PEs	Configuration	M = 16			M = 32		M = 64
		m = 16	m = 32	m = 48	m = 32	m = 64	m = 64
1	nolb_noex	57.77	248.44	553.56	885.15	2738.19	
2	lb	33.67	137.16	299.10	535.46	2095.07	8401.88
	lb_noex	33.32	134.24	292.04	538.01	2096.38	7553.68
	lb_noex_ABKU	33.02	142.10	303.53	537.89	2125.26	7938.18
	nolb	31.41	131.28	291.50	516.11	2056.58	7992.80
	nolb_noex_ABKU	31.52	147.78	323.92	516.56	2058.75	7568.18
4	lb	10.71	34.55	73.59	131.17	483.59	2006.93
	lb_noex	10.54	33.47	71.76	132.40	486.65	1969.86
	lb_noex_ABKU	10.90	37.95	76.06	132.39	503.26	1998.43
	nolb	12.10	40.74	87.71	159.37	597.68	2552.75
	nolb_noex_ABKU	12.39	48.59	106.96	162.15	676.49	2370.51
8	lb	8.63	22.19	46.68	70.95	271.11	1003.34
	lb_noex	8.21	19.72	41.07	70.63	258.05	1000.05
	lb_noex_ABKU	8.82	25.34	43.42	72.42	279.38	1003.11
	nolb	12.00	32.24	71.92	129.68	494.68	2296.43
	nolb_noex_ABKU	12.32	34.25	74.70	131.57	553.18	2320.82
12	lb	8.15	15.04	30.11	54.59	180.04	683.60
	lb_noex	8.26	14.76	31.37	52.56	181.61	684.13
	lb_noex_ABKU	17.55	20.56	33.47	89.40	193.59	756.86
	nolb	8.53	21.88	44.29	94.74	330.67	1342.02
	nolb_noex_ABKU	15.61	24.10	54.07	97.63	348.71	1383.19

Table 1: Average execution times.

References

1. Y. Azar, A.Z. Broder, and A.R. Karlin. On-line load balancing (extended abstract). In *33rd Annual Symposium on Foundations of Computer Science*, pages 218–225, Pittsburgh, Pennsylvania, 24–27 October 1992. IEEE.

2. Max Böhm. *Verteilte Lösung harter Probleme: Schneller Lastausgleich*. PhD thesis, Universität zu Köln, 1996.

3. E. W. Dijkstra. Cooperating sequential processes. *Programming Languages*, 1965.

4. O. Krone, M. Aguilar, and B. Hirsbrunner. PT-PVM: Using PVM in a multithreaded environment. In *2nd PVM European Users' Group Meeting*, Lyon, September 13–15 1995.

5. F. C. H. Lin and R. M. Keller. The gradient model load balancing method. *IEEE Transactions on Software Engineering*, 13(1):32–38, January 1987.

6. T. Ludwig. *Lastverwaltungsverfahren für Mehrprozessorsysteme mit verteiltem Speicher*. PhD thesis, Technische Universität München, München, Dezember 1992.

7. Trevorr E. Meyer, James A. Davis, and Jennifer L. Davidson. Analysis of Load Average and its Relationship to Program Run Time on Networks of Workstations. *Journal of Parallel and Distributed Computing*, 44(2):141–146, August 1997.

8. Martin Raab. Entwicklung eines Lastverwaltungssystems für vernetzte Arbeitsplatzrechner. Master's thesis, University of Fribourg, 1997.

9. Sun Microsystems, Mountain View, California. *SunOS 5.3 Guide to Multithread Programming*, November 1993.

10. V.S. Sunderam. PVM: A framework for parallel distributed computing. *Concurrency: Practice and Experience*, 2(4):315–339, December 1990.

11. S. White, A. Alund, and V.S. Sunderam. Performance of the NAS Parallel Benchmarks on PVM-Based Networks. *Journal of Parallel and Distributed Computing*, 26(1):61–71, 1995.

12. Niklaus Wirth. Tasks versus Threads: An Alternative Multiprocessing Paradigm. *Software - Concepts and Tools*, (17):6–12, 1996.

13. C. Xu, B. Monien, R. Lüling, and F. Lau. An analytical comparison of nearest neighbor algorithms for load balancing in parallel computers. In *Proc. of the 9th International Parallel Processing Symposium (IPPS '95)*, April 1995.

Creation of Reconfigurable Hardware Objects in PVM Environments

G.M. Megson, R.S. Fish, and D.N.J. Clarke

Parallel Emergent and Distributed Architcetures Lab (PEDAL),
Dept Computer Science, The University of Reading,
Whiteknights, Reading, Berkshire,
RG6 6AY, UK
{G.M.Megson, R.S.Fish, D.N.J.Clarke}@reading.ac.uk
http://www.cs.reading.ac.uk/cs/

Abstract. The concept of using reconfigurable hardware such as FP-GAs in a PVM enviroment is considered. The Dynamic Reconfiguration of Protocol Stacks (DRoPs) system allowing adaptable protocols and the Reading Template Interface Compiler (RTIC) for specify regular parallel frameworks with PVM are introduced as essential mechanisms for supporting the generation and use of Hardware Objects. How these systems could be augmented to provide Reconfigurable Hardware Objects within PVM is then briefly discussed.

1 Introduction

In the recent past researchers from many disciplines have show that computationally intensive tasks with simple and regular structures can be placed directly in hardware to produce dramatic performance gains. More recently there has been significant work on reconfigurable hardware platforms and the development of so-called harwdare-software codesign systems [10]. In the former Hardware Objects are algorithms implemented as hardware designs using downloadable configurations and SRAM-style Field programmable Gate Arrays (FPGAs) [9]. In the latter designers combine software with hardware by delaying the moment of commitment to Software or Hardware objects as long as possible. Thus to convert an algorithm into an hardware object requires the integration of higher level language compilers, lower level schematic capture tools, and hardware description lauguages such as VHDL.

Thus far the emerging technology of hardware-software co-design systems has been targeted at niche markets for embedded systems where the Hardware Object can be downloaded and run many times. In this paper we explore the possibilities of extending the principle to parallel systems based on PVM style programming. The idea is to identify regular structures in both parallel programs which can exploit FPGA capabilities and to also use this resource to optimise the message passing features of PVM as the state of an algorithm and its run-time enviroment changes over time.

Below two developments, the DRoPs system and the RTIC compiler are described. The former produces adaptable protocols that could make use of Hardware Objects. The second tools for defining parallel objects which could the be synthesized or refined by Hardware-Software Codesign systems to generate compute intensive parts of subroutines as Hardware Objects and swap them in and out of reconfigurable hardware on demand.

2 PVM and adaptable communication protocols

Modern distributed applications, such as PVM, are being limited by unwieldy historical communication systems. As distributed applications have evolved and interconnection technology matured, it has become apparent that *legacy* communication protocol suites, such as IP, are unable to efficiently serve modern distributed applications. The deficiency of these systems may be attributed to the increasing diversity of application requirements and operating environments. Historically, distributed applications, such as file transfer, conveyed traffic with relatively simple requirements. However, modern applications perform diverse tasks with contrasting and potentially continuously evolving communication requirements. Communication services, such as IP, are unable to satisfy such a broad range of requirements in a single system and are therefore unable to provide optimal communication performance. A solution is to implement a tailored communication system for each application. Whilst this is the best solution for embedded safety critical systems, such as flight control or rail signaling, it is impractical for generic applications. The lack of a single, globally consistent protocol, leads to problems with interoperability and an inability to compensate for varying connection characteristics. An alternative solution is to implement a protocol, able to adapt its functionality at runtime to suit an applications requirements and operating environment. This class of communication system, is known as an *adaptable protocol* and allows a single protocol to serve applications with diverse requirements and operating environments.

2.1 The Reading adaptable protocol system

The Dynamic Reconfiguration of Protocol Stacks project (DRoPS) provides an infrastructure for the implementation and operation of multiple runtime adaptable communication protocols [1, 2]. Mechanisms are provided to initialise a protocol, configure an instantiation for each connection, manipulate the configuration over the lifetime of a connection and maintain consistent configurations at all end points. Embedded within the Linux operating system, the architecture is accessible through standard interfaces, such as sockets, and benefits from a protected environment with realtime scheduling capabilities.

Protocol construction DRoPS provides an infrastructure supporting the composition of adaptable protocols from fundamental protocol processing mechanisms called microprotocols [3]. Each microprotocol implements a protocol processing operation, the complexity of which may range from a simple function, such as a checksum, to a complex layer of a protocol stack, such as TCP. Kernel loadable modules encapsulate microprotocols, allowing code to be dynamically loaded and executed within the protected operating system environment. A *protocol* defines a bag of microprotocols from which individual transport systems are fabricated. Mechanisms are provided to define a separate, dynamic route through this bag for each connection. This is known as a *protocol stack* and provides a tailored communication service for its connection. Interaction takes place through an Application Programming Interface (API) which is a combination of the BSD socket interface, UNIX *ioctl* interface and a custom DRoPS interface. Data exchange takes place through the socket interface whilst the manipulation of a protocol stack may take place through the ioctl or DRoPS.

Automatic control of adaption Manual reconfiguration can only be performed by applications augmented with the DRoPS API or ioctl equivalent. Consequentially, the use of an adaptable protocol with *legacy* applications, unable to perform manual reconfiguration, is redundant. Automatic adaption remedies this, associating each connection with an agent that endeavors to maintain an appropriate protocol configuration. The agent executes a heuristic control mechanism, called an *adaption policy*, that determines the most appropriate protocol configuration for each stack at arbitrary times. Adaption policies are encapsulated within a loadable module, are stackable, hot swappable and may be supplied by a protocol or application. If a policy determines that adaption is necessary, reconfiguration requests are posted to DRoPS and are propagated to all end points of communication. Research has identified various methods for controlling automatic adaption and studied the feasibility of using neural networks as a generic control mechanism [1].

2.2 Implications of protocol adaption for PVM systems

PVM applications typically require transport services that guarantee data integrity. This conflicts with the requirements of typical multimedia applications, such as voice transfer and video conferencing, that can tolerate certain levels of data loss and corruption. These rigid, unvarying requirements somewhat restricts the flexibility of an adaptable protocol and bound its ability to deliver improved performance. However, a number of areas are identified where a system such as DRoPS could provide tangible benefits to PVM applications.

PVM applications can be classified as *non real time, non time critical* distributed systems [3]. They are typically sensitivity to connection latency, data loss and bursts, have variable sensitivity to data order and exhibit a moderate average data throughput. A generic set of runtime protocol optimisations can be derived from these requirements and include the adaption of acknowledgment schemes, error detection algorithms, reassembly and order processing. For example, in a high delay environment, a *forward error control*[1] scheme performs better

---

[1] Redundant data is sent with each packet and errors are corrected at the receiver.

than a go back N^2 or selective repeat scheme [3]. The connection characteristics that effect these requirements vary continuously and a tailored communication service can quickly become inappropriate. Adaption policies are able to monitor these characteristics, evaluate how different protocol configurations would better satisfy the applications requirements and initiate adaption.

Manual runtime reconfiguration is performed by an application and based on domain specific knowledge such as remote host locality, architecture and expected communication patterns. For example, if communication remains within a local cluster, the algorithms that control acknowledgments, sequencing, fragmentation and reassembly, addressing, software checksums and buffer allocation may be optimised. The exact optimisation depends on the underlying network topology and the services, such as hardware broadcasting and checksumming, that it may provide. Knowledge of the remote host architecture allows the optimisation of data packing routines, and details of communication patterns allow the optimisation of buffer allocation, fragmentation, reassembly and acknowledgment routines [2]. The PVM daemon stores little more about remote hosts than their compile architecture and makes no attempt to identify the underlying interconnection hardware. Similarly, DRoPS does not automatically profile interconnection devices, rather it delegates this task to the adaption policies.

Any attempt to use an alternative protocol under PVM involves convoluted changes to core PVM functions. DRoPS supports *protocol masquerading*, allowing the substitution of one kernel level protocol for an adaptable equivalent. This scheme allows PVM applications to benefit from an adaptable protocol without modification or recompilation of the PVM layer. The concept, mechanisms, merits and pitfalls of masquerading are explained further in [2]. Combined with the process of automatic adaption, masquerading provides a transparent network service that will remain appropriately configured to the underlying connection characteristics and network architecture.

3 Parallel Programming with an Interface Compiler

Recently a number of languages have been proposed which support the application programmer in the development of well structured parallel programs, most notably the Pisa Parallel Programming Language [6] (P3L) from the University of Pisa. Most initiatives base their work on Cole [5], who stated that many parallel programs are commonly composed of regular communication patterns.

At the University Of Reading the ongoing Reading Template Interface Compiler (RTIC) project[7] is a modular approach to the solution of parallel problems. The approach involves the programmer declaring the problem communication requirements through an interface language. An interface compiler translates the information contained therein into a library of functions tailored specifically to support structured implementation of the program through PVM.

---

[2] All packets after and including the offending one are retransmitted.

[3] Only the lost or corrupt packet is retransmitted.

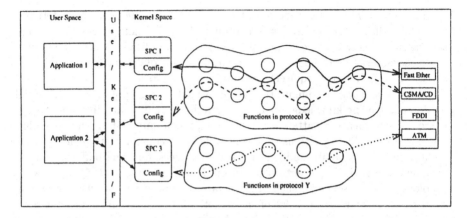

Fig. 1. Two applications with multiple connections through two adaptable protocols.

3.1 The Interface Language

An interface is used to declare the communications requirements of a message-passing parallel program. A non-trivial MIMD program is typically composed of several distinct steps, with all or a subset of tasks taking part in every step; all take part in at least one step. A communication step involves tasks communicating messages with other tasks. As Cole [5] observed, commonly these communications have regular patterns. We represent six of the most common: *One-To-Many, All-To-All, Ring, Pipe, Grid* and *Toric-Grid*. The topological definition of each can be found in Cosnard and Trystram[8]. We refer to each as a *framework*, and define each in terms of *task* and *channel* types. A framework has a set of rules governing how tasks should be connected to each other through channels. The programmer's declaration of a framework is made in terms of *name, type*, and *size*; size being the number of tasks in the framework. Messages are associated with frameworks and travel in one direction or another on a particular channel. The *combine* mechanism allows the tasks of one framework to be included within another framework. For example, a particular task of a *Toric-Grid* framework could also act as the *master*, and the remaining tasks act as the *slaves* of a *One-To-Many* framework. The combine construct facilitates the mapping. The set of tasks in each framework have a default order and individual tasks within the set are given a fixed label which is its position coordinate within that ordering. Consider two different frameworks x and y that have the same number of tasks. Writing x ONTO y ensures that the tasks of x are mapped onto those of y using the default ordering of each. The programs communication sequence is declared, that is, the order in which the communications will be made. Each item in the ordering is a reference to a declaration made through the *use* construct. A complete order will take the form: *use x, use y, use z*. Tasks of the base framework, that is, the framework which is not mapped onto another, are instead mapped to executable programs through which they are implemented. These are the binaries generated from the imperative source code written in C or Fortran with embedded RAPI and PVM calls.

3.2 The Application Programmers Interface

The RTIC Applications Programmers Interface (RAPI) is a set of functions and parameters supporting structured SPMD programming through the message-passing paradigm. Logical communication and identity are the core functions of the RAPI. PVM has no support for logical frameworks, thus programs implemented with PVM must map logical to actual identifiers for communication, and from actual to logical for determining their own identity.

As communication requirements are diverse, especially in heterogeneous systems. Without detailed static program scheduling it is impossible to select appropriate arguments for PVM functions automatically. So rather than impede performance, our functions either produce arguments for PVM functions or accept PVM functions as arguments. In this way we are able to fulfill our requirement of structured programming support whilst leaving intact those details concerned with scheduling and communication efficiency. Communication is supported by *initsend, send, recv, pack_?,* and *unpack_?. initsend* creates an RTIC message and serves as a direct replacement for *pvm_initsend. send* and *recv* are functions which provide the identifier, *tid,* of the task with which to communicate for *pvm_send* and *pvm_recv,* and accept arguments of framework, channel, label, and message. *pack_?* and *unpack_?* functions are generated to marshall each type of message declared as communication requirements. Each includes a number of *pvm_pk?* and *pvm_upk?* calls in order to marshall a message, they provide an simple alternative to individually packing a messages elements. Identity determination is provided for by *istask, label,* and *cartesian. label* accepts only framework as argument and returns the label of the caller within it. *istask* takes a framework and task type as arguments and returns a boolean value of true, if the caller is of the argued type and belongs to the specified framework. *cartesian* is for use with the two dimensional frameworks: *Grid* and *Toric-Grid,* accepting only framework as argument and returning the *cartesian coordinates* of the caller task within it.

Clarke et al.[7], demonstrates that benchmarks implemented with RAPI are only nominally less efficient than the equivalent PVM implementations.

```
Example - RTIC interface for the Conjugate Gradient benchmark Bailey et al
INTERFACE CG;
  CONST N = 3, NITPM = 15, NITCG = 25 ;
  MESSAGE   ... ;
TEMPLATE
  GRID cg SIZE N BY N;
  ONETOMANY RowSum[N] SIZE N, ColScatter[N] SIZE N, ScatGather SIZE N*N;
  FOR i:=1 TO N DO
    COMBINE RowSum[i] ONTO cg{ROW(i)} END;
```

```
FOR i:=1 TO N DO
  COMBINE ColScatter[i]{1} ONTO cg{i+(i-1)*N};
  COMBINE ColScatter[i]{2..i} ONTO cg{i..(N*(i-2))+i BY N};
  COMBINE ColScatter[i]{i+1..N} ONTO cg{N*i+i..(N-1)*N+i BY N} END;
COMBINE ScatGather ONTO cg;
FOR i:=1 TO N DO
  USE ROWSUMS_RAW ON RowSum[i].MS_CH OF M_TASK TO S_TASK;
  USE ROWSUMS_FINISHED ON RowSUm[i].MS_CH OF S_TASK TO M_TASK END;
FOR i:=1 TO N DO
  USE PJTYPE0 ON ColScatter[i].MS_CH OF M_TASK TO S_TASK END;
USE NZA,ASUM,MY_MAXZELT,MY_DP ON ScatGather.MS_CH OF M_TASK TO S_TASK;
USE NEW_DP,NEW_ZETA ON ScatGather.MS_CH OF S_TASK TO M_TASK;
SEQ
  ScatGather.NZA; ScatGather.ASUM;
  FOR i:=1 TO NITPM
    ScatGather.MY_DP; ScatGather.NEW_DP;
    FOR ii:=1 TO NITCG
      ColScatter.PJTYPE0; RowSum.ROWSUMS_RAW;RowSum.ROWSUMS_FINISHED
    END;
    ScatGather.MY_MAXZELT; ScatGather.NEW_ZETA
  END;
  RowSum
END
END CG.
```

4 Hardware Objects and PVM

The need and use of Hardware objects with PVM enviroments occurs in two main contexts at the user level and kernel level in Figure 1. In the former we look to accelerating compute intensive sub-programs and nested loops with algorithm specific hardware maps. In the second we require predefined Hardware objects which can be quickly dowloaded into reconfigurable resources. Such resources can take the form of co-processors, accelerator boards, or be included as part of the main processor (on a single chip).

In user space applications the RTIC compiler needs to be extended to allow tagging of code with hardware objects. This includes references to load maps in predefined libraries of fast ciruits (equivalent to software such as numerical libraries). These maps not only include the Hardware Configuration but iterface information for communicating and buffering of data between the board and the main processor. In static cases compiler and synthesis techniques such as those based on loop nested (e.g SUIF) and polyhedral domain manipulation (MMAlpha) when linked with tools such as VHDL allow specific maps for hardware objects to be compiled. Reconfiguration allows the same hardware to be used for a range of applications and so be cost effective while realising some of the performance advantages of algorithmically specialised architectures. More dynamic problems such as irregular problems arising in combinatorics (for example involving large search trees) can be used to change the hardware as the load and emphasis of the computation changes with execution. Clearly the time for generating (or choosing) an Hardware Object and downloading must be small compared with the actual run-time of the object on a data set. Consequently we envisage relatively slow change of architecture under an application.

At the kernel level the emphasis is on pre-compiled Hardware Objects which can be selected from a library of Objects. In DRoPs one way to manage this is to associate separate objects with each microprotocol. The functions of an adaptable protocol, the circles in Figure 1 would then require information on the local map and the interface between the Harwdare Object through the reconfigurable object. A single FPGA device could contain several microprotocol Hardware Objects. Consequently to facilitate the DRoPs approach a dynamically reconfigurable FPGA resource would be required to maintain the functionality. These Hardware Objects could service several communications simultaneously or operate as a hardware protocol stack in which the hardware object for a layer of the stack could be changed dynamically thus adapting the circuit as the protocol adapts. Since the use of the stack would be relatively long lived in a PVM application compared to the set up time for the Hardware Object such an approach should be extremely efficient.

References

1. R.S.Fish and R.J.Loader. *Architectural support for runtime adaptable protocols*, ICAST'98, 1998.
2. R.S.Fish and R.J.Loader. *DRoPS: kernel support for runtime adaptable protocols*, To be presented at 24th Euromicro Workshop on Netoworked Computing August 25th 1998
3. M.Zitterbart. *A model for flexible high performance communication subsystems*, Journal on Selected Areas in Communication, Vol 11, pp 507, May 1993.
4. A. Beguelin, J.Dongarra, G.A.Geist, W.Jiang, R.Manchek, V.Sunderam. *PVM: Parallel Virtual Machine, A User's Guide and Tutorial for Networked Parallel Computing*, MIT Press, Cambridge, MA., 1994.
5. M.Cole. *Algorithmic Skeletons: Structured Management of Parallel Computation*, MIT Press, Cambridge, MA., 1989.
6. S.Pelagatti. *Structured Development of Parallel Programs*, Taylor & Francis Ltd, ISBN 0-7484-0655-7, 1998.
7. D.N.J.Clarke, J.M.Graham, R.J.Loader, and S.A.Williams. *Paradigms for the Parallel Programming of Heterogeneous Machines through an Interface Compiler*, ParCo '97, Bonn, Germany, 1997.
8. M.Cosnard and D.Trystram *Parallel Algorithms and Architectures*, International Thomson Computing Press, ISBN 1-85032-125-6, 1995 pp 71-106.
9. S. Casselman, M. Thorburg, J. Schewel *Creation of Hardware Objects in a Reconfigurable Computer*, Virtual Computer Corporation, technical note.
10. IEE, *Hardware-Software Cosynthesis for reconfigurable Systems*, IEE Digest No : 96/036, Feb 1996.

Implementing MPI with the Memory-Based Communication Facilities on the SSS–CORE Operating System*

Kenji Morimoto, Takashi Matsumoto, and Kei Hiraki

Department of Information Science, Faculty of Science
University of Tokyo
7-3-1 Hongo, Bunkyo-ku, Tokyo 113–0033, Japan
{morimoto, tm, hiraki}@is.s.u-tokyo.ac.jp

Abstract. This paper describes an efficient implementation of MPI on the Memory-Based Communication Facilities; *Memory-Based FIFO* is used for buffering by the library, and *Remote Write* for communication with no buffering. The Memory-Based Communication Facilities are software-based communication mechanisms, with off-the-shelf Ethernet hardware. They provide low-cost and highly-functional primitives for remote memory accesses.

The performance of the library was evaluated on a cluster of workstations connected with a 100Base-TX network. The round-trip time was $71\,\mu s$ for 0 byte message, and the peak bandwidth was $11.86\,$Mbyte/s in full-duplex mode. These values show that it is more efficient to realize the message passing libraries with the shared memory model than with the message passing model.

1 Introduction

MPI is a widely used standard library for writing message passing programs, especially on parallel machines with distributed memory [1]. It has been implemented on various platforms such as clusters of workstations and MPPs. In the message passing model, a communication path is established between each pair of tasks, and communication among tasks is performed by applying *send* and *receive* operations to those paths. This model is an abstraction of actual communication paths. In the shared memory model, on the other hand, address spaces of all tasks are mapped into a unified address space, and *load* and *store* operations[1] to that shared space correspond to communication. This model considers an address space as an object, and is called 'memory-based'.

When these two models are considered as communication models, they are exchangeable, that is, one can emulate the other. Thus the two models are equivalent in expressiveness. So far, the message passing model is widely used because

---

* This work is partly supported by Information-technology Promotion Agency (IPA) Japan and by Real World Computing Partnership (RWCP) Japan.

[1] These operations are not necessarily fine-grain memory accesses by a *load* or *store* machine instruction.

that model is believed to be more efficient, and many implementations are supplied as libraries. However, when considered as a functionality provided by a system (hardware and operating system), it has been argued that the shared memory model is superior to the message passing model from the viewpoint of optimization, efficiency, and flexibility [2]. This is because shared memory communication directly utilizes architectural support such as MMU. For this reason, parallel machines should provide an efficient communication functionality based on the shared memory model, rather than the message passing model.

The SSS–CORE is a general-purpose massively-parallel operating system [3, 4] being developed at our laboratory. The Memory-Based Communication Facilities (MBCF) [5, 6] are provided in the SSS–CORE as mechanisms for accesses to remote memory. The MBCF directly support programs which are written based on the shared memory model.

In this paper, communication functions of MPI Ver. 1.1 [1] were implemented with the MBCF on a cluster of workstations. The rest of this paper is organized as follows. Section 2 gives introduction of the MBCF. A detailed explanation of the implementation of MPI is presented in Sect. 3. Section 4 shows performance of the implemented library. We discuss related works in Sect. 5, and conclude in Sect.6.

2 MBCF: Memory-Based Communication Facilities

2.1 Features of MBCF

The MBCF is a software-based mechanism for accessing remote memory. Details of the MBCF are as follows.

1. *Direct access to remote memory*
   The MBCF communicates by reading from and writing to remote memory directly, not by sending messages to some fixed buffer for communication. At the same time, by using architectural memory management mechanisms such as MMU, protection of memory and abstraction of accesses are achieved at clock-level speed.
2. *Use of off-the-shelf network hardware*
   The MBCF is a software-based mechanism, and does not need such dedicated communication hardware as many of MPPs have. In order to achieve high performance, however, it is preferable that the following mechanisms are provided.
   - Switching of address spaces with low overhead
   - TLB which allows many contexts to be mixed
   - Page alias capability
   - High-speed processor cache with physical address tags
   All of these mechanisms are available on most of the latest microprocessors.
3. *Channel-less communication*
   Unlike channel-oriented communication such as user memory mapping with the Myrinet [7], the MBCF achieves abstraction and protection dynamically by system calls for communication.

4. *Highly-functional operations for remote memory*
   Since a receiver of an MBCF packet handles it with software, such compound operations as *swap*, *FIFO write*, and *fetch and add* are available as well as *read* and *write*.

5. *Guarantee for arrival and order of packets*
   Because a system takes care of lost or out-of-order packets, users can make communication as if they were on a reliable network.

2.2 Performance of MBCF

The performance of the MBCF was evaluated on a cluster of workstations connected with a 100Base-TX network. The following machines were used for measurement; Axil 320 model 8.1.1 (Sun SPARCstation 20 compatible, 85 MHz SuperSPARC × 1), Sun Microsystems Fast Ethernet SBus Adapter 2.0 on each workstation, SMC TigerStack 100 5324TX (non-switching HUB), and Bay Networks BayStack 350T (switching HUB with full-duplex mode). The one-way latency and the peak bandwidth between two nodes were measured.

The one-way latency is the time from the invocation a system call for remote write to the arrival of the data at the destination task (including the overhead of reading the data). Table 1 shows the one-way latency of *Remote Write* (MBCF_WRITE) and *Memory-Based FIFO* (MBCF_FIFO) for various data-sizes on a HUB.

Table 1. One-way latency of MBCF's remote accesses with 100Base-TX

data-size (byte)	4	16	64	256	1024
MBCF_WRITE (μs)	24.5	27.5	34	60.5	172
MBCF_FIFO (μs)	32	32	40.5	73	210.5

The peak bandwidth is measured by invoking remote accesses continuously. Table 2 shows peak bandwidth of *Remote Write* and *Memory-Based FIFO* for various data-sizes on a HUB (half-duplex) and on a switching HUB (full-duplex).

Both of the results show that the performance of the MBCF is very close to that of the network itself. The MBCF is superior in efficiency to the communication functions of MPPs, which have dedicated communication hardware of higher-potential [6].

3 Implementation of Communication Functions

In this section, the details of the implementation of two point-to-point communication functions, MPI_Isend() and MPI_Irecv(), are described. All other communication functions can be explained on the analogy of these two functions.

Table 2. Peak bandwidth of MBCF's remote accesses with 100Base-TX

data-size (byte)	4	16	64	256	1024	1408
MBCF_WRITE, half-duplex (Mbyte/s)	0.31	1.15	4.31	8.56	11.13	11.48
MBCF_FIFO, half-duplex (Mbyte/s)	0.31	1.14	4.30	8.53	11.13	11.45
MBCF_WRITE, full-duplex (Mbyte/s)	0.34	1.27	4.82	9.63	11.64	11.93
MBCF_FIFO, full-duplex (Mbyte/s)	0.34	1.26	4.80	9.62	11.64	11.93

The behavior of these two functions varies according to the order of matching two invocations of send and receive functions. In the followings, two cases are described separately; the case where the invocation of MPI_Isend() precedes that of MPI_Irecv() and the reversed case[2].

3.1 The Case Where MPI_Isend() Precedes MPI_Irecv()

When MPI_Isend() gets started before the invocation of the corresponding MPI_Irecv(), the sender does not know which buffer the receiver specifies for incoming data. Therefore the sender should transmit a message to some fixed buffer in the receiver's address space[3]. The MBCF's *Memory-Based FIFO* (*MB_FIFO*) is used for this fixed buffer.

MB_FIFO is one of variations of *Remote Write* (stated in Sect. 3.2). The buffer for a FIFO-queue is taken from the receiving-user's address space, which is specified by the user in advance. The user can make as many queues as space permits. The sender transmits an *MB_FIFO* packet, designating the objective queue by the destination address. The trap handler (managed by the system) on the receiver's side tries to enqueue that packet, and notifies the sender whether the trial succeeded or not, if it is required by the sender to return the state.

In this implementation, the number of *MB_FIFO*'s queues for messages corresponds to the number of processes in the group of MPI_COMM_WORLD. When the sender's rank in MPI_COMM_WORLD is i, the sender transmits a message to the receiver's i-th queue. The receiver searches the i-th queue for a message from the sender of rank i (in MPI_COMM_WORLD). By preparing many queues, it becomes easier to examine message matching and to manage the order of messages.

The sequence of communication is shown in Fig. 1. The left side is the sender's execution flow, and the right is the receiver's. At first the sender enqueues a message to the receiver's *MB_FIFO* queue (because no matching special message has come from the receiver; see Sect. 3.2), and then the receiver dequeues that message when it becomes necessary.

---

[2] When MPI_Isend() and MPI_Irecv() are invoked at the same time, it follows the former case. This is detected by assigning sequential numbers to messages.

[3] The sender can choose to transmit a special short message to the receiver (without transmitting the actual message), which tells the receiver to take the message away with *remote read* by itself. This protocol is suitable only for long messages.

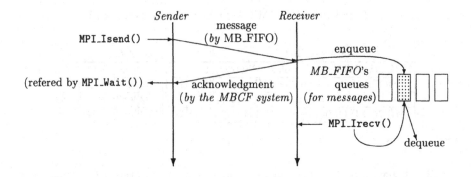

Fig. 1. Communication sequence where `MPI_Isend()` precedes `MPI_Irecv()`

The message may be divided into pieces before transmission owing to the constraint of communication hardware. In order to reduce acknowledgments, notifications of successful enqueueing are not issued, except for the notification for the last packet in a message.

3.2 The Case Where `MPI_Irecv()` Precedes `MPI_Isend()`

When `MPI_Irecv()` is invoked before `MPI_Isend()`, the receiver is able to tell the address of the receiving buffer to the sender, so that the sender can transmit a message directly to that buffer by *Remote Write*. To notify the invocation of `MPI_Irecv()`, another set of *MB_FIFO* queues is used in addition to one used for buffered messages in Sect. 3.1.

The sender of *Remote Write* transmits an MBCF packet with an argument of the destination address represented in receiver's virtual address space. The trap handler on the receiver's side tries to write that packet to the specified address, and returns the resulting state if necessary.

Figure 2 shows the communication sequence. At first the receiver enqueues a special message to the sender's *MB_FIFO* queue which requests the sender to transmit a message directly (because no matching message has come from the sender). `MPI_Isend()` on the sender checks queues of requests for sending, and responds to a matching request. For this *Remote Write*, acknowledging messages are not needed because it is guaranteed that the *Remote Write* succeeds.

4 Performance

This section shows the performance of the MPI library implemented on the SSS–CORE with the MBCF. The performance was evaluated on a cluster of workstations connected with a 100Base-TX network. The same equipments were used as in Sect. 2.2.

For comparison, the performance of the MPICH Ver. 1.1 [8] on the SunOS 4.1.4 was also evaluated with the same system configuration. The MPICH is an

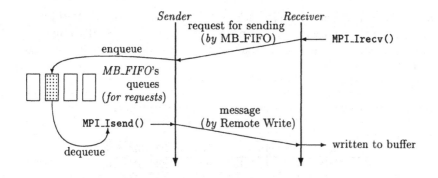

Fig. 2. Communication sequence where MPI_Irecv() precedes MPI_Isend()

implementation of MPI being developed at the Argonne National Laboratory and the Mississippi State University. The MPICH on a cluster of workstations uses TCP sockets for communication, which are based on the message passing model. For the SunOS 4.1.4, the network switch can not be used in full-duplex mode owing to the constraint of the device driver.

Let our implementation be called "MPI/MBCF," and the MPICH be called "MPICH/TCP." In order to see the effect of using *Remote Write*, there are two different versions for MPI/MBCF implementation. One issues "requests for sending (SendReqs)" as stated above, and another does not. The latter treats MPI_Isend() and MPI_Irecv() as if MPI_Isend() always preceded MPI_Irecv(). As a consequence, there are five cases, as shown below.

NSRH MPI/MBCF without SendReqs in half-duplex mode (HUB)
SRH MPI/MBCF with SendReqs in half-duplex mode (HUB)
NSRF MPI/MBCF without SendReqs in full-duplex mode (switching HUB)
SRF MPI/MBCF with SendReqs in full-duplex mode (switching HUB)
MPICH MPICH/TCP in half-duplex mode (HUB)

First we measured the round-trip time. In the evaluation program, two processes issue MPI_Irecv()'s in advance. And then one process calls MPI_Isend(), MPI_Wait() (for sending), and MPI_Wait() (for receiving), and another does MPI_Wait() (for receiving), MPI_Isend(), and MPI_Wait() (for sending). The time in the former process from the beginning of MPI_Isend() to the end of MPI_Wait() (for receiving) is measured as a round-trip time. For MPI/MBCF, the time is measured for every iteration by $0.5\,\mu$s-resolution counter, and the minimum value is taken as a round-trip time. For MPICH/TCP, unfortunately, this counter is not available, and the minimum value of average times is taken.

Table 3 shows the round-trip time for various message sizes. Since there is large penalties and little benefit to the round-trip time in full-duplex mode, NSRF and SRF are omitted. NSRH and SRH are much faster than MPICH. The difference between NSRH and SRH is caused by the difference between *MB_FIFO* and *Remote Write*; *Remote Write* is faster, and much easier to manage because it does not require explicit acknowledgments. Because the MPI library needs additional operations such as message matching, the SRH's round-trip time $71\,\mu s$ is within a reasonable range compared with the MBCF's one-way latency $24.5\,\mu s$.

Table 3. Round-trip time of MPI with 100Base-TX

message size (byte)	0	4	16	64	256	1024	4096
NSRH (μs)	112	137	139	154	223	517	1109
SRH (μs)	71	85	85	106	168	438	1026
MPICH (μs)	968	962	980	1020	1080	1255	2195

The peak bandwidth was measured for various message sizes by sending messages in one direction, shown in Table 4. MPI/MBCFs gained higher bandwidth than MPICH/TCP, especially for small messages. The difference between NSRH and SRH reveals that the additional packets of "requests for sending" interfere with the communication of actual data. In full-duplex mode, however, the undesirable influence of "requests for sending" is not so clear as in half-duplex mode.

Table 4. Peak bandwidth of MPI with 100Base-TX

message size (byte)	4	16	64	256	1024	4096	16384	65536	262144	1048576
NSRH (Mbyte/s)	0.14	0.54	1.89	4.92	8.54	10.21	10.34	10.43	10.02	9.96
SRH (Mbyte/s)	0.14	0.53	1.82	4.72	8.08	9.72	10.15	9.78	9.96	10.00
NSRF (Mbyte/s)	0.15	0.59	1.98	5.51	10.58	11.70	11.78	11.81	11.82	11.82
SRF (Mbyte/s)	0.14	0.57	1.90	5.33	10.22	11.68	11.77	11.85	11.85	11.86
MPICH (Mbyte/s)	0.02	0.09	0.35	1.27	3.54	6.04	5.59	7.00	7.77	7.07

5 Related Work

To reduce the buffering overhead, MPIAP [9] uses *put* and *get* of AP3000, and CRI/EPCC MPI [10] uses Shared Memory Access of T3D. They send a special message from the sender, perform message matching only on the receiver's side, and issue remote read. This method increases latency. MPI-EMX [11] uses *remote memory write* of EM-X, but all of them are implementations with dedicated communication hardware on MPPs.

6 Summary

An MPI library has been implemented for the SSS–CORE operating system by the use of the MBCF. The MBCF's *MB_FIFO* is used for buffering by the library, and *Remote Write* for direct transmission with no buffering. When the receiver precedes, *Remote Write* reduces the latency of communication. Even when the sender precedes, *MB_FIFO* efficiently transmits the message to the receiver.

The performance of the library was evaluated on a cluster of workstations connected with a 100Base-TX network. The round-trip time was 71 μs (for 0 byte message) and the peak bandwidth was 10.15 Mbyte/s (in half-duplex mode) and 11.86 Mbyte/s (in full-duplex mode). These values show that the additional overhead of the library is small, and that it is efficient to use the MBCF as a base of mechanisms for message passing. More generally, it is effective to use software-implemented virtual-address-based shared memory communication as a base of a communication system of parallel machines with distributed memory.

References

[1] Message Passing Interface Forum. MPI: A Message-Passing Interface Standard. http://www.mpi-forum.org/, June 1995.

[2] T. Matsumoto and K. Hiraki. Shared memory vs. message passing (in Japanese). In *IPSJ SIG Reports 97-ARC-126, Vol. 97, No. 102*, pages 85–90, October 1997.

[3] T. Matsumoto, S. Furuso, and K. Hiraki. Resource management methods of the general-purpose massively-parallel operating system: SSS–CORE (in Japanese). In *Proc. of 11th Conf. of JSSST*, pages 13–16, October 1994.

[4] T. Matsumoto, S. Uzuhara, and K. Hiraki. A general-purpose scalable operating system: SSS–CORE. In *Proc. of 20th Int. Conf. on Software Engineering (2)*, pages 147–152, April 1998.

[5] T. Matsumoto, T. Komaarashi, S. Uzuhara, S. Takeoka, and K. Hiraki. A general-purpose massively-parallel operating system: SSS–CORE — implementation methods for network of workstations — (in Japanese). In *IPSJ SIG Notes 96-OS-73, Vol. 96, No. 79*, pages 115–120, August 1996.

[6] T. Matsumoto and K. Hiraki. MBCF: A protected and virtualized high-speed user-level memory-based communication facility. In *Proc. of Int. Conf. Supercomputing '98 (to be appeared)*, July 1998.

[7] H. Tezuka, A. Hori, Y. Ishikawa, and M. Sato. PM: An operating system coordinated high performance communication library. In B. Hertzberger and P. Sloot, editors, *High-Performance Computing and Networking*, volume 1225 of *Lecture Notes in Computer Science*, pages 708–717. Springer Verlag, April 1997.

[8] W. Gropp, E. Lusk, N. Doss, and A. Skjellum. A high-performance, portable implementation of the MPI Message-Passing Interface Standard. *Parallel Computing*, 22(6):789–828, September 1996.

[9] D. Sitsky and P. Mackerras. System developments on the Fujitsu AP3000. In P. Mackerras, editor, *Proc. of 7th Parallel Computing Workshop*, September 1997.

[10] K. Cameron, L. Clarke, and G. Smith. CRI/EPCC MPI for CRAY T3D. http://www.epcc.ed.ac.uk/t3dmpi/Product/, September 1995.

[11] O. Tatebe, Y. Kodama, S. Sekiguchi, and Y. Yamaguchi. Efficient implementation of MPI using remote memory write (in Japanese). In *Proc. of Joint Symp. on Parallel Processing '98*, pages 199–206, June 1998.

PVM on Windows and NT Clusters

Stephen L. Scott[1,+], Markus Fischer[2], and Al Geist[1]

[1] Oak Ridge National Laboratory, Computer Science and Mathematics Division, P.O. Box
2008, Bldg. 6012, MS-6367, Oak Ridge, TN 37831.
scottsl1@ornl.gov, geist@msr.epm.ornl.gov
[2] Paderborn Center for Parallel Computing, University of Paderborn, 33100 Paderborn,
Germany. getin@uni-paderborn.de

Abstract. This paper is a set of working notes[1] based on recent experience using PVM on NT clusters and Windows machines. Included in this document
are some techniques and tips on setting up your own cluster as well as some of
the anomalies encountered during this work.

1 Introduction

Cluster computing over a network of UNIX workstations has been the subject of
research efforts for a number of years. However, this familiar environment of expensive workstations running UNIX has begun to change. Interest has started to focus on
off-the-shelf Intel based Pentium class computers running Microsoft's NT Workstation and NT Server operating systems. The NT operating system is a departure in
both function and philosophy from UNIX. Regardless of the differences, this interest
is being driven by a combination of factors including: the inverse relationship between price and performance of the Intel based machines; the proliferation of NT in
industry and academia; and the new network technologies such as Myrinet, Easynet,
and SCI. However, lacking in this equation is much of the effective cluster computing
software developed in the past for the UNIX environment - that is with the notable
exception of PVM. PVM[1] has been available from ORNL for the Windows and NT
world for approximately 2-years. However, the transition from UNIX to the W/NT[2]

+ This research was supported in part by an appointment to the Oak Ridge National Laboratory
  Postdoctoral Research Associates Program administered jointly by the Oak Ridge National
  Laboratory and the Oak Ridge Institute for Science and Education.
[1] As "working notes" implies - updated information may be found from links at
  http://www.epm.ornl.gov/~sscott and http://www.epm.ornl.gov/pvm/pvm_home.html
[2] W/NT is used to represent both Windows and NT operating systems. In general one may
  assume that all comments represent both the Windows and NT environment. This document
  will explicitly specify Windows or NT in those cases where the discussion is relevant to only
  that one.

world has not been without problems. The nature of the Windows operating system makes PVM installation and operation simple yet not secure. It is this lack of security that provides both of these *benefits* by making all Windows users the equivalent of UNIX root. The NT operating system, on the other hand, comes with a plethora of configuration and security options. When set properly, these options make NT far more secure than Windows. However, when used improperly they can render a system insecure and unusable.

First is a look into the ORNL computing environment used to generate the information of this report. This provides an example of tested hardware and software for constructing an NT cluster. This is followed by a variety of cluster configuration options that have been tried along with comments regarding each.

2 The Oak Ridge Cluster Environment

The Oak Ridge NT cluster is a part of the Tennessee / Oak Ridge Cluster (TORC) research project. This effort is designed to look into Intel architecture based common off the shelf hardware and software. Each cluster varies in both specific hardware configuration and in the number of machines running NT and Linux operating systems. UTK/ICL administers the University of Tennessee portion of the cluster and the Distributed Computing group at ORNL administers their cluster.

2.1 Hardware and Operating System Environment

The Oak Ridge portion of this effort consists of dual-Pentium 266MHZ machines using Myrinet, gigabet Ethernet, and fast Ethernet network hardware. For testing purposes, three machines are always running the NT 4.0 operating system. The other machines in the cluster are generally running Red Hat Linux. However, if additional NT machines are desired, Linux machines may be rebooted to serve as NT cluster nodes.

Of the three machines always running NT, Jake is configured as NT 4.0 Server and performs as NT Domain server for both the cluster and any remote Domain logins. The other two machines, Buzz and Woody, are configured with NT 4.0 Workstation. Any machine on the network or internet for that matter may access the cluster. However, for this work it was generally accessed via the first author's desktop NT machine (U6FWS) running 4.0 Workstation. Also used in this work was a notebook Pentium providing the Windows 95 component.

Further information and related links regarding the TORC cluster may be found at the ORNL PVM web page.

2.2 Supporting Software

In addition to PVM 3.4 beta-6 for Intel machines, there are two software packages that were used extensively during this work. First is Ataman RSHD software that is used to provide remote process execution. This is a reasonably priced shareware package available at http://www.ataman.com. A RSHD package is required for the use of PVM on W/NT systems. Second is the freeware VNC (Virtual Network Computing) available from ORL at http://www.orl.co.uk. Although, not required for PVM's operation, VNC provides a simple and free way to perform remote administration tasks on W/NT systems.

Ataman RSHD

There are three versions of this software - one for NT on Intel systems (version 2.4), a second for NT on Alpha systems (version 2.4 - untested here), and a third for Windows 95 systems (version 1.1). At this writing it is unknown if the Windows 95 version will work for 98 or for that matter if it is even needed for Windows 98. All indications are that the NT version will operate on NT 5.0 should it ever be released. This section will become a moot point should Microsoft decide to field RSHD software. However, all indications are that they are not interested in doing so.

Although the Ataman RSHD software is a straightforward installation, it MUST be installed and configured on each machine. This is not difficult but is time consuming. One way to simplify the configuration of multiple machines with the same user and host set is to do one installation and propagate that information to the other machines. For a setup with many users or many machines this procedure will save some time. However, not much is gained in the case of few users or few machines. Furthermore, this process can only be done on machines with the same operating system. For example - NT 4.0 on Intel to NT 4.0 on Intel.

After successfully installing on one machine (the donor machine) perform the following steps while logged in as the NT Administrator or from an account with Administrator privileges:
1. From the donor machine, copy the entire directory that contains the Ataman software suite to the same location on the target machine.
2. On the donor machine, run the register editor (regedit) and export the entire Ataman registry branch to a file. This branch is located at {HKEY_LOCAL_MACHINE\SOFTWARE\Ataman Software, Inc.}
3. Move the exported file to a temporary location on the target machine or if you have shared file access across machines it may be used directly from the donor machine.
4. On the target machine, run the registry editor - go to the {HKEY_LOCAL_MACHINE\SOFTWARE} level in the registry and perform an import registry file using the donor's file.
5. On the target machine, perform installation per instructions in Ataman manual.
6. On the target machine, invoke Ataman icon from the windows control panel folder and reenter all user passwords. Granted, reentering all passwords is a lengthy process, but not as lengthy as reentering user information for every user.

VNC - Virtual Network Computer

Although, the Virtual Network Computer software is not necessary for the operation of a PVM cluster, it greatly simplifies the administration of a group of remote W/NT machines. This software package provides the ability to remotely operate a W/NT machine and control it as if you were sitting in front of the local keyboard and monitor. While there are some commercial packages that provide the same services as VNC, none tested performed any better than this freeware package.

There are a number of versions of VNC available including W/NT, Unix, and Macintosh. There are also two sides to the VNC suite. One is the VNCviewer and the other is the VNCserver. VNCviewer is the client side software that runs on the local machine that wants to remotely operate a W/NT machine. VNCserver must be running on a machine before VNCviewer can attach for a session. It is recommended that all remote machines have VNCserver installed as a service so that it will be automatically restarted when the W/NT reboots. When installed as a service, there will be one VNC password that protects the machine from unauthorized access. User passwords are still required if no one is logged in at the time a remote connection is established. CAUTION: a remote connection attaches to a machine in whatever state it is presently in. This can present a large security problem if someone has the VNC machine password and connects to a machine that another person has left active. However, restricting VNC access to only administrator access users should not present a problem since it is a package essentially designed for remote administration.

One other warning regarding VNC. The VNChooks (see VNC documentation) were activated on one Windows 95 machine. Error messages were generated during the installation process. Although the software was uninstalled, there are still some lingering problems on that machine that did not exist prior to the hook installation. While it is not known for certain that the VNChooks caused problems, it is recommended that this option be avoided until more information is known.

3 W/NT Cluster Configuration

There are a number of factors to consider when implementing a cluster of computers. Some of these factors are thrust upon the cluster builder by virtue of the way W/NT machines tend to be deployed. Unfortunately it is not always the case that there is a dedicated W/NT cluster sitting in the machine room. Unlike in the UNIX environment, PVM's installation and use is directly affected by W/NT administration policy. Users in the UNIX world are easily insulated from one another. W/NT unfortunately does not provide this insulation. Thus, when setting up a W/NT computing cluster one must consider a number of factors that a UNIX user may take for granted.

The three basic configuration models for PVM W/NT clusters are the *local*, *server*, and *hybrid* models. Adding to the complexity of these three models are the three cluster computing models that one must consider. These are the *cooperative cluster*, the *centralized cluster*, and the *hybrid cluster*. At first glance, it appears that there is a one-to-one mapping of PVM model to cluster model. However, the decision is not that simple.

3.1 Cluster Models

The first cluster model is that of the *cooperative* or adhoc cluster. The cooperative environment is where a number of users, generally the machine owner, agree to share their desktop resources as part of a virtual cluster. Generally, in this environment, each owner will dictate the administrative policy for those resources they are willing to share. The second cluster model is that of the *centralized* cluster. Generally a centralized cluster is used so that the physical proximity of one machine to another can be leveraged for administrative and networking purposes. The centralized cluster is usually a shared general computing resource and frequently individual machines do not have monitors or other external peripherals. The third cluster model is the *hybrid* cluster. The hybrid cluster is generally what most researchers will use. This cluster environment is a combination of a centralized cluster with the addition of some external machines as the cooperative cluster component. Many times the cooperating machines are called into the cluster as they have special features that are required or advantageous for a specific application. Examples would include special display hardware, large disk farms, or perhaps a machine with the only license for a visualization application.

The ORNL cluster consists of a centralized cluster and the addition of remote machines makes the tested configuration a hybrid cluster.

3.2 PVM Models

First is the *local* model where each machine has a copy of PVM on a local disk. This method has the benefit of being conceptually the most direct and producing the quickest PVM load time. The downside is that each machine's code must be individually administered. While not difficult or time consuming for a few workstations the administration quickly becomes costly, cumbersome, and error prone as the number of machines increases. Second is the *server* model where each local cluster of machines contains a single instance of PVM for the entire cluster. This method exhibits the client-server benefit of a centralized software repository providing a single point of software contact. On the negative side, that central repository represents a single point of failure as well as a potential upload bottleneck. Even with these potential negatives, the centralized server approach is generally the most beneficial administration technique for the cluster environment. Third is the *hybrid* model that is a mixture of the local and server models. An elaborate hybrid configuration will be very time consuming to administer. PVM and user application codes will have to be copied and maintained throughout the configuration. The only significantly advantageous hybrid configuration is to maintain a local desktop copy of PVM and application codes so that work may continue when the cluster becomes unavailable.

3.3 Configuration Management

This is where the W/NT operating system causes the operation of PVM to diverge from that of the UNIX environment. These difficulties come from the multi-user and remote access limitations of the W/NT operating system and not PVM.

One such difference is that the W/NT operating system expects all software to be administrator installed and controlled. Since there is only one registry in the W/NT system, it is maintained by the administrator and accessed by all. Thus, registry values for PVM are the registry values for all users of PVM. Essentially, this means that there is no such thing as an individual application. While it is possible to have separate individual executables, and to restrict access to an application through file access privileges, it is not possible to install all of these variants without a great deal of confusion and overhead. Thus, for all practical purposes, W/NT permits only one administrator installed version of PVM to be available. This is a direct departure from the original PVM philosophy that individual users may build, install, and access PVM without any special privileges. Furthermore, each PVM user under UNIX had the guarantee of complete autonomy from all other users including the system itself. This meant that they could maintain their own version of PVM within their own file space without conflicting with others or having system restrictions being forced on them. It is important to note that PVM on W/NT, as on UNIX, does not require privileged access for operation. However, it is very important to remember that a remote user of a Windows machine has complete access to all machine resources as if they were sitting directly in front of that machine.

Another problem is that local and remote users of W/NT share the same drive map. This means that all users will immediately see and may be affected by the mapping of a drive by another user. This also limits the number of disks, shared disks, and links to less than 26 since drives on W/NT machines are represented as a single uppercase character. This is a major departure from the UNIX world where drives may be privately mounted and links created without affecting or even notifying other users. It also goes directly against the original PVM philosophy of not having the potential to affect other users.

4 Anomalies

PVM in the Windows and NT environment is somewhat temperamental. At times it appears that the solution that worked yesterday no longer works today. Here are some of the documented deviations of PVM behavior on Windows and NT systems versus its UNIX counterpart.

4.1 Single Machine Virtual Machine

Because PVM embodies the virtual machine concept, many people develop codes on a single machine and then move the application to a network of machines for increased performance. When doing so, beware of the following failure when invoking PVM from the start menu on a stand-alone machine. The PVM MS-DOS window will freeze blank and the following information is written to the PVM log file in the temporary directory.

```
[pvmd pid-184093] readhostfile() iflist failed
[pvmd pid-184093] master_config() scotch.epm.ornl.gov: can't gethostbyname
[pvmd pid-184093] pvmbailout(0)
```

This error occurs when the network card is not present in the machine. The first encounter of this error was on a Toshiba Tecra notebook computer running Windows-95 with the pcmcia ethernet card removed. The error was fixed by simply replacing the pcmcia ethernet card and rebooting. The card need only be inserted into the pcmcia slot and does not require connection to a network. So, when developing codes on the road, remember the network card.

4.2 NT User Domains

The Domain user is a feature new to the NT operating system that does not exist in the Windows world. Windows only has the associated concept of work groups. Using NT Domains intermixed with machines using work groups has great potential for creating conflicts and confusion.

While it is possible to have the same user name within multiple domains as well as various work groups on NT systems it is not recommended that you do so. This is guaranteed to cause grief when using the current version of PVM. The multiple domain problem is in both the Ataman software as well as PVM. However, the only symptoms observed throughout testing presented themselves as PVM startup errors. Ataman user documentation warns against using user accounts with the same name even if they are in different domains.

The symptoms are exhibited from the machine where PVM refuses to start. Generally, there will be a pvml.userX file in the temporary directory from a prior PVM session. Under normal circumstances this file is overwritten by the next PVM session for userX. However, if (userX / domainY) created the file, then only (userX / domainY) can delete or overwrite the file as it is the file owner. Thus all other userX are prevented from starting PVM on that machine since they are unable to overwrite the log file.

This problem was encountered most frequently when alternating where PVM is initially started. For example when experimenting with NT Domain Users on Jake, Woody, and Buzz while U6FWS was running as a local user. Experience to date has shown that there are fewer problems when workgroups are used instead of domains.

Unfortunately this means that a PVM user will have to have a user account on every machine to be included in the virtual machine. Perhaps with more NT experience we can resolve this issue. Administrator access is required to solve this lockout problem, as the pvml.userX file must be deleted.

Related to this is the use of NT Domain based machines mixed with Windows machines. This presents a problem since Windows 95 does not support user domains. The difficulty occurs when a Windows machine attempts to add an NT machine with user domains. PVM is unable to add the NT to the virtual machine. However, an NT with or without user domains is able to successfully add and use a Windows machine. This access is permitted, as Windows does not validate the user within a user domain.

5 Conclusion and Future Work

This paper provided some insights as how to construct, install, and administer a cluster of W/NT machines running PVM. Obviously there is much more information that could be included in a paper such as this. However, due to time and space constraints it is impossible to do so.

First we need more time to explore all the intricacies of the W/NT operating systems. Of course this is a moving target as Windows 98 has already been released and NT 5.0 has been promised for some time. Furthermore, we are unsure that all problems can be resolved so that PVM behaves exactly on W/NT as it does on Unix.

The space problem is easily resolved today via the WWW. Look to the web links provided throughout this paper for more current and up to date information.

References

1. Geist, A., Beguelin, A., Dongarra, J., Jiang, W., Manchek, R, Sunderam, V.: PVM: Parallel Virtual Machine - A Users' Guide and Tutorial for Networked Parallel Computing, MIT Press, Boston, 1994.

Java and Network Parallel Processing

Nenad Stankovic and Kang Zhang
Department of Computing
Macquarie University, NSW 2109, Australia
{nstankov, kang}@mpce.mq.edu.au

Abstract. Parallel computing on a network of workstations (NOW) is receiving a lot of attention from the research community. Recently, Java has emerged as a language of choice for programming on the Internet. However, there is still a lack of tools for developing and running parallel applications on a NOW environment. The Visper tool incorporates the advantages of Java with the established techniques and practices of parallel processing on the network. The aim of the project is to develop a visual software-engineering environment for portable parallel programs based on the MPI standard. We present the design and implementation of a parallel extension to Java that consists of remote process and group creation and message-passing communications.

1 Introduction

Parallel processing community has recognized that *the network is the computer* and provided tools and libraries to foster the use of networks of heterogeneous hardware to run parallel applications. Different solutions for MIMD environments have been proposed and implemented; the most popular being the message-passing model with libraries like MPI [9] and PVM [7]. However, the problem with such systems is that programmers have to deal with different hardware and software when building their programs. This requires a considerable effort when programming and setting up a parallel-processing environment. The problems vary from technical to structural. Some of the technical problems are:

- programmers have to build different executable, one for each target platform and operating system, with, possibly, a different compiler
- there must be a shareable file system between the networked workstations, for the executable to be available to each running kernel
- users must have an account available at each computer.

The structural problems stem from the fact that this computing environment is usually heterogeneous in both software and hardware and shareable between many users. In a multiprocessor system, the workload is more predictable and it is easier to restrict users' access to the system. On the other hand, the load on each networked computer can vary from time to time, as one cannot control other programs running on a computer or on a network. Therefore, the same program, for different runs, is likely to have different execution time and produce different trace data, even on the same computer. This problem is compounded for nondeterministic programs, because it is difficult to isolate programming mistakes from the nondeterminism caused by the runtime environment.

A number of tools have been built to help with these issues. The primary objective of Phred [1] is to encourage writing deterministic rather than nondeterministic programs, even though the latter can yield better performance. The engine behind the tool asists with the process, by automatically detecting potential sources of nondeterminism in the program. HeNCE [2] is a visual programming environment for composing and running PVM programs. It provides a GUI that keeps a consistent mental and visual image for the programmer while programming and running parallel programs, even though it uses two similar visual representations. On the other hand, CODE [11] is more concerned with program composition and compilation than with runtime analysis. It has a hierarchical graph and an object-oriented architecture that facilitate the process of adding new target architecture to a PVM environment.

In this paper we present a novel tool for MPI programming on the network called Visper. Similar to HeNCE, it is conceived as an integrated software-engineering tool that provides the services to design, develop, test and run parallel programs. It comes with a MPI-like communication library, and features to spawn and control processes from within the environment. It provides a single visual formalism for program design and testing based on the space-time diagram [10]. Being implemented in Java, Visper encourages object-oriented parallel programming but, in the same time, does not obscure the traditional approach based on the process identity that was adopted by MPI. In the paper, we first look at the related work regarding the use of Java and parallel processing on the Internet. Then, in Section 3 we describe the services provided by the tool to support the environment, and in Section 4 the design and implementation of the communication library, the process and group abstractions, and the proposed programming model for meta-parallel processing. Finally, a summary is given of the project's current status.

2 Related Java Projects

Recent developments in networking, the advent of Java and the Internet have motivated new approaches to distributed and parallel computing. Java has earned its recognition as the Internet programming language of choice, being, in the same time, a general-purpose object-oriented programming language. So far, a typical distributed or parallel application would consist of one user, processes and data that are bound to a particular architecture or file system and resources to which the user has access. There have been a number of projects that aim at making this concept more flexible. For example, Netsolve [3] provides a Java based system for exporting computational resources and libraries of preconfigured modules to solve computationally intensive problems. Other systems like IceT [8] and InfoSphere [4] see the Internet as a cooperative or group environment in which multiple users can work together. The IceT project has also done some work at providing a PVM like environment for parallel processing. The main drive behind these projects was the recognition of the *write once run many* capability of the Java environment.

Parallel to this type of research, there have been efforts to enable popular message-passing libraries like MPI and PVM to run under the Java Virtual Machine (JVM). JavaPVM [16] and MPI Java [5] provide wrappers for the native C-calls by using the Java native methods capability. The gain in performance of such an approach is offset by the availability of a native MPI or PVM library that drives the messaging. JPVM [6] is a PVM library written in Java. It offers features such as thread safety, multiple communication end-points per task, and direct message routing that are not found in standard PVM. However, it is not interoperable with standard PVM applications.

3 The Tool and User Interface

Architecturally, the Visper tool consists of a console, a system interface and a network of computers running daemons. Both, the console and the daemon are designed and built as standalone Java applications. Figure 1 shows the main components. With the *Design Tool* the programmer draws the *process communication graph* (PCG) [12], where the nodes in the graph represent communication primitives and the arcs represent communication channels. The process communication graph describes the structural aspects of the application, independent from the target hardware. The *Group Tool* allows manual configuration of the network in terms of the resources being used and the *Run Tool* starts and controls the parallel program execution. The monitoring systems collects run-time data. There are two tools that allow the data visualization. The *Debug Tool* displays a space-time diagram, while the *Performance Tool* displays information about the hardware, e.g. process and process group activity and group configuration.

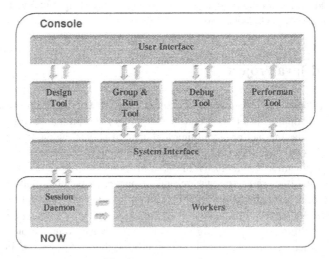

Fig. 1. Visper Architecture

The network of workstations consists of a number of daemons that upload, control and execute a parallel program. The system interface comprises a communication library and utilities to control and monitor the NOW environment.

3.1 The Console

From the user's perspective, the console provides a graphical user interface to interact with the parallel-processing environment. To the user, console is the only tangible component of the tool. It can be described as a multi-threaded "rather" thin Java client. When a console starts up, a window like the one in Figure 2 (Visper: Console) pops up. It has a menu bar located at the top and a message area below it. The message area displays messages generated by the system.

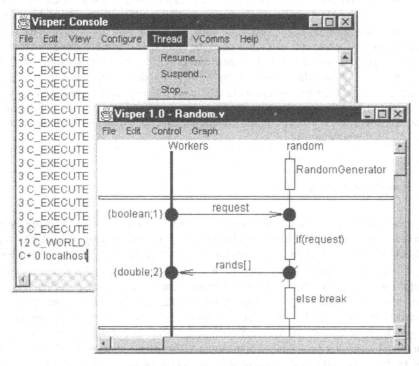

Fig. 2. Console and PCG Editor

From the menu bar, the programmer can select different actions. For example, the *File* menu allows connecting to a daemon, starting a parallel program and exiting from the Visper. The *Thread* menu provides a manual mechanism to control the execution of processes in the environment, while the *VComms* menu allows selective enabling of runtime trace data collection. The *PCG Editor* makes use of the process communication graph to compose a message-passing program (Figure 2). The vertical lines represent processes or group of processes. The blocks represent sequential code, while the nodes and arcs represent communication channels. The annotation is used to define the data, data types and message tags. The pair of hollow horizontal lines designates an iteration.

3.2 The Daemon

The daemon is a multi-threaded, fully equipped message-passing virtual computer that runs within its own JVM. To make a computer available to Visper a copy of the daemon must run on that computer. To create a new session, a console must establish connection to a daemon. Each console can run only one parallel program at a time, and can be connected to only one daemon. We call that daemon a *leading* or *session* daemon. Each session will typically have multiple *working* daemons or *workers*, to execute Java bytecodes. Just as a console talks to a session daemon, all daemons can communicate between themselves. Apart from the communication channel between console and session daemon, there is no other difference between the daemons. Each session remains active and intact as long as the console is running. Subsequent runs of the same program use the cached classes from previous runs. It is, however, possible to refresh the cached data upon request, without terminating the session. It is also possible to run different programs within the same session, but not at the same time.

Multiple consoles could run on the same network, and each has its own session daemon and a set of workers. In the current implementation, daemons are not shared across session boundaries.

4 Implementation

Visper builds upon traditional parallel computing techniques and paradigms to include novel aspects that have been brought about by the evolving technologies like object-oriented design and programming, multi-threading, rapid prototyping and architectural neutrality. It has been completely implemented in Java and does not require any platform specific extension libraries. The advantage of Java is that it is not just another programming language but is in fact a self-contained environment, independent of the underlying operating system or architecture. Java comes with a wide range of classes, such as networking protocols and graphical user interface building blocks that are fundamental to Visper. The instant solutions provided by Java range from the portability and remote execution of the Java bytecodes to the elementary security model [15] provided by the *SecurityManager* class. While the security itself may not be a major issue in parallel processing, it eliminates the requirement for the users to be trusted when starting up processes on remote computers. The daemon, just as a Java enabled web browser, limits the scope of operations a process can perform to those that will not violate security of the host system. The *soft-installation* of Java bytecodes by the *ClassLoader* class removes the *rsh-rlogin* mechanism to start processes on remote computers, as in MPI. It also enables execution of a parallel program on a NOW without a shared file system.

4.1 Message-Passing Primitives

At the API level, Visper provides a communication class called *VComms* that follows the MPI standard, but also takes advantage of the features like function overloading and object serialization [13] available in Java. To simplify the marshaling of data, all messages consist of serializable Java objects that are communicated via sockets. When serializing data, the programmer does not have to define the data type or the array size. Being properties of the data types, that is taken care of by the serialization mechanism itself. These features simplify the signature of the MPI calls in our implementation and reduce the possibility of errors. The implementation supports blocking and non-blocking point-to-point and collective messaging, together with synchronization capabilities in a raw and trace mode. At the moment, the inter-group communication is enabled only in the point-to-point mode. Synchronous and asynchronous calls can be combined together, at both ends of the communication channel.

As in MPI, each message has a tag, a process ID and a group to which the sending or receiving process belongs. These three attributes are combined into an object of the *VData* class. All calls that send data take another argument that represents the contents. For example, a blocking send call is defined as:

```
Send(VDataSend(tag,toProcID,group),userData);
```

and the matching blocking receive:

```
UserData data = Recv(VDataRecv(tag,fromProcID,group));
```

where:

      VDataSend and *VDataRecv* are derived from *VData*.

In point-to-point communications, the programmer may use wildcards on the receiving side to receive messages of any tag or from any source.

4.2 Remote Processes, Groups and Threads

Parallel programs consist of many processes (i.e. threads of execution). In Visper, each process that runs on a remote computer encapsulates a thread and a state. There is a one-to-one mapping between *remote processes* and *remote threads*. Each remote thread is a well-defined, self-contained, and self-sufficient module that runs within its own process, and interacts with other remote threads by sending messages. It can be initialized by passing in user defined arguments at runtime and controlled by its process.

To create remote processes Visper provides 2 abstractions. The *VRemoteProcess* class creates a process with a thread running on a remote computer. In addition, we define the *VRemoteGroup* class that is used to fork a uniform group of remote processes. The following example shows how to instantiate a remote group of threads:

```
VGroup gr = new VGroup(groupName,parentGroup,4);
```

```
VLoaderURL lu = new VLoaderURL(path,RemoteThread,argv);
```

```
VRemoteGroup rgrp = new VRemoteGroup(lu,gr);
```

First, the parent thread creates a new group of 4 processes, followed by a loader mode object. The loader mode object defines the top remote thread class to be loaded, and the path to it and other classes the thread is using. It also allows passing in the user-defined arguments, similar to the command line arguments in MPI. Visper provides different modes to upload remote threads. The *VLoaderURL* relies on the uniform resource locator and http daemon. To minimize the network traffic, a loader check for the cached classes before it tries to fetch the requested class or resolve it. Finally, the remote group of process is forked off. The initial state of all the processes is changed to running, by default.

Instances of the *VRemoteProcess* and *VRemoteGroup* classes serve as peers when referring to a process or a whole group. To change state, the interface consists of public methods; for example, to suspend a process or a group, we use:

```
rgrp.Suspend();
```

For convenience, the same operations are available from the *Thread* menu (Figure 2).

Groups in Visper play two roles. Firstly, they are used to allocate processes to the system, because each process must belong to a group before it can run a thread. Secondly, similar to MPI, groups are used to define communication scope. All communication and synchronization events take place within or among groups. This mechanism, however, does not obscure the Remote Method Invocation [14] provided by Java, or similar.

5 Conclusion

Visper is a novel Java based, visual software engineering environment for MIMD parallel programs. It combines new features provided by Java with the standard practices and techniques pioneered by the systems like MPI and PVM. A program in Visper consists of a series of specialized modules that perform well-defined actions. At runtime, these modules are represented by processes on a NOW. Visper allows for the dynamic transfer of data and processes to a dynamic and modifiable pool of computational resources. In addition, it enables the remote processes to be controlled by the program or user at runtime, by changing their state of execution and enabling or suspending the trace data collection on per group or per process basis. Because the remote thread model allows the state of the computation to be modeled directly, a continuous interaction with the environment is possible for monitoring and control of applications.

The communication primitives follow the MPI standard. They allow synchronous and asynchronous modes of communication between processes. Programmers can choose between point-to-point and collective communications. Basic intra group synchronization is enabled by the barrier call.

References

1. Beguelin, A. L.: Deterministic Parallel Programming in Phred. PhD Thesis, University of Colorado, at Boulder (1990)
2. Beguelin, A. L., Dongarra, J. J., Geist, G. A., Manchek, R., Sunderam, V. S.: HeNCE: Graphical Development Tools for Network-Based Concurrent Computing. *SHPCC-92 Proceedings of Scalable High Performance Computing Conference.* Williamsburg, Virginia (1992) 129-136
3. Casanova, H., Dongarra, J. J.: Netsolve: A Network Solver for Solving Computational Science Problems. Technical Report CS-95-313, University of Tennessee (1995)
4. Chandy, K. M, Rifkin, A., Sivilotti, P. A. G., Mandelson, J., Richardson, M., Tanaka, W., Weisman, L.: A World Wide Distributed System Using Java and the Internet, http://www.infospheres.caltech.edu
5. Chang, Y-J., Carpenter, B.: MPI Java Wrapper Download Page (March 27, 1997) http://www.npac.syr.edu/users/yjchang/javaMPI
6. Ferrari, A.: JPVM. http://www.cs.virginia.edu/~ajf2j/jpvm.html
7. Geist, G. A., Beguelin, A., Dongarra, J. J., Jiang, W., Manchek, R., Sunderam, V. S.: PVM 3 User's Guide and Reference Manual. Technical Report ORNL/TM-12187, Oak Ridge National Laboratory (1993)
8. Gray, P., Sunderam, V.: The IceT Project: An Environment for Cooperative Distributed Computing. http://www.mathcs.emory.edu/~gray/IceT.ps
9. Gropp, W., Lusk, E., Skjellum, A.: *Using MPI, Portable Parallel Programming with the Message-Passing Interface.* The MIT Press (1994)
10. Lamport, L.: Time, Clocks, and the Ordering of Events in a Distributed System. *Communication of the ACM.* Vol. 21, No. 7 (1978) 558-565
11. Newton, P., Browne, J. C.: The CODE 2.0 Graphical Parallel Programming Language. *Proceedings of ACM International Conference on Supercomputing* (1992) http://www.cs.utexas.edu/users/code
12. Stankovic, N., Zhang, K.: Graphical Composition and Visualization of Message-Passing Programs. SoftVis'97, Flinders University, Adelaide, South Australia (1997).35-40
13. Sun Microsystems, Inc.: Java Object Serialization Specification. Revision 1.4 (July 3, 1997) http://java.sun.com
14. Sun Microsystems, Inc.: Java Remote Method Invocation Specification. Revision 1.42 (October 1997) http://java.sun.com
15. Sun Microsystems, Inc.: Java Security Architecture (JDK 1.2). Revision 0.7 (October 1, 1997) http://java.sun.com
16. Thurman, D.: JavaPVM. http://homer.isye.gatech.edu/chmsr/JavaPVM

Part 4
Tools

A Tool for the Development of Meta-applications Supporting Several Message-Passing Programming Environments

R. Baraglia, R. Ferrini, D. Laforenza, R. Sgherri

CNUCE - Institute of the Italian National Research Council
Via S. Maria, 36 - I56100 Pisa (Italy)
Phone +39-50-593111 - Fax +39-50-904052
e-mail: R.Baraglia@cnuce.cnr.it, D.Laforenza@cnuce.cnr.it
URL: http://miles.cnuce.cnr.it

Abstract. This paper presents the extensions made to WAMM (Wide Area Metacomputer Manager) in order to manage a metacomputer composed of hosts on which several message-passing programming environments run. Initially, WAMM only permitted the execution of meta-applications consisting of PVM components. To allow the execution of meta-applications composed of PVM and MPI tasks, WAMM has been extended by means of PLUS. PLUS is one of the main components of the MOL Project. It provides an efficient, easy-to-use interface among various communication libraries.

The paper is organized as follows: after the introduction, Sections 2 and 3 describe WAMM and PLUS respectively. Section 4 presents some implementation details related to the new WAMM functionalities, and Section 5 describes some performance measurements related to the new version of WAMM. Section 6 concludes the paper.

1 Introduction

A large-scale application running on a metacomputer may involve several co-operating computational components; some of them could be existing modules specialized to solve a particular computational task. There are many examples of applications of this type [1, 2]. Cooperation among the components may be obtained by means of *message-passing* libraries. The implementation of a meta-application could entail using existing components, each of which is written using different message-passing libraries (hereafter this kind of application will be called a *heterogeneous* meta-application). Several message-passing environments are currently available. Some are proprietary (e.g., MPL[3], PARIX[4]) and are characterized by a low degree of portability. Others are public domain products (e.g., PVM [5], MPI [6]). They are portable and, therefore, available for several platforms and operating systems. Unfortunately, none of these environments permits communication among processes belonging to different message-passing environments. Mechanisms are thus needed to permit communication among the meta-applications' components in a transparent way. Several libraries that can get round this problem have been implemented (e.g., Nexus [7] and PLUS [9]). Nexus is a joint project of Argonne National Laboratory and USC Information Sciences Institute. Nexus is a portable library providing the multi-threading, communication, and resource management facilities required to implement advanced languages, libraries, and applications in heterogeneous parallel and distributed computing environments. Nexus is intended for use by compiler writers and library developers, rather than application programmers. The Globus [8] project builds on Nexus mechanisms to provide software infrastructure for high-performance distributed computing.

PLUS represents one of the main components of the MOL Project [10] whose goal is to create a metacomputer through the definition of interfaces that can interact with several existing autonomous software tools. Plus will be described in more detail in Section 3.

The development of a meta-application requires tools providing a user interface that incorporates the essential tools for the development of parallel applications. The main goal of such an interface is to facilitate the management of a metacomputer which helps the user during the application development phases [11, 12]. In particular, the compilation and the execution of a meta-application usually entails writing source files on a local node, copying them onto remote hosts, and manually starting compilations on each machine: thus a great deal of time-consuming, error-prone operations. WAMM[1] [13, 14, 18] can help to alleviate these problems. For this reason, in the framework of the MOL Project, WAMM was selected for this purpose. In its initial design, WAMM only permitted the execution of a meta-application consisting of components written using PVM. In order to permit the execution of heterogeneous meta-applications this was an unacceptable limitation, more so considering the growing number of MPI applications in the scientific computing environment. To overcome this problem a new version of WAMM integrating PLUS has been implemented.

2 WAMM: A Short Description

Developed by CNUCE-CNR, WAMM is a graphical tool built on top of PVM. It provides users with a graphical interface to assist in repetitive and tedious tasks such as host add/check/removal, process management, remote compilation, and remote commands execution. Figure 1 shows a snapshot of the WAMM interface.

WAMM is written in ANSI C with calls to OSF/Motif and XPM[2] routines. To use WAMM, users have to prepare a configuration file which contains the description of the nodes that can be inserted into the metacomputer. This configuration file contains information to organize the hosts as tree-structured subnetworks, where:

– the leaves represent single hosts;

---

[1] see at http://miles.cnuce.cnr.it/pp/wamm11/version.html

[2] XPM is a freely distributable library simplifying the image management in *X Windows applications*; it is available via anonymous FTP at koala.inria.fr, /pub/xpm.

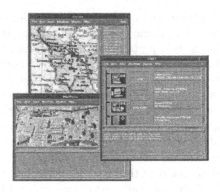

Fig. 1. A snapshot of WAMM.

- the leaves are grouped into LANs (Local Area Networks);
- the LANs are grouped into MANs (Metropolitan Area Networks) or into a WAN (Wide Area Network);
- the MANs are grouped into a WAN, which is the root of the tree.

This file is read at the start of the interface. The organization of the hosts into the subnetworks is typically decided on the basis of its geographical position, e.g. all hosts belonging to the same computing center might be included in the same LAN. A MAN could be used to group the computer centers of a city. The metacomputer configuration can be dynamically changed by executing interface commands (just by clicking on icons).

3 The PLUS Protocol

The PLUS system provides an efficient, easy-to-use interface between different communication models. Here, the term 'communication model' is used in its more general sense to comprise both worlds: standard message passing environments such as PVM, MPI, and vendor-specific communication libraries like MPL, and PARIX. For PLUS it makes no difference whether vendor-specific or standard communication methods are used. The PLUS system itself consists of daemons and a modular library that is linked to the application code. Using only four new commands makes it easy to integrate PLUS into an existing code:

- plus_init() to sign on at the nearest PLUS daemon;
- plus_exit() to log off;
- plus_spawn() to spawn a task on another (remote) system;
- plus_info() to obtain information on the accessible (remote) tasks.

Figure 2 gives an example, where a C/MPI code communicates via PLUS with a C/PVM application. After the initialization, remote processes are able

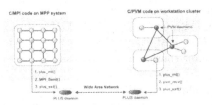

Fig. 2. PLUS Architecture.

to communicate with each other via PLUS. From the MPI application, the communication is made by calling the original MPI_Send() with a process ID that is greater than the last (maximum) process ID managed by MPI in the corresponding communicator group. Generally speaking, PLUS recognizes an external communication by using the original communication function (e.g. MPI_Send(), or pvm_send()) by a process ID that lies outside the ID range managed by the corresponding programming model. Within PLUS, all process IDs are specified in relation to the number of active tasks. User processes can identify external processes by means of the plus_info() function. Most of the PLUS system code is contained in the daemons. It was thus possible to keep the PLUS library small. The daemons are used to hide the user processes from slow Internet communication. Whenever a message has to be transferred between different environments, it is first sent to the nearest PLUS daemon, which immediately acknowledges the message to allow for message latency hiding. The daemon then takes responsibility for delivering the message while the user process proceeds with its computation. Currently, PLUS supports communication between PVM, MPI and the PARIX programming environment. Moreover, PLUS was designed in a modular way to allow easy extensions to other, new communication methods. Only a few communication routines in the modular PLUS library have to be adapted to include a new programming model in the PLUS system. For programming environments that do not provide a process model (such as MPI-1, and PARIX) PLUS provides the functions plus_system() and plus_info() to spawn new processes and to obtain information on remote processes, respectivelly. PLUS is public domain software [3] and is distributed as ANSI C source code.

4   New WAMM Functionalities

The first version of WAMM only allowed the inclusion of PVM hosts; the new version also manages MPI hosts supporting MPI/CH [15]. The new functionalities are: *management of hosts running MPI, execution of MPI applications,* and *control and monitoring of MPI processes.* The control and monitoring of

---

[3] The code can be downloaded via WWW at http://www.uni-paderborn.de /pc2/projects/mol/index.htm

MPI processes required the implementation of a library (mpi_info) [16] which has to be linked by users at compile time. WAMM was extended to permit the insertion/removal of MPI hosts as well as PVM hosts, while maintaining a uniform look&feel. The same considerations are valid for the remote commands and compilation execution.

To run an MPI application, MPI/CH provides a command named mpirun. The user has to give some input parameters, e.g. number of execution copies, hosts required. Using MPI/CH with mpirun, the list of the metacomputer hosts must be written in a configuration file; at run time the processes are allocated to the hosts in a round-robin fashion. To run different applications requires as many configuration files as the different groups of hosts. When mpirun is entered, the user has to specify the required file. Using WAMM, the user does not have to execute mpirun, because it is the responsibility of the interface to issue this command automatically, using the configuration file containing the hosts selected by the user during the metacomputer definition. Moreover, WAMM permits MPI processes to be spawned either on a set of hosts or on the hosts belonging to an architectural class selected by the user.

PVM provides functionalities to produce useful information on the status of the processes being executed. MPI/CH does not support either notification mechanisms or the redirection of the output of the processes. In order to implement these capabilities a new library (mpi_info) was implemented. mpi_info gives information describing the MPI processes being executed as well as that obtainable by the PVM_notify mechanism. Using WAMM, users can receive information on PVM and MPI processes running on the metacomputer. They can also receive the output of the processes in separate windows and store them in a file. The use of mpi_info does not preclude the use of other tools based on MPI since it only uses native Unix mechanisms. Note that, even with the addition of the MPI host support, the new version of WAMM remains a PVM application. Consequently, at its start-up at least one PVM host is required: the local host. The main components of the new WAMM version are:

- GUI: manages windows, pull-down menus, etc.;
- PVMHoster: manages the insertion/removal of PVM hosts in the metacomputer;
- MPITasker/PVMTasker: executes remote commands and collects information on the MPI/PVM processes being executed on the metacomputer;
- MPIMaker/PVMMaker: controls the parallel compilation of a meta-application.

GUI and PVMHoster are executed only on the local host. Figure 3 shows an example of an allocation of the WAMM components on a metacomputer consisting of PVM and MPI hosts.

PLUS supports both the communication between the MPI hosts and the graphical interface, along with the spawning of MPI processes. At compile time the use of mpi_info adds specific code, before and after the occurrences of MPIInit() and MPIFinalize() primitives, which permits the enrolling/exit of a process to/from the MPI environment. At run time, for each MPI process, a

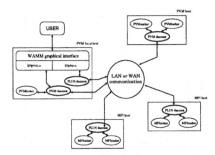

Fig. 3. Example of an allocation of WAMM components.

new file is opened. This file is used to store useful information, e.g., Tid, host on which the process is running, and the name of the file in which the output of the process will be redirected. The periodical sending of these files and the redirection of the MPI processes output towards the interface to be displayed are the responsibility of the MPITasker. When a process leaves MPI the corresponding file is cancelled.

5 Evaluation of the New WAMM Functionalities

In order to evaluate the overheads introduced by the PLUS integration into WAMM, tests were conducted using some kernel programs that implement point-to-point communications among tasks of a meta-application. In particular, the tests model an application composed of: PVM tasks alone, MPI tasks alone, PVM tasks communicating by means of PLUS, and MPI tasks communicating by means of PLUS. Note that the above tests do not include a case where MPI and PVM tasks communicate. This because it is impossible to measure the overhead incurred in an MPI-PVM application without support for PLUS. All tests were run on a metacomputer composed of two workstations, connected by Ethernet on which MPI, PVM, and PLUS were installed. As shown in Figure 4, for each test the communication times are compared by varying the message length. The figure shows that the overhead incurred when the MPI tasks communicate via PLUS is negligible with respect to the case in which the communication is native (without PLUS). On the other hand, communication among PVM tasks is sensitive whether operated with or without PLUS. In these cases, the overhead measured remains constant in all the tests and is about 30%.

6 Conclusions

The new version of WAMM can manage a metacomputer composed of hosts on which several message-passing environments are used. This removes the limitations of the previous version, which was designed to work only in a PVM

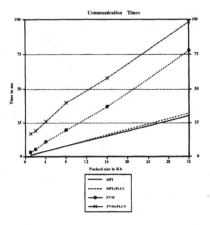

Fig. 4. Measurement of the overheads introduced by the PLUS integration into WAMM.

environment. WAMM currently supports MPI and PVM. This meets the initial goal of the MOL Project. Moreover, it constitutes another step towards developing a multi-environment tool for metacomputing management. WAMM may be useful for creating a meta-application which requires the integration of several applications written by using several message-passing libraries. This means that a target machine could be chosen which best matches the computational requirements of the application without constraints on the use of a particular message-passing environment. Moreover, this approach permits a better reuse of code. To support monitoring functionalities WAMM was extended by integrating PVaniM [17, 18], which was designed specifically to monitor PVM applications. The current version of WAMM does not permit performance monitoring of MPI processes.

7 Acknowledgments

We would like to thank Matthias Brune, Alexander Reinefeld and all the members of the PLUS team of the Paderborn Center for Parallel Computing of University of Paderborn for their help during the design and development of the new version of WAMM.

References

1. G. C. Fox, R. D. Williams, and P. C. Messina. *Parallel Computing Works!* Morgan Kaufmann Publishers, Inc., 1994.
2. T. DeFanti, I. Foster, M. Papka, R. Stevens, and T. Kuhfuss. Overview of the I-WAY: Wide area visual supercomputing. *International Journal of Supercomputer Application*, 10:123–130, 1996.

3. IBM. *Parallel Environment for AIX: Operation and Use.* IBM Corporation, August 1997.

4. Parsytec Computer GmbH. *Parix 1.2 Documentation and Reference Manual.*

5. A. Geist, A. Beguelin, J. Dongarra, W. Jiang, B. Manchek, and V. Sunderam. *PVM: Parallel Virtual Machine - A User's Guide and Tutorial for Network Parallel Computing.* MIT Press, 1994.

6. MPIF. MPI: A Message Passing Interface Standard. Final Report, Version 1.1. Message Passing Interface Forum. Available via WWW: www.mcs.anl.gov, /Projects/mpi/standard.htm, June 1995.

7. I. Foster, C. Kesselman, and S. Tuecke. The Nexus Approach to Integrating Multithreading and Communication. *Journal of Parallel and Distributed Computing,* 37:70–82, 1996.

8. I. Foster and C. Kesselman. The Globus Project: A Status Report. *to appear in the proceedings of IEEE Heterogeneous Computing Workshop, Orlando, USA,* 1998.

9. A. Reinefeld, J. Gehring, and M. Brune. Communicating Across Parallel Message-Passing Environments. In *Journal of Systems Architecture, special issue on Cluster Computing, Elsevier,* 1997.

10. A. Reinefeld, R. Baraglia, T. Decker, J. Gehring, D. Laforenza, F. Ramme, T. Römke, and J. Simon. The MOL Project: An Open Extensible Metacomputer. In *Proceedings of Sixth IEEE Heterogenous Computing Workshop (HCW 97),* pages 17–31. IEEE Computer Society Press, 1997.

11. J.E. Devaney, R. Lipman, M. Lo, W.F. Mitchell, M.Edwards, and C.W. Clark. *The Parallel Applications Development Environment (PADE), User's Manual.* National Institute of Standards and Technology, November 1995.

12. J.A. Kohl and G.A. Geist. *XPVM 1.0 Users' Guide, Technical Report ORNL/TM-12981.* Computer Science and Mathematical Division, Oak Ridge National Laboratory, TN, USA, April 1995.

13. R. Baraglia, G. Faieta, M. Formica, and D. Laforenza. WAMM: A visual interface for managing metacomputers. In *EuroPVM,* pages 137–142. Ecole Normale Supérieure de Lyon, Lyon, France, September 14-15 1995.

14. R. Baraglia, G. Faieta, M. Formica, and D. Laforenza. Experiences with a Wide Area Network Metacomputing Management Tool using SP-2 Parallel Systems. *Concurrency: practice and experience,* 9(3):223–239, March 1997.

15. W. Gropp, E. Lusk, N. Doss, and A. Skjellum. A High-Performance, Portable Implementation of the MPI Standard. Available via WWW: http://www.mcs.anl.gov, /mpi/mpich/indexold.html, 1996.

16. R. Sgherri. Integrazione di WAMM (Wide Area Metacomputer Manager) nel Progetto MOL (Metacomputer On Line). Master's thesis, University of Pisa (Italy), October 1997.

17. B. Topol, J. Stasko, and V. Sunderam. Monitoring and Visualization in Cluster Environments. Technical Report GIT-CC-96-10, Georgia Institute of Technology, Atlanta, March 1996.

18. R. Baraglia, M. Cosso, D. Laforenza, and M. Nicosia. Integrating PVaniM into WAMM for Monitoring Meta-Applications. In *Lecture Notes in Computer Science,* volume 1332, pages 226–233. Springer-Verlag, 1997.

Cross-Platform Parallel Debugging and Performance Analysis Tools

Shirley Browne

University of Tennessee, Knoxville TN 37996, USA
browne@cs.utk.edu

1 Introduction

Versatile and easy-to-use parallel debuggers and performance analysis tools are crucial for the development of correct and efficient high performance applications. Although vendors of HPC platforms usually offer debugging and performance tools in some form, it is desirable to have the same interface across multiple platforms so that the user does not have to learn a different tool for each platform. Furthermore, a tool should have an easy-to-use interface that intuitively supports the debugging and performance analysis tasks the user needs to carry out, as well as the parallel programming language and paradigm being used.

This paper describes a survey and evaluation of cross-platform debugging and performance analysis tools. In addition, we describe a current project which is developing a cross-platform API for accessing hardware performance counters. This paper necessarily represents a snapshot in time and as such will become out-of-date as new tools and new versions of existing tools are released. Current information and up-to-date evaluations of parallel debugging and performance analysis tools may be found at the Parallel Tools Library web site at http://www.nhse.org/ptlib/.

2 Cross-platform Debuggers

2.1 TotalView

The only parallel debugger that we have found to be currently available and supported on multiple HPC platforms is TotalView which is a commercial product available from Dolphin Interconnect Solutions.

TotalView can be used for debugging programs written in C, C++, Fortran 77, Fortran 90, and HPF, and it supports the PVM and MPI message passing libraries. TotalView runs on Sun Solaris and SunOS, IBM AIX, Digital UNIX, and SGI IRIX 6 platforms. It can only be used in homogeneous environments, however, in that all processes of the parallel or distributed application to be debugged using TotalView must be running on the same architecture with the same version of the operating system. TotalView has a graphical user interface but no command-line interface.

TotalView can manage multiple processes, and multiple threads within a process. TotalView displays each process in its own window, showing the source code, stack trace, and stack frame for one or more threads in the process. TotalView can be used to debug distributed programs which can consist of multiple remote programs running on different machines, provided all machines have the same machine architecture and operating system.

TotalView allows setting both source-level and machine-level breakpoints. By default, breakpoints are shared by all processes in the share group (i.e., same executable), and when any process reaches the breakpoint, all processes in the program group are stopped, but these default settings can be changed. You can also define evaluation points, which are points in your program where TotalView evaluates a code fragment. The code fragment can include debugger variables and built-in statements, as well as a subset of the source program language.

TotalView has what it calls a "Diving" facility for displaying more information about an object. The user "dives" into an object by clicking on it with the "Dive" (right) mouse button. Diving into a variable causes the contents of the variable to appear in a separate variable window. If the variable is a pointer, structure, or array, one can dive further into the contents, using a "nested dive". One can do this repeatedly, creating a "dive stack". TotalView supports display of Fortran 90 data types, as well as basic Fortran 77 and C data types. TotalView can display subsections of arrays, which are called *slices*. Arrays and array slices can be displayed in a variable window, one element per line, but this display is unwieldy for large arrays or slices. However, TotalView includes a Visualizer that allows you to create graphic images of array data. You can launch the Visualizer from TotalView or run it from the command line to visualize data dumped to a file from a previous TotalView session. The TotalView Visualizer restricts the type of data it can visualize to one or two dimensional arrays of character, integer, or floating point data. Both graph and surface visualization are available, and the images can be manipulated – e.g., by rotating, scaling, translating, and zooming.

We have tested version 3.7.7 of TotalView on an IBM SP2 and version 3.7.10-3 on an SGI/Cray Origin 2000. TotalView has excellent features and capabilities and is quite robust, although it does have a rather steep learning curve. However, we highly recommend it for users who can afford it and for whom a graphical user interface is not a problem.

There is a different version of TotalView for the Cray T3D/T3E, but this version branched off from the Dolphin version a few years ago, was developed independently by Cray, and has a somewhat different look and feel. The Cray version has both command-line and graphical user interfaces.

2.2 High Performance Debugging (HPD) Standard

In view of the fact that easy-to-use cross-platform parallel debuggers are not widely available and of user dissatisfaction with the current state of parallel debugging tools, an effort was begun in late 1996 to define a cross-platform parallel debugging standard that included the features and interface users wanted. The

High Performance Debugging Forum (HPDF) was formed as a Parallel Tools Consortium (PTools) project and met several times throughout 1997, with participation from vendors, academic and government researchers, and HPC users. The effort culminated in the HPD Version 1 specification for a standard functionality, semantics, and syntax for a command-line parallel debugger. Special attention was paid to features for scalability, such as aggregating output from multiple processes. HPD Version 1 was released from public comment at SC '97, and work is now underway to produce reference implementations for the IBM SP and the SGI/Cray Origin 2000. More details about HPD can be found at the Ptools web site at http://www.ptools.org/.

3 Cross-Platform Performance Analysis Tools

The reasons for poor performance of parallel message-passing codes can be varied and complex, and users need to be able to understand and correct performance problems. Performance tools can help by monitoring a program's execution and producing performance data that can be analyzed to locate and understand areas of poor performance.

We have investigated a number of performance tools, both research and commercial, that are available for monitoring and/or analyzing the performance of message-passing parallel programs written in Fortran or C. Some of these tools also support F90, C++, and/or HPF, or are language-independent. The most prevalent approach taken by these tools is to collect performance data during program execution and then provide post-mortem analysis and display of performance information. Some tools do both steps in an integrated manner, while other tools or tool components provide just one of these functions. A few tools also have the capability for run-time analysis, either in addition to or instead of post-mortem analysis. We investigated the following tools:

- AIMS - instrumentors, monitoring library, and analysis tools
- MPE logging library and Nupshot performance visualization tool
- Paradyn - dynamic instrumentation and run-time analysis tool
- SvPablo - integrated instrumentor, monitoring library, and analysis tool
- VAMPIRtrace monitoring library and VAMPIR performance visualization tool

We attempted to use each tool to analyze the same C and Fortran test programs. Our set of evaluation criteria consisted of *robustness, usability, scalability, portability*, and *versatility*. The following sections present a summary of our evaluation of these tools. A more detailed evaluation, including an expansion of the above criteria and pictures of analysis of our test programs using the tools, may be found in [1].

3.1 AIMS

AIMS is a software toolkit for measurement and analysis of Fortran 77 and C message-passing programs written using the NX, PVM, or MPI communication libraries [3]. AIMS currently runs on the IBM SP with IBM MPI or MPICH, on Sun, SGI, and HP workstations with MPICH, and on the SGI Power Challenge with SGI MPI or MPICH. The developers of AIMS are working on a port for the SGI Origin 2000, and ports to other platforms are being considered.

Source code can be instrumented using either the xinstrument graphical user interface or the batch_inst command-line instrumentor. The AIMS instrumentation is rather fragile with respect to the source language, which must be standard Fortran 77 or ANSI C. Free-format Fortran is poorly supported, and most F90 constructs are not parsed correctly. The instrumentors also have trouble with include files. The xinstrument GUI allows the user to select specific source code constructs to be instrumented. xinstrument is quite flexible in allowing the user to specify what constructs should be instrumented. Because the AIMS instrumentation API is not meant to be called by the user, there is no way provided to turn tracing on and off under program control during program execution. Either Monitor Mode, which generates a trace file, or Statistics Mode, which generates a much smaller file of summary statistics, may be selected from xinstrument.

After the instrumented application source files are compiled and linked with the AIMS monitor library, they can be run in the usual manner to produce trace and/or statistics files. AIMS generates separate files for each process and then automatically collects and merges the per-process files to create a single trace or statistics file. Trace files can be analyzed using the View Kernel (VK) and the tally statistics generator. VK has VCR-like controls for controlling tracefile playback. The user can also set breakpoints by time or on specific source code constructs. VK has timeline view called OverVIEW and a view called Spokes that animates messages passed between tasks while showing the state of each task. In the OverVIEW, each process is represented by a horizontal bar, with different colors for different instrumented subroutines and white space to indicate blocking due to a send or receive. Messages between processes are represented by lines between bars. Both bars and message lines can be clicked on for additional information, including source code click back to the line that generated the event. The OverVIEW display can be toggled to show two additional views: I/OverVIEW for I/O activity and MsgVIEW for message activity. In these views, heights of the bars are used to represent size of I/O or messages, respectively. Although the playback of the trace file can be controlled with the VCR controls, and the time range of the timeline can be adjusted, there is no way to scroll backward or to zoom in this view.

tally reads a trace file and generates resource-utilization statistics on a node-by-node and routine-by-routine basis. tally also reports the percentage of execution time spent in communication. The output from tally can be used as input to statistical analysis packages such as Excel. We discovered a problem in that tally currently always reports mpi_waitall as Send Blocking, even though this function generates both Send Blocking and Recv Blocking. This problem is supposed to be fixed in the next release.

3.2 nupshot

Nupshot is a performance visualization tool that displays logfiles in the alog format or the PICL version 1 format. The user can create customized logfiles for viewing with nupshot by inserting calls to the various MPE logging routines in his/her source code. A standard MPI profiling library is also provided that automatically logs all calls to MPI functions. MPE logging and nupshot are part of the MPICH distribution and come with their own configure scripts to set them up. MPE logging and nupshot are also distributed separately from MPICH from Parallel Tools Library (PTLIB) and can be used with vendor MPIs. Nupshot needs to have the Tcl 7.3 and Tk 3.6 libraries to compile it successfully.

Nupshot includes three visualization displays: Timelines, Mountain Ranges, and state duration histograms. The Timelines and Mountain Ranges views can be toggled on and off using the pulldown Display menu. A state duration histogram display for each state can be invoked by clicking on the button for that state on the main display. The Timelines view is present initially by default. Each line represents states of the process whose identifier appears along the left edge. Clicking on a bar with the left mouse button brings up an info box that gives the state name and duration. Messages between processes are represented by arrows. Clicking on a message line does not have any effect. The Mountain Ranges view gives a color-coded histogram of the states that are present at a given time. One can zoom in or out to stretch the Timeline and Mountain Ranges views along the horizontal axis. The initial scale can be restored by the Reset button. When zoomed in, the entire width of the display can be scrolled.

nupshot is fairly robust except on the SGI PCA and Origin 2000 platforms, where it crashes frequently in Tk routines, apparently due to instability on these platforms of the version of Tcl/Tk that it is using. On other platforms nupshot seems fairly robust. On the SGI platforms using MPE logging with SGI MPI, we experienced problems with test programs that used communicators, in that the alog files produced sometimes had bad values for sources of messages or did not appear to have sends and receives matched properly. We are unsure at this point whether the problem is due to the MPE logging library or to SGI MPI. We did not experience any problems in producing trace files with the MPE logging library on other platforms.

3.3 SvPablo

SvPablo, which stands for Source view Pablo, is a different approach from the previous Pablo components, which are no longer supported, in that the instrumentation, trace library, and analysis are combined in the single SvPablo component. The SvPablo "project" concept provides a way to organize your source code as well as to collect and organize traces done in the past. The current release supports ANSI C programs and HPF programs compiled with the Portland Group HPF compiler pghpf. HPF programs are automatically instrumented by the pghpf compiler when the appropriate flags are used. SvPablo has been ported to and tested on Sun Solaris and SGI IRIX 6 platforms.

C programs can be instrumented interactively using the SvPablo GUI which allows selective instrumentation of outer loops and function calls. SvPablo generates an instrumented version of the source code which is then linked with the SvPablo trace library and executed in the usual manner. For a C MPI program, the per-process SDDF performance files must then be collected and combined using the SvPablo CCombine utility before the merged performance file can be analyzed using the SvPablo GUI.

After the performance file has been loaded, the SvPablo GUI allows the user to view performance summary statistics for each instrumented routine and loop. To the left of the name for each instrumented routine, SvPablo shows two color-coded columns summarizing the number of calls made to the routine and the cumulative time for the routine. Detailed statistical information about a routine can be seen by clicking the mouse buttons. Selecting a function name for which SvPablo has access to the source code displays the source code along with color-coded performance information for instrumented constructs. Again, clicking on the colored boxes displays more detailed information. On the SGI/Cray Origin 2000 platform, SvPablo supports access to the MIPS R10000 hardware performance counters.

3.4 Paradyn

The purpose of the Paradyn project is to provide a performance measurement tool that scales to long-running programs on large parallel and distributed systems and that automates much of the search for performance bottlenecks [2]. The Paradyn designers wished to avoid the space and time overhead typically associated with trace-based tools. Their approach is to dynamically instrument the application and automatically control the instrumentation in search of performance problems. Paradyn starts by looking for high-level problems (such as too much total synchronization blocking, I/O blocking, or memory delays), using only a small amount of instrumentation. Once a general problem has been found, more instrumentation is selectively inserted to find specific causes of the problem. The Performance Consultant module, which automatically directs the placement of instrumentation, has a knowledge base of performance bottlenecks and program structure so that it can associate bottlenecks with specific causes and with specific parts of a program.

The PVM version of Paradyn works on Sun SPARC. The MPI version works on IBM RS6000 and SP with AIX 4.1 or greater. There is also a version of Paradyn for Windows NT. The developers are currently porting Paradyn to the SGI/Cray Origin 2000. The dyninst library that provides a machine-independent interface for runtime program instrumentation is also available separately. Dyninst is used in Paradyn but can also be used to build other performance tools, debuggers, simulators, and steering systems.

Before running the program, the user can first define performance visualizations. These are defined in terms of metric-focus pairs. For example, the user might specify a histogram visualization with a metric of CPU time and a focus of a particular subset of processes executing a particular procedure. More than one metric-focus pair can be displayed in the same visualization. Alternatively or in addition, the user can start up the Performance Consultant. The Performance Consultant automatically enables and disables instrumentation for specific metric-focus pairs as it searches for performance bottlenecks. One can then start a visualization to display performance data corresponding to a bottleneck found by the Performance Consultant.

3.5 VAMPIR

VAMPIR is a commercial trace visualization tool from PALLAS GmbH. VAMPIRtrace, also available from PALLAS, is an instrumented MPI library. In addition to C and Fortran, VAMPIRtrace works with HPF compilers that emit MPI. VAMPIRtrace is provided for every HPC platform we know of, and VAMPIR for most of them.

Instrumentation is done by linking your application with the VAMPIRtrace library which interposes itself between your code and the MPI library by means of the MPI profiling interface. Running the instrumented code produces a merged trace file that can be viewed using VAMPIR. The VAMPIRtrace library also has an API for stopping and starting tracing and for inserting user-defined events into the trace file. The trace files generated by the MPI processes when the program is run are automatically collected and merged into a single trace file.

VAMPIR includes three main categories of visualization displays, which can be configured by the user by using pull-down menus to change options which are saved to a configuration file. The Process State Display displays every process as a box and displays the process state at one point in time. The Statistics display shows the cumulative statistics for the complete trace file in pie chart form for each process. The Timeline display shows process states over time and communication between processes by drawing lines to connect the sending and receiving process of a message. The VAMPIR Timeline display shows the time during which a process has constant state as a colored bar along the horizontal axis. One can obtain additional information about a state (or message) by selecting Identify State (or Identify Message) from the popup menu and then clicking on a colored bar (or message line). Selecting Communication Statistics from the popup menu diplays a matrix showing the cumulative lengths of messages sent between pairs of processes. By default, the Process State and Statistics displays summarize the complete history of the tracefile, but if the timeline display is open, the "Use Timeline Portion" option can be selected. In this mode, the displays show statistics about the time interval displayed in the timeline window and track changes in the timeline window.

3.6 Comparison

Based on the testing and observations described in the individual tool reviews, we provide the following summary of our evaluation of each tool on each of the evaluation criteria.

	Robustness	Usability	Portability	Scalability	Versatility
AIMS	Fair	Good	Fair	Good	Good
nupshot	Good	Good	Good	Good	Good
Paradyn	Fair	Good	Fair	Good	Good
SvPablo	Good	Good	Fair	Good	Good
VAMPIR	Excellent	Good	Excellent	Excellent	Good

If one can afford to buy a commercial tool, then VAMPIR is clearly a good choice because of its availability on all important HPC platforms and because it works well and has excellent support. All the tools we reviewed should continue to be of interest, however, because each offers unique capabilities.

4 Current Work on Hardware Performance Counter API

Although trace-based performance analysis tools with timeline views are useful for analyzing communication performance, attention should be paid first to optimizing single-processor performance. All known processors include hardware performance counters that can provide information needed for tuning single-processor performance, but some vendors do not provide APIs for accessing these counters, and for those that do provide them, the APIs are platform-specific and inconsistent between platforms. The goal of our project is to specify a standard application programmer interface (API) for accessing hardware performance counters. The specification will include a standard set of definitions for a common set of performance metrics that provide the information that most affects how we tune applications. Reference implementations of the API are planned for the IBM SP and the SGI/Cray Origin 2000. The reference implementations will be layered over the existing vendor-specific APIs for those platforms. The goal is to eventually encourage vendors to implement the standard API for their platforms. This is a Parallel Tools Consortium (Ptools) sponsored project, and more information may be found at the Ptools web site at http://www.ptools.org/.

References

1. S. Browne, J. Dongarra, and K. London. Review of performance analysis tools for MPI parallel programs. Technical Report PET TR 98-02, CEWES MSRC, Jan. 1998. Also available at http://www.cs.utk.edu/ browne/perftools-review/.
2. B. P. Miller, M. D. Callaghan, J. M. Cargille, J. K. Hollingsworth, R. B. Irvin, K. L. Karavanic, K. Kunchithapadam, and T. Newhall. The Paradyn parallel performance measurement tools. *IEEE Computer*, 28(11), Nov. 1995.
3. J. Yan, S. Sarukhai, and P. Mehra. Performance measurement, visualization and modeling of parallel and distributed programs using the AIMS toolkit. *Software – Practice and Experience*, 25(4):429–461, Apr. 1995.

Debugging Point-To-Point Communication in MPI and PVM

Dieter Kranzlmüller, Jens Volkert

GUP Linz, Johannes Kepler University Linz
Altenbergerstr. 69, A-4040 Linz, Austria/Europe
kranzlmueller@gup.uni-linz.ac.at
http://www.gup.uni-linz.ac.at:8001/

Abstract. Cyclic debugging of nondeterministic parallel programs requires some kind of record and replay technique, because successive executions may produce different results even if the same input is supplied. The NOndeterministic Program Evaluator NOPE is an implementation of record and replay for message-passing systems. During an initial record phase, ordering information about occurring events is stored in traces, which preserve an equivalent execution during follow-up replay phases. In comparison to other tools, NOPE produces less overhead in time and space by relying on certain properties of MPI and PVM. The key factor is the non-overtaking rule which simplifies not only tracing and replay but also race condition detection. In addition, an automatic approach to event manipulation allows extensive investigation of nondeterministic behavior.

1 Introduction

Debugging of parallel programs is concerned with location and correction of computational bugs and run-time failures in parallel code. The set of possible errors includes all bugs known from sequential debugging as well as additional obstacles introduced by process interaction (e.g. deadlocks [11]). As a consequence, a parallel debugger has to provide special capabilities to cope with communication errors and synchronization bugs.

A critical example are *race conditions* [9]. These are places in the code, where different event-ordering may occur, leading to different runtime-behavior. Thus, their existence introduces nondeterminism, which manifests itself through variations in program results during successive program runs, even if the same input data are supplied. The main problem of races is the "irreproducibility effect" [11], which means, that program executions cannot be reproduced easily. Furthermore, it is not ad hoc possible to guarantee, that repeated executions of the program reveal all possible results and errors. Both problems are equally important and have to be addressed in order to produce reliable software.

The focus of this paper is the solution of *NOPE*, the *NO*ndeterministic *P*rogram *E*valuator. NOPE is integrated in the Monitoring And Debugging environment MAD [4], a toolset for error detection and performance analysis of message-passing programs. Originally intended for the nCUBE 2 multiprocessor, MAD has now been transferred to the standard Message-Passing Interface MPI [8], with preparations for the Parallel Virtual Machine PVM [3]. During the design of the module NOPE, extensive studies of the communication libraries MPI and PVM were required, which influenced the resulting implementation through certain simplifications. The outcome is a record and replay mechanism, which produces less overhead in time and space than previous approaches.

The paper is organized as follows. The next section describes the relation between nondeterministic program behavior in message-passing programs and the debugging cycle in general. Afterwards an introduction of message-races in MPI and PVM is presented, which leads to the simplifications as implemented in NOPE. Section 4 describes the operation of NOPE and its integration into the debugging cycle. Conclusions and an outlook on future goals of this project summarize the paper.

2 Nondeterminism in Message-Passing Programs

The traditional approach to error detection is *cyclic debugging*. The program is executed again and again with the same input, allowing the user to gain more insight about program states and intermediate results with the debugger. The basic idea is as follows [12]: determine the results y of the arbitrary function F with a given input x. If x is a valid input for F, and the input/output pair $\langle x|y \rangle$ does not represent a correct computation of F, the error is located somewhere in function F. For that reason, F is split up into subfunctions $f0$, $f1$,... fn and repeated executions of F are used to determine the correct states between these subfunctions by analyzing intermediate results.

A simple sequential program is sketched in figure 1. The function F is split up into $f0$, $f1$, and $f2$, which perform the desired computation. The resulting output y is determined by the computation of F, the provided input x and the interaction with the system environment. If the input is the same and system-interactions can be reproduced, each iteration of the debugging cycle would yield the same output, and intermediate results can be analyzed with breakpoints and single-stepping.

In parallel programs the situation is more difficult, because subfunctions of F are executed on concurrent processes and all process-interactions are influenced by the computer system. The parallel program of figure 1 is executed on two processes. The function F is split up into $f0$, $f1$, and $f2$ on process 0, as well as $g0$, $g1$, and $g2$ on process 1. The output is again determined by the computation of F, the input x, and all system interactions. Since communication and synchronization are carried out by the system, even small changes in the system state (processor speed, scheduling decisions, or cache contents [4]) may trigger different behavior. Unfortunately several of these environmental parameters cannot be controlled by a debugger and thus may lead to changes in the execution path of a program.

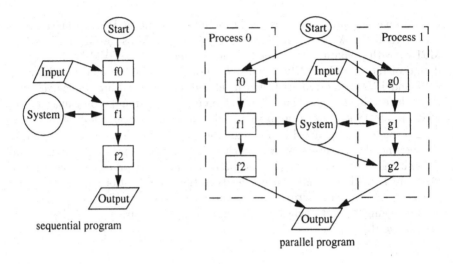

Fig. 1. Comparison of sequential and parallel program influences

In message-passing programs process interaction takes place through functions for sending and receiving messages. Basic operations are point-to-point communication with *send* and *receive*, and similar functions are provided by most message-passing libraries. For example, a function for blocking receive, where the process is blocked until a message arrives, is similar in MPI (*MPI_Recv* [8]), in PVM (*pvm_recv* [3]), and in vendor-specific libraries like for the nCUBE 2 multiprocessor machine (*nread*). As the main characteristics of these functions are the same for each of these systems, a (universally valid) primitive for a blocking receive operation can be defined as follows:

```
receive(buffer, source, tag, ...)
```

The identifier `buffer` provides the address for the incoming message, whereas `source` determines the origin of the message. The parameter `tag` is used to classify the contents of a message. Of course, additional parameters necessary for correct operation of message transmission or for use of additional functionality may be available depending on the message-passing system.

With the receive primitive defined as above a message can only be received if it matches the `source` and `tag` values specified by the receive operation. Additionally, the receiver may specify a wild card for `source` (e.g. ANY_SOURCE) and/or for `tag` (e.g. ANY_TAG), indicating that any `source` and/or `tag` are acceptable. However, due to the possible use of the wild card, a receive is a place in the code where nondeterminism may be introduced because of a message race [9]. This means, that two or more messages might race for acceptance at a particular receive and the order of their arrival may alter subsequent computations.

A simple example for a nondeterministic message-passing program is given in figure 2. When executing this code on 3 processes, process P0 receives the

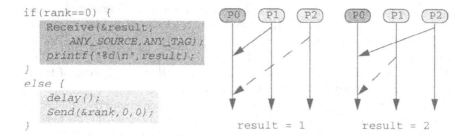

```
if(rank==0) {
    Receive(&result,
        ANY_SOURCE,ANY_TAG);
    printf("%d\n",result);
}
else {
    delay();
    Send(&rank,0,0);
}
```

Fig. 2. Simple nondeterministic message-passing program

message `result` from either process P1 or process P2 depending on which is faster. Afterwards `result` is printed, which reveals nondeterministic behavior.

In this simple example the source of nondeterminism seems clear. It is the function `delay()` before the send operation. Yet there are several reasons which could delay any process participating in a race. Among them are obviously different computational loads or branches in the code. Other causes are variations in processor speeds, load imbalances, and scheduling decisions, as well as conflicts on the communication network.

This means that manifold reasons for different message ordering may exist, but there is primarily one group of statements - the message receive operations - where nondeterministic behavior is observable. Furthermore, if programmers wouldn't use wild card receives, program behavior would be deterministic. However, there are reasons for programmers to introduce nondeterminism. An example is performance improvement, because paradigms like first-come first-served are often applied as optimizations. Another reason is reality itself, which can often be nondeterministic or chaotic and the same behavior has to be included in computational models.

3 Record and Replay Techniques

A solution for cyclic debugging of nondeterministic programs is provided by *record and replay techniques* [6]. During the record phase a program's execution is observed by a monitor, which stores relevant ordering information about occurring events in trace files. These traces are used to perform trace-driven replay of the program under the constraint of an equivalent execution [7].

First approaches of record and replay methods recorded the contents of each message as it is received [1], which introduced the problem of requiring significant monitor and storage overhead. An improvement was proposed with the *Instant Replay* technique that traced only the relative order of significant events instead of data associated with these events [6]. Other improvements were proposed by [9] and [10], which use on-the-fly analysis for further trace reduction.

The set of events that are important for all these approaches are communication events like send and receive. Ordering information of such events is usually generated with some kind of clock counters which number the occurrence of events. For example, [10] uses Lamport clocks [5] to obtain a partial order, while [9] applies vector clocks to perform on-the-fly race detection. The drawback is that calculating and updating these clock counters introduces additional monitor overhead and memory requirement. However, instead of tracing every event, only critical events need to be stored.

The approach of NOPE does not require any clock counters, while at the same time it traces only a subset of all communication events. This is achieved by taking advantage of a special characteristic available in MPI and PVM, which guarantees non-overtaking of point-to-point communication (see [8], section 3.5, and PVM man-page for pvm_send): If a sender sends two messages in succession to the same destination, and both match the same receive, then this operation cannot receive the second message if the first one is still pending.

Figure 3 contains three examples of point-to-point communication between processes. The graph (a) shows message transfer as guaranteed by MPI and PVM. On the other hand graph (b) is not possible (if the message tag is the same). However, indirect overtaking as shown in graph (c) is allowed and must be reproduced during replay.

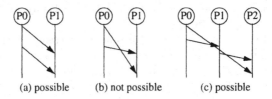

(a) possible   (b) not possible   (c) possible

Fig. 3. Overtaking rules in message-passing systems

Due to this non-overtaking characteristic, message-passing code is deterministic if the wild card is not used in receives. Besides that, nondeterministic programs follow a deterministic ordering of events on each process up to the point where the first wild card receive occurs. At that point several possibilities exist due to possible message races. During the record phase the first message to arrive will be accepted. If the replay phase guarantees the same message to be accepted instead of any available message, an equivalent execution is performed. Therefore an identifier for the incoming message must be stored during the record phase. Since overtaking of messages is not possible, this identifier is just the return value of parameter **sender**, which indicates the address of the sending process. Thus, a record and replay mechanism based on simple point-to-point communication can apply the following simplifications:

- Send events are not traced. They will always be in the same order.
- Receive events are traced only if the parameter sender contains a wild card.
- It is sufficient to store the id of the sender. The message tag can be neglected.
- Clock counters are not needed due to implicit ordering of messages based on the non-overtaking rule.

In addition, NOPE also instruments system calls to the random number generator. This has been implemented in order to research replay mechanisms including sources of sequential nondeterminism.

4 NOPE - Nondeterministic Program Evaluator

The simplifications derived from the non-overtaking rule of point-to-point communication are the basis of the record and replay technique used in NOPE. The application of NOPE to programs is rather simple and operates in three steps:

1. Instrument receive events and system calls (e.g. random number generator).
2. During the initial record phase generate initial traces by storing
   - sender id as accepted by wild card receive events, and
   - return values of system calls.
3. After the initial record phase subsequent replay phases can be used to generate complete traces.

The advantages of this method are that monitoring only occurs at places where nondeterminism may influence the program (receives, system calls). For example, no monitor overhead is generated at send events. Besides that the monitor performs only few and simply activities. Firstly, at receives the parameter **sender** has to be checked. Only if its value is a wild card, the monitor has to store the sender id of the incoming message. By using one trace file per process, only one integer value per wild card receive is required. Secondly, there is no need to update and store any clock counters, nor to attach any counters to the transmitted messages, which reduces the overhead significantly.

Step 3 is important for the analysis. The partial traces of the initial record phase are only needed to perform a correct replay of the program. Therefore it is necessary to generate all additional data for program analysis during subsequent replay phases. However, since the initial trace guarantees equivalent execution during replay, exhaustive analysis can be performed as necessary.

In MAD the analysis of traces is based on a communication graph visualization (see figure 4). Various possibilities for analysis are imaginable and have already been implemented in many tools. For race condition detection, wild card receives and racing messages can be colored, directing the user's attention to places of nondeterminism.

Again the non-overtaking rule is useful when determining message race candidates. As mentioned before, racing messages are all messages that may be accepted at a particular wild card receive. If overtaking is allowed, this leads to an enormous set of messages. In the non-overtaking case, the set is limited to all first messages that did not *happen before* [5] the receive (compare frontier races in [9]). Messages that happened before a particular receive are those that have already been accepted. The next message transmitted from each process to the target is then a possible candidate for a wild card receive. Consider each receive in figure 4 to be a wild card receive, then the set of racing messages for each receive contains at most $log(p) = 3$ elements.

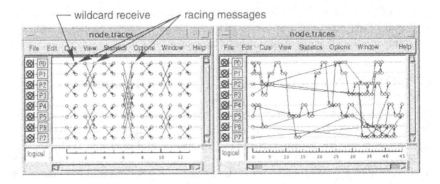

Fig. 4. Example event-graphs of a nondeterministic program's execution

A major problem is that the observed results do not necessarily represent the only valid execution of the program [2]. For example, in programs computing nondeterministic scenarios of reality (e.g. chaos models, crash simulations,...) several valid solutions may exist. Additionally, different execution paths of a program may compute the same results, while others may contain erroneous behavior. Without a suitable steering mechanism it may not be possible to find all prospective solutions, even if a large number of program runs are initiated.

With NOPE it is possible to uncover all possible execution paths of a nondeterministic program. Starting with either a correct pattern or any other pattern, NOPE can automatically generate the remaining patterns. Firstly, all possible race conditions of an initial program run are computed. Secondly, event manipulation is used to exchange the ordering of events and replay steps are initiated for each combination of message arrival at each wild card receive. Of course, this has to be done iteratively, because follow-up executions may contain additional race candidates. An example is given in figure 4. The left side shows a communication graph that has been traced during the first execution. With repeated event manipulation and replay, all possible combinations of message arrival are generated. The right graph contains another example of the same program.

5   Conclusion

This paper introduced *NOPE*, the *NO*ndeterministic *P*rogram *E*valuator for message-passing parallel programs. It allows cyclic debugging of nondeterministic code and improves previous record and replay approaches by taking advantage of the non-overtaking characteristic of point-to-point communication protocols as provided by MPI and PVM. Based on the non-overtaking characteristic, the monitor overhead of the record phase is decreased and the calculation of message-race candidates is simplified. If other message-passing mechanisms like collective communication or global operations are implemented under the same constraint, NOPE should be usable without major changes.

The future goals in this project are concerned with combinatorial testing of possible execution paths in nondeterministic programs. Simple toy applications can already be tested automatically. The main problem is not the size of the traces, but the number of replay steps needed, which can be enormous. However, in cases were it is possible to distinguish between intended and unintended races, promising results have already been obtained. Furthermore, investigations concerning the probability of messages being actually exchanged lead to further reduction of test cases.

References

1. Curtis, R.S. and Wittie, L.D.: BugNet: A Debugging System for Parallel Programming Environments. Proc. 3rd Intl. Conf. Distributed Computing Systems, Miami, FL, pp. 394-399 (Oct. 1982).
2. Damodaran-Kamal, S.K. and Francioni, J.M.: Testing Races in Parallel Programs with an OtOt Strategy. Proc. 1994 Intl. Symp. on Software Testing and Analysis, Seattle, WA (1994).
3. Geist, A., Beguelin, A., Dongarra, J., Joang, W., Manchek, R., Sunderam, V.: PVM 3 User's Guide and Reference Manual. Techn. Rep. ORNL/TM-12187, Oak Ridge Natl. Lab., Oak Ridge, TN (May 1994).
4. Kranzlmüller, D., Grabner, S. and Volkert, J.: Debugging with the MAD Environment. Parallel Computing, Vol. 23, Nos. 1-2, pp. 199-217 (Apr. 1997).
5. Lamport, L.: Time, Clocks, and the Ordering of Events in a Distributed System. Comm. ACM, pp. 558 - 565 (July 1978).
6. LeBlanc, T.J. and Mellor-Crummey, J.M.: Debugging Parallel Programs with Instant Replay. IEEE Trans. on Comp., Vol. C-36, No. 4, pp. 471-481 (1987).
7. Leu, E., Schiper, A., and Zramdini, A.: Execution Replay on Distributed Memory Architectures. Proc. 2nd IEEE Symp. on Parallel & Distributed Processing, Dallas, TX, pp. 106-112 (Dec. 1990).
8. Message Passing Interface Forum: MPI: A Message-Passing Interface Standard - Version 1.1. http://www.mcs.anl.gov/mpi/ (June 1995).
9. Netzer, R.H.B. and Miller, B.P.: Optimal Tracing and Replay for Message-Passing Parallel Programs. Supercomputing '92, Minneapolis, MN (Nov. 1992).
10. Ronsse, M.A. and Kranzlmüller, D.: RoltMP - Replay of Lamport Timestamps for Message Passing Systems. Proc. 6th EUROMICRO Workshop on Parallel and Distributed Processing, Madrid, Spain, pp. 87-93, (Jan. 21-23, 1998).
11. Snelling, D.F. and Hoffmann, G.-R.: A comparative study of libraries for parallel processing. Proc. Intl. Conf. on Vector and Parallel Processors, Computational Science III, Parallel Computing, Vol. 8 (1-3), pp. 255-266 (1988).
12. Wasserman, H. and Blum, M.: Program result-checking: a theory of testing meets a test of theory. Proc. 35th IEEE Symp. Foundations of Computer Science, pp. 382-392 (1994).

Monitoring PVM Programs Using the DAMS Approach

José C. Cunha and Vítor Duarte

Universidade Nova de Lisboa, Faculdade de Ciências e Tecnologia
Departamento de Informática *
2825 Monte de Caparica, Portugal
{jcc,vad}@di.fct.unl.pt

Abstract. Monitoring tools are fundamental components of a development environment as they provide basic support for performance evaluation, debugging, and program visualization. We describe our experiments with several monitoring tools for PVM, namely XPVM, developed at ORNL, Tape/PVM, developed at IMAG Lab, and DAMS, developed at UNL. These tools are compared and their use is described to support instrumentation and monitoring of a high level distributed language, PVM-Prolog, an extension to Prolog that provides an interface to PVM. This language is being used for the implementation of multi-agent systems, and it provides support for heterogeneous programs, built from C and Prolog components that communicate using PVM.

1 Introduction

In order to support the monitoring of parallel and distributed applications many tools have been developed in the recent past for distinct platforms and programming environments. In many cases PVM [2] is being used as the basic programming layer that provides an adequate degree of portability, architecture and operating system independence, and rapid prototyping. Such increased use was accompanied by efforts to provide monitoring support for PVM programs. Among the existing tools there are a large diversity of supported functionalities, often offered in a very monolithic way. Basic monitoring support such as code instrumentation and event generation, buffering, transfer, storage, and presentation, is tightly coupled with some given mode of operation, and it is not easy or possible to adapt or modify. For example, XPVM [5] includes built-in support for execution tracing, a PVM control console, and a display tool.

In this paper we discuss an alternative approach, which is based on a software architecture, called DAMS [3], that provides an infrastructure for the implementation of monitoring, debugging, and resource management that can be adapted according to user and application requirements. We describe our experimentation with the above approaches that we have used to instrument and monitor

* Thanks to B. Moscão, J. Vieira, D. Pereira. To EU COPERNICUS SEPP(CIPA-C193-0251), HPCTI(CP-93-5383), the Portuguese CIENCIA, PRAXIS XXI PRO-LOPPE and SETNA-ParComp, and DEC EERP PADIPRO(P-005).

programs in the PVM-Prolog language [7]. This allowed us to compare those tools in a practical setting and exercise important aspects such as information gathering, buffering, transfer, processing, and archiving, as well as information analysis, interpretation, and visualization.

The paper is organized as follows. In section 2 we present an overview of the main requirements for a monitoring tool. In Section 3 we describe the DAMS approach. Section 4 discusses our experimentation with the monitoring of PVM-Prolog programs, using XPVM, Tape/PVM, and DAMS, and compare such experiments. In Section 5 we comment related work, and finally we present some conclusions.

2 PVM Monitoring Tools

The goal of the monitoring activity is to gather runtime information about a target computation. This information may be used by tools at distinct levels of a computing system and for very different purposes such as program visualization, program testing and debugging, and performance evaluation.

Event Identification and Generation. Ideally, one would like to have a high-level user interface for the specification of the events to be monitored. This depends on the type of instrumentation that is applied into the target program (into the source code, into the library code, into the object code, or at the kernel level code). A significant example of an advanced tool that supports automatic probe insertion and dynamic instrumentation of parallel programs, including support for PVM applications, is Paradyn [8]. In XPVM [5] the instrumentation of the PVM library is supported so that the only requirement is for the user to select the PVM calls that should be monitored. Tools like Tape/PVM and PGPVM are also based on the instrumentation of the PVM library and allow to trace specific classes of PVM calls or specific program source modules. Such tools additionally support the specification of user-defined events, but this must be explicitly programmed by the user. PVaniM [10] also supports on-line monitoring based in periodic sampling of some values. The sampling rate is defined by the user as a compromise between the update rate of the visualizations and the application perturbation.

Event Buffering, Transfer, and Processing. Local event buffering allows to maintain the collected events in the local memory of each node, so that the monitoring communication overhead can be kept as low as possible. Possibly, event transfer to a central monitoring and storage node can take place in the end of the execution. However, there is the problem of local memory overflow so periodic flushing of events may become necessary during runtime. The amount of collected information can also be restricted to user-defined events. Concerning the user, an operation mode supporting on-line event transfer may be required to allow further event interpretation and visualization to proceed during runtime.

In XPVM, the frequent event transfer to the central XPVM daemon using PVM messages is related to the typical use of XPVM for on-line program visualization. Alternatively, XPVM allows the user to select a post-mortem visualization mode but this doesn't disable the on-line event transfer and visualization. In Tape/PVM and PGPVM, post-mortem event transfer is the only option. Besides sampling, PVaniM event generation can also rely on tracing. Such options are under user control, as well as the specification of off-line or on-line event processing and visualization.

Event Storage and Presentation. Event storage in a central monitoring node is required in order to support further event processing, analysis and interpretation. Some related issues concern the formats of the event traces, their efficient storage, manipulation and access by other tools, and the management of causally consistent event orderings [11]. In XPVM, event storage in a trace file is performed in a meta-format (SDDF) allowing flexibility in event processing. The events are reordered if necessary to preserve the causality between send and receive events. In Tape/PVM, event storage takes place in the end of the execution, in a specific format. There is a monitoring starting phase that performs a first physical clock synchronization, allowing more "consistent" timestamp information on the event records, although it can take some time. An upper limit can be imposed by the user. An ending phase performs a final adjustment of the timestamps. By relying on off-line event transfer and storage, and this type of synchronization, Tape/PVM can compensate the intrusion effect. In PVaniM, a separate command reorders the events in the end to preserve the causality in the final trace.

2.1 Flexibility of the Monitoring Architecture

A monitoring system should have a flexible internal architecture, allowing easy configuration, and adaptation to specific low-level platforms. Concerning PVM monitoring tools, hardware and operating system heterogeneity are typically supported, even if most of the tools depend on the specific PVM version being used. Additionally, concerning easy configuration and tailoring to the application needs, most of the tools are not so flexible because their architectures are more or less based on the PVM internal mechanisms. Also, the user sees them as monolithic blocks with a closed set of functionalities. For example XPVM provides built-in PVM control console, trace execution, and on-line display. There are few possibilities of changing its internal event processing strategies.

Similar considerations would apply to the other mentioned tools. Their reconfiguration to meet new functionalities would require great knowledge and internal changes to their architectures.

2.2 Tool Interfacing and Integration

Efforts on the definition of more uniform and standard monitoring interfaces are essential towards the successful support of environments that integrate many high level tools. In order to handle the distinct and evolving requirements posed by such tools, a monitoring layer should provide well-defined interfaces, and support easy definition of new services. This goal motivates the search for an extensible set of basic mechanisms for event handling, including accessing, filtering, searching, which can be met for example by object-oriented interfaces to manipulate meta-formats like SDDF[1].

Concerning tool interfacing, several requirements should be satisfied:

1. On-line interaction of the monitoring tool and an external observer such as the detected events are passed on to the observer, according to several possible modes of operation. On-line interaction between an external controller or observer such as a debugger, and the target computation.
2. Support of dynamic attachment and detachment of observer and controller tools. Support of multiple tools, acting upon the same ongoing computation, and requiring coordination and synchronization.

Concerning the PVM monitoring tools under analysis, namely XPVM, Tape/PVM, PGPVM, PVaniM, tool interaction can only be achieved through the trace file, so this always implies an off-line processing and interpretation of events. None of the above requirements is satisfied.

3 The DAMS

The DAMS system (Distributed Applications Monitoring System) supports the monitoring and control of applications consisting of distributed Target Processes. It has the software architecture shown in Figure 1.

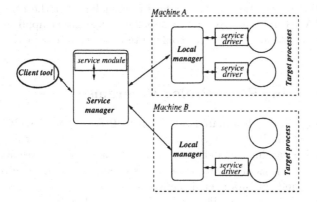

Fig. 1. DAMS Architecture

DAMS is organized as a set of Local Manager Processes (LM), one on each physical node. They supervise the local processes and the communication with the central Service Manager Process (SM). The SM process does not directly handle the application commands. These commands are forwarded to Service Modules that are responsible for their interpretation, according to each service (e.g. debugging, profiling or resource management). On each node, Local Managers act as intermediate between the SM and the Driver processes, by passing commands to the Drivers and sending the replies back to the SM. The Drivers apply the client commands to each Target Process.

DAMS provides well-defined interfaces between the client tools, the SM, the LM processes, and the Drivers, in the form of an internal message-based protocol which is architecture and system independent. It can be mapped onto different underlying communication platforms such as PVM, MPI or TCP/IP sockets. Each DAMS implementation assures there is no interference between the internal DAMS messages and the messages exchanged by the target processes.

DAMS includes a basic built-in set of commands so that the SM can launch, interact and destroy configurations of LM and Driver processes, and the Drivers can be dynamically attached to target processes. Asynchronous event notification is also supported so that each client tool can define an handler to be invoked on event occurrence. This can be used for tool synchronization e.g. involving a debugger and a visualization tool. DAMS does not include any other built-in services. Each service must be explicitly added by specifying a pair (Service Module, Driver). Actually, each Service Module contains the functions defining a specific service, and this code is linked with the Service Manager on system configuration. During execution, each existing service can be accessed by the client tools through an interface library that passes the client requests to the corresponding SM. Multiple concurrent client tools can coexist in a DAMS configuration. The current prototype runs on top of PVM, on a heterogeneous Ethernet LAN with Linux/PC's, and a FFDI-based cluster of OSF/1 DEC Alpha processors. It allows the exploitation of the Alpha Ethernet links for the communications between DAMS managers, at the same time as the target application can use the FDDI connections. This can contribute to a reduction in the monitoring intrusion.

4 Monitoring PVM-Prolog Programs

PVM-Prolog [7] is a distributed extension to Prolog that provides a complete interface to PVM. The interface was already used to implement an agent-based language [9]. Reasoning models based on distributed agents are also being developed for diagnosis applications, and this experimentation requires a flexible development and execution environment. Besides supporting rapid prototype development, PVM-Prolog allows to bridge the gap between such high level abstractions and actual PVM execution:

PVM Interface. This is based on a set of built-in Prolog predicates for the spawning of independent Prolog evaluators (as PVM tasks), in local and remote processors. This includes the passing of top goals to such tasks and PVM-like communication of Prolog terms.

Language heterogeneity. A lower level set of Prolog predicates gives access to
all PVM functions, namely to spawn PVM tasks that can execute Prolog or
any kind of executable files. This also supports the communication between
PVM-Prolog and C/PVM tasks, by packing, passing and converting Prolog
terms to C structures.

Multi-threading. A multi-threaded model supports internal concurrency with
user-level threads. Each thread solves an individual goal within a PVM-
Prolog task. Communication between threads is supported by shared queues
using specific predicates.

User-defined Prolog and thread predicates, and PVM-like predicates are supported by C code. The latter require argument conversion and passing to the
C/PVM functions. Some predicates for spawning and communication have distinct parameters than the PVM functions. For example, there is a predicate to
spawn a Prolog task and pass a Prolog goal as an argument, and the implementation must launch the Prolog task as an executable file, and pass the PVM
arguments.

Several experiments were performed in order to support monitoring of PVM-
Prolog programs. One goal was to trace events related to user-defined Prolog
predicates; PVM predicates; and thread predicates. Another goal was to access
and visualize the trace by using existing off-line and on-line visualization packages at the same abstraction level as defined by the application and not only at
the PVM level.

4.1 Using Some PVM Monitoring Tools

XPVM. As the supported instrumentation is present in PVM there is no need
to change the PVM-Prolog system or the application. The user selects PVM calls
for monitoring through the XPVM GUI. Even if the user is only using the PVM-
Prolog level, one must know about PVM so to understand the relation between
the PVM calls presented by the XPVM and the PVM related predicates. Then
the application must be launched from the XPVM console. One cannot attach
XPVM to already running applications, without using the GUI. As XPVM runs
synchronously with the application it introduces great perturbation but allows
on-line visualization. In the end the user can make a post-mortem analysis.

Tape/PVM. We had to build an instrumented PVM-Prolog version. Code for
the starting/ending phases of the Tape/PVM monitoring was added. A rewrite of
the C code of each PVM-Prolog predicate was required, replacing each PVM call
with its instrumented version as supplied by the Tape/PVM library. New event
descriptions, corresponding to PVM-Prolog user-defined and thread predicates
can be inserted in the trace file using a specific Tape function in specified points
of the PVM-Prolog code. Selective monitoring of certain classes of PVM calls
and modules of the source code (C) can be specified by the user. Interaction with
other tools is only possible through the final trace file. An existing filter has been
used to obtain a NPICL[12] format enabling visualization using Paragraph[4].

A Monitoring Service in DAMS. Based on the ability to include new Service Modules we implemented a monitoring service on the DAMS that is supported by a "Service Module" (SM), a "Driver" in each machine and a user console for controlling the service. A library that is linked with each target process supports the interaction with the driver, and the instrumentation of the application code.

The following components were implemented:

The SM manages the monitoring service, including functions to start the drivers in all the machines, detecting the end of the monitoring phase and collecting the traces from each driver;

The Driver stores the trace data generated by the instrumentation library in the local processes. The information is buffered locally until requested by the "Service Module".

The Instrumentation library interacts with the local driver to connect the target process to the driver, to collect the event descriptions and to close the connection.

The Console allows the user to launch the monitoring system and its components in all the machines, and provides status information. During runtime, the user can request the already collected trace for each individual machine or process.

The PVM-Prolog predicates were instrumented to generate events corresponding to the start and end of each predicate call. The event description includes time-stamp, process identifier, identification of the call and information on the call parameters and result. The current monitoring service module asks for the trace in the end or by user request. Automatic on-line transfer is easily achieved. A conversion program enabled the generation of a NPICL trace obtaining a global trace preserving a causality consistent event ordering, and allowing the use of ParaGraph for post-mortem program visualization.

5 Related Work

There are other monitoring systems for PVM that could have been tested. Some have a similar architecture to the Tape/PVM. They allow the monitoring of the PVM calls and use some traditional techniques for reducing the perturbation. Other systems, as Paradyn [8], represent a pioneering effort to separate the interfacing services and their implementation, as well as providing well-defined interfaces between separate modules. The On-line Monitoring Interface Specification (OMIS) [6] is another effort to provide a built-in standard interface. Its goal is to allow faster tool development and portability by decoupling the tools and the monitor. OMIS also allows adding new library services.

DAMS follows a more basic approach as it just provides the infrastructure and the basic mechanisms. Monitoring and debugging services can be replaced or modified freely, in part or all, according to the user and tool needs. Additionally it eases the implementation of these services in distinct platforms including heterogenous ones.

6 Conclusions and Ongoing Work

We briefly compared some PVM monitoring tools and described their use to support the monitoring of a distributed programming language. We have presented the main motivation to the DAMS approach, and showed how it was used to implement a monitoring service for that language. Due to its neutrality concerning both the client tools and the target processes, DAMS provides a flexible and easily extensible environment. It supports on-line interaction between the target application and the tools and dynamic attachment of multiple concurrent tools. DAMS is an ongoing project. Its open organization is allowing us to increase its functionalities in many directions. It has been used to support a distributed process-level debugging service [3], and it is being extended to support a thread-level debugger, and a thread visualization service. DAMS supports the monitoring and control of heterogeneous applications, with PVM and MPI components. A distributed debugger for PVM-Prolog is also being developed as a DAMS service.

References

[1] R. A. Aydt. The pablo self-defining data format. Technical report, DCS-University of Illinois, 1992.

[2] A. Beguelin, J. J. Dongarra, G. A. Geist, R. Manchek, and V. S. Sunderam. A user's guide to PVM parallel virtual machine. Technical Report ORNL/TM-118266, Oak Ridge National Laboratory, 1991.

[3] J. C. Cunha, J. Lourenço, J. Vieira, B. Moscão, and D. Pereira. A framework to support parallel and distributed debugging. In *To apperar in Proc. of HPCN'98, Amesterdan*, 1998.

[4] M. T. Heath and J. A. Etheridge. ParaGraph: A tool for visualizing performance of parallel programs. Univ. of Illinois and Oak Ridge National Lab., 1992.

[5] J. A. Kohl and G. A. Geist. XPVM 1.0 user's guide. Technical Report ORNL/TM-12981, Oak Ridge National Laboratory, 1995.

[6] T. Ludwing, R. Wismüller, V. Sunderam, and A. Bode. OMIS – on-line monitoring interface specification. 1997.

[7] R. Marques and J. C. Cunha. Using PVM with logic programming interface. In *Proc. of 2nd EuroPVM User's Meeting*, Lyon, France, 1995.

[8] B. P. Miller, J. K. Hollingsworth, and M. D. Callaghan. The paradyn parallel performance tools and PVM. Technical report, Department of Computer Sciences, University of Wisconsin, 1994.

[9] M. Schroeder, R. Marques, G. Wagner, and J. C. Cunha. CAP - concurrent action and planning: Using PVM-Prolog to implement vivid agents. In *Proc. of PAP'97*, London, U.K., 1997.

[10] B. Topol, J. Stasko, and V. Sunderam. PVaniM 2.0 - online and postmortem visualization support for PVM. Technical report, Georgia Inst. Tech. and Emory University, 1995.

[11] M. van Riek, B. Tourancheau, and X.-F. Vigouroux. General approach to the monitoring of distributed memory multicomputers. Technical Report UT-CS-93-204, epartment of Computer Science, University of Tennessee, 1993.

[12] P. H. Worley. A new picl trace file format. Technical Report ORNL/TM-12125, Oak Ridge National Laboratory, 1992.

Functional Message Passing with OPAL–MPI

Thomas Nitsche[*] and Wolfram Webers

Institut für Informations- und Kommunikationstechnik, Technische Universität Berlin,
Franklinstr. 28/29, Sekr. FR5-13, 10587 Berlin, Germany,
{nitsche,wwebers}@cs.tu-berlin.de

Abstract This paper presents OPAL-MPI, our integration of the message passing interface into the functional programming language OPAL. It describes the problems occurring when the functional style with MPI are combined. One of them is the presence of dynamic data structures which requires the creation of an internal communication buffer where the data is packed.

The resulting programmer interface is more abstract and high-level than in MPI as data types and sizes need not to be passed as parameters to the communication operations. It allows arbitrary data types and even functions to be send quite easily.

However, due to the lack of a request handling in MPI 1.1 non-blocking receives cannot be implemented efficiently with full overlapping of computation and communucation.

1 Introduction

For distributed memory machines like most massively parallel processing systems (MPP) or workstation clusters message passing is used for data exchange between the different processors. As most vendors support MPI [6] or PVM [4] implementations, these standard libraries can be used for platform independent parallel programming. The interfaces are defined for commonly used imperative languages like Fortran, C and C++. This article presents the integration of the message passing interface into the world of functional programming languages.

Our implementation is based on OPAL [2,1], a strongly typed, higher-order functional language with a distinctive algebraic flavour. In a pure functional language the result of a function only depends on its arguments. However, communication has inherently side-effects as data is received from an external processor. These I/O side-effects are encapsulated with the so-called *command-monad* [7], a special data type com[data] which describes an I/O operation and yields a result of type data when executed. For optimisation purposes and for the integration of system libraries the OPAL compiler offers an interface for a direct call of C-functions from OPAL programs [5]. In the current OPAL library e.g. UNIX processes and Tcl/Tk are integrated this way. Thus the MPI library routines can be incorporated as well.

---

[*] The work is being supported by a scholarship from the German Research Foundation (DFG).

2 Communication Buffer

The two main problems of the integration of MPI into functional languages are the data types and access to memory.

A functional language allows recursive data types which in general are dynamic types like lists or trees which results in pointer structures. In addition parameterisation yields to complex types where elements are structured and possibly dynamic as well. MPI, on the other side, assumes in principle the data to be stored in a contiguous memory block. More formally, a datatype is specified by a sequence of basic data types and displacements which allows strides or structures as well. Compared to the flexibility of functional data types, the MPI data types are restricted to regular, static structures while a functional data type is in general dynamic. Thus the functional data has to be transformed to an MPI type in order to be transferable.

The second problem is that the message passing routines require an address of a communication buffer, where the data is read in case of send and stored in case of receive, while functional languages does not support direct memory access. The memory is managed automatically and the user has no control over where a certain value is stored.

To solve these problems we encode an arbitrary OPAL object into a *communication buffer*. This is an abstract data type which can only be accessed by pack and unpack routines simular to communication in PVM. In addition we provide a function to create a buffer of a certain size. Internally it is implemented as a byte array, so it can be directly given to a MPI routine as a parameter.

```
SIGNATURE MpiBuffer[data]
   SORT data                          -- parameter type
   SORT buffer                        -- communication buffer

   FUN pack: data → buffer            -- code data
   FUN unpack: buffer → data          -- restore data

   FUN make_buf : int → buffer        -- buffer of fixed size
   FUN pack_size: buffer → int        -- size of a buffer
```

The encoding and decoding of an OPAL object is possible as the OPAL system tags data objects simular to object-oriented languages with structure information. Consider for example an array of sequences. As sequences are dynamic data structures, we cannot just give the array as a parameter to MPI_Send. This would only send the pointers to the target processor but not the lists itself. Thus we have to pack the data first.

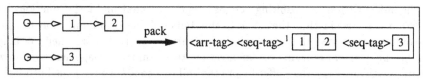

---

[1] Actually not a seq-type flag is stored here but a structured element flag, its size etc.

In the same way even functions can be encoded and therefore transfered with MPI. This feature is supported by the OPAL system through dynamic linking. Unfortunately the MPI library is statically linked so the communication of functions is currently restricted to those functions which code is available on the receiving side as in SPMD style programs. This enables an easy implementation of master-slave applications with distributed dynamic data objects. Only the different initialization or worker functions have to be send to the slaves.

The advantage of this communication buffer type is the abstraction of data type and size arguments which are required by the communication functions of MPI. The programmer does not have to care how OPAL objects are given to MPI. On the other hand, we cannot take advantage of a possible optimisation for certain MPI data types, as due to the presence of dynamic data types we always have to pack the data into a standard format.

3 Low-level Point-to-Point Communication

The blocking communication functions can be integrated quite easily using the abstract communication buffer described above. For the recv-command we have to provide a buffer as parameter and get a modified buffer with the received data as a result, while the send-command yields nothing (void).

```
SIGNATURE MpiPt2pt   --low − level  interface

SORT request

          --send (data _buf , target , tag , comm )
FUN send : buffer × int × int × communicator → com[void]
FUN recv : buffer × int × int × communicator → com[buffer]

FUN isend : buffer × int × int × communicator → com[request]
FUN irecv : buffer × int × int × communicator → com[request]

FUN wait : request → com[buffer × status]
FUN test : request → com[option[buffer] × status]
```

More interesting are the non-blocking functions. Here we have the problem that the communication buffer will only later be filled with data, so it should only be read after receiving the data. To overcome this side-effect we encapsulate the buffer within the resulting request type. The test and wait functions have to be changed in that they deliver this buffer if the communication has been completed. In case that the same buffer variable is used in another call before finishing the non-blocking communication, the memory management system will automatically copy the buffer before the call to isend/irecv. Thus both buffers can be used independently without any side-effects.

4 High-level Programmer Interface

The use of the communication buffer within the programmer interface is not optimal. As for a receive operation a buffer has to be provided, the receiver has to create a buffer using pack on some dummy data or make_buf with a certain size. This means the programmer explicitly has to take care of memory management which is in contrast to the pure functional paradigm and should be avoided if possible.

The second problem is that the necessary size of a reception buffer can hardly be estimated by the user. Even if he knows the data he will receive the buffer size is compiler dependent, as the pack function stores in the buffer not only the data itself but also structure information necessary for the reconstruction of the data object. This behaviour is inadequate for functional programs, as another processor may create a possible error due to not enough buffer size, i.e. a side-effect, which is (sometimes) unpredictable from the program code.

Thus we implemented a higher level interface where no buffers but directly the data are given as parameters

```
SIGNATURE Pt2pt[data]   --high − level interface
SORT data   --parameter type

        --send (value , target , tag , comm )
FUN send: data × int × int × communicator → com[void]
FUN recv: int × int × communicator → com[data]

FUN isend: data × int × int × communicator → com[request]
FUN irecv: int × int × communicator → com[request]

FUN wait: request → com[data × status]
FUN test: request → com[option[data] × status]
```

The programmer does not have to take care of buffers and memory or which data type to communicate, he can just write

$$\text{send}(\text{value}, \text{target}, \text{tag}, \text{comm}).$$

Internally the data will be packed, handed over to MPI and the buffer will be released afterwards. However, in order to avoid a buffer overflow runtime error we have to tell the receiver the buffer size needed for reception. To achieve this, two protocols are possible.

4.1 Two-step Protocol

This protocol sends the buffer size and afterwards the data buffer itself. So the receiver can allocate the buffer in between. The buffers will be de-allocated automatically by the run-time system if they are no longer used.

Sender	Receiver

```
         Sender                              Receiver
data_buf = pack(value)
size = pack_size(data_buf)
size_buf = pack(size)                 size_buf = pack(< dummy_int >)
send(size_buf, ...)            ⟶ recv(size_buf, ...)
                                      size = unpack(size_buf)
                                      data_buf = make_buf(size)
send(data_buf, ...)           ⟶ recv(data_buf, ...)
                                      unpack(data_buf)
```

As this protocol always sends two messages we have higher communication costs. Especially for small messages the time may nearly double.

4.2 Fixed-size Protocol

In order to avoid the overhead of the first protocol the receiver can create a buffer of fixed block_size. The sender splits the message into a first part of maximal block_size and a rest which is only sent if the message is too big to fit into the first block. The current message size will be added at the beginning of the first block:

```
         Sender                              Receiver
data_buf = pack(value)            data_buf = make_buf(block_size)
size = pack_size(data_buf)
(first, rest) =
    split([size, data_buf],
          block_size)
send(first, ...)                  ⟶ recv(data_buf, ...)
                                      [size, data_buf] = [data_buf]
if size > block_size                  if size > block_size
                                         rest = make_buf(size − block_size)
    send(rest, ...)               ⟶      recv(rest, ...)
                                      unpack([data_buf, rest])
```

For small messages this protocol has nearly no overhead as only one message is sent. Note that only the data itself and one integer for the size information but not a full block_size block is transfered. Big messages are split into two messages and we therefore have one additional latency time as overhead. However, if block_size is big enough this time becomes neglectable relative to the total communication time. Due to its minimal overhead this protocol has been used for our implementation. The choice of block_size is a tradeoff between communication time and memory requirements.

4.3 Non-blocking Communication

The protocols described so far work properly for blocking communication. For non-blocking communication a call to irecv should issue a communication request which can operate overlapping with some computation. Unfortunately we can only issue the first of possible two message receives of our protocol as the second receive can only be started if the first has finished due to the unknown buffer size. If we would make the first receive blocking, we would have to wait for the message to arrive before the high-level `irecv` can return. This includes at least the network latency but also the time until the corresponding send operation has started. If both processors issue an `irecv` first this may even deadlock. That is why we have to use a non-blocking irecv for the first (`block_size`) message. In that case the `test` function has not only to check if the message has arrived but also to start the second message receive in case of a big data transfer and test for its completion.

The problem is that without an intermediate call of `test` only the first message can arrive by the time we finally call a closing `wait`. Thus it might be that the second message only starts if `wait` is called, so the overlapping of computation and communication is limited to the first message block. What we actually want is an overlapping with both messages. So the second message should start automatically via an interrupt to a service routine as soon as the first communication operation has finished and thus the necessary buffer size is available. This could not be done as our current implementation is based on MPI 1.1 which does not provide such capabilities and therefore does no allow an efficient implementation of the high-level abstraction. MPI-2 [3] request handles shall provide this capability.

4.4 Collective Operations

For the collective communication operations the abstraction of the data type in the interface is even more notable. The programmer is completely freed from the task to calculate proper offsets and displacements which are normally necessary under MPI.

```
SIGNATURE Collective[data]
  SORT data    --parameter type

  FUN bcast : data × int × communicator → com[data]

  FUN scatter : seq[data] × int × communicator → com[data]
  FUN gather : data × int × communicator → com[seq[data]]

        --reduce (value , op , commute , root , comm )
  FUN reduce : data × (data × data → data) × bool
               × int × communicator → com[data]
```

Internally `scatter` packs the sequence of data objects into a single buffer and sends it using MPI_Scatterv, as the different objects may have different sizes.

The reduce operation under MPI normally applies an operation on a (standard) data type onto multiple values *in parallel*, which is used to combine multiple small messages. As in OPAL a data object may be arbitrary complex and large, this is not really necessary anymore. Therefore we apply the operator to a single - but complex - data element rather than to a list of (simple) data. As the buffer size may change during the reduce operation we cannot use MPI_Reduce which requires fixed messages sizes. For that reason reduce had to be re-implemented in OPAL.

5 Performance

We wrote some benchmarks to compare the C and the OPAL implementation. There are basically taken from the **mpbench** [8] program. The *latency* benchmark measures the time to launch a send operation. The *roundtrip* benchmark measures how long it takes a message to be echoed by the destination node. Next we look for the throughput of our implementation. We send a message to one node and receive a small ack packet. The result reflects the *bandwidth* in MB per second. The last benchmark *broadcasts* portions of the communication buffer the all other nodes and receives for each broadcast a small ack packet.

All the benchmarks allocate a communication buffer of size 8MB and transfer portions of it. To be able to compare the OPAL version with the C version we use the OPAL datatype *denotation* which represents a continues character array. Further it uses an initial communication buffer size of 20KB with an increment of 1KB which is used for dynamically growing buffers. Note, these benchmarks represent only the overhead of the OPAL implementation in comparison to the equivalent C version. They do not reflect the real performance of the architecture. All measurements were done with 2 nodes resp. 4 nodes for broadcast and 100 iterations on a Cray T3E.

	Latency ms		Roundtrip Transact./sec.		Bandwidth MB/sec.		Broadcast MB/sec.	
Size	C	OPAL	C	OPAL	C	OPAL	C	OPAL
64KB	0.34	0.88	1111.2	329.5	193.7	65.7	133.1	34.3
256KB	1.19	2.64	304.4	111.1	202.6	89.6	135.5	50.5
512KB	2.37	5.06	154.3	59.4	203.3	96.4	134.1	54.9
1MB	4.74	9.82	77.9	31.0	203.6	99.0	133.7	57.6
4MB	19.00	38.62	19.5	7.8	186.9	100.0	133.4	58.9
8MB	25.15	64.25	9.9	3.9	156.0	62.2	133.2	56.5

6 Conclusion

We described OPAL-MPI, our integration of the message passing interface as library routines into the functional programming language OPAL. There we concentrated on the basic communication functions. Other routines like e.g. communicator handling or MPE trace logging are more or less a direct mapping of OPAL-MPI calls to MPI calls and therefore omitted here.

Due to the nature of functional languages with its automatic handling of dynamic and parameterised data types, we always have to consider dynamic data structures (i.e. pointers) as elements of a data object. This required the creation of a communication buffer where the data is packed. The advantage is that the user does not have to handle the data types in a communication call, as this will be done automatically by OPAL-MPI. The high-level interface which even hides the buffer from the user is therefore easier to use than the standard MPI interface and allows arbitrary data types to be sent just with send(value, target, ...). Even functions can be communicated in SPMD style programs.

However, as the receiver has to know how much buffer space he has to provide, a protocol was needed which may cause a split into two messages for big data transfers. Due to the lack of a request handling like active messages or callbacks in MPI 1.1 non-blocking receives cannot be implemented efficiently with full overlapping of computation and communication.

The described interface of OPAL-MPI will be used for the implementation of *data distribution algebras* [9], a concept of parallel abstract data types with overlapping data parts.

References

1. Klaus Didrich, Andreas Fett, Carola Gerke, Wolfgang Grieskamp, and Peter Pepper. OPAL: Design and Implementation of an Algebraic Programming Language. In Jürg Gutknecht, editor, *Programming Languages and System Architectures, International Conference, Zurich, Switzerland, March 1994*, volume 782 of *Lecture Notes in Computer Science*, pages 228–244. Springer, 1994.
2. Klaus Didrich, Wolfgang Grieskamp, Christian Maeder, and Peter Pepper. Programming in the Large: the Algebraic-Functional Language Opal 2α. In *Proceeding of IFL'97: 9th. International Workshop on Implementation of Functional Languages , St Andrews, Scottland*, volume 1497 of *Lecture Notes in Computer Science*, pages 323–244. Springer, September 1997.
3. Message Passing Interface Forum. MPI-2: Extensions to the Message-Passing Interface. Technical report, University of Tennessee, Knoxville, Tenn., July 1997. ftp://ftp.mpi-forum.org/pub/docs/mpi-20.ps.
4. A. Geist, A. Beguelin, J. Dongarra, W. Jaing, R. Mancheck, and V. Sundram. *PVM: A Users' Guide and Tutorial for Networked Parallel Computing*. MIT Press, 1994.
5. Wolfgang Grieskamp and Mario Südholt. *Handcoder's Guide to OCS Version 2*. The OPAL Language Group, February 1994.
6. W. Gropp, E. Lusk, and A. Skellum. *Using MPI: Portable Parallel Programming with the Message Passing Interface*. MIT Press, 1995.
7. Simon Peyton Jones and Philip Wadler. Imperative functional programming. In *20'th Symposium on Principles of Programming Languages*. ACM Press, Charlotte, North Carolina, January 1993.
8. Philip J. Mucci. Mpbench version 3.1. a program to measure the performance of some essential operations of implementations of MPI and PVM. http://www.cs.utk.edu/mucci/mpbench.
9. Mario Südholt. *The Transformational Derivation of Parallel Programs using Data Distribution Algebras and Skeletons*. PhD thesis, Fachgruppe Übersetzerbau, Fachbereich Informatik, Technische Universität Berlin, August 1997.

An MPI–Based Run–Time Support to Coordinate HPF Tasks

Salvatore Orlando[1] and Raffaele Perego[2]

[1] Dip. di Matematica Appl. ed Informatica, Università Ca' Foscari di Venezia, Italy
[2] Istituto CNUCE, Consiglio Nazionale delle Ricerche (CNR), Pisa, Italy

Abstract. This paper describes $COLT_{HPF}$, an MPI–based run–time support for the coordination of concurrent and communicating HPF tasks. $COLT_{HPF}$ is conceived for use by a compiler of a high-level coordination language to structure a set of data-parallel HPF tasks according to popular forms of *task-parallelism*. Since it requires only small changes to the run–time support of the HPF compiler used, $COLT_{HPF}$ is easily portable among different compilation systems. The paper outlines design and implementation issues, and reports the results of experiments conducted on an SGI/Cray T3E.

1 Introduction

Due to its simplicity, the data-parallel programming model allows high-level parallel languages such as HPF [9] to be designed, which hide low-level programming details and let programmers to concentrate on the high-level exploitation of data parallelism. The compiler manages data distribution and translates the annotated source program into an SPMD code with explicit interprocessor communications and synchronizations. Unfortunately, many important parallel applications do not fit a pure data-parallel model and can be more efficiently implemented by exploiting both task and data parallelism [4]. The advantage of exploiting both forms of parallelism is twofold. On the one hand the capability of integrating task and data parallelism in a single framework allows the number of addressable applications to be enlarged. On the other hand, the exploitation of parallelism at different levels may significantly increase the scalability of applications which may exploit only a limited amount of data parallelism [7].

The promising possibility of integrating task parallelism within the HPF framework recently attracted much attention [10, 6, 14, 3]. A new standard for HPF was proposed, HPF 2.0, which introduces task parallelism by allowing TASK_REGION blocks to be specified [10]. Within a TASK_REGION, we may specify through ON blocks that a set of HPF tasks has to be executed concurrently on disjoint subsets of processors, where each task only accesses data distributed on the associated processor subset. Communications between tasks are accomplished by simple (array) assignments outside ON blocks, but inside the outer TASK_REGION block. The main disadvantage of the approach is its lacking in generality due to the strong restriction in the task interaction capabilities. In fact, the use of explicit assignments for inter-task communications does not allow programmers to specify an HPF task which, non-deterministically, waits for input data from several other HPF tasks, even though this communication pattern may occur very often in task-parallel programs. Other approaches which also requires changes to the original HPF 1.0 language were proposed [14, 6]. In these cases programmers have to specify an input/output list for all the HPF tasks involved rather than explicitly providing assignments to express communications. Here tasks can be either PURE HPF-like subroutines or simple statements. Since programmers don't specify either the allocation of tasks on specific subsets of processors, or explicit communications/assignments between tasks, the compiler has to (1) extract a data dependencies graph of the tasks, (2) decide the best allocation of these tasks, and (3) insert the proper communications between tasks. This approach is much more high-level than the one proposed for HPF 2.0, but it does require sophisticated compiling techniques for task allocation [14]. Nevertheless, the type of task interaction that can be specified is still deterministic. A different approach regards the design of an HPF binding for MPI, proposed by Foster et al. [5]. They propose a framework in which concurrent HPF tasks communicate by means of a restricted subset of MPI communication primitives. We believe that the exploitation of a message-passing interface is too much of a "low-level" approach for introducing task parallelism into HPF. The programmer is charged of all the efforts needed to exploit task parallelism, thus loosing most advantages deriving from the use of a high-level parallel language like HPF.

In this paper we present $COLT_{\text{HPF}}$ (COordination Layer for Tasks expressed in HPF), an MPI–based coordination/communication layer for HPF tasks. $COLT_{\text{HPF}}$ provides suitable mechanisms for starting distinct HPF data-parallel tasks on disjoint groups of processors, along with optimized primitives for inter-task communication where data to be exchanged may be distributed among the processors according to user-specified HPF directives. Although $COLT_{\text{HPF}}$ can be exploited to implement libraries of *skeletons*, it was primarily conceived for use by a compiler of a high-level coordination language to structure a set of data-parallel HPF tasks according to popular *task parallel paradigms*, such as *pipelines* and *processor farms* [8, 11]. The proposed high-level coordination language is described elsewhere [12]. Here we focus on $COLT_{\text{HPF}}$ implementation details, and we present some performance results. Although the framework is very different, many implementation issues addressed in the paper are common to those discussed by Foster et al [5]. A detailed discussion of the main differences between the two approaches can be found in [12].

2 $COLT_{\text{HPF}}$ implementation

We implemented $COLT_{\text{HPF}}$ on top of MPI and Adaptor HPF compilation system [2]. We believe that our technique is very general, so that a similar binding might easily be made with other HPF compilation systems that use MPI too.

The main issue to face for coordinating HPF tasks, are: (1) allowing distinct HPF tasks to be started concurrently on the same (MPI) virtual machine; (2) managing the communication of data distributed within HPF tasks. Note that the communication of data distributed among the task processors entails several point-to-point communications and, when the data and processor layouts of the sender and receiver tasks differ, it also requires the redistribution of the data exchanged; (3) providing an efficient support for signaling events between tasks, where these signals may be received non-deterministically to implement dynamic policies (e.g. dynamic scheduling techniques [12]).

In the following we discuss how $COLT_{HPF}$ adresses these three important issues. Note that most $COLT_{HPF}$ functionalities are implemented as HPF_LOCAL EXTRINSIC subroutines [9]. This means that when one of our primitives is invoked by an HPF task, all the processors executing the task switch from the single thread of control provided by HPF to an SPMD style of execution. According to the language definition, HPF_LOCAL subroutines have to be written in a restricted HPF language where, for example, it is not possible to transparently access data stored on remote processors.

Group definition and task loading

HPF compilers that use MPI as underlying communication layer exploit one or more MPI *communicators*, a powerful MPI abstraction that permits one to specify communications to occur only within groups of specific processors. Adaptor produces a code which exploits the MPI predefined global communicator MPI_COMM_WORLD to perform communications and also to ask for the rank identifying each processor and the total number of processors actually involved. Similar run-time inquiries are present in the code produced by any HPF compiler in order to arrange the logical processor layout onto the physical processor grid and consequently distribute data and computations among the physical processors actually involved. In order to permit Adaptor to support task parallelism, we had to slightly modify its run-time support. In particular our modified version of Adaptor produces an executable MPI code which:

1. reads during the initialization a *configuration file* containing mapping information. The file specifies the number M of HPF tasks constituting the parallel application as well as the name of the HPF subroutine executed by each task. Moreover, for each task t_i, $i = 1, \cdots, M$, it specifies the number N_i of processors reserved for its execution. Our simple mapping function associates HPF task t_i with the logical processors whose MPI ranks are in the range $[K_{i-1}, K_i)$, where $K_0 = 0$ and $K_i = K_{i-1} + N_i, \forall 1 \le i \le M$;

2. creates, M different MPI communicators, one for each group of processors executing an HPF task. At this purpose MPI provides a powerful primitive, MPI_Comm_split, which creates all the communicators we need simultaneously, all of them with the same name (MPI_LOCAL_COMM_WORLD). MPI_Comm_split is called by each MPI processor with a *color* parameter equal to its own task identifier $t_i, i = 1, \cdots, M$.

3. uses MPI_LOCAL_COMM_WORLD in all Adaptor-related MPI calls. In this way each HPF task still exploits a self-contained environment, and any HPF communication or collective operation only affects the appropriate processors. On the other hand, inter-task communications provided by $COLT_{HPF}$ exploit MPI_COMM_WORLD.

Once a suitable MPI environment has been created, we have to start the distinct HPF codes onto the disjoint MPI groups of processors. To this end, since according to the static SPMD model provided by MPI the same program has to be loaded on each node, the main entry point of the task-parallel HPF program is a "loader", which invokes the right HPF code on each group of processors. At the beginning the loader invokes the Adaptor initialization routine which create the disjoint MPI groups. Then, the loader, which is dynamically built on the basis of the configuration file described above, forces all the processors belonging to a task (i.e. the corresponding processor *group*) to call the appropriate HPF subroutine. HPF tasks have thus to be written as HPF subroutines, where the task local data are defined within the subroutines themselves.

Channel initialization and data transmission

$COLT_{HPF}$ associates a *descriptor* with each communication channel used to transmit a distributed array. Such descriptors are used to store information which is subsequently used to optimize communications. To fill the descriptors, all the processors of both the sender and receiver groups, by invoking suitable $COLT_{HPF}$ initialization primitives, have to carry out the following steps for each distributed array D to be exchanged:

1. inquire the HPF run-time support to find out the layout of D on the HPF processor grid associated with their own processor group. To this end, HPF provides an appropriate intrinsic subroutine [9];
2. exchange mapping information so that each processor involved knows the layout of D at both the sender and receiver sides;
3. on the basis of the information exchanged at the previous step, compute the intersections between D distributions at the sender and receiver sides. To this end, we adopted the *pitfalls* algorithm [13];
4. build, on the basis of the result of the *pitfalls* algorithm, the *Communication Schedule* that is used each time a communication actually occurs to pack (unpack) the elements of D, and send (receive) them to (from) each destination (source) processor. The *Communication Schedule* is stored by each processor in the descriptor associated with the communication channel.

When a $COLT_{HPF}$ send primitive is invoked to transmit a distributed structure, array data are packed by each processor of the sender group on the basis of the information stored in the channel descriptor, and sent to the processors of the receiver group. In the worst case each processor of the sender group may need to communicate with all the processors of the receiver one. However, the channel descriptor contains all the information needed, so that the processors involved carry out the "minimum" number of point-to-point communications needed to complete the task-to-task communication. Data are sent by means of asynchronous MPI send primitives that are invoked in an order which prevent several processors from simultaneously sending messages to the same destination. On the receiver side, the processors involved receive the messages and unpack the data still on the basis of the information stored in their descriptor. The exchange of scalar values between tasks is simpler. No channel setting is needed in this case. Since HPF scalars are replicated on all the processors of a given task, the send primitive is invoked by all the sender processors, but only the root processor of the source group actually broadcasts the scalar to the processors of the receiver group.

Special messages and non-determinism

Messages often need to be received in a non-deterministic way. For example, an HPF task may need to receive data from a task non-deterministically chosen among several possibilities. The problem is that to ensure correctness the same non-deterministic choice must be globally made by all the processors executing the receiving task. In other words, if a task $\bar{t}$ non-deterministically decides to receive first from task t_i, and then from t_j, this order must be maintained in the point-to-point communications performed by all the processors of $\bar{t}$ in order to accomplish the overall communication. Hence our layer provides an appropriate receive primitive (along with a corresponding send) that causes only the root processor of the receiver group to make the non-deterministic choice of the sender, and then to broadcast its choice to all the other processors of its own group. Only when this choice has been signaled to the other receiving processors, can they invoke the right point-to-point receive primitives and actually receive the data from the selected source task as discussed above.

3 Experimental results

In order to characterize the performance of $COLT_{\text{HPF}}$ we implemented both synthetic micro-benchmarks and a sample task/data-parallel application. All the experiments were conducted on an SGI/CRAY T3E.

The first micro-benchmark measures the time required to exchange a distributed array between two data-parallel tasks. We executed this sort of "ping-pong" program with 1-D arrays distributed (BLOCK) in the source task and (CYCLIC) in the destination task, and 2-D arrays distributed (*,BLOCK) and (BLOCK,*) in the source and destination tasks, respectively. We varied both the array size and the number of processors per-task. The plots reported in Figure 1.(a) show the time required to communicate 1-D arrays. As can be seen, there is a small increase in the communication times when two processors per-task are exploited. This is due to the different data layout exploited which, if several processors are used for each task, entails packing "non-contiguous" data before sending them. Moreover, communication latencies increase with the number of per-task processors for small array sizes, while the opposite effect was measured in the tests involving large volumes of data. This behavior can also be noted in the plots shown in Figures 1.(b) and 1.(c), which report the results obtained with 2-D arrays. In all these plots communication latency decreases up to a minimum and then tends to increase slightly. With very large arrays (e.g. 8, 32 MB) the decrease is constant up to the maximum number of per-task processors tested. The curves thus behave as expected: for small data volumes the communication startup time dominates the overall latency, while for larger arrays the main contribution to communication latency is given by the message transfer time.

Note that this transfer time is directly proportional to the length of messages transmitted and thus indirectly proportional to the number of processors onto which the exchanged array is distributed.

The other micro-benchmark implemented demonstrates the effectiveness of supporting non-deterministic choices for the reception of incoming messages. To this end we built a simple pipeline application composed of three stages. The first stage produces a stream of arrays and sends one array to the next stage every T_1 secs. The second stage is replicated in five copies: each replica performs, on each array received, a dummy computation C before forwarding it to the third stage. Finally, the third stage simply consumes, every T_3 secs, an element of the stream received from the various replicas of the second stage. It is worth noting that the replicated second stage entails exploiting a processor farm structure within the original pipeline. The first stage, in fact, besides computing its own dummy job, has to dispatch the various arrays of the stream to the various replicas of the second stage (i.e. the farm workers), while the third stage collects the results from them. This application was implemented in two different ways: the first version exploits a *Round Robin* (RR) technique to dispatch the arrays to the five replicas of the second stage, while the second version exploits a dynamic *Self Scheduling* (SS) technique. Moreover, with both the versions we conducted three series of experiments, by changing the cost of the dummy computation C. In the first series of experiments the C's costs were determined according to an exponential distribution with average μ, while a uniform distribution with the same average μ was instead used for the second series of experiments. Finally, the costs used in the third series were exactly equal to μ for all the stream elements. The value of μ was forced to be equal to 0.2, 0.4 and 0.8 secs, while T_1 and T_3 were fixed to $\mu/5$ (μ divided by the number of workers) to balance the pipeline stages. We used four processors within each data-parallel task, and we fixed to 400 the number of stream elements processed, where each element is a 256×256 array of 8 byte integers. The SS version gave performances from 13% to 14% better than the RR one for exponentially distributed costs. The improvements ranged instead from 11% to 12% in the case of uniformly distributed costs, while in the balanced case, the difference between the results of the two implementations was negligible with a slight performance loss measured for the SS version. These results demonstrate the utility of employing dynamic scheduling strategies when the computational costs are *unbalanced* and unknown until run-time. On the other hand, when execution times are *balanced*, and thus no dynamic scheduling should be needed, the overheads introduced by our implementation of self scheduling are negligible.

The sample application implemented is a 2-D Fast Fourier Transform, (2-D FFT) which is probably the most used example of the utility of exploiting a mixture of task and data parallelism [4, 5, 12]. Table 1 shows the per-input array execution times (in secs) for different problem sizes. The results are reported as a function of P, the number of processors used. Hence the mixed task and data-parallel version ($COLT_{HPF}$) exploits $P/2$ processors for each of the two communicating HPF tasks implementing the 2-D FFT. As can be seen, the $COLT_{HPF}$ version considerably outperforms the HPF one. The columns labeled **Ratio** reports the ratio between the pure HPF and the $COLT_{HPF}$ execution times. The performance improvement obtained is significant, and ranges from 11% to 134%. The largest improvements were obtained when 32 or 64 processors were used on small/medium sized problems. These results are particularly interesting because many image and signal processing applications require 2-D FFTs to be applied in real-time to streams of data sets of limited size [7].

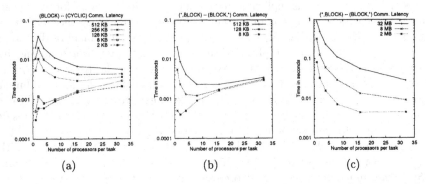

(a)   (b)   (c)

Fig. 1. Average task-to-task communication latencies as a function of the size of the data exchanged and the number of per-task processors.

Table 1. 2-D FFT execution times obtained with HPF and $COLT_{HPF}$.

Procs	256 × 256			512 × 512			1024 × 1024		
	HPF	$COLT_{HPF}$	Ratio	HPF	$COLT_{HPF}$	Ratio	HPF	$COLT_{HPF}$	Ratio
2	0.118	0.106	1.11	0.451	0.367	1.23	1.834	1.452	1.26
4	0.058	0.052	1.12	0.229	0.193	1.19	0.919	0.747	1.23
8	0.029	0.026	1.11	0.115	0.096	1.20	0.468	0.375	1.25
16	0.018	0.014	1.28	0.058	0.047	1.23	0.236	0.190	1.24
32	0.014	0.009	1.51	0.034	0.025	1.36	0.123	0.093	1.32
64	0.017	0.007	2.34	0.028	0.016	1.78	0.074	0.050	1.48

4 Conclusions

In this paper we have discussed $COLT_{HPF}$, a run-time support to coordinate HPF tasks, implemented on top of MPI and Adaptor compilation system. We have also presented some encouraging performance studies, conducted on an SGI/Cray T3E. Although $COLT_{HPF}$ can be exploited to implement parallel libraries (*skeletons*), it was primarily conceived for use by a compiler of a simple high-level coordination language [12]. The main idea behind this language is to allow programmers to coordinate HPF tasks according to specific paradigms for task parallelism. These paradigms, for example pipelines and processors farms, are the most commonly encountered in parallel applications, and, more importantly, can be associated with simple analytic performance models that, on the basis of profiling information, can be used to automatically solve the problem of optimal resource allocation [1]. However, other less structured forms of task parallelism could be supported as well (e.g. computations modeled by general task graphs), where heuristic techniques can be exploited for task allocation and resource optimization [14]. According to this approach, programmers have only to specify the HPF source code of each task, and the high-level constructs which specify the coordination among the various tasks. The associated compiler, depending on the specific paradigm, generates the suitable "system" code for carrying out task creation and interaction, and integrates the HPF user-provided code with the compiler-generated $COLT_{HPF}$ calls for inter-task communications. For example, if the paradigm is a pipeline, it generates the code to process streams of data, while, for a processor farm paradigm, it produces the code which dynamically schedules incoming stream elements in order to balance the workload.

Acknowledgments. We wish to thank Thomas Brandes of GMD-SCAI, and the support of PQE2000 project and CINECA Consortium.

References

1. B. Bacci, M. Danelutto, S. Orlando, S. Pelagatti, and M. Vanneschi. P^3L: a Structured High-level Parallel Language and its Structured Support. *Concurrency: Practice and Experience*, 7(3):225–255, 1995.
2. T. Brandes. ADAPTOR Programmer's Guide Version 5.0. Internal Report Adaptor 3, GMD-SCAI, Sankt Augustin, Germany, April 97.
3. B.M. Chapman, H.P. Zima, M. Haines, P. Mehrotra, and J. Van Rosendale. OPUS: A Coordination Language for Multidisciplinary Applications. TR 95-6, Inst. or Software Technology and Parallel Systems, Univ. of Vienna, Oct. 1995.
4. P. Dinda, T. Gross, D. O'Halloron, E. Segall, E. Stichnoth, J. Subhlok, J. Webb, and B. Yang. The CMU task parallel program suite. Technical Report CMU-CS-94-131, School of Computer Science, Carnegie Mellon University, March 1994.
5. Ian Foster, David R. Kohr, Jr., Rakesh Krishnaiyer, and Alok Choudhary. A Library-Based Approach to Task Parallelism in a Data-Parallel Language. *J. of Parallel and Distr. Comp.*, 45(2):148–158, Sept. 1997.
6. T. Gross, D. O'Hallaron, and J. Subhlok. Task parallelism in a high performance fortran framework. *IEEE Parallel and Distributed Technology*, 2(2):16–26, 1994.
7. T. Gross, D. O'Halloron, E. Stichnoth, and J. Subhlok. Exploiting task and data parallelism on a multicomputer. In *ACM SIGPLAN Symposium on Principles and Practice of Parallel Programming*, pages 13–22, May 1993.
8. A.J.G. Hey. Experiments in MIMD Parallelism. In *Proc. of Int. Conf. PARLE '89*, pages 28–42, Eindhoven, The Netherlands, June 1989. LNCS 366 Spinger-Verlag.
9. HPF Forum. *HPF Language Specification*, May 1993. Ver. 1.0.
10. HPF Forum. *HPF Language Specification*, Jan. 1997. Ver. 2.0.
11. H.T. Kung. Computational Models for Parallel Computers. C.A.R. Hoare editor, *Scientific applications of multiprocessors*, pages 1–17. Prentice-Hall Int., 1988.
12. S. Orlando and R. Perego. $COLT_{HPF}$, a Coordination Layer for HPF Tasks. Technical Report TR-4/98, Dipartimento di Mat. Appl. ed Informatica, Università di Venezia, March 1998. Available at http://raffaele.cnuce.cnr.it/papers.html.
13. S. Ramaswamy and P. Banerjee. Automatic generation of efficient array redistribution routines for distributed memory multicomputers. In *Frontiers '95: The Fifth Symp. on the Frontiers of Massively Par. Comp.*, pages 342–349, Feb. 1995.
14. S. Ramaswamy, S. Sapatnekar, and P. Banerjee. A Framework for Exploiting Task and Data Parallelism on Distributed Memory Multicomputers. *IEEE Trans. on Parallel and Distr. Systems*, 8(11):1098–1116, Nov. 1997.

Dynamic Visualization and Steering Using PVM and MPI[*]

P.M. Papadopoulos and J.A. Kohl

Oak Ridge National Laboratory
Computer Science and Mathematics Division
Oak Ridge, TN, 37831-6367, USA

Abstract. This paper describes a middleware, called CUMULVS, that allows users to dynamically attach multiple visualization and steering programs to a running parallel simulation. It further develops possible strategies for enabling dynamic attachment to MPI-based simulations using hybrid (PVM and MPI) and MPI-only schemes. The hybrid schemes retain the full range of CUMULVS' dynamic capabilities while MPI-only schemes reduce these dynamics and eliminate any possibility of fault-tolerance. However, both solutions are important, especially on platforms where PVM and MPI cannot co-exist in the same application (on some monolithic MPPs, for example).

CUMULVS manages the attachment protocols so that subsets of distributed data can be extracted from the simulation and aggregated into a single array for consistent presentation to the viewer/steerer, termed "front-ends." The software can be simply understood as a translator from distributed data residing within the parallel program to a single monolithic array residing in the front-end memory. The attachment of front-ends is performed on-demand at runtime. The protocols are fault-tolerant allowing both the parallel program and the viewer to recover in the event of failure. Because of this, front-end viewers can appear and disappear throughout the lifetime of a long-running simulation without adversely affecting the simulation code.

1   Introduction

Scientific simulation programs have evolved from single CPU serial operation to parallel computing on a heterogeneous collection of machines. Many scientists are now comfortable developing PVM- [1] or MPI-based [8] parallel applications for their core computation. However, they are forced to utilize inflexible post-processing techniques for visualizing program data due to a lack of tools that understand the distributed nature of the data fields. Issues such as extracting distributed data across processors and insuring time coherency of a global view hinder the use of on-line visualization and steering.

---

[*] Research supported by the Mathematical Sciences Research Program, Office of Energy Research, U.S. Department of Energy, under contract No. DE-AC05-96OR22464 with Lockheed Martin Energy Research Corporation.

CUMULVS [2] is an infrastructure library that allows these programmers to insert "hooks" that enable real-time visualization of ongoing parallel applications, steer program-specified parameters, and provide application-directed checkpointing and recovery. CUMULVS allows any number of "front-end" visualization tools and/or steering programs to dynamically attach to a running simulation and view some or all of the data fields that a simulation has published. One key to the success of the CUMULVS software is that *commercial* visualization packages can be used to provide the graphical processing. CUMULVS can be thought of as a translation layer that accumulates parallel data so that traditional visualization packages can be used for processing. The libraries handle all of the connection protocols, insure consistency of both steered parameters and visualized data across the parallel computation, and recover in the face of network (or program) failure. The fault-tolerant nature of the attachment protocols insure that a running simulation will not hang if an attached "viewer[2]" becomes unresponsive via an (unexpected) exit or network failure.

Clearly, one critical point in porting CUMULVS to a variety of platforms is the application's message passing layer. The middleware currently uses PVM to pass data to/from the application and the front-end viewers. Applications written in MPI can be used with CUMULVS if both runtime systems are available. This "full overlay" scheme is straightforward and is discussed in Section 3. Additionally, partial overlay schemes with proxies (Section 3.1) and MPI-only schemes (Section 4) are considered. The conclusion is that for the full range of dynamics to be supported for MPI-based applications, an additional messaging substrate (e.g., PVM, Nexus, or sockets) must be implemented. Nevertheless, an all-MPI solution (with reduced functionality) can be very useful for environments where this is the only messaging supported.

2 Fault-Tolerant Dynamic Attachment

Viewers and steerers can dynamically attach to running parallel applications. Since the viewers are generic, they must gather information from the parallel program and reliably make a connection to it. In CUMULVS, this connection differs from a standard peer-to-peer connection in that it is a gather connection (from application to viewer) in one direction and a multicast source (from viewer to application) in the other. This connection sequence is also fault-tolerant. It is expected that applications run for relatively long periods of time, and special care is taken to insure that the application will not hang due to a dead viewer. Attaching a viewer (or steerer) to a running application goes through the following steps:

1. *Lookup.* Find the location of the simulation program. The viewer uses a name server to find instance 0 of a named simulation program. The "name" of the simulation is defined by the simulation and must be known before a lookup can start.

---

[2] "Viewer" is a generic phrase to describe a program for visualizing *or* steering an application.

2. *Request Information.* The viewer requests information from the application about defined data fields and steerable parameters. Information such as data field names, decompositions, and data types is returned from this query.

3. *Request a Field.* Based on the information gathered in the previous step, a field (or a group of fields and parameters) is requested for viewing.

4. *Time-step Synchronization.* The nodes in a parallel process are at various "arbitrary" time steps. CUMULVS uses a "loose" synchronization scheme so that it can assemble data in a time-consistent frame. The synchronization is termed loose because an explicit barrier is not used.

5. *Viewing.* CUMULVS expects an iterative program. Once attached, a viewer renders frames of data as they are produced from the simulation. The viewer can adjust the size and granularity of the subset of data being viewed.

6. *Detachment.* Whenever possible, detachment is done with a a message from the viewer. However, if the viewer is determined to have failed, the application-side detachment protocol is executed.

3 Hybrid PVM and MPI

It is quite reasonable to use PVM for all viewer-to-application messaging even if the application uses only MPI for its internal messaging. On clusters of work-stations, for example, a virtual machine must be constructed that includes the hosts where the MPI application will be started. MPI startup can be used for the application and PVM will only come into play when CUMULVS is initialized. Essentially each node in the application program is both an MPI and PVM node. As long as the underlying mechanisms for realizing the messaging libraries do not collide, this is a simple solution. The powerful messaging modes of MPI can be fully utilized for the application while the dynamic capabilities of PVM and notification functions can used to realize the full dynamics of the CUMULVS infrastructure. Figure 1 shows this "full overlay" mode where all nodes of the MPI application are also members of a PVM virtual machine. This approach has been successfully demonstrated for a three-dimensional compressible computational fluid dynamics flow code. The only runtime difficulty is managing a virtual machine along with a specific MPI startup mechanism.

3.1 Using Proxy Nodes

A second hybrid approach is to split the CUMULVS messaging between PVM and MPI. A viewer would use PVM to talk to one (or more) "proxy" nodes in the MPI application (See Figure 2). This approach could be thought of as a "partial overlay" of PVM and MPI where only a small portion of the parallel application must utilize two types of messaging. Steering/Viewing requests go to the proxy nodes over PVM, are translated to MPI, and then are forwarded to interior nodes. For full advantage, native MPI routines could be used to gather data subfields onto the proxies. The proxies would then forward the gathered data to the viewer. The advantage of this approach is that it may be possible

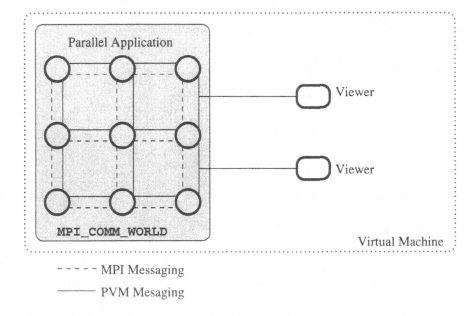

- - - - - MPI Messaging
———— PVM Mesaging

Fig. 1. Hybrid PVM and MPI with full overlay. All MPI nodes in the parallel application are also processes in a PVM virtual machine. Viewers communicate directly with each task in the simulation.

to leverage more efficient MPI communications at some steps of the gathering process. In a proxy design, the communication between a viewer and all nodes in the simulation is hierarchical. The hierarchy increases the number of data copies (one additional copy for each level of the hierarchy), but in general exhibits better scaling properties. One minor drawback of this design is that gathering of data is split into multiple levels, increasing the complexity of the gathering (or accumulation) process.

4 MPI only

MPI-1 programs are *statically configured.* The strong message encapsulation laid out in the MPI specification is, in fact, problematic for the dynamic attachments/detachments used in CUMULVS. If one desires an MPI-only system, then each visualization front-end must be part of the base communicator at start up. Figure 3 illustrates this with an enlarged MPI_COMM_WORLD. Viewers may still "dynamically attach" to a the simulation, but they must physically remain in memory for the duration of the program run. Also, Step 1 of the attachment process is implicit because the entire structure is static. Because it is non-standard and non-portable to change the size of the base communicator once it has been formed, a new communicator must be defined that delineates

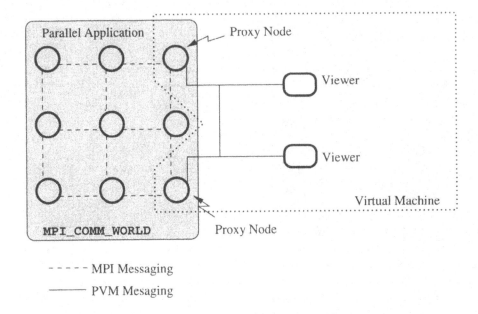

Fig. 2. Hybrid PVM and MPI with partial overlay. Only *proxy* nodes are both MPI and PVM processes. Viewers communicate only with proxies, which forward requests to the MPI-only nodes and send responses back to the PVM-based viewers.

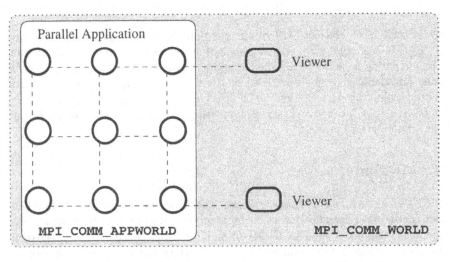

Fig. 3. MPI-only message passing. Viewers must exist for the entire duration of the parallel simulation. MPI_COMM_WORLD is expanded requiring a new communicator MPI_COMM_APPWORLD to be defined.

the application program from any viewers. Common programming practice produces programs that configure themselves at run time to the size of the base communicator. The solution described below introduces a new communicator called MPI_COMM_APPWORLD which is simply MPI_COMM_WORLD with the nodes used for visualization taken out. Codes would then use MPI_COMM_APPWORLD as their base communicator from which all their internal groupings would be derived. In theory, this is an acceptable solution. However, the clear downside is that applications must add (at least one) extra nodes to accommodate the viewers. Programs that have run in "power of 2" partitions, for example, will now be "oddly" sized. While MPI-1 has proven to be useful and efficient for computational components, its static nature is a severe handicap for interactive steering and visualization. It is perhaps simpler and better to have some of the application nodes double as proxies and use PVM, Nexus, or even just TCP sockets to connect a viewer to the application. In this way, desktop viewers can come and go during a long simulation, thus taking full advantage of the dynamic infrastructure. Clearly, MPI-2 will alleviate this static constraint, but no full-fledged public MPI-2 implementations yet exist (at the time of this writing, Fujitsu has the only commercial implementation of which the authors are aware).

5 Availability

CUMULVS is an ongoing project. The authors have made the software source available for download. Please visit http://www.epm.ornl.gov/cs/cumulvs.html for the latest updates and news.

6 Summary

This paper has described a visualization and steering infrastructure called CUMULVS that supports dynamic attachment of viewers to a running parallel simulation. It further describes the steps that CUMULVS goes through to make a connection to an application. Finally, it describes several approaches to integrating MPI-based applications into CUMULVS. The full PVM and MPI overlay approach is the simplest, but will not work when the two systems cannot coexist. The proxy approach exhibits better scalability but at the cost of increased complexity and extra memory copies. This approach is expected to yield favorable results and be the preferred method for both hybrid and monolithic messaging substrates. An all-MPI approach was discussed and illustrated some limitations for dynamic attachment. The MPI approach also showed that MPI_COMM_WORLD would have to be enlarged to allow viewers to communicate and this might have program logic ramifications. A suggested approach is to define MPI_COMM_APPWORLD and have an application derive all of its contexts from this communicator.

References

1. A. Begulin, J. Dongarra, G. A. Geist, W. Jiang, R. Manchek, V. Sunderam, *PVM: Parallel Virtual Machine, A User's Guide and Tutorial for Networked Parallel Computing*, MIT Press, Cambridge, MA, 1994.
2. G. A. Geist, J. A. Kohl, P. M. Papadopoulos, "CUMULVS: Providing Fault-Tolerance, Visualization and Steering of Parallel Applications," SIAM, August 1996.
3. G. A. Geist II, J. A. Kohl, R. Manchek, P. M. Papadopoulos, "New Features of PVM 3.4, " 1995 EuroPVM User's Group Meeting, Lyon, France, September 1995.
4. J. A. Kohl, G. A. Geist, "XPVM 1.0 User's Guide," Technical Report ORNL/TM-12981, Oak Ridge National Laboratory, Oak Ridge, TN, April, 1995.
5. J. A. Kohl, G. A. Geist, "The PVM 3.4 Tracing Facility and XPVM 1.1," Proceedings of the 29th Hawaii International Conference on System Sciences (HICSS-29), Heterogeneous Processing Minitrack in the Software Technology Track, Maui, Hawaii, January 3-6, 1996.
6. N. Carriero and D. Gelernter. "Linda and Message Passing: What Have We Learned?" Technical Report 984, Yale University Department of Computer Science, Sept. 1993.
7. J. Pruyne and M. Livny, "Interfacing Condor and PVM to Harness the Cycles of Workstation Clusters", Journal on Future Generations of Computer Systems, Vol. 12, 1996
8. Message Passing Interface Forum. MPI: A message-passing interface standard. "International Journal of Supercomputer Applications and High Performance Computing", International Journal of Supercomputer Applications and High Performance Computing, Volume 8, Number 3/4, 1994.

A PVM-Based Library for Sparse Matrix Factorizations *

Juan Touriño and Ramón Doallo

Dep. of Electronics and Systems, University of A Coruña, Spain
{juan,doallo}@udc.es

Abstract. We present *3LM*, a C *L*inked *L*ist *M*anagement *L*ibrary for parallel sparse factorizations on a PVM environment which takes into account the fill-in, an important drawback of sparse computations. It is restricted to a mesh topology and is based on an SPMD paradigm. Our goal is to facilitate the programming in such environments by means of a set of list and vector-oriented operations. The result is a pseudo-sequential code, in which the interprocessor communications and the sparse data structures are hidden from the programmer.

1 Introduction

Sparse matrix operations appear in many scientific areas. Many libraries have been developed for managing sparse matrices, specially in linear algebra; for instance, the *NIST sparse BLAS* library [5] provides computational kernels for fundamental sparse matrix operations. This library is based on compressed storage formats which do not consider fill-in operations. Moreover, many linear algebra applications need to be solved in parallel due to memory and CPU requirements; so, parallel libraries such as *ScaLAPACK* [1], mainly oriented to dense computations, were developed. The *3LM* library was originally designed taking advantage of our experiences in programming sparse QR factorization algorithms on distributed-memory multiprocessors [6]. However, the routines of the library may be applied, without loss of generality, to several kinds of sparse algorithms involving fill-in (Cholesky, LU ...).

This paper is organized as follows: in §2 we describe the data structures and distributions available to users; §3 presents the programming model with *3LM*, focusing on the loop mapping. Different subsets of useful routines we have developed are briefly described in §4. A practical example of the use of *3LM* is shown in §5 and, finally, conclusions and future work are discussed in §6.

2 Library Data Structures and Distributions

The Linked List Column/Row Scatter scheme (*LLCS/LLRS*) was selected for representing sparse matrices, in order to support fill-in operations in a flexi-

---

* This work was supported by the Ministry of Education of Spain (project CICYT TIC96-1125-C03), Xunta de Galicia (XUGA20605B96) and by the Training and Mobility of Researchers Programme of the EU (ICARUS project at CINECA, Italy)

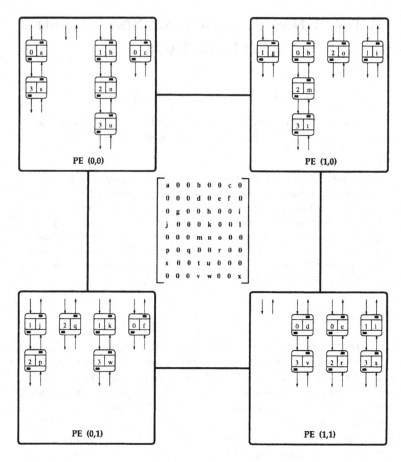

Fig. 1. *LLCS* scheme

ble way. It includes a data structure: linked lists, each one of them represents a column/row of the matrix, and a data distribution, a pseudo-regular cyclic distribution. This is accomplished by means of this *3LM* routine:

```
int  lll_dcs (char *file_n, int cols, dll *list_id)
```

where `file_n` is the name of the file in which the matrix is stored in Harwell-Boeing format [3] or in coordinate format; if `file_n=0` (or NULL), the structure is only set up (this is necessary for sparse matrices which are generated at run-time); `cols` is the number of columns of the matrix, and `list_id` is an identifier of the matrix which contains the list orientation and an array of pointers to the beginning and to the end of the lists. In Figure 1, an 8×8 matrix is distributed onto a 2×2 mesh using this scheme. Similar routines have been developed [6] for a row-oriented scheme (`lll_drs`), for singly-linked lists (`lll_scs`, `lll_srs`), and for two-dimensional linked lists (`lll_srcs`, `lll_drcs`).

In matrix algebra, vector operations such as scalar-vector multiplication, vector addition, dot product, vector multiply or saxpy operation are very common. Besides, the characteristics of many problems force the programmer to manage vectors distributed (and even replicated) in a row or column of processors of the virtual mesh to take advantage of data locality and to minimize communications. In order to make this kind of operations easier, we use the routine:

```
void *lll_InitVector (char *file_n, int nels, vector *vec_id,
                      int dir, int dtype)
```

which distributes a dense vector of `nels` entries, stored in `file_n`, onto a mesh in a cyclic way, on each row or column of processors (that is, replicated), depending on `dir` (`XDirection` or `YDirection`); `dtype` is the data type of the elements: `DataInt`, `DataFloat`, `DataDouble` (predefined constants). This routine stores in `vec_id` (vector identifier) the following information: orientation of the vector (row-oriented or column-oriented), type of the elements and a pointer to the beginning of the vector, which is also returned by the routine.

A complete set of routines for data redistribution or reorientation, both for sparse matrices and for dense vectors, has been also developed in [6].

3 Loop Mapping

Let us assume a mesh topology in which each processor is identified by coordinates *(pidx, pidy)*. *3LM* programs must begin with the sentence:

```
lll_BeginMesh (npex, npey, progname)
```

which sets a mesh of dimensions `npey`×`npex` and executes the program `progname` in all the processors, using a PVM environment, for a cluster of workstations or for a Cray T3D/T3E multiprocessor (by setting `progname=0/NULL`). Programs must end with `lll_EndMesh()`.

As an example, considering that a matrix A is stored in an *LLCS* format, a double loop which performs a column access, is mapped on a double local loop, as shown in Figure 2.

For instance, let us consider the operation of multiplying the elements of the submatrix $A_{a:c,b:d}$ by a scalar constant named `value`. The corresponding pseudo-sequential *3LM* code is expressed as:

```
for (j=fcol(b); j<fcol(d+1); j++)
    lll_doper(j, listA_id, value, OpMul, frow(a), frow(c+1));
```

where `listA_id` is the matrix A identifier, `OpMul` is the operation (product) of each element of the list with `value`, from global row index `a` up to index `c`. The procedure `lll_doper` goes only through the links of the corresponding lists instead of traversing the whole iteration space `a:c`.

A similar procedure for vectors is `lll_voper`, which has a vector identifier `vec_id` as parameter instead of a scalar `value`; it operates each entry of list `j` with the corresponding entry of `vec_id`. There are predefined operations: `OpAdd`, `OpSub`, `OpMul`, `OpDiv`, `Nop`, as well as user-defined ones.

$$
\boxed{
\begin{array}{ll}
\text{for } (j=j1;\ j<j2;\ j++) & \text{for } (j=f_{col}(j1);\ j<f_{col}(j2);\ j++) \\
\quad \text{for } (i=i1;\ i<i2;\ i++) \implies & \quad \text{for } (i=f_{row}(i1);\ i<f_{row}(i2);\ i++) \\
\quad\quad A_{ij} = \cdots & \quad\quad A_{ij} = \cdots
\end{array}
}
$$

being

$$
f_{col}(x) = \left\lfloor \frac{x}{npex} \right\rfloor + \begin{cases} 1 \text{ if } pidx < (x \bmod npex) \\ 0 \text{ otherwise} \end{cases}
$$

$$
f_{row}(x) = \left\lfloor \frac{x}{npey} \right\rfloor + \begin{cases} 1 \text{ if } pidy < (x \bmod npey) \\ 0 \text{ otherwise} \end{cases}
$$

Fig. 2. Mapping global loops onto local loops

4 Library Routines

The *3LM* routines we have shown above and the ones we will see next, have been specified for column-oriented operations, that is, using an *LLCS* distribution for lists and using column vectors (YDirection). This was accomplished in order to simplify their explanation. There exist analogous procedures for singly-linked lists (lll_s*) and for 2-D linked lists (lll_2d*, lll_2s*) [6].

However, the same routines can be also applied to row-oriented operations (when using an *LLRS* scheme and row vectors) because these routines obtain the orientation from the identifiers of lists and vectors, and they operate accordingly.

Next, we introduce additional subsets of routines we found interesting for helping the user to program parallel algorithms in our application context.

4.1 Replication Operations

Sometimes, a column (in an *LLCS* distribution) of the matrix is required to perform calculations with data located in other processors.

The procedure lll_drepl(j, list_id, vec_id, low, high) replicates column (list) j of the matrix on the corresponding processors. This column is stored in the vector defined by vec_id, from entry with index low up to entry high (not inclusive). Internally, this procedure broadcasts a compressed vector instead of a full-size vector to reduce the size of the message to be broadcast. There are analogous procedures to replicate dense vectors (lll_vrepl).

4.2 Gather Operations

They are used for vectors which are distributed on each row (or column) of processors, and other processors need to obtain non-local data of these vectors. Function lll_vgather(vec_id, j1, j2) returns the value of entry j1 of vector identified by `vec_id` to the processors which own entry j2. If j2=All (All is a predefined constant of the library), this value is returned to all the processors.

4.3 Reduction Routines

3LM provides a set of reduction instructions, both for lists and for dense vectors. For instance: `lll_vmaxval/lll_vminval(vec_id, low, high)` returns the maximum/minimum element of vector `vec_id`, from index `low` up to index `high`. Similarly, `lll_vmaxloc/lll_vminloc(vec_id, low, high)`, returns the index of the maximum/minimum element. There are also reduction routines for other operations such as sum, product ..., and for user-defined operations.

4.4 Fill-in Routines

In the sparse computations we are considering, an important drawback is the generation of new nonzero entries in the matrix, with the corresponding problems of storage and treatment of these entries. This is solved by means of the linked list data structure. Let us consider the following iteration space:

for (j=b; j<d+1; j++)
    for (i=a; i<c+1; i++)
        $A_{ij} = A_{ij} + vec_i$

where *vec* is a vector distributed and replicated in each column of processors. Fill-in appears in this computation and is confined in the local processor which executes its own set of iterations. We can solve this fact by using this routine:

for (j=fcol(b); j<fcol(d+1); j++)
    lll_dfillin(j, listA_id, vec_id, OpAdd, frow(a), frow(c+1));

where `OpAdd` is the operation between the entries of the list and vector vec. Generalizing, an operation g_{oper} can be a predefined or a user-defined function. According to this, the procedure `lll_dfillin` carries out the following actions:

$$If \ A_{ij}^* \leftarrow g_{oper}(A_{ij}, vec_i) \begin{cases} \neq 0 \ and \ A_{ij} \neq 0 & Entry \ A_{ij} \ updated \ in \ the \ list \ as \ A_{ij}^* \\ \neq 0 \ and \ A_{ij} = 0 & New \ entry \ A_{ij}^* \ inserted \ in \ the \ list \\ 0 & Entry \ A_{ij} \ deleted \ of \ the \ list \\ A_{ij} & No \ actions \ are \ taken \end{cases}$$

The routine `lll_dupdate(i, j, aij, list_id)` sets element (i, j) in the matrix identified by `list_id` to `aij` (insertion and deletion operations are assumed depending on the value of `aij`).

4.5 Swapping Operation

In many matrix calculations, explicit pivoting operations are required. This feature is a drawback in sparse computations due to the storage scheme and to the fill-in, which changes the number of elements per column of the matrix. A high-level swap operation is implemented to make the programming easier:

```
lll_dswap(j1, j2, list_id, rows)
```

being j1 and j2 the global indices of the columns to be swapped in the mesh according to the *LLCS* scheme, and rows is the row dimension of the matrix. Compressed vectors are used to reduce message sizes.

4.6 Other Routines

More remarkable procedures for list management, among others developed, are: lll_dvdp(j, list_id, vec_id, low, high) returns to all the processors which own list (column) j the dot product of that column and vector vec_id. lll_dunpack(j, list_id, vec_id, low, high) copies elements of list (column) j, from index low up to index high on the corresponding positions of the column vector defined by vec_id; the rest of entries of this vector are zero.

There are also *3LM* low-level routines [6] to handle directly the data structures, as well as to determine the actions on each processor of the mesh, for special operations which cannot be performed with the high-level set described above.

5 Sparse QR Factorization: an Application Example

The code of Figure 3 shows an example of the use of the *3LM* routines for the rank-revealing sparse Modified Gram-Schmidt (MGS) QR algorithm, with column pivoting. An m×n matrix A is decomposed into the product of an orthogonal matrix Q (which is originally matrix A) and an upper triangular matrix R (consult [4, Chap.5]). Lines 27-37 of Figure 3 correspond with the column pivoting stage of the algorithm. The generation of each row k of matrix R is performed in line 40: $R_{k,k} \leftarrow pivot$, and in line 47: $R_{k,k+1:n-1} \leftarrow Q_{0:m-1,k}^T Q_{0:m-1,k+1:n-1}$. Finally, the core of the stage of updating matrix Q is carried out in line 41: $Q_{0:m-1,k} \leftarrow Q_{0:m-1,k}/pivot$, and principally in line 51, where fill-in appears: $Q_{0:m-1,k+1:n-1} \leftarrow Q_{0:m-1,k+1:n-1} - Q_{0:m-1,k}R_{k,k+1:n-1}$.

A detailed parallel implementation which uses message-passing routines explicitly is described in [2]. As we can see, the *3LM* code is not very broad, whereas the corresponding parallel code mentioned above can fill about 2000 lines.

Figure 4 shows the efficiencies obtained for the code of Figure 3 on a Cray T3E, for five sparse matrices selected from the Harwell-Boeing collection [3]. A strategy to preserve sparsity during the factorization was also included. The legend of this figure indicates the dimensions of the matrices, as well as the number of nonzero entries. As we can see, the algorithm scales rather well. Nevertheless, the execution times are not good in comparison with the implementation which uses message-passing explicitly. This is because that implementation is very optimized and the *3LM* routines are generic, not specific for a particular algorithm. The ease of programming using *3LM* involves higher execution times.

This library has been also used to program other sparse orthogonal factorizations, such as Householder reflections and Givens rotations, using *LLCS* and *LLRS* schemes, respectively [6]. A 2-D linked list (*LLRCS* scheme) would be suitable for a right-looking LU factorization. Sparse Cholesky factorization can also be approached by means of the *3LM* library, using an *LLCS* distribution.

```
1    #include "lll.h"
2
3    void main()
4    {
5     int m, n, pesx, pesy;
6     int i, j, k, rank, pivot_index;
7     double pivot, tempnorm;
8     double *norm, *vsum, *vcol, *temp;
9     vector norm_id, vsum_id, vcol_id, temp_id;
10    dll listQ_id, listR_id;
11
12    pesx=4; pesy=4;
13    lll_BeginMesh(pesx, pesy, "qr_mgs");
14    m=1000; n=1000;
15    norm=lll_InitVector(0, n, &norm_id, XDirection, DataDouble);
16    vsum=lll_InitVector(0, n, &vsum_id, XDirection, DataDouble);
17    vcol=lll_InitVector(0, m, &vcol_id, YDirection, DataDouble);
18    temp=lll_InitVector(0, m, &temp_id, YDirection, DataDouble);
19    lll_dcs("matrix.dat", n, &listQ_id);
20    lll_dcs(NULL, n, &listR_id);
21    rank=n;
22    for (j=fcol(0); j<fcol(n); j++) {
23       lll_dunpack(j, listQ_id, temp_id, frow(0), frow(m));
24       norm[j]=lll_dvdp(j, listQ_id, temp_id, frow(0), frow(m));
25       }
26    for (k=0; k<n; k++) {
27       pivot=lll_vmaxval(norm_id, fcol(k), fcol(n));
28       pivot_index=lll_vmaxloc(norm_id, fcol(k), fcol(n));
29       if (pivot < 1.0e-20) {
30          rank=k; break;
31          }
32       lll_dswap(k, pivot_index, listQ_id, m);
33       lll_dswap(k, pivot_index, listR_id, n);
34       tempnorm=lll_vgather(norm_id, k, pivot_index);
35       for (j=fcol(pivot_index); j<fcol(pivot_index+1); j++)
36          norm[j]=tempnorm;
37       pivot=sqrt(pivot);
38       for (j=fcol(k); j<fcol(k+1); j++) {
39          for (i=frow(k); i<frow(k+1); i++)
40             lll_dupdate(i, j, pivot, listR_id);
41          lll_doper(j, listQ_id, pivot, OpDiv, frow(0), frow(m));
42          }
43       lll_drepl(k, listQ_id, vcol_id, 0, m);
44       for (j=fcol(k+1); j<fcol(n); j++) {
45          vsum[j]=lll_dvdp(j, listQ_id, vcol_id, frow(0), frow(m));
46          for (i=frow(k); i<frow(k+1); i++)
47             lll_dupdate(i, j, vsum[j], listR_id);
48          norm[j]=norm[j]-vsum[j]*vsum[j];
49          for (i=frow(0); i<frow(m); i++)
50             temp[i]=vcol[i]*vsum[j];
51          lll_dfillin(j, listQ_id, temp_id, OpSub, frow(0), frow(m));
52          }
53       }
54    lll_EndMesh();
55  }
```

Fig. 3. Sparse MGS code using *3LM* routines

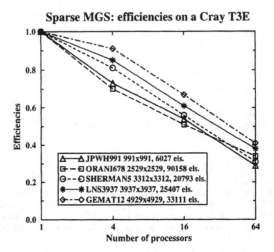

Fig. 4. Efficiencies for the MGS algorithm using *3LM* routines

6 Conclusions and Future Work

3LM provides an environment to develop effortlessly codes in the field of sparse direct factorizations and their applications (linear systems of equations, least squares problems ...). Besides, some of these routines can be used to extend the capabilities of a data-parallel compiler to handle sparse matrix computations [6]. As future work, we intend to code this library using Fortran 90/MPI, as well as to extend the library to include a wider class of problems.

References

1. Choi, J., Demmel, J., Dhillon, I., Dongarra, J., Ostrouchov, S., Petitet, A., Stanley, K., Walker, D., Whaley, R.C.: ScaLAPACK: a Portable Linear Algebra Library for Distributed Memory Computers -Design Issues and Performance. Tech. Report CS-95-283, Dep. Computer Science, University of Tennessee (1995).
2. Doallo, R., Fraguela, B.B., Touriño, J., Zapata, E.L.: Parallel Sparse Modified Gram-Schmidt QR Decomposition. In Int'l Conference on High-Performance Computing and Networking, HPCN'96, Brussels. Lecture Notes in Computer Science, Vol. 1067, Springer-Verlag (1996) 646–653.
3. Duff, I.S., Grimes, R.G., Lewis, J.G.: User's Guide for the Harwell-Boeing Sparse Matrix Collection. Tech. Report TR-PA-92-96, CERFACS (1992).
4. Golub, G.H., van Loan, C.F.: Matrix Computations. The Johns Hopkins University Press, second edition (1989).
5. Remington, K.A., Pozo, R.: NIST Sparse BLAS User's Guide. National Institute of Standards and Technology (1996).
6. Touriño, J.: Parallelization and Compilation Issues of Sparse QR Algorithms. PhD Thesis, Dep. of Electronics and Systems, University of A Coruña, Spain (1998).

On-Line Monitoring Support in PVM and MPI [*]

Roland Wismüller

Lehrstuhl für Rechnertechnik und Rechnerorganisation (LRR-TUM)
Informatik, Technische Universität München, D-80290 München, Germany
email: wismuell@in.tum.de

Abstract. PVM and MPI have often been compared regarding their functionality and performance from the users' point of view. In this paper, however, we will present some comparison from a tool developer's point of view. We will show how a supporting infrastructure – the OMIS compliant monitoring system OCM – can be implemented for both PVM and MPI. Thus, we will put light onto those features of PVM and MPI that support the implementation of on-line tools.

1 Introduction

In the community of parallel computer users, there is a broad agreement that there should be tool environments that are uniform across different hardware platforms and programming libraries [SMP95]. A closer analysis shows that the fact that we usually don't have such environments is mainly caused by the tools' *monitoring systems*, which are responsible for observing and possibly manipulating the run-time behavior of an application program (called the *target program* or *target application*). While monitoring systems for off-line tools need only interact with the parallel programming library and therefore are portable across hardware platforms, those supporting on-line tools also have to interact with operating system and hardware. Thus, these systems are typically not portable.

At LRR-TUM, we tried to solve this problem by defining a common interface for on-line monitoring systems that is independent of the supported hardware and parallel programming library and is usable for a large variety of different on-line tools. The OMIS project (On-line Monitoring Interface Specification) has shown that it is possible to identify a large set of services that are independent of the target platform, so we only need small, well-defined extensions to allow for different programming models etc.

We achieved this by using an abstract object based model of a parallel system. In this model, the system basically consists of a set of compute nodes (which may have multiple processors) and a set of processes distributed across these nodes. In addition, processes may consist of several threads. In message passing systems we have two additional objects, namely messages and message queues. This abstract model allows to invoke most monitoring services without having

---

[*] This work is partly funded by *Deutsche Forschungsgemeinschaft*, Special Research Grant SFB 342, Subproject A1.

to know whether we actually have a PVM process on a SUN workstation node, or an MPI process on a CRAY. Although the implementation of these services might differ, the interface is the same, so tools do not need to be adapted. Thus, a set of OMIS-based tools is available for a new platform as soon as one monitoring system is available.

Tools interact with the monitoring system by specifying requests, which consist of an optional event definition and a list of actions. The action list is executed whenever the monitoring system detects the specified event. For example, the following request defines a simple breakpoint, which stops each target process when it reaches address 0x1234:

```
thread_reached_address([], 0x1234): thread_stop([$proc])
```

We can not go further into the details of OMIS here; the interested reader is referred to [LWSB97] and [LW97].

In addition to specifying the interface, we implemented the OMIS compliant monitoring system OCM [WTL98] for PVM on networks of workstations, which is currently being ported to MPI. In the rest of this paper, we will first present the coarse structure of the OCM. We will then focus on the necessary interactions between the OCM and the programming library, i.e. PVM or MPI. In this way, we will put light onto those features of PVM and MPI that support the implementation of on-line tools.

2 The OMIS Compliant Monitoring System OCM

As the OCM must monitor a distributed system, it must itself be distributed, i.e. we need local monitoring components on each node. We decided to use one additional process per node, which enables the monitoring system to react on events, independently of the state of the target program. Operating system support for debugging also requires the use of an additional process.

Because each monitor process can operate on its local node only, but OMIS allows tools to issue requests relating to multiple nodes, we need another component, called Node Distribution Unit (NDU), that analyzes each request and splits it into pieces that can be processed locally [WTL98]. The NDU also assembles the partial results and returns them to the tool. As shown in Fig. 1, the NDU is currently implemented as a central process, which communicates with the tools and the local monitor processes via message passing.

The communication uses buffered send and interrupt-driven receive operations. We need interrupt-driven receives (or comparable concepts such as Active Messages) to avoid blocking of the monitor processes. It would result in the inability to timely react on occurrences of other important events. A polling scheme is not feasible, as it consumes too much CPU time.

3 Interactions Between the OCM and PVM/MPI

In the following, we will identify the interactions necessary between the OCM and the PVM [GBD+94] and MPI [For95,For97] environments. Although we

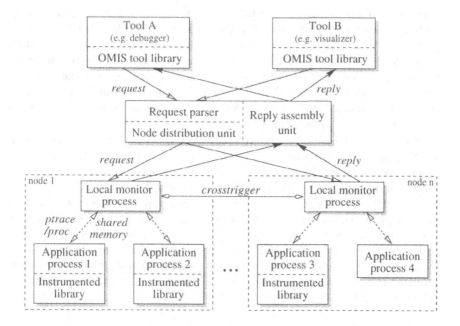

Fig. 1. Coarse Structure of the OCM

will only talk about the OCM, the results apply to on-line monitoring systems in general. Interaction between the OCM and the programming library[1] is mainly necessary for three activities:

1. for start-up and initialization,
2. for acquiring the state of the target program and the programming library,
3. for the detection of events related to the programming library.

In addition, the OCM may be able to just *use* the programming library, e.g. for its internal communication.

Since it turns out that the MPI specification does not support these interactions sufficiently, we have to use implementation specific interfaces. In the following descriptions we will refer to mpich version 1.1 [GLDS96].

3.1 Start-up and Initialization

When an on-line tool is started, we have to distinguish between two different scenarios: (1) the tool starts the target program (via the OCM), or (2) the tool (and the OCM) connects to an already running program.

---

[1] In the following discussions, the term "programming library" also includes the accompanying run-time environment, e.g. the PVM daemons.

Starting an application. In principle, starting the target program can be achieved by calling pvm_spawn or MPI_Comm_spawn_multiple (MPI-2 only) from within the OCM. However, this leads to a couple of possible problems: First, the OCM itself must be a PVM/MPI application, which may be undesirable[2]. Second, the behavior of the target application may change, since the processes now have a parent process within PVM or MPI, which may not be the case with the normal startup. For MPI-1, this kind of startup is not possible at all, since there is no dynamic process creation.

Thus, in the OCM for PVM, we start the target program the same way as a UNIX shell does, i.e. a monitor process forks a child process that execs the proper executable file. This process then eventually registers as a PVM task and dynamically creates other PVM tasks (see Section 3.3).

For MPI, establishing the connection between a monitoring system and its target application must be integrated into the mpirun program. In mpich, mpirun already contains an option for starting the totalview debugger [Dol]. This option can be used for the OCM, too, as it allows the monitoring system to fork/exec one process (the master process). mpirun then starts all other (slave) processes in a way that blocks their execution in MPI_Init until the monitoring system has achieved control over them.

Connecting to an application. The situation after the start-up is very similar to the one, where the OCM must attach to a running application. We will therefore not distinguish between these cases in the following discussion. The most important information now needed by the OCM is, which components (i.e. nodes and processes) must be monitored. Since we should not force the user of a tool to specify this information in detail, it must be retrieved from the programming library. The minimum information required consists of:

1. A list of all nodes that can be used by the target application. For workstation nodes, the minimum information needed is their host name.
2. A list of all processes in the target application. For each process, the minimum information needed is: its processing node, its local UNIX PID, the full (local) path to its executable file, and its global ID assigned by the programming library (e.g. the PVM TID or the rank in MPI_COMM_WORLD).

Any further information can be acquired via operating system services when host name and PID are known. Unfortunately, the path to the executable cannot be safely determined in this way, but it is needed e.g. to access symbol tables. The process ID assigned by the programming library is not really necessary for monitoring, but is important for the user of a tool in order to identify processes.

With PVM, it is trivial to get this information, provided that at least one monitor process is a PVM task. In this case, it can just call pvm_config to get the necessary information on the nodes, and pvm_tasks for the process infor-

---

[2] We will show some of the resulting problems later.

mation[3]. However, we can see that precisely because pvm_tasks is available, a monitoring system should not contain any PVM tasks: If it does, it might modify the behavior of the target application, as it may depend on the result of pvm_tasks. In addition, the PVM TIDs may change w.r.t. an unmonitored run. This can be a serious problem when e.g. TIDs have been stored in a log file and a user tries to debug a suspicious process in a second (monitored) run.

The MPI standard does not specify functions to retrieve the information listed above. As a consequence, it is impossible to build on-line tools for MPI that can be used with all MPI implementations. However, mpich provides a special interface allowing to acquire the configuration data in the following way:

1. When invoked with the debugging option, mpirun starts the master process under control of the monitoring system. The monitor now must place a breakpoint on a special function (MPIR_Breakpoint) and start the process.
2. The master process calls MPI_Init, which creates all other processes. For each created process, MPI_Init adds a data block to a process list, containing the name of the host where the process has been started, its local PID, and the path to its executable. In addition, detailed information on MPI communicators is preserved.
3. When the start-up has completed, the master process calls MPIR_Breakpoint and thus triggers the breakpoint set in step 1.
4. Using symbol table information of the master process, the monitoring system can now read the process and communicator lists. However, it is still not trivial to obtain a mapping between processes and their rank in MPI_COMM_WORLD.

3.2 Acquisition of State Information

There are two different kinds of state information stored in the programming library that are of interest for on-line tools:

1. The target application's configuration, i.e. nodes and processes. We have already discussed this above.
2. The state of the communication subsystem, i.e. message queues, blocked processes etc.

Neither PVM nor MPI/mpich offers sufficient support for the last item, so the only solution is to extract this information from internal and undocumented data structures in the programming library. Of course, this is not a satisfactory solution, since in this way the monitoring system becomes extremely sensitive to changes in the programming library's implementation.

3.3 Event Detection

Library Calls. Most events related to the programming library can be detected by monitoring the entry into and the exit from library functions. A common

---

[3] There is actually a slight difficulty in getting the full path names, however, it is beyond the scope of this paper to discuss the solution.

technique is to insert *hooks*, i.e. small pieces of monitoring code that are executed immediately before and after the actual library function. A major concern is how to insert hooks without having to recompile the programming library or the target application.

In MPI, an elegant method is used to achieve this: The MPI standard requires that each MPI function provides two entry points. One of these entry points has the usual name starting with MPI_, the other one uses the prefix PMPI_. With a few additional requirements, which are outlined in the standard, this so-called profiling interface allows to easily incorporate hooks by just linking the target application against an additional library. This library contains functions starting with MPI_, which perform some monitoring work and call the original MPI routines via their second entry point PMPI_. The application code now calls these new functions instead of the original ones.

In PVM, no such mechanism exists. Thus, we have to use *binary wrapping* [CM92] to achieve the same effect. The basic idea is to create differently named entry points in an existing binary version of a library by changing the names in its linker symbol table. We can then proceed as explained above.

Process creation. This event that cannot be detected in the way outlined above. By instrumenting e.g. pvm_spawn, we can only detect that (1) a process wants to create other processes (hook at the function's beginning), or (2) it successfully created other processes (hook at the end). However, we cannot catch the new processes: at point (1), they are not yet existent, while at point (2) they already started execution and may even have terminated. However, being able to monitor new processes from their very beginning is essential for debugging.

PVM therefore defines the *tasker* interface [BDG+95]. A tasker is a PVM task responsible for starting new processes on its local node. Thus, it can prepare the new process in a way that keeps it from running until the monitoring system is ready to control it. Although the tasker interface offers the only way to immediately obtain control over new processes without having to modify PVM, its use leads into some trouble: First, all monitor processes now have to be PVM tasks, since we need a tasker on every node. As stated in Section 3.1, this may influence the behavior of the target application. Second, when a tasker terminates, its child processes are killed. This means that although we can dynamically attach the OCM to a target application, we cannot simply detach it again. Finally, when the tasker is informed by the PVM system, the new task does not have a TID yet, which leads to an assignment problem inside the OCM.

For mpich, process creation doesn't seem to be an issue at all, as there is no dynamic process creation in MPI-1. However, this is not true. During the start-up phase, the monitoring system gets immediate control over the master process only (see Section 3.1). From the viewpoint of the monitoring system, the slave processes are created dynamically. In order to prevent them from running too far, mpirun starts them with a special option that results in an endless loop inside MPI_Init. The monitoring system can free a process again by changing a variable inside that process. A drawback of this method is that it is impossible to monitor activities prior to the call to MPI_Init. Thus, applications should call MPI_Init as the very first statement in their main function[4].

3.4 Using PVM/MPI Within the OCM

In principle, PVM and MPI may also be used to implement the communication inside the OCM. Unfortunately, neither of the two offers the interrupt-driven (or handler-driven) receives required by the OCM. However, if communication is implemented using TCP sockets, the sockets can be manipulated, such that a signal handler is called when a message arrives. The OCM then can call available non-blocking receive functions to read the message. Accessing the socket is easy in PVM, since there is a library call (pvm_getfds) returning its file descriptor. In MPI, there is no such call.

There is another stringent reason why the OCM can't use MPI for its communication: When a tool is started, it must be able to connect to the OCM, even when the OCM is already running. However, even with MPI-2, it is impossible for an independent process to join an already running MPI application.

3.5 Consequences for the OCM

As a consequence of the above discussions, the OCM for PVM *must* be a PVM application (due to the use of pvm_config, pvm_tasks, and the tasker interface) and also *can* be a PVM application (since new processes can connect to a running PVM application). Despite the disadvantages already mentioned, the OCM for PVM is implemented this way.

On the other hand, for the MPI version of the OCM there is neither a necessity nor a possibility to use MPI for internal purposes. All the information on the target application can be retrieved without the need for the monitors being MPI processes. MPI also does not offer some essential features needed for the communication within the OCM. This is not astonishing, since MPI has been designed purely for parallel applications, while the OCM is a typical distributed application with accordingly different requirements.

We have therefore designed a tiny communication interface specifically adapted to the needs of the OCM. It has been implemented both on top of PVM, and (for the MPI version of the OCM) by using plain TCP/IP socket connections.

4 Conclusion

As a conclusion, we can state that both PVM and mpich offer sufficient support for building on-line monitoring systems and tools. In a direct comparison, the PVM support wins, however, we also have shown some problematic details. mpich allows to retrieve all necessary information, too, but the interface is more complex and a bit cumbersome. On the other hand, MPI and mpich support features that are missing in PVM, e.g. the profiling interface.

---

[4] However, in C++ programs constructors may be invoked even before main.

In summary, the experience with the OCM has shown that parallel programming libraries should at least provide the following features to support on-line monitoring: A list of nodes (with host names), a list of processes (with node, PID, global ID, path to executable), a means to intercept process creation, and a second entry point for each library function. In the ideal case, a monitoring system should be able to use this functionality, even if it is *not* an application of this programming library.

References

[BDG+95] A. Beguelin, J. Dongarra, A. Geist, R. Manchek, and V. Sunderam. Recent Enhancements to PVM. *International Journal of Supercomputing Applications and High Performance Computing*, 9(2), 1995.

[CM92] J. Cargille and B. P. Miller. Binary Wrapping: A Technique for Instrumenting Object Code. *ACM SIGPLAN Notices*, 27(6):17-18, June 1992.

[Dol] Dolphin Interconnect Solutions, Inc. TotalView Overview. WWW page. http://www.dolphinics.com/tw/tvover.htm.

[For95] The MPI Forum. MPI: A Message-Passing Interface Standard, Version 1.1. Technical report, Univ. of Tennessee, Knoxville, TN, June 1995. http://www.mpi-forum.org/docs/mpi-11.ps.Z.

[For97] The MPI Forum. MPI-2: Extensions to the Message-Passing Interface. Technical report, Univ. of Tennessee, Knoxville, TN, July 1997. http://www.mpi-forum.org/docs/mpi-20.ps.Z.

[GBD+94] A. Geist, A. Beguelin, J. Dongarra, W. Jiang, R. Mancheck, and V. Sunderam. *PVM: Parallel Virtual Machine. A Users' Guide and Tutorial for Networked Parallel Computing*. MIT Press, 1994.

[GLDS96] W. Gropp, E. Lusk, N. Doss, and A. Skjellum. A High-Performance, Portable Implementation of the MPI Message Passing Interface Standard. Technical report, Argonne National Lab, July 1996. http://www.mcs.anl.gov/mpi/mpicharticle/paper.html.

[LW97] T. Ludwig and R. Wismüller. OMIS 2.0 – A Universal Interface for Monitoring Systems. In M. Bubak et al., editors, *Proc. 4th European PVM/MPI Users' Group Meeting*, volume 1332 of *Lecture Notes in Computer Science*, pages 267-276, Crakow, Poland, November 1997. Springer Verlag. http://www.in.tum.de/~wismuell/pub/europvm97b.ps.gz.

[LWSB97] T. Ludwig, R. Wismüller, V. Sunderam, and A. Bode. *OMIS — On-line Monitoring Interface Specification (Version 2.0)*, volume 9 of *LRR-TUM Research Report Series*. Shaker Verlag, Aachen, Germany, 1997. http://wwwbode.informatik.tu-muenchen.de/~omis/OMIS/Version-2.0/version-2.0.ps.gz.

[SMP95] T. Sterling, P. Messina, and J. Pool. Findings of the Second Pasadena Workshop on System Software and Tools for High Performance Computing Environments. Technical report, Center of Excellence in Space Data and Information Sciences, NASA Goddard Space Flight Center, Greenbelt, Maryland, 1995. http://cesdis.gsfc.nasa.gov/PAS2/findings.html.

[WTL98] R. Wismüller, J. Trinitis, and T. Ludwig. OCM — A Monitoring System for Interoperable Tools. In *Proc. 2nd SIGMETRICS Symposium on Parallel and Distributed Tools*, Welches, OR, USA, August 1998. To appear.

Part 5
Algorithms

Coarse Grained Parallel Monte Carlo Algorithms for Solving SLAE using PVM

V. Alexandrov[1], F. Dehne[2], A. Rau-Chaplin[3], and K. Taft[1]

[1] Department of Computer Science, University of Liverpool,
Chadwick Building, Peach Street, Liverpool, L69 7ZF, UK
{vassil, keitht} @csc.liv.ac.uk
[2] School of Computer Science, Carleton University,
Ottawa, Canada, K1S 5B6
dehne@scs.carleton.ca
[3] Faculty of Computer Science, DalTech, Dalhousie University,
P.O. Box 1000, Halifax NS, Canada B3J 2X4
arc@cs.dal.ca

Abstract. The problem of solving System of Linear Algebraic Equations (SLAE) by parallel Monte Carlo numerical methods is considered. Three Monte Carlo algorithms are presented. In case when copy of the matrix is sent to each processor the execution time for solving SLAE by Monte Carlo on p processors is bounded by $O(nNT/p)$ (excluding the initial loading of the data) where N is the number of chains and T is the length of the chain in the stochastic process, which are independent of matrix size n.
Numerical tests are performed for a number of dense and sparse test matrices using PVM on a cluster of workstations.

1 Introduction

It is known that Monte Carlo methods give statistical estimates for the components of the solution vector of SLAE by performing random sampling of a certain random variable whose mathematical expectation is the desired solution [9, 10]. We consider Monte Carlo methods for solving SLAE since: **firstly,** only $O(NT)$ steps are required to find an element of the inverse matrix (MI) or component of the solution vector of SLAE (N is a number of chains and T is a measure on the chains length in the stochastic process, which are independent of n) and **secondly,** the sampling process for stochastic methods is inherently parallel. In comparison, the direct methods of solution require $O(n^3)$ sequential steps when the usual elimination or annihilation schemes (e.g non-pivoting Gaussian Elimination, Gauss-Jordan methods) are employed [3]. Consequently the computation time for very large problems or for real-time problems can be prohibitive and prevents the use of many established algorithms. Therefore due to their properties, their inherent parallelism and loose data dependencies Monte Carlo algorithms can be implemented on parallel machines very efficiently and thus may enable us to solve large-scale problems which are sometimes difficult or prohibitive to be solved by the well-known numerical methods.

Generally three Monte Carlo methods for Matrix Inversion (MI) and finding a solution vector of System of Linear Algebraic Equations (SLAE) can be outlined: with absorption, without absorption with uniform transition frequency function, and without absorption with almost optimal transition frequency function.

In the case of **fine grained** setting, recently Alexandrov, Megson and Dimov have shown that an $n \times n$ matrix can be inverted in $3n/2 + N + T$ steps on regular array with $O(n^2 NT)$ cells [8]. Alexandrov and Megson have also shown that a solution vector of SLAE can be found in $n + N + T$ steps on regular array with the same number of cells [2]. A number of bounds on N and T have been established, which show that these designs are faster than the existing designs for large values of n [8, 2].

The **coarse grained** case for MI is considered in [1]. In this paper we extend this implementation approach for SLAE in MIMD environment, i.e. a cluster of workstations under PVM in our case. We also derive an estimate on time complexity using CGM model.

The **Coarse Grained Multicomputer** model, or $CGM(n, p)$ for short, which is the architectural model to be used in this paper is a set of p processors with $O(\frac{n}{p})$ local memory each, connected to some arbitrary interconnection network or a shared memory. The term "**coarse grained**" refers to the fact that (as in practice) the size $O(\frac{n}{p})$ of each local memory is defined to be "considerably larger" than $O(1)$. Our definition of "considerably larger" will be that $\frac{n}{p} \geq p$. This is clearly true for all currently available coarse grained parallel machines. For determining time complexities we will consider both, local computation time and inter-processor communication time, in the standard way.

For parallel algorithms for SLAE to be relevant in practice, such algorithms must be **scalable**, that is, they must be applicable and efficient for a wide range of ratios $\frac{n}{p}$. The use of CGM helps to ensure that the parallel algorithms designed are not only efficient in theory, but also they result in efficient parallel software with fast running time on real data . Experiments have shown that in addition to the scalability, the CGM algorithms typically quickly reach the point of optimal speedup for reasonable data sets. Even with modest programming efforts the actual results obtained for other application areas have been excellent [4].

In this paper we focus mainly on the case when a copy of the matrix is sent to each processor. We are currently testing different strategies for efficiently parallelising Monte Carlo algorithms for the case of large matrices when the matrix is partitioned and distributed among the processors as well as different ways of minimising the number of chains required to find the solution. We expect to report these results in the near future.

2 Stochastic methods and SLAE

Assume that the system of linear algebraic equations (SLAE) is presented in the form:

$$x = Ax + \varphi \tag{1}$$

where A is a real square $n \times n$ matrix, $x = (x_1, x_2, ..., x_n)^t$ is a $1 \times n$ solution vector and $\varphi = (\varphi_1, \varphi_2, ..., \varphi_n)^t$ is a given vector. (If we consider the system $Lx = b$, then it is possible to choose non-singular matrix M such that $ML = I - A$ and $Mb = \varphi$, and so $Lx = b$ can be presented as $x = Ax + \varphi$.) Assume that A satisfies the condition $\max_{1 \leq i \leq n} \sum_{j=1}^n |a_{ij}| < 1$, which implies that all the eigenvalues of A lie in the unit circle. The matrix and vector norms are determined as follows: $\|A\| = \max_{1 \leq i \leq n} \sum_{j=1}^n |a_{ij}|$, $\|\varphi\| = \max_{1 \leq i \leq n} |\varphi_i|$.

Suppose that we have Markov chains with n - states. The random trajectory (chain) T_i of length i starting in state k_0 is defined as $k_0 \to k_1 \to \cdots \to k_j \to \cdots \to k_i$ where k_j is the number of the state chosen, for $j = 1, 2, \cdots, i$. The following probability definitions are also important: $P(k_0 = \alpha) = p_\alpha$, $P(k_j = \beta | k_{j-1} = \alpha) = p_{\alpha\beta}$ where p_α is the probability that the chain starts in state α and $p_{\alpha\beta}$ is the transition probability to state β from state α. Probabilities $p_{\alpha\beta}$ define a transition matrix P. We require that $\sum_{\alpha=1}^n p_\alpha = 1$, $\sum_{\beta=1}^n p_{\alpha\beta} = 1$ for any $\alpha = 1, 2, ..., n$, the distribution $(p_1, ..., p_n)^t$ is acceptable to vector g and similarly the distribution $p_{\alpha\beta}$ is acceptable to A [9].

Consider the problem of evaluating the inner product of a given vector g with the vector solution of (1)

$$(g, x) = \sum_{\alpha=1}^n g_\alpha x_\alpha \qquad (2)$$

It is known [9] that the mathematical expectation $E\Theta^*[g]$ of random variable $\Theta^*[g]$ is:

$$E\Theta^*[g] = (g, x)$$

$$\text{where } \Theta^*[g] = \frac{g_{k_0}}{p_{k_0}} \sum_{j=0}^\infty W_j \varphi_{k_j} \qquad (3)$$

$$\text{and} \quad W_0 = 1, \quad W_j = W_{j-1} \frac{a_{k_{j-1} k_j}}{p_{k_{j-1} k_j}}$$

We use the following notation for a partial sum (3) $\theta_i[g] = \frac{g_{k_0}}{p_{k_0}} \sum_{j=0}^i W_j \varphi_{k_j}$. According to the above conditions on the matrix A, the series $\sum_{j=0}^\infty W_j \varphi_{k_j}$ converges for any given vector φ and $E\theta_i[g]$ tends to (g, x) as $i \longrightarrow \infty$. Thus $\theta_i[g]$ can be considered an estimate of (g, x) for i sufficiently large.

Now we define the Monte Carlo method. To find one component of the solution, for example the r-th component of x, we choose $g = e(r) = (0, ..., 0, 1, 0, ..., 0)$ where the one is in the r-th place. It follows that $(g, x) = \sum_{\alpha=1}^n e_\alpha(r) x_\alpha = x_r$ and the corresponding Monte Carlo method is given by

$$x_r \approx \frac{1}{N} \sum_{s=1}^N \theta_i[e(r)]_s \qquad (4)$$

where N is the number of chains and $\theta_i[e(r)]_s$ is the value of $\theta_i[e(r)]$ in the s-th chain.

The **probable error** of the method, is defined as $r_N = 0.6745\sqrt{D\theta/N}$, where $P\{|\bar\theta - E(\theta)| < r_N\} \approx 1/2 \approx P\{|\bar\theta - E(\theta)| > r_N\}$, if we have N independent realizations of random variable (r.v.) θ with mathematical expectation $E\theta$ and average $\bar\theta$ [9].

It is clear from the formula for r_N that the number of chains N can be reduced by a suitable choice of the transition probabilities that reduces the variance for a given probable error. This idea leads to Monte Carlo methods with minimal probable error.

The key results concerning minimization of probable error and the definition of **almost** optimal transition frequency for Monte Carlo methods applied to the calculation of inner product via iterated functions are presented in [8]. According to [8, 7] and the principal of collinearity of norms [8] we can choose $p_{\alpha\beta}$ proportional to the $|a_{\alpha\beta}|$.

In case of Monte Carlo with absorption, assuming as before $\|A\| < 1$, we have [1, 2, 7]:

$$p_{\alpha\beta} = |a_{\alpha\beta}| \text{ for } \alpha, \beta = 1, 2, ..., n.$$

and the absorption probability

$$p_{\alpha n+1} = p_\alpha = 1 - \sum_{\beta=1}^{n} p_{\alpha\beta}$$

is the probability that the trajectory ends in state α.

In case of Monte Carlo without absorption we have two possibilities [1, 2] :

– Almost Optimal Monte Carlo method:

$$p_{\alpha\beta} = \frac{|a_{\alpha\beta}|}{\sum_\beta |a_{\alpha\beta}|} \text{ for } \alpha, \beta = 1, 2, ..., n.$$

– Usual Monte Carlo method:

$$p_{\alpha\beta} = 1/n \text{ for } \alpha, \beta = 1, 2, ..., n$$

In case of $\|A\| \geq 1$ or very close to 1 we can use the Resolvent Monte Carlo method [5] to reduce the matrix norm and to speedup the computations.

3   Parameters Estimation and Discussion

We will outline the method of estimation of N and T in case of **Monte Carlo method without absorbing states** since it is known that these methods require less chains than the methods with absorption to reach the same precision [2, 1]. In case of Monte Carlo with absorption the parameter estimation can be done in the same way. We will consider Monte Carlo methods with uniform (UM) and with almost optimal (MAO) transition frequency function. Let us consider Monte Carlo method with almost optimal (MAO) transition frequency function. We assume that the following conditions $\sum_{\beta=1}^{n} p_{\alpha\beta} = 1$ for any $\alpha = 1, 2, ..., n$

must be satisfied and transition matrix P might have entries $p_{\alpha\beta} = \frac{|a_{\alpha\beta}|}{\sum_\beta |a_{\alpha\beta}|}$ for $\alpha, \beta = 1, 2, ..., n$.

The estimator Θ^* for SLAE was defined as follows

$$E\Theta^*[g] = (g, x),$$

$$\text{where } \Theta^*[g] = \frac{g_{k_0}}{p_{k_0}} \sum_{j=0}^{\infty} W_j \varphi_{k_j} \tag{5}$$

$$\text{and } W_0 = 1, \quad W_j = W_{j-1} \frac{a_{k_{j-1}k_j}}{p_{k_{j-1}k_j}}.$$

The sum for Θ^* must be dropped when $|W_i \varphi_{k_i}| < \delta$ [9].
Note that

$$|W_i \varphi_{k_i}| = \left| \frac{a_{\alpha_0\alpha_1} \cdots a_{\alpha_{i-1}\alpha_i}}{\frac{|a_{\alpha_0\alpha_1}|}{\|A\|} \cdots \frac{|a_{\alpha_{i-1}\alpha_i}|}{\|A\|}} \right| \|\varphi_{k_i}\| = \|A\|^i \|\varphi\| < \delta.$$

Then it follows that

$$T = i \leq \frac{\log\left(\delta / \|\varphi\|\right)}{\log \|A\|}.$$

It is easy to find [9] that $|\Theta^*| \leq \frac{\|\varphi\|}{(1 - \|A\|)}$, which means that variance of r.v. Θ^* is bounded by its second moment: $D\Theta^* \leq E\Theta^{*2} = \frac{\|\varphi\|^2}{(1-\|A\|)^2} \leq \frac{f^2}{(1-\|A\|)^2}$. According to the Central Limit Theorem for the given error ϵ

$$N \geq \frac{0.6745^2 D\eta^*[g]}{\epsilon^2} \quad \text{and} \quad \text{thus} \quad N \geq \frac{0.6745^2}{\epsilon^2} \frac{f^2}{(1-\|A\|)^2} \tag{6}$$

is a lower bound on N which is independent of n.

It is clear that T and N depend only on the matrix norm and precision. Furthermore, the size of N can be controlled by an appropriate choice of ϵ once P and A are known.

Consider N and T as functions of $\frac{1}{(1-\|A\|)}$. It is obvious from (6) that $T = O(\sqrt{(N)})$. In addition there are computational experiments in [8] showing this fact that for sufficiently large N we can take $T \approx \sqrt{N}$.

4 Parallel Implementation

We implement parallel Monte Carlo algorithms on a cluster of workstations under PVM. We assume virtual star topology and we apply master/slave approach.

Inherently, Monte Carlo methods for solving SLAE allow us to have minimal communication, i.e. to pass the full matrix A to every processor, to run the algorithm in parallel on each processor computing $\lceil n/p \rceil$ components of the solution vector and to collect the results from slaves at the end without any communication between sending A and receiving partitions of x. The only communication is at the beginning and at the end of the algorithm execution which allows us to obtain very high efficiency of parallel implementation. Therefore, by allocating the master in the central node of the star and the slaves in the remaining nodes, the communication is minimized.

Therefore since we need to compute n components of the vector solution each requiring N chains of length T on p processors in parallel the time is $O(nNT/p)$ excluding the initial loading of the data.

5 Numerical tests

The numerical tests are made on a cluster of 48 Hewlett Packard 900 series 700 Unix workstations under PVM. The workstations are networked via 10Mb switched ethernet segments and each workstation has at least 64Mb RAM and run at least 60 MIPS.

The numerical tests are made using methods without absorption, since they require less chains to reach given precision in comparison with methods with absorption [1]. We have used dense and sparse balanced matrices (which have nearly equal sums of elements per row). In the example presented, the matrix is dense with norm 0.98 when the convergence of the method is slow. The results for the average time and efficiency are given in tables 1 and 2. The relative accuracy is 10^{-2}.

Table 1. Time in seconds

Processors Matrix Size	1	2	3	4	6	8	10
50	36.108	18.159	12.359	9.153	7.427	5.419	4.006
100	286.318	143.397	104.428	72.178	52.302	40.271	32.93
200	581.628	286.244	192.719	144.356	105.609	80.828	62.699
300	855.506	445.109	358.114	229.093	162.159	124.316	103.430
400	1150.567	574.193	385.461	302.706	219.099	174.823	166.83
500	1494.473	741.936	564.527	409.003	280.916	224.696	210.679

The experiments show that the computation time is a **linear function** of the matrix size n which is in accordance with the theoretical estimates.

The **parallel efficiency** E as, a measure that characterize the quality of the proposed algorithms is defined as:

$$E(X) = \frac{ET_1(X)}{pET_p(X)},$$

where X is a Monte Carlo algorithm, $ET_p(X)$ is the expected value of the computational time for implementation the algorithm X on a system of p processors.

Table 2. Efficiency

Processors Matrix Size	1	2	3	4	6	8	10
50	1	0.994	0.974	0.986	0.810	0.833	0.9013
100	1	0.9985	0.914	0.992	0.912	0.889	0.869
200	1	1.016	1.006	1.007	0.918	0.8995	0.928
300	1	0.961	0.796	0.9335	0.879	0.86	0.827
400	1	1.0015	0.995	0.95	0.875	0.823	0.6897
500	1	1.007	0.891	0.9135	0.877	0.831	0.7094

6 Conclusion

In our parallel implementation we have to compute n components of the solution vector of SLAE in parallel. To compute a component of the solution vector we need N independent chains with length T, and for n components in parallel we need nN such independent chains of length T, where N and T are the mathematical expectations of the number of chains and chain length, respectively. So the execution time on p processors for solving SLAE by Monte Carlo is bounded by $O(nNT/p)$ (excluding initialization communication time). According to the discussion and results above N and T depend only on the matrix norm and precision and do not depend on the matrix size. Therefore the Monte Carlo methods can be efficiently implemented on MIMD environment and in particular on a cluster of workstations under PVM.

In particular it should be noted that the Monte Carlo methods are well suited to large problems where other solution methods are impractical or impossible for computational reasons, for calculating quick rough estimate of the solution vector, and when only a few components of the solution vector are desired. Consequently, if massive parallelism is available and if low precision is acceptable, Monte Carlo algorithms could become favourable for $n >> N$.

7 Acknowledgements

Thanks to the British Council for the partial support.

References

1. V.Alexandrov and S. Lakka *Comparison of three Parallel Monte Carlo Methods for Matrix Inversion*, Proc. of EUROPAR96, Lyon, France, Vol II, pp. 72-80.
2. V.Alexandrov and G.M. Megson *Solving Sytem of Linear algebraic Equations by Monte Carlo Method on Regular Arrays*, Proc. of PARCELLA96, 16-20 September, Berlin, Germany, pp. 137-146, 1996.
3. Bertsekas D.P. and Tsitsiklis , *Parallel and Distributed Computation* , Prentice Hall, 1989

4. F. Dehne, A. Fabri, and A. Rau-Chaplin, Scalable parallel geometric algorithms for multicomputers, *Proc. 7th ACM Symp. on Computational Geometry*, 1993.

5. I. Dimov and V.Alexandrov A New Highly Convergent Monte Carlo Method for Matrix Computations, Proc. of IMACS Monte Carlo Seminar, April 1-4, 1997, Belgium (in print).

6. G. H. Golub, Ch. F. Van Loon, *Matrix Computations*, **The Johns Hopkins Univ. Press**, Baltimore and London, 1996.

7. J.H. Halton, *Sequential Monte Carlo Techniques for the Solution of Linear Systems*, **TR 92-033**, University of North Carolina at Chapel Hill, Department of Computer Science, 46 pp., 1992.

8. G.M.Megson, V.Aleksandrov, I. Dimov *Systolic Matrix Inversion Using Monte Carlo Method*, J. Parallel Algorithms and Applications , Vol.3, pp.311-330, 1994.

9. Sobol' I.M. *Monte Carlo numerical methods*. Moscow, Nauka, 1973 (Russian)(English version Univ. of Chicago Press 1984).

10. Westlake J.R., *A Handbook of Numerical Matrix Inversion and Solution of Linear Equations*, John Wiley and Sons, New York, 1968.

Parallel Quantum Scattering Calculations Applied to the Dynamics of Elementary Reactions

Alessandro Bolloni, Antonio Riganelli,
Stefano Crocchianti, Antonio Laganà

Dipartimento di Chimica
Università di Perugia
via Elce di Sotto, 8
06123 Perugia (Italy)

Abstract. A consolidated approach to the problem of integrating the full dimensional time independent Schrödinger equation consists of expanding the solution in terms of surface functions of the bond coordinates. The construction of these functions is a computational task difficult to parallelize. In this paper we discuss a successful attempt adopting a processors farm parallel model implemented using MPI.

1   Introduction

The integration of the full dimension (3D) Schrödinger equation describing the evolution of an atom diatom reactive system is a challenging computational problem of the many body type as well as a key step of several technological and environmental modelling. Mathematically, this is a 9 dimension problem that, after separating the center of mass motion and expanding the solution in partial waves, can be reduced to the integration of the following 3D problem:

$$H\Psi^{JMpn} = E\Psi^{JMpn}. \tag{1}$$

In the hyperspherical coordinate formulation the Hamiltonian H reads:

$$H = T_\rho + T_h + T_r + T_c + V(\rho, \theta, \chi_i) \tag{2}$$

with ρ, θ, χ_i being the three internal coordinates and

$$T_\rho = -\frac{\hbar^2}{2\mu\rho^5} \frac{\partial}{\partial\rho} \rho^5 \frac{\partial}{\partial\rho}, \tag{3}$$

$$T_h = -\frac{\hbar^2}{2\mu\rho^2} \left(\frac{4}{\sin 2\theta} \frac{\partial}{\partial\theta} \sin 2\theta \frac{\partial}{\partial\theta} + \frac{1}{\sin^2\theta} \frac{\partial^2}{\partial\chi_i^2} \right), \tag{4}$$

$$T_r = AJ_x^2 + BJ_y^2 + CJ_z^2, \tag{5}$$

$$T_c = -\frac{i\hbar\cos\theta}{\mu\rho^2\sin^2\theta} J_y \frac{\partial}{\partial\chi_i} \tag{6}$$

and $A^{-1} = \mu\rho^2 (1 + \sin\theta)$, $B^{-1} = 2\mu\rho^2 \sin^2\theta$, $C^{-1} = \mu\rho^2 (1 - \sin\theta)$.

The partial wave Ψ^{JMpn} is expanded as products of Wigner rotational functions $\hat{D}^J_{\Lambda M}$ of the three Euler angles α, β, γ and surface functions Φ of the two internal hyperangles θ and χ_i:

$$\Psi^{JMpn} = 4 \sum_{t,\Lambda} \rho^{-\frac{5}{2}} \psi^{Jpn}_{t\Lambda}(\rho) \Phi^{Jp}_{t\Lambda}(\theta, \chi_i; \rho_\epsilon) \hat{D}^{Jp}_{\Lambda M}(\alpha, \beta, \gamma). \quad (7)$$

To carry out the numerical integration we use a computer code (APH3D) based on the APH coordinate formalism of R. T Pack and G. A. Parker[1] [2], where the ρ interval is divided into several sectors. For each sector ϵ a set of surface functions $\Phi^{Jp}_{t\Lambda}(\theta, \chi_i; \rho_\epsilon)$ is calculated at the sector midpoint ρ_ϵ. These surface functions, which serve as a local basis set, are independent of ρ within the sector but change for different sectors.

The first computational step consists of the integration of the following two dimensional bound state equation:

$$\left[T_h + \frac{15\hbar^2}{8\mu\rho_\epsilon^2} + \hbar^2 G_J + F\hbar^2 \Lambda^2 + V(\rho_\epsilon, \theta, \chi_i) - \varepsilon^{Jp}_{t\Lambda}(\rho_\epsilon) \right] \Phi^{Jp}_{t\Lambda}(\theta, \chi_i; \rho_\epsilon) = 0 \quad (8)$$

where $G_J = \frac{1}{2}J(J+1)(A+B)$ and $F = C - (A+B)/2$.

The second computational step consists of the integration, sector by sector and from small ρ values to the asymptotes, of the following set of coupled differential equations:

$$\left[\frac{\partial^2}{\partial\rho^2} + \frac{2\mu E}{\hbar^2} \right] \psi^{Jpn}_{t\Lambda}(\rho) = \frac{2\mu}{\hbar^2} \sum_{t'\Lambda'} \langle \Phi^{Jp}_{t\Lambda} \hat{D}^{Jp}_{\Lambda M} | H_i | \Phi^{Jp}_{t'\Lambda'} \hat{D}^{Jp}_{\Lambda' M} \rangle \psi^{Jpn}_{t'\Lambda'}(\rho) \quad (9)$$

where the Hamiltonian H_i reads:

$$H_i = T_h + T_r + T_c + \frac{15\hbar^2}{8\mu\rho^2} + V(\rho, \theta, \chi_i). \quad (10)$$

Once the integration is performed, the solution is mapped into the space of the Delves coordinates, asymptotic conditions are imposed and fixed **J** S matrix elements are evaluated.

The related computational procedure is very demanding in terms of computer resources and computing time. For this reason it has been articulated into several programs. The most demanding of these programs, i.e. the program performing the calculation of fixed ρ eigenvalues and surface functions of the two internal hyperangles (ABM), as well as the program performing the fixed total angular momentum **J** propagation along the reaction coordinate ρ for a set of energy values (LOGDER), are being considered for parallelization.

2 The parallel computational model

We focus here on the ABM program. The scheme of the serial ABM program is articulated as follows:

```
Input data
Calculate quantities of common use
LOOP on sectors
    Calculate the value of ρ
    LOOP on Λ
        Calculate surface functions
        IF(not first ρ) calculate overlaps with previous sector
    END the Λ loop
    Calculate and store the coupling matrix
END the sector loop
```

In the input step, the program reads the input data needed to calculate the surface functions. Then, the program performs a main loop over the index of all ρ values. After the initialization of ρ, there is a loop over the Λ index (the projection of the total angular momentum $\mathbf{J}$ on the z axis of the BF frame of reference). Inside this loop, the program calculates the fixed ρ and Λ surface functions of θ and χ using the Analytical Basis Method. For sectors higher than $\epsilon=1$ the program calculates also the overlap and the coupling matrices between surface functions at the current value of the hyperradius and those of the preceeding one to be used by the LOGDER program.

The order dependency associated with the calculation of the overlap and coupling integrals is an obstacle to the parallelization of the ABM code. To cope with this difficulty, in a previous work[3] the program was parallelized by statically assigning a block of sectors to each node (the number of sectors is equal to the number of nodes used for the calculation). To decouple the calculations of different blocks, the last sector of each block was taken also as the first sector of the next block. Each node writes the calculated block of the coupling matrix on disk. After completing ABM, the various blocks are appended in a single file.

To develop the parallel version of ABM discussed in this paper, use was made of the MPI package [4] (so as to guarantee the portability of the code) and a task farm model[5] was adopted with a dynamical assignment of the work to the nodes. The scheme of the slave program reads as follows:

```
call MPI_RECV(ρ_ε)
if(first ρ_ε) then
    initrho=ρ_ε
    endrho=ρ_ε
else
    initrho=ρ_ε-1
    endrho=ρ_ε
endif
loop on Λ
```

```
do count=initrho,endrho
   Solve the Schrödinger equation for ρ=count
   Store eigenvalues and surface functions
enddo
if(not first ρ) calculates overlap
end loop on Λ
Calculate the coupling matrix
Store the coupling matrix
```

To implement the task farm model it was necessary to deeply restructure the program because the surface functions are stored in huge matrices, causing memory problems. The model allows a node to act as a master and to distribute fixed ρ calculations of the surface functions to all other nodes as soon as they complete the previously assigned work. The slave processes compute and store eigenvalues and surface functions for the previous and current values of ρ, and then construct the overlap integrals and the related section of the coupling matrix.

3 Performance measurements

The parallel ABM code was implemented on the Cray T3E at EPCC and CINECA.
Calculations were performed for a realistic reaction model (Li+FH) by dividing the ρ interval into 230 sectors and using a basis set of 277 functions. Elapsed time measured for individual processors are plotted in Figure 1 as a function of the node number.

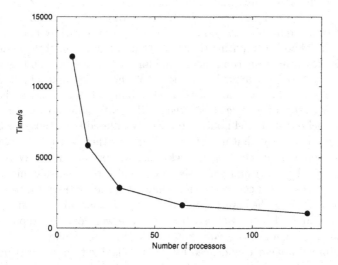

Fig. 1. Elapsed time for the ABM program.

Information of Figure 1 is complemented by the plot of the speedup (solid line) calculated for the same number of processors given in Figure 2.

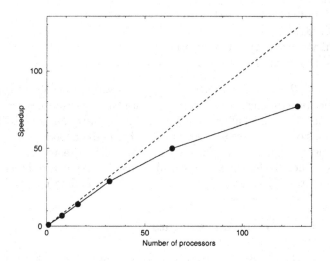

Fig. 2. Speedup of the ABM program

The sequential time used for calculating the speedup has been approximated by defect by summing the individual time of all sectors (82449 s). As apparent from the figure the program scales fairly well since the measured speedup is still about 70 % the ideal value (dashed line).

To analyze in more detail the performance parameters of ABM we have also measured the amount of time spent in computing by the variuos nodes. In Figure 3 the individual node computing time is plotted as a function of the node number for a typical 32 processors run (above) and for a 64 processors run (below). Both plots show a two level articulation. Most of the nodes take about the same computing time, while a small fraction take about 300 s more. This is the first difference with regard to times measured for the static assignment. For the static parallel model results for 64 nodes significantly differed from those for 32 nodes. The reason for this was that in a static assignment there are two sources of load unbalance: some nodes get larger blocks (230 sectors are unevenly partitioned among 32 or 64 nodes) and some sectors (usually the lowest numbered ones) require more time to get converged eigenvalues. On the contrary, for the task farm model a dispersion of the lowest numbered sectors among all nodes automatically guarantees a more democratic distribution of the workload. On top of that, the dynamical assignment of the work further levels the workload.

The remaining imbalance evidenced by Figure 3 is due to nodes getting the last sectors to run when all others have almost completed their job. This is confirmed by a detailed analysis of the individual node workloads for a typical run.

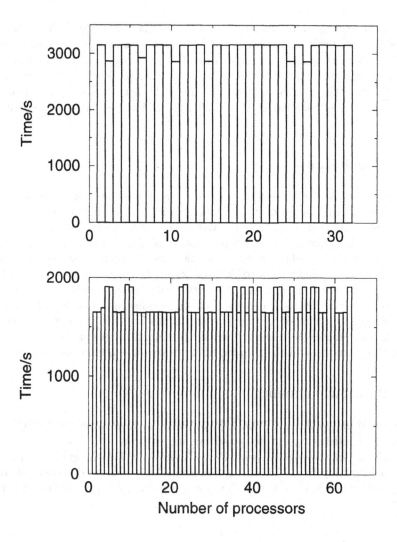

Fig. 3. Time spent in the ABM program by each node for a 32 processors run (above) and for a 64 processors run (below).

As an example, by taking a 32 nodes run, the analysis shows that for the first sector calculation (a slow convergent *sc* one not having to calculate the coupling matrix) is performed by all slave nodes to set the initial value of several variables. With the calculation parameters of the model chosen here, this is a time ranging from 453 s to 457 s. Then, calculations for sectors 2 to 32 (these are also *sc*) are distributed to the 31 slave nodes taking from 606 s to 610 s each. Next, the remaining 13 *sc* calculations are distributed to the first 13 slave nodes ending their jobs. The remaining 18 nodes get large ρ (faster convergent *fc*) calculations.

Since the average computing time of *sc* sectors is about 600 s while that of *fc* is 300 s, there will be another batch of 18 nodes running *fc* calculations while the 13 nodes running the *sc* ones are still completing their job. Then, almost at the same time all the 31 nodes will end their work and get a new one of the *fc* type. The last batch of calculations will start, therefore, just before the remaining nodes complete their work. This leads for these nodes to a delay time of about 300 s.

4 Conclusions

We investigated the possibility of parallelizing the ABM program which is devoted to the calculation of surface functions for a three dimensional time independent quantum approach for reactive atom diatom probabilities.

Our work has shown that an adoption of a task farm model with a dynamical assignment of the load to the slaves has significant advantages over models based on a static assignment of the work. This despite the fact that one node has been dedicated to act as master, that first sector calculations have to be repeated by all nodes to evaluate some quantities of common use and that the calculation of the surface functions of the previous sector has been replicated for all sectors. Work is in progress to refine the model and minimize all sources of inaccuracy. The chosen model and the adopted MPI library allow a high portability.

5 Acknowledgments

We would like to thank CINECA (Casalecchio di Reno, Italy) and EPCC (Edinburgh, United Kingdom) for providing access to the Cray T3E.
A. Bolloni acknowledges a grant form CINECA, a TRACS grant from EPCC and a fellowship from INFN. A grant from INFN is also acknowledged by A. Riganelli, while S. Crocchianti acknowledges a grant from the University of Perugia.

References

1. R. T Pack, G. A. Parker, J. Chem. Phys. **87** (1987) 3888-3921.
2. G. A. Parker, A. Laganà, S. Crocchianti, R. T Pack, *A detailed three dimensional quantum study of the Li+FH reation*, J. Chem. Phys. **102** (1995) 1238-1250.
3. A. Laganà, S. Crocchianti, G. Ochoa de Aspuru, R. Gargano, G.A. Parker, *Parallel time independent quantum calculations of atom diatom reactivity*, Lecture Notes in Computer Science **1041** (1995) 361-370.
4. M. Snir, S. Otto, S. Huss-Lederman, D. Walker, J. Dongarra, *MPI: The complete reference*, The MIT Press, Cambridge, Mass. (1996).
5. G. C. Fox, M. Johnson, G. Lyzenga, S. Otto, J. Salmon, D. Walker, *Solving problems on concurrent processors*, Prentice Hall, Englewood Cliff (1988).

On the PVM Computations of Transitive Closure and Algebraic Path Problems

Ken Chan[1], Alan Gibbons[1], Marcelo Pias[3], and Wojciech Rytter[1,2]

[1] Department of Computer Science, University of Liverpool, Liverpool L69 7ZF, U.K.
{kjc,amg,rytter}@csc.liv.ac.uk
[2] Institute of Informatics, Warsaw University, Warsaw, Poland
W.Rytter@mimuw.edu.pl
[3] Department of Computer Science, Fundacao Universidade de Rio Grande, Brazil
mpias@acm.org

Abstract. We investigate experimentally, alternative approaches to the distributed parallel computation of a class of problems related to the generic *transitive closure* problem and the *algebraic path problem*. Our main result is the comparison of two parallel algorithms for transitive closure,

- a straightforward coarse-grained parallel implementation of the War-shall algorithm named Block-Processing (which also extends to the stronger algebraic path problem) and
- a coarse-grained Three-Pass algorithm, introduced in this paper. Although this latter algorithm is more complicated, it behaves better for large problem sizes.

We show the relationship between the transitive closure problem and matrix multiplication - the latter problem has especially efficient PVM implementations which can be applied here. The synchronous shared memory model and several known intricate systolic algorithms are a good starting point for distributed implementations. We discuss alternative implementations and the suitability of the PVM model.

1 Introduction

The generic transitive closure problem (*TC*, for short) and the algebraic path problem (*APP*, for short) are useful algorithmic schemes having important applications in areas such as graph theory and dynamic programming. Matrix multiplication is well suited to parallel implementation in PVM - by reducing the APP and TC problems to instances of matrix multiplication, we can gain efficiency (through parallelism) for solving these problems.

The TC and APP can be defined using an abstract notion of a *semiring* with operations $\oplus$ and $\otimes$, see [1] for formal definitions. In both problems there are two operations $\oplus$ and $\otimes$, we sum the values of the paths from a given vertex i to a given vertex j using the generalised summation operation $\oplus$ and the value of each path is the multiplication of the values of its edges in terms of the generalised multiplication operation $\otimes$. In the case of the TC problem we sum only simple paths - simple means that no vertex appears twice, except possibly the first and the last one.

Our main problem is the **Generic Transitive Closure Problem, TC**:
    Instance: a matrix A with elements from a semiring S
    Output: the matrix A^*, $A^*(i,j)$ is the sum of all **simple** paths from i to j.
The second problem is the **Algebraic Path Problem, APP**:
    Instance: a matrix A with elements from a closed semiring S
    Output: the matrix whose (i,j)th entry is the sum of **all** paths from i to j.

Two straightforward applications of the TC problem are the *boolean closure* of the matrix (where $\oplus$ and $\otimes$ are the boolean *OR* and boolean *AND* operations respectively) and *all-pairs shortest paths* computation in graphs (where $\oplus$ and $\otimes$ are the *MIN* and $+$ operations). Less clear-cut is the computation of *minimum spanning* trees [8]: if we consider $\oplus$ and $\otimes$ as *MIN* and *MAX* then the minimum spanning tree consists of all edges (i,j) such that $A(i,j) = A^*(i,j)$, assuming that all initial weights $A(i,j)$ are distinct.

An example of an application of the APP is the analysis of nondeterministic finite automata (computing regular expressions describing paths between pairs of states of the automaton), see [1].

In this paper we show that the coarse-grained computation of the TC problem can be also considered as an instance of the APP problem. The best known sequential algorithm for the TC problem is the *Warshall* algorithm [10] which takes $O(n^3)$ time steps to compute. Our first algorithm, called *Block-Processing*, uses a straightforward coarse-grained parallel implementation of the Warshall algorithm. Our second algorithm, *Three-Pass*, is more complicated and uses the ideas of the Guibas-Kung-Thompson systolic algorithm [4], [6], [7] and [9]. Systolic array of processors can compute the TC problem in $O(n)$ time steps but require $O(n^2)$ processing elements.

2   The Block Processing Algorithm

The classical algorithm for computing the the transitive closure is the Warshall algorithm and works on the elements of matrix A as follows ...

Warshall Algorithm
for k := 1 **to** n **do**
    for i := 1 **to** n **do**
        for j := 1 **to** n **do**
            $A(i,j) = A(i,j) \oplus A(i,k) \otimes A(k,j)$

The APP can be computed similarly; by replacing $A(i,k) \otimes A(k,j)$ with $A(i,k) \otimes A(k,k)^* \otimes A(k,j)$, the algorithm is transformed into a version of Kleene's algorithm, see [1]. A simplistic parallel implementation of the Warshall algorithm is

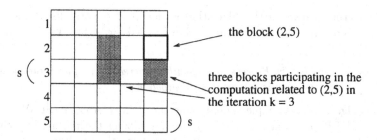

Fig. 1. The partitioning of the matrix: the case when $s = \frac{n}{5}$

to partition the matrix A into blocks $\tilde{X}_{i,j}$ of size $s \times s$, see Figure 1, and perform on blocks $\tilde{X}_{i,j}$ similar operations as for $A(i,j)$. This algorithm, we call *Naive Blocks-Processing*, is unfortunately incorrect!

Naive Blocks-Processing Algorithm
(incorrect version)
for k := 1 to $\frac{n}{s}$ do
    for all $1 \leq$ i,j $\leq \frac{n}{s}$ **parallel do**
        $\tilde{X}_{i,j} = \tilde{X}_{i,j} \oplus \tilde{X}_{i,k} \otimes \tilde{X}_{k,j}$

If we consider the matrix A given below with $s = 3$ then the output of the algorithm Naive Blocks-Processing is incorrect, as shown below ...

$$A = \begin{bmatrix} 1 & 0 & 0 & 0 & 0 & 1 \\ 1 & 1 & 0 & 0 & 0 & 0 \\ 0 & 0 & 1 & 1 & 0 & 0 \\ 0 & 1 & 0 & 1 & 0 & 0 \\ 0 & 0 & 1 & 0 & 1 & 0 \\ 0 & 0 & 0 & 0 & 0 & 1 \end{bmatrix} \quad (expected)\ A^* = \begin{bmatrix} 1 & 0 & 0 & 0 & 0 & 1 \\ 1 & 1 & 0 & 0 & 0 & 1 \\ 1 & 1 & 1 & 1 & 0 & 1 \\ 1 & 1 & 0 & 1 & 0 & 1 \\ 1 & 1 & 1 & 1 & 1 & 1 \\ 0 & 0 & 0 & 0 & 0 & 1 \end{bmatrix} \quad (actual)\ A^* = \begin{bmatrix} 1 & 0 & 0 & 0 & 0 & 1 \\ 1 & 1 & 0 & 0 & 0 & 1 \\ 0 & 0 & 1 & 1 & 0 & 0 \\ 1 & 1 & 0 & 1 & 0 & 0 \\ 1 & 1 & 1 & 1 & 1 & 0 \\ 0 & 0 & 0 & 0 & 0 & 1 \end{bmatrix}$$

The corrected version, named *Blocks-Processing*, results from incanting an additional statement - the proof of correctness is omitted due to space limitations.

Blocks-Processing Algorithm
(correct version)
for k := 1 to $\frac{n}{s}$ do
    for all $1 \leq$ i,j $\leq \frac{n}{s}$ **parallel do**
        compute $\tilde{X}_{k,k}^*$;
        $\tilde{X}_{i,j} = \tilde{X}_{i,j} \oplus \tilde{X}_{i,k} \otimes \tilde{X}_{k,k}^* \otimes \tilde{X}_{k,j}$

An interesting feature of this algorithm is that it also works for the algebraic path problem even though the initial fine grained algorithm was incorrect for this problem.

Lemma 1. *The Blocks-Processing algorithm correctly computes the transitive closure problem as well as algebraic path problem.*

This algorithm was implemented using the PVM MASTER/SLAVE model. The MASTER program is responsible for initializing the mesh of processors, sending/receiving blocks from slaves and assembling the resultant matrix. Each SLAVE receives from the MASTER program the blocks it needs for computation, computes and sends back the results.

The MASTER program

1. The MASTER process initializes the mesh of processors. It sends $\tilde{X}^k$ to all SLAVE processors, in such way that each receives only the blocks needed for its local computation. For instance, the processor P_{11} receives the **blocks** needed to compute $\tilde{X}_{11}^1$, $\tilde{X}_{11}^2$, $\tilde{X}_{11}^3$ ...
2. Each SLAVE process sends back to the MASTER the resulting blocks.
3. The MASTER process updates the resultant matrix.

The SLAVE program

1. Each SLAVE process receives some setting parameters from the MASTER process for initialization.
2. The SLAVE process does its local computation:
   $\tilde{X}_{ij}^k \leftarrow \tilde{X}_{ij}^{k-1} \oplus \tilde{X}_{ik}^{k-1} \otimes \tilde{X}_{kk}^* \otimes \tilde{X}_{kj}^{k-1}$
3. The SLAVE process sends the results back to the MASTER process.

3 The Three-Pass Algorithm

Matrix multiplication can be done in parallel in a very simple way:

for all i, j **parallel do**

$$A(i,j) = \sum_{k=1}^n A(i,k) \otimes A(k,j).$$

There are n^2 (long) scalar products which can be computed independently - the more independence the better from the point of view of distributed computing. We need a parallel algorithm for the transitive closure having also $O(n^2)$ independent scalar products.

Let us first define some sets of entries of the matrix.

$$Strip1(k) = \{(i,j) \ : \ \min(i,j) = k\}; \quad Strip2(k) = \{(i,j) \ : \ \max(i,j) = k\}$$

Fine-Grained Three-Pass Algorithm

Pass I
for k := 1 to n do
    for all $i, j \in STRIP1(k)$ **parallel do**

$$A(i,j) := A(i,j) \oplus \sum_{k=1}^{\min(i,j)-1} A(i,k) \otimes A(k,j);$$

Pass II
for k := 1 to n do
    for all $i, j \in STRIP2(k)$ **parallel do**

$$A(i,j) := A(i,j) \oplus \sum_{k=\min(i,j)}^{\max(i,j)-1} A(i,k) \otimes A(k,j);$$

Pass III
    for all i, j **parallel do**

$$A(i,j) := A(i,j) \oplus \sum_{k=\max(i,j)}^{n} A(i,k) \otimes A(k,j)$$

Observation. The algorithm performs the transitive closure using at most $3n^2$ independent scalar products.

Lemma 2. *The algorithm Fine-Grained Three-Pass is correct.*

Proof. (sketch)
Denote by $min(i,j)$-path a path from i to j such that each internal node of this path is smaller than $\min(i,j)$, and by $max(i,j)$-path a path from i to j such that each internal node of this path is smaller than $\max(i,j)$ It can be shown that after Pass 1 the sum of all simple $\min(i,j)$ paths for all i, j is computed and after Pass 2 the sum of all simple $\max(i,j)$ paths for all i, j is computed. Then each path from i to j consists of a $\max(i,k)$ and $\max(k,j)$ path for some k. Hence after Pass 3 the correct value of A^* is computed.

We now describe the coarse grained implementation of the last algorithm. Assume that the matrix A is stored in $s \times s$ blocks, one block per machine. Denote by '$\|$' the programming construction which means that the statements connected by $\|$ are performed in parallel and are independent of each other. The parts Pass I, Pass II, Pass III are now implemented in terms of multiplication of sub-matrices.

Observation. The resulting algorithm is similar to the LU-decomposition of matrices but differs crucially in the mechanism by which the actions are independent of each other. Such independence is the most desirable aspect of the algorithm when running on a distributed system.

Coarse-Grained Three-Pass Algorithm

Pass I

{ the sub-matrices are as in Figure 2. Pass 1 }

for k := 1 **to** $\frac{n}{s}$ **do**

$$B_{k+1} := F_k \otimes E_k \oplus B_k \parallel C_{k+1} := D_k \otimes G_k \oplus C_k \parallel A_{k+1} := F_k \otimes G_k \oplus A_k;$$
$$A_{k+1} := A_k^*;$$
$$B_{k+1} := A_k \otimes B_k \oplus B_k \parallel C_{k+1} := C_k \otimes A_k \oplus C_k;$$

Pass II

{ the sub-matrices are as in Figure 2. Pass 2}

for k := 1 **to** $\frac{n}{s}$ **do**

$$B_{k+1} := E_k \otimes B_k \oplus B_k \parallel C_{k+1} := C_k \otimes D_k \oplus C_k \parallel A_{k+1} := C_k \otimes B_k \oplus A_k;$$
$$A_{k+1} := A_k^*;$$
$$B_{k+1} := B_k \otimes A_k \oplus B_k \parallel C_{k+1} := A_k \otimes C_k \oplus C_k;$$

Pass III

construct the upper triangular matrix U by filling left triangular part of A with zeros, similarly create the lower triangular part L; then use a (PVM) subroutine with a given number of processors as a parameter and perform:
$A := A \oplus U \otimes L$

We use a PVM subroutine for matrix multiplication which can find corresponding blocks of the partitioned matrix amongst machines to calculate parts of A.

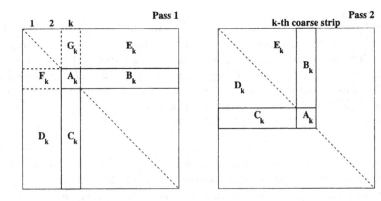

Fig. 2. in iteration k

In the coarse-grained representation, the set $STRIP1(k)$ consists of blocks with indices (i,j), where $\min(i,j) = k$, similarly $STRIP2(k)$ consists of blocks $(1,k),(2,k),\dots(k,k),(k,k-1),\dots(k,1)$, see Figure 2.

Lemma 3. *The Coarse-Grained Three-Pass algorithm computes correctly the transitive closure problem as well as the algebraic path problem.*

4 Experimental Comparison of Algorithms

In this section we compare the practical behaviour of the sequential Warshall algorithm, Blocks-Processing and Three-Pass algorithms. All experiments were performed on a cluster of Hewlett Packard 720 Unix workstations networked via a switched 10Mb Ethernet using PVM version 3.4.6. PVM was used in preference to MPI as previous experience had shown MPI to exhibit unusual anomalies [2] rendering it unusable in our workstation environment.

Table 1 shows the elapsed time in seconds for the sequential Warshall algorithm to complete on a single CPU for matrices ranging in size from 240 x 240 to 1920 x 1920 elements. The times show an expected increase as the problem size increases.

Matrix Size	Elapsed time
240	4.2
480	30.2
960	221.5
1920	1690.2

Table 1. The (sequential) Warshall algorithm

Table 2 shows the elapsed time in seconds for the Block and Three-Pass algorithms for the same sized matrices as above and varying CPU cluster size. The times demonstrate a useful, though limited, speed up over the sequential case.

No. of CPUS	240 x 240		480 x 480		960 x 960		1920 x 1920	
	Block alg.	3-Pass alg.	Block alg.	3-Pass alg.	Block alg.	3-Pass alg.	Block alg.	3-Pass alg.
4	8.1	3.6	51.7	19.6	338.1	113.7	3236.1	2335.6
9	4.9	4.2	27.6	14.6	176.3	106.5	1728.7	1484.6
16	3.6	5.2	23.9	12.9	125.2	72.0	894.5	551.5
25	4.3	6.3	21.8	12.7	104.1	57.6	786.4	524.3
36	5.1	7.9	25.1	12.7	110.2	47.1	558.3	313.4

Table 2. Blocks-Processing and Three-Pass Algorithms

Apart from the 240 x 240 case, the Three-Pass algorithm consistently out performs the Block algorithm. The poor behavior for the inputs of sizes 240 x 240 displayed by the Three-Pass algorithm was almost certainly due to the more expensive, initial communication times required to distribute blocks of data amongst machines. Indeed, communications times were observed to *swamp* the smaller input experiments and accounted for one-third of the elapsed time as the number of processors were increased.

5 Conclusions

We have shown how matrix multiplication is related to the algebraic path problem and transitive closure problem and have implemented two different coarse-grained algorithms to investigate their relative merits. Our experiments show that the Three-Pass algorithm performs better than the Block-Processing algorithm for larger problems. The reason for the efficiency of this algorithm is the greater independence of large coarse-grained subcomputations related to sub-matrix multiplications. We have shown the significance of two important properties of the distributed algorithm: the *degree* of coarse-graininess and the *degree* of independence.

An interesting observation is that fine-grained algorithms for the transitive closure (which are incorrect for the algebraic path problem) after transforming them into coarse-grained ones solve the algebraic path problem correctly.

A systolic transitive closure algorithm also deserving a coarse-grained distributed implementation is the systolic algorithm from [11] based on the concept of *circular waves*.

References

1. A.Aho, J.Hopcroft, J.Ullman, The design and analysis of computer algorithms, Addison-Wesley (1974)
2. V. Alexandrov, K. Chan, A. Gibbons, W. Rytter, On the PVM/MPI computations of dynamic programming recurrences, EuroPVM-MPI'97, Lecture Notes in Comp. Science, Springer Verlag, 1997
3. A.Gibbons, W.Rytter, Efficient parallel algorithms, Cambridge University Press (1988)
4. L.Guibas, H.Thompson, C.Thompson, Direct VLSI implementation of combinatorial algorithms, Caltech Conf. on VLSI (1979)
5. H.T.Kung and Jaspal Subhlok, A new approach for automatic parallelization of blocked linear algebra computations, 122–129, Supercomputing '91. Proceedings of the 1991 Conference on Supercomputing, 1992
6. Sun-Yuan Kung, Sheng-Chun Lo, Paul.S.Lewis, Optimal Systolic Design for the Transitive Closure and the Shortest Path Problems, IEEE Transactions on Computers, C-36, 5, 603–614, 1987
7. Hans-Werner Lang, Transitive Closure on the Instruction Systolic Array, 295-304, Proc. Int. Conf. on Systolic Arrays, San Diego,
8. B. Maggs, S. Plotkin, Minimum cost spanning trees as a path finding problem, IPL 26 (1987) 191-293
9. Gunter Rote, A systolic array algorithm for the algebraic path problem, Computing, 34, 3, 191–219, 1985
10. S. Warshall, A Theorem on Boolean Matrices, J. Assoc. Comput. Mach. Vol 9 (1962)
11. F.L. Van-Scoy, The parallel recognition of a class of graphs, IEEE trans. Comp. C-29, (7) (1980) 563-570

Implementation of Monte Carlo Algorithms for Eigenvalue Problem Using MPI

I. Dimov[1], V. Alexandrov[2] and A. Karaivanova[1]

[1] Central Laboratory for Parallel Processing, Bulgarian Academy of Sciences,
Acad. G. Bonchev St.,bl. 25 A, 1113, Sofia, Bulgaria,
dimov@amigo.acad.bg, anet@copern.acad.bg,
WWW home page: http://www.acad.bg/BulRTD/math/dimov2.html
[2] Department of Computer Science University of Liverpool
Chadwick Building Peach Street, Liverpool, L69 7ZF, UK
vassil@csc.liv.ac.uk

Abstract. The problem of evaluating the dominant eigenvalue of real matrices using Monte Carlo numerical methods is considered.
Three almost optimal Monte Carlo algorithms are presented:
- Direct Monte Carlo algorithm (DMC) for calculating the largest eigenvalue of a matrix A. The algorithm uses iterations with the given matrix.
- Resolvent Monte Carlo algorithm (RMC) for calculating the smallest or the largest eigenvalue. The algorithm uses Monte Carlo iterations with the resolvent matrix and includes parameter controlling the rate of convergence;
- Inverse Monte Carlo algorithm (IMC) for calculating the smallest eigenvalue. The algorithm uses iterations with inverse matrix.

Numerical tests are performed for a number of large sparse test matrices using MPI on a cluster of workstations.

1 Introduction

Monte Carlo methods give statistical estimates for the functional of the solution by performing random sampling of a certain random variable whose mathematical expectation is the desired functional. They can be implemented on parallel machines efficiently due to their inherent parallelism and loose data dependencies. Using powerful parallel computers it is possible to apply Monte Carlo method for evaluating large-scale irregular problems which sometimes are difficult to be solved by the well-known numerical methods.

Let J be any functional that we estimate by Monte Carlo method; θ_N be the estimator, where N is the number of trials. The probable error for the usual Monte Carlo method [5] is defined as parameter r_N for which $Pr\{|J - \theta_N| \geq r_N\} = 1/2 = Pr\{|J - \theta_N| \leq r_N\}$. If the standard deviation is bounded, i.e. $D(\theta_N) < \infty$, the normal convergence in the central limit theorem holds, so we have

$$r_N \approx 0.6745 D(\theta_N) N^{-1/2}. \tag{1}$$

In this paper we present Monte Carlo algorithms for evaluating the dominant eigenvalue of large real sparse matrices and their parallel implementation on a cluster of workstations using MPI. These three algorithms use the idea of the Power method combined with Monte Carlo iterations by the given matrix, the resolvent matrix and the inverse matrix correspondingly. In [6], [5], [3], [4] one can find Monte Carlo methods for evaluation the dominant (maximal by modulus) eigenvalue of an integral operator. In [7], [8] Monte Carlo algorithms for evaluating the smallest eigenvalue of real symmetric matrices are proposed. Here we generalize the problem.

Power method.

Suppose $A \in R^{n \times n}$ is diagonalizable, $X^{-1}AX = diag(\lambda_1, \ldots, \lambda_n)$, $X = (x_1, \ldots, x_n)$, and $|\lambda_1| > |\lambda_2| \geq \ldots \geq |\lambda_n|$. Given $f^{(0)} \in C^n$, the *power method* ([1]) produces a sequence of vectors $f^{(k)}$ as follows:

$$z^{(k)} = Af^{(k-1)},$$
$$f^{(k)} = z^{(k)}/\|z^{(k)}\|_2,$$
$$\lambda^{(k)} = [f^{(k)}]^H Af^{(k)}, \quad k = 1, 2, \ldots.$$

Except for special starting points, the iterations converge to an eigenvector corresponding to the eigenvalue of A with largest magnitude (*dominant eigenvalue*) with rate of convergence:

$$|\lambda_1 - \lambda^{(k)}| = O\left(\left|\frac{\lambda_2}{\lambda_1}\right|^k\right). \tag{2}$$

Consider the case when we want to compute the smallest eigenvalue. To handle this case and others, the power method is altered in the following way: The iteration matrix A is replaced by B, where A and B have the same eigenvectors, but different eigenvalues. Letting σ denote a scalar, then the three common choices for B are: $B = A - \sigma I$ which is called the *shifted power method*, $B = A^{-1}$ which is called the *inverse power method*, and $B = (A - \sigma I)^{-1}$ which is called the *inverse shifted power method*.

Table 1. Relationship between eigenvalues of A and B

B	Eigenvalue of B	Eigenvalue of A
A^{-1}	$\frac{1}{\lambda_A}$	$\frac{1}{\lambda_B}$
$A - \sigma I$	$\lambda_A - \sigma$	$\lambda_B + \sigma$
$(A - \sigma I)^{-1}$	$\frac{1}{\lambda_A - \sigma}$	$\sigma + \frac{1}{\lambda_B}$

Computational Complexity: Having k iterations, the number of arithmetic operations in Power method is $O(4kn^2 + 3kn)$, so the Power method is not suitable for large sparse matrices. **In order to reduce the computational complexity we propose a Power method with Monte Carlo iterations.**

2 Monte Carlo algorithms

2.1 Monte Carlo iterations

Consider a matrix $A = \{a_{ij}\}_{i,j=1}^{n}, A \in R^{n \times n}$, and vectors $f = (f_1, \ldots, f_n)^t \in R^{n \times 1}$ and $h = (h_1, \ldots, h_n)^t \in R^{n \times 1}$. The algebraic transformation $Af \in R^{n \times 1}$ is called *iteration* and plays a fundamental role in iterative Monte Carlo methods.

Consider the following Markov chain:

$$k_0 \to k_1 \to \ldots \to k_i, \tag{3}$$

where $k_j = 1, 2, \ldots, n$ for $j = 1, \ldots, i$ are natural numbers. The rules for constructing the chain (3) are:

$$Pr(k_0 = \alpha) = \frac{|h_\alpha|}{\sum_{\alpha=1}^{n} |h_\alpha|},$$

$$Pr(k_j = \beta | k_{j-1} = \alpha) = \frac{|a_{\alpha\beta}|}{\sum_{\beta=1}^{n} |a_{\alpha\beta}|}, \quad \alpha = 1, \ldots, n.$$

Such a choice of the initial density vector and the transition density matrix leads to *almost optimal* Monte Carlo algorithms for matrix computations.

Now define the random variables W_j using the following recursion formula:

$$W_0 = \frac{h_{k_0}}{p_{k_0}}, \quad W_j = W_{j-1} \frac{a_{k_{j-1}k_j}}{p_{k_{j-1}k_j}}, \quad j = 1, \ldots, i. \tag{4}$$

2.2 Direct Monte Carlo Algorithm

The dominant eigenvalue can be obtained using the iteration process mentioned in the Introduction:

$$\lambda_{max} = lim_{i \to \infty} \frac{(h, A^i f)}{(h, A^{i-1} f)},$$

where we calculate scalar products having in mind (see, [5], [6], [2]) that

$$(h, A^i f) = E\{W_i f_{k_i}\}, \quad i = 1, 2, \ldots. \tag{5}$$

Thus we have

$$\lambda_{max} \approx \frac{E\{W_i f_{k_i}\}}{E\{W_{i-1} f_{k_{i-1}}\}}$$

2.3 Inverse Shifted Monte Carlo Algorithm (Resolvent MC Method)

Now consider an algorithm based on Monte Carlo iterations by the resolvent matrix $R_q = [I - qA]^{-1} \in R^{n \times n}$. The following presentation holds

$$[I - qA]^{-m} = \sum_{i=0}^{\infty} q^i C_{m+i-1}^i A^i, |qA| < 1.$$

Having in mind that (see, [3], [7])

$$([I - qA]^{-m} f, h) = E \left\{ \sum_{i=0}^{\infty} q^i C_{m+i-1}^i (A^i f, h) \right\}, \qquad (6)$$

we have the following Monte Carlo algorithm:

$$\lambda_{min} \approx \frac{1}{q} \left(1 - \frac{1}{\mu^{(m)}} \right) = \frac{(A[I - qA]^{-m} f, h)}{([I - qA]^{-m} f, h)} =$$

$$\frac{E \sum_{i=1}^{\infty} q^{i-1} C_{i+m-2}^{i-1} W_i f(x_i)}{E \sum_{i=0}^{\infty} q^i C_{i+m-1}^i W_i f(x_i)} = \frac{E \sum_{i=0}^{l} q^i C_{i+m-1}^i W_{i+1} f(x_{i+1})}{E \sum_{n=0}^{l} q^i C_{i+m-1}^i W_i f(x_i)}, \qquad (7)$$

where $W_0 = \frac{h_{k_0}}{p_{k_0}}$, W_i are defined by (4) and C_i^j are binomial coefficients.

Let us note that if $q > 0$ the algorithm evaluates λ_{max}, if $q < 0$, the algorithm evaluates λ_{min} without matrix inversion. This parameter may be used as parameter controlling the convergency.

The coefficients C_{n+m}^n are calculated using the formula

$$C_{i+m}^i = C_{i+m-1}^i + C_{i+m-1}^{i-1}.$$

The RMC algorithm has strong requirements about matrices for which it can be applied: the error from the Power method applied on the resolvent matrix determines the value of the parameter m; the error which comes from the representation of the resolvent matrix as a series determines the value of the parameter l, and also the values of m and l are not independent, since they determine the binomial coefficients $C_{m=l-1}^l$ which grow exponentially with l.

2.4 Inverse Monte Carlo Algorithm

This algorithm can be applied when A is a non-singular matrix. The algorithm has high efficiency when the smallest by modulus eigenvalue of A is much smaller than the other eigenvalues. This algorithm can be implemented in two ways:

– **First,**

1. Calculate the inversion of matrix A. For example, an efficient algorithm for evaluating the inverse matrix is proposed in [9].

2. Apply the Direct Monte Carlo Algorithm using the iterations with the inverse matrix.

Remark. It is not allways necessary to calculate A^{-1} because the vectors f_k can be evaluated by solving the following systems of equations:

$$Af_j = f_{j-1}, j = 1, \ldots, i,$$

where $f_j = A^{-j} f_{j-1}$ and f_0 is the starting vector.

– **Second,** to apply Resolvent Monte Carlo algorithm with $q = -1$, i.e.

$$\lambda_{min} \approx \frac{E \sum_{i=0}^{l} C_{i+m-1}^{i} W_{i+1} f(x_{i+1})}{E \sum_{n=0}^{l} C_{i+m-1}^{i} W_i f(x_i)}$$

2.5 Balancing of errors

There are two kind of errors in Power method with Monte Carlo iterations:

– systematic error (from Power method, see (2)):

$$O\left(\left|\frac{\mu_2}{\mu_1}\right|^k\right),$$

where $\mu_i = \lambda_i$ if $B = A$, $\mu_i = \frac{1}{\lambda_i}$ if $B = A^{-1}$, $\mu_i = \lambda_i - \sigma$ if $B = A - \sigma I$, $\mu_i = \frac{1}{\lambda_i - \sigma}$ if $B = (A - \sigma I)^{-1}$ and λ_i and μ_i are the eigenvalues of A and B correspondingly;

– stochastic error (because we calculate mathematical expectations approximately, see (1)):

$$O(D(\theta_N) N^{-1/2})$$

To obtain good results the stochastic error must be approximately equal to the systematic one. (It is not necessary to use "a large" number of realizations N in order to have "a small" stochastic error if the systematic error is "big".)

2.6 Computational Complexity

The mathematical expectation of the total number of operations for the Resolvent MC Method ([7], [8]) is:

$$ET_1(RMC) \approx 2\tau \left[(k + \gamma_A)l_A + \frac{1}{2} dl_L\right] lN + 2\tau n(1 + d), \tag{8}$$

where l is the numbers of moves in every Markov chain, N is the number of Markov chains, d is the mean value of the number of non-zero elements per row, γ_A is the number of arithmetic operations for calculation the random variable (in our code-realization of the algorithm $\gamma_A = 6$), l_A and l_L are arithmetic and logical suboperations in one move of the Markov chain, k is the number of arithmetic operations for generating the random number (k is equal to 2 or 3).

The main term of (8) does not depend on the matrix size n. This means that the time required for calculating the eigenvalue by RMC practically does not depend n. The parameters l and N depend on the spectrum of the matrix, but does not depend on its size n. The above mentioned result was confirmed for a wide range of matrices during the realized numerical experiments (see Table 3).

3   Numerical tests

The numerical tests are made on a cluster of 48 Hewlett Packard 900 series 700 Unix workstations under MPI (version 1.1). The workstations are networked via 10Mb switched ethernet segments and each workstation has at least 64Mb RAM and run at least 60 MIPS. Each processor executes the same program for N/p number of trajectories, i.e. it computes N/p independent realizations of the random variable (here p is the number of processors). At the end the host processor collects the results of all realizations and computes the desired value. The computational time does not include the time for initial loading of the matrix because we consider our problem as a part of bigger problem (for example, *spectral portraits of matrices*) and suppose that every processor constructs it.

The test matrices are sparse and storaged in *packed row format* (i.e. only nonzero elements). The results for average time and efficiency are given in tables 2 and 3 and look promising. The relative accuracy is 10^{-3}.

We consider the *parallel efficiency E* as a measure that characterize the quality of the proposed algorithms. We use the following definition:

$$E(X) = \frac{ET_1(X)}{pET_p(X)},$$

where X is a Monte Carlo algorithm, $ET_i(X)$ is the expected value of the computational time for implementation the algorithm X on a system of i processors.

4   Conclusion

Parallel Monte Carlo algorithms for calculating the eigenvalues are presented and studied. They can be applied for well balanced matrices (which have nearly equal sums of elements per row) in order to provide good accuracy.

We propose to use them when one have to calculate the dominant eigenvalue of very large sparse matrices since the computational time is almost independent of the dimension of the matrix and their parallel efficiency is superlinear.

5   Acknowledgements

This work was partially supported by the Ministry of Science, education and Technology of Bulgaria under grant I501/95 and by the European Community

Table 2. Implementation of **Direct Monte Carlo Algorithm** using MPI (number of trajectories - 100000).

	1pr. $T(ms)$	2pr. $T(ms)$	2pr. E	3pr. $T(ms)$	3pr. E	4pr. $T(ms)$	4pr. E	5pr. $T(ms)$	5pr. E
matrix n = 128	34	17	1	11	1.03	8	1.06	7	0.97
matrix n = 1024	111	56	0.99	37	1	27	1.003	21	1.06
matrix n = 2000	167	83	1	56	1	42	1	35	0.96

Table 3. Implementation of **Resolvent Monte Carlo Algorithm** for evaluation of λ_{max} using MPI (number of trajectories - 100000; $q > 0$).

	1pr. $T(ms)$	2pr. $T(ms)$	2pr. E	3pr. $T(ms)$	3pr. E	4pr. $T(ms)$	4pr. E	5pr. $T(ms)$	5pr. E
matrix n = 128	18	9	1	6	1	4	1.1	3	1.2
matrix n = 1024	30	15	1	10	1	7	1.06	6	1
matrix n = 2000	21	11	0.99	7	1	5	1.04	4	1.04

grant CP960237 (Study of Stability of Physical Systems Using Parallel Computers).

References

1. G. H. Golub, Ch. F. Van Loon, *Matrix Computations*, **The Johns Hopkins Univ. Press**, Baltimore and London, 1996.
2. J.H. Halton, *Sequential Monte Carlo Techniques for the Solution of Linear Systems*, **TR 92-033**, University of North Carolina at Chapel Hill, Department of Computer Science, 46 pp., 1992.
3. G.A. Mikhailov, *A new Monte Carlo algorithm for estimating the maximum eigenvalue of an integral operator*, **Docl. Acad. Nauk SSSR, 191**, No 5 (1970), pp. 993 – 996.
4. G.A. Mikhailov, Optimization of the "weight" Monte Carlo methods (Nauka, Moscow, 1987).

5. I.M. Sobol, *Monte Carlo numerical methods*, **Nauka**, Moscow, 1973.
6. V.S.Vladimirov, *On the application of the Monte Carlo method to the finding of the least eigenvalue, and the corresponding eigenfunction*, of a linear integral equation, in Russian: **Teoriya Veroyatnostej i Yeye Primenenie, 1**, No 1 (1956),pp. 113 – 130.
7. I. Dimov, A. Karaivanova and P. Yordanova, *Monte Carlo Algorithms for calculating eigenvalues*, **Springer Lectur Notes in Statistics, v.127** (1998) (H. Niederreiter, P. Hellekalek, G. Larcher and P. Zinterhof, Eds)), pp.205-220.
8. I. Dimov, A. Karaivanova *Parallel computations of eigenvalues based on a Monte Carlo approach*, **Journal of MC Methods and Appl.**, 1998 (to appear).
9. Megson, G., V. Alexandrov, I. Dimov, *Systolic Matrix Inversion Using a Monte Carlo Method*, **Journal of Parallel Algorithms and Applications** , 3, No 1 (1994), pp. 311-330.

Running an Advection-Chemistry Code on Message Passing Computers

K. Georgiev[1] and Z. Zlatev[2]

[1] Central Laboratory for Parallel Processing, Bulgarian Academy of Sciences,
Acad. G. Bonchev Str. Bl. 25-A, 1113 Sofia, Bulgaria
e-mail georgiev@parallel.bas.bg
[2] National Environmental Research Institute,
Frederiksborgvej 399, P. O. Box 358, DK-4000 Roskilde, Denmark
e-mail: luzz@sun2.dmu.dk

Abstract. Studying high pollution levels in different regions of Europe is an important environmental problem. Large mathematical models can successfully be used in the treatment of this problem. However, the use of large mathematical models in which all physical and chemical processes are adequately described leads, after the application of appropriate discretization and splitting procedures, to the treatment of huge computational tasks: in a typical simulation one has to perform several hundred runs, in each of these run one has to carry out several thousand time-steps and at each time-step one has to solve numerically systems of ODE's containing up to $O(10^6)$ equations. Therefore, it is difficult to treat numerically such large mathematical models even when modern computers are available. Runs of an important module of a large-scale air pollution model on parallel message passing machines will be discussed in this paper. Numerical results will be presented.

1 Mathematical description of a large air pollution model

Large air pollution models are normally described by systems of partial differential equations (PDE's):

$$\frac{\partial c_s}{\partial t} = -\frac{\partial(uc_s)}{\partial x} - \frac{\partial(vc_s)}{\partial y} - \frac{\partial(wc_s)}{\partial z} \tag{1}$$

$$+\frac{\partial}{\partial x}\left(K_x\frac{\partial c_s}{\partial x}\right) + \frac{\partial}{\partial y}\left(K_y\frac{\partial c_s}{\partial y}\right) + \frac{\partial}{\partial z}\left(K_z\frac{\partial c_s}{\partial z}\right)$$

$$+E_s - (\kappa_{1s} + \kappa_{2s})c_s + Q_s(c_1, c_2, \ldots, c_q), \quad s = 1, 2, \ldots, q.$$

where (i) the concentrations of the chemical species are denoted by c_s, (ii) u, v and w are wind velocities, (iii) K_x, K_y and K_z are diffusion coefficients, (iv) the emission sources are described by E_s, (v) κ_{1s} and κ_{2s} are deposition coefficients and (vi) the chemical reactions are denoted by $Q_s(c_1, c_2, \ldots, c_q)$ (the CBM IV chemical scheme, which has been proposed in [5], is actually used in the model).

1.1 Splitting the large model into simpler sub-models

It is difficult to treat the system of **PDE's** (1) directly. This is the reason for using different kinds of splitting. A splitting procedure, based on ideas proposed in [9] and [10], leads, for $s = 1, 2, \ldots, q$, to five sub-models, representing respectively the horizontal advection, the horizontal diffusion, the chemistry (together with the emission terms), the deposition and the vertical exchange:

$$\frac{\partial c_s^{(1)}}{\partial t} = -\frac{\partial(u c_s^{(1)})}{\partial x} - \frac{\partial(v c_s^{(1)})}{\partial y} \tag{2}$$

$$\frac{\partial c_s^{(2)}}{\partial t} = \frac{\partial}{\partial x}\left(K_x \frac{\partial c_s^{(2)}}{\partial x}\right) + \frac{\partial}{\partial y}\left(K_y \frac{\partial c_s^{(2)}}{\partial y}\right) \tag{3}$$

$$\frac{dc_s^{(3)}}{dt} = E_s + Q_s(c_1^{(3)}, c_2^{(3)}, \ldots, c_q^{(3)}) \tag{4}$$

$$\frac{dc_s^{(4)}}{dt} = -(\kappa_{1s} + \kappa_{2s})c_s^{(4)} \tag{5}$$

$$\frac{\partial c_s^{(5)}}{\partial t} = -\frac{\partial(w c_s^{(5)})}{\partial z} + \frac{\partial}{\partial z}\left(K_z \frac{\partial c_s^{(5)}}{\partial z}\right) \tag{6}$$

1.2 Space discretization

If the model is split into sub-models (2) - (6), then the discretization of the spatial derivatives in the right-hand-sides of the sub-models will lead to the solution (successively at each time-step) of five ODE systems ($i = 1, 2, 3, 4, 5$):

$$\frac{dg^{(i)}}{dt} = f^{(i)}(t, g^{(i)}), \qquad g^{(i)} \in R^{N_x \times N_y \times N_z \times N_s}, \qquad f^{(i)} \in R^{N_x \times N_y \times N_z \times N_s}, \tag{7}$$

where N_x, N_y and N_z are the numbers of grid-points along the coordinate axes and $N_s = q$ is the number of chemical species. The functions $f^{(i)}$, $i = 1, 2, 3, 4, 5$, depend on the particular discretization methods used in the numerical treatment of the different sub-models, while the functions $g^{(i)}$, $i = 1, 2, 3, 4, 5$, contain approximations of the concentrations (more details are given in [16]).

1.3 The size of the ODE systems

The size of any of the five ODE systems (7) is equal to the product of the number of the grid-points and the number of chemical species. It grows very quickly when the grid-points and/or the chemical species is increased; see Table 1.

Sometimes it is necessary to perform long simulation processes consisting of several hundreds of runs (see, for example, [3] or [18]). At present these problems are solved by the operational two-dimensional version of the Danish Eulerian Model (see [16]). In this version the following values of the parameters are used: $N_x = 96$, $N_y = 96$, $N_z = 1$, $N_s = 35$. This leads to the treatment of four ODE systems per time-step; each of them contains 322560 equations. It is desirable to solve these systems in a more efficient way. It is even more desirable to use the three-dimensional version of the model ([17]) in such runs and/or to implement chemical schemes containing more species (a chemical scheme with $N_s = 56$ will be used in this paper). This is why the search for more efficient numerical methods is continuing (the need of such methods is emphasized, for example, in [14] and [16]). It is also very important to exploit better the great potential power of the modern supercomputers.

Number of species	$(32 \times 32 \times 10)$	$(96 \times 96 \times 10)$	$(192 \times 192 \times 10)$
1	10240	92160	368640
2	20480	184320	737280
10	102400	921600	3686400
35	358400	3225600	12902400
56	573440	5160960	21381120
168	1720320	15482880	61931520

Table 1. Numbers of equations per system of ODE's that are to be treated at every time-step. The typical number of time-steps is 3456 (when meteorological data covering a period of one month + five days to start up the model is to be handled). The number of time-steps for the chemical sub-model is even larger, because smaller step-sizes have to be used in this sub-model.

2 The advection-chemistry module

It is very difficult to achieve high performance on a message passing parallel architecture when a large application code is to be run. Therefore, it is useful to carry out the experiments needed in the efforts to improve the performance on a simplified module of the model which contains the most time-consuming parts of the work. The advection and the chemistry sub-models are the most time-consuming parts of the Danish Eulerian Model. A module consisting of these two sub-models was constructed and tested on many different parallel machines in [8] and [16]. Such an advection-chemistry module is a very flexible tool for testing (i) the performance and the accuracy in the case where only advection is used, (ii) the performance and the accuracy in the case where only the chemical reactions are active, (iii) the performance and the accuracy of the combination of the advection process and the chemical process, (iv) some of the effects of the using splitting (in connection with the treatment of both the advection and the chemistry). This module, which was tested in [8] and [16], will also be used in this paper. Its governing PDE system is:

$$\frac{\partial c_s}{\partial t} = -(1-y)\frac{\partial c_s}{\partial x} - (x-1)\frac{\partial c_s}{\partial y} + Q_s(c_1, c_2, \ldots, c_q), \qquad (8)$$

where

$$s = 1, 2, \ldots, q, \qquad 0 \leq x \leq 2 \qquad and \qquad 0 \leq y \leq 2. \qquad (9)$$

2.1 Three applications of the advection-chemistry module

The use of the same splitting procedure as in (1) leads to two sub-models of the same type as (2) and (4). Three types of tasks can be solved by using of the advection-chemistry module:

Pure advection tests can be carried out by solving only the system corresponding to (2). In this case the module is in fact reduced to the classical test proposed in [4] and [11] (see more details in [16]).

Pure chemical tests can be carried out by solving only the system corresponding to (4).

The most important case is **the treatment of both the advection and the chemistry**, by solving successively (2) and (4) at each time-step.

2.2 Checking the accuracy of the numerical algorithms

Not only is the module a simplified version of the model (1), but it also allows us to carry out some checks of the accuracy of the results. The accuracy tests will not be discussed here. However, these have been discussed in several studies; see, for example, [8] and [16]).

3 Parallel algorithms for the advection-chemistry module

Two parallel algorithms will be shortly described in this section together with several improvements of the second algorithm. It will be assumed that linear one-dimensional finite elements are used in the advection part (see [12], [13] and [16]), while the QSSA (Quasi Steady State Approximation) algorithm, which has been proposed for air pollution models in [7] will be used in the chemical part with some improvements made in [1].

The parallel computer used in the experiments is an IBM SP architecture. It was possible to use up to 32 processors on the available computer (at the Danish Computing Centre for Research and Education, UNI-C). The theoretical top-performance of each processor is 0.48 GFLOPS. MPI (Message Passing Interface) has been used in the efforts to exploit the parallelism; see, for example, [6]. This means that the proposed algorithms can easily be implemented also on some other message passing parallel computers.

3.1 Exploiting the parallelism arising after the splitting procedure

Assume that the combined advection-chemistry module is to be treated. Then the PDE system (8) is split into two PDE systems, which are of the same form as (2) and (4). The ODE systems, arising from (2) and (4) after the application of some discretization procedure, are successively solved at each time-step.

Consider first the system (2). This system is formed by q independent sub-systems (one sub-system per each chemical compound). Thus, there are q tasks which can be run in parallel. There is a perfect load balance (the same computational work has to be performed for each of these tasks) if q is a multiple of the number p of processors. We used a chemical scheme with $q = 56$. The load balance is perfect for $p = 2, 4, 7, 8, 14, 28, 56$. Therefore, this simplest way to achieve concurrency is not a very good solution when p is large (and not equal to one of the above figures).

Consider now system (4). This systems consists of $N_x \times N_y$ independent sub-systems (one per each grid-point). If $N_x = N_y = 96$, then the number of parallel tasks is 9216. Each sub-system contains $q = 56$ equations. Thus, there are a lot of parallel tasks and the load balance will be very good also when the number p of processors is large.

There is no need for communications when only (2) is solved (the pure advection problem) or when only (4) is solved (the pure chemistry problem). However, the most important case is the combined problem where both the advection and the chemistry are handled. It is necessary to solve (2) and (4) successively at every time-step in this situation. This causes communication problems. A careful examination shows that the only large array of data that is needed both when (2) and (4) are solved is the array containing the concentrations c. Assume that this array is denoted by C and dimensioned as $C(9216, 56)$. Assume also, for the sake of simplicity, that the number of processors is $p = 8$. Every processor needs 7 columns of array C when (2) is solved and 1152 rows of this array when (4) is solved. This means that parts of the contents of array C must be communicated among the processors before the beginning of the solution of (2) and before the beginning of the solution of (4). This is the only communication which is needed.

Although data from only one large array have to be communicated, the communication time is rather large. Pipelining can be used to hide a part of the communication time. This means that the computations can be started as soon as some minimal amount of the necessary data is received (the remaining data is communicated simultaneously with the computations). The computations in the advection part, the solution of (2), can be started when the processor under consideration receives one column of array C. The computations in the chemical part, the solution of (4), can be started when the processor under consideration receives one row of array C. It should however be noted that the IBM SP is not able to overlap fully communications with computations. Thus, one should expect better results on architectures which can perform the communications without involving the CPU. Nevertheless, the experiments show that the exploitation of the possibility of pipelining the communications with the computations leads to improvements of performance also on the IBM SP; some results are given in [2].

3.2   Creating parallelism by using sub-domains

Let us again start with the advection process. The concentrations can be considered as an array of the form: $C(96, 96, 56)$. Assume, for the simplicity sake only, that the number of processors is $p = 4$. Array C can be divided into four sub-arrays $C_1(1 : 25, 96, 56)$, $C_2(24 : 49, 96, 56)$, $C_3(48 : 73, 96, 56)$ and $C_4(72 : 96, 96, 56)$. For every chemical compound s, $s = 1, 2, \ldots, q$, the sub-arrays C_1 and C_4 contain 25 rows, while the sub-arrays C_2 and C_3 contain 26 rows (in both cases each row contains 96 elements). The advection process can be carried out concurrently for each sub-array (assuming here that the wind velocities and the arrays containing the matrices induced by the application of the finite elements are appropriately divided into sub-arrays). It is necessary to update (both in the advection part and in the chemical part) the concentrations of rows 1-24 for C_1, rows 25-48 for C_2, rows 49-72 for C_3 and rows 73-96 of C_4. This means that the concentrations of row 25 are only used as an inner boundary condition in the calculations involving C_1, the concentrations of rows 24 and 49 are only used as inner boundary conditions during the calculations involving C_2, the concentrations of rows 48 and 73 are only used as inner boundary conditions during the calculations involving C_3 and, finally, the concentrations of row 72 are only used as an inner boundary condition in the calculations involving C_4. Since explicit integration methods, described in [15] and [16] are used to treat the systems of ODE's arising after the finite element discretization, the values of the concentrations obtained during the last application of the chemical procedure can be used in the inner boundary conditions. Both the advection part and the chemical part can treated concurrently for every sub-domain (defined by the four sub-arrays) as in the sequential case provided that the inner boundaries are treated by taking the last updates of the concentrations in the chemical procedure. This means that the following communications must be done after the chemical partr: (i) the contents of row 24 must be communicated from the first processor to the second one, while the contents of row 25 must be communicated from the second processor to the first one, (ii) the contents of row 48 must be communicated from the second processor to the third one, while the contents of row 49 must be communicated from the third processor to the second one and (iii) the contents of row 72 must be communicated from the third processor to the fourth one, while the contents of row 73 must be communicated from the fourth processor to the third one. Thus, communications take place only once per step (twice in the previos algorithm) and, moreover, at most two rows are to be communicated by each processors.

It must be emphasized that quite similar ideas can be applied when the number of processors is different from four.

3.3   Need for further improvements in the second algorithm

The computing times are reduced considerably when the second algorithm is used (compare the first and the second lines in Table 2). However, the efficiency achieved (measured as the ratio of the GFLOPS actually achieved and the maximal number of GFLOPS that can be achieved on the configuration used) is very low. Therefore, it is necessary to try to improve the second algorithm.

A careful study of the results shows that the advection times are much less than the chemical times. The chemical times are about three times greater than the advection times on IBM SP. Therefore it is more important to try to increase the efficiency in the chemical part by exploiting better the cache memory. This can be done be rearranging both the computations and the arrays where the data is stored in an attempt to use the same amount of data as long as possible.

It is again convenient to describe the approach by using the example where the number of processors used is $p = 4$ (the same ideas can be used for any other value of p). The concentrations treated by any of the four processors are stored, as in Sub-section 3.2, in an array $C_i(2304, 56)$, where $i = 1, 2, 3, 4$. Instead of using directly this array in the computations, one can introduce a small array $CSMALL(NSIZE, 56)$, where $NSIZE$ is a divisor of 2304. Assume that $NCHUNKS$ is such that $NCHUNKS * NSIZE = 2304$. Then the computations in the chemical part can be organized as follows. A loop from 1, to $NCHUNKS$ is carried out and the following steps are successively performed at every sweep of this loop:

Step 1. Information from array C_i is copied in array $CSMALL$.

Step 2. Array $CSMALL$ and five other arrays ($C1SMALL$, $C2SMALL$, $RCSMALL$, $DJSMALL$ and $EMISSMALL$) of the same dimension are used to carry out the chemical reactions.

Step 3. The modified in Step 2 contents of array $CSMALL$ are copied back to the appropriate positions of array C_i.

It is clear that small portions of data are used in the main step of the computations (the second step). This will in general lead to a better exploitation of the cache and, thus, to an increase of the performance.

The algorithm described in this section has one additional advantage: the big working arrays $C1, C2, RC, DJ$ and $EMIS$ are replaced with the small arrays $C1SMALL, C2SMALL, RCSMALL, DJSMALL$ and $EMISSMALL$, which leads to considerable savings of storage.

4 Numerical results

Let us introduce the following abbreviations: (i) **ALG1** for the algorithm from Sub-section 3.1, (ii) **ALG2A** for the algorithm from Sub-section 3.2 and (iii) **ALG2B** for the algorithm from Sub-section 3.3 (in fact, this algorithm is further enhanced by some traditionally used devices; such as reordering some operations, uniting some loops, etc.). The computing times obtained when these algorithms are used are given in Table 2 (**ALG2B** is used with chunks of size 48). The speed up ratios, the computational speeds (measured in GFLOPS; i.e. billions of floating point operations per second) and the efficiency ratios (in percent) are given in Table 3, Table 4 and Table 5 respectively. The efficiency is measured by the ratio of the GFLOPS that are actually obtained and the theoretical peak-performance of the configuration under consideration.

It is clearly seen that the third algorithm, ALG2B, is the most efficient among the algorithms tested. It must also be added that the communication time is negligible. This time does not depend on the number of processor p that are used when $p > 2$. If this is the case, i.e. if $p > 2$, then the communication time is about 5 seconds.

Algorithm	2 procs	4 procs	8 procs	16 procs	32 procs
ALG1	6056	3051	1554	855	456
ALG2A	3977	1703	869	474	272
ALG2B	2370	1168	606	330	193

Table 2. Computing times (measured in seconds) obtained in runs on IBM SP.

Algorithm	4 procs	8 procs	16 procs	32 procs
ALG1	1.98	3.90	7.08	13.28
ALG2A	2.34	4.58	8.39	14.62
ALG2B	2.04	3.92	7.19	12.36

Table 3. Speed-ups ratios.

Algorithm	2 procs	4 procs	8 procs	16 procs	32 procs
ALG1	0.080	0.158	0.311	0.565	1.059
ALG2A	0.121	0.284	0.556	1.019	1.776
ALG2B	0.204	0.414	0.797	1.464	2.503

Table 4. Computational speeds (measured in GFLOPS).

Algorithm	2 procs	4 procs	8 procs	16 procs	32 procs
ALG1	8.3%	8.2%	8.1%	7.3%	6.9%
ALG2A	12.7%	14.8%	14.5%	13.3%	11.6%
ALG2B	21.2%	21.5%	20.8%	19.1%	16.3%

Table 5. Efficiency ratios (in percent).

5 Concluding remarks and plans for future work

Several algorithms for achieving parallel computations when an important module of a large-scale air pollution model is run of high-speed computers have been discussed in the previous sections. The main conclusions from these runs as well as several ideas for further improvements of the performance are summarized in the following remarks.

Remark 1. As a rule, it is not very difficult to obtain good speed-ups when large scale tasks arising from applications from different fields of science and engineering are to be solved on parallel computers. However, it is normally not sufficient to obtain large speed-ups. Consider the speed-ups obtained by using **ALG1** as an illustration of this statement. The speed-ups obtained when **ALG1** is used are very good, but the computing times obtained by this algorithm are rather large. This is why one should look at the efficiency of the computations with regards to the theoretical top-performance of the configuration of the architecture used in the runs. The objective should be not only to get large speed-ups, but also to obtain great efficiency.

Remark 2. It has been shown that **ALG2** can be improved in several ways. These improvements have been achieved by doing modifications only in the chemical part. Nevertheless, the results in Table 2 - Table 5 show that the improvements are rather considerable. The results can be further improved by carrying out similar transformations in the advection part. However, the improvements will be considerably smaller, because the advection part is not so time-consuming as the chemical part.

Remark 3. Some modifications by which **ALG1** can be improved can also be performed. However, the situation here will be a little more complicated. One have to do changes in some subroutines which are called by other subroutines. This will lead to do also modifications in the calling subroutines. In this way the main advantage of **ALG1** (the performance can be improved considerably and good speed ups can be achieved with only very small modifications in the code) will be lost.

Acknowledgments

This research was supported by the NATO Scientific Programme under the projects ENVIR.CGR 930449 and OUTS.CGR.960312, by the EU ESPRIT Programme under projects WEPTEL and EUROAIR and by NMR (Nordic Council of Ministers) under a common project for performing sensitivity studies with large-scale air pollution models in which scientific groups from Denmark, Finland, Norway and Sweden are participating. Furthermore, a grant from the Danish Natural Sciences Research Council gave us access to all Danish supercomputers.

References

1. Alexandrov, V., Sameh, A., Siddique, Y. and Zlatev, Z., Numerical integration of chemical ODE problems arising in air pollution models, Environmental Modelling and Assessment, Vol. 2 (1997), 365-377.
2. Bendtsen, C. and Z. Zlatev, Z., Running air pollution models on message passing machines, in: Parallel Virtual Machine and Message Passing Interface (M. Bubak, J. Dongarra and J. Wasniewski, eds.), pp. 417-426. Springer-Verlag, Berlin, 1997.
3. Bastrup-Birk, A., Brandt, J., Uria, I. and Zlatev, Z., Studying cumulative ozone exposures in Europe during a seven-year period, Journal of Geophysical Research, Vol. 102 (1997), 23917-23935.

4. Crowley, W. P., "Numerical advection experiments", Monthly Weather Review, Vol. 96 (1968), 1-11.

5. Gery, M. W., Whitten, G. Z., Killus, J. P. and Dodge, M. C., A photochemical kinetics mechanism for urban and regional computer modeling, Journal of Geophysical Research, Vol. 94 (1989), 12925-12956.

6. Gropp, W, Lusk, E. and Skjellum, A., Using MPI: Portable programming with the message passing interface, MIT Press, Cambridge, Massachusetts, 1994.

7. Hesstvedt, E., Hov, Ø. and Isaksen, I. A., Quasi-steady-state approximations in air pollution modelling: comparison of two numerical schemes for oxidant prediction, International Journal of Chemical Kinetics, Vol. 10 (1978), 971-994.

8. Hov,Ø., Zlatev, Z., Berkowicz, R, Eliassen, A. and Prahm, L. P., Comparison of numerical techniques for use in air pollution models with non-linear chemical reactions, Atmospheric Environment, Vol. 23 (1988), 967-983.

9. Marchuk, G. I., Mathematical modeling for the problem of the environment, Studies in Mathematics and Applications, No. 16, North-Holland, Amsterdam, 1985.

10. McRae, G. J., Goodin, W. R. and Seinfeld, J. H., Numerical solution of the atmospheric diffusion equations for chemically reacting flows, Journal of Computational Physics, Vol. 45 (1984), 1-42.

11. Molenkampf, C. R., Accuracy of finite-difference methods applied to the advection equation, Journal of Applied Meteorology, Vol. 7 (1968), 160-167.

12. Pepper, D. W. and Baker, A. J., A simple one-dimensional finite element algorithm with multidimensional capabilities, Numerical Heath Transfer, Vol. 3 (1979), 81-95.

13. Pepper, D. W., Kern, C. D. and Long, Jr., P. E., Modelling the dispersion of atmospheric pollution using cubic splines and chapeau functions, Atmospheric Environment, Vol. 13 (1979), 223-237.

14. Peters, L. K., Berkowitz, C. M., Carmichael, G. R., Easter, R. C., Fairweather, Ghan, G, S. J., Hales, J. M., Leung, L. R., Pennell, W. R., Potra, F. A., R. D. Saylor, R. D. and Tsang, T. T., The current state and future direction of Eulerian models in simulating the tropospherical chemistry and transport of trace species: A review. Atmospheric Environment, Vol. 29 (1995), 189-221.

15. Zlatev, Z., Application of predictor-corrector schemes with several correctors in solving air pollution problems, BIT, Vol. 24 (1984), pp. 700-715.

16. Zlatev, Z., Computer treatment of large air pollution models, Kluwer Academic Publishers, Dordrecht-Boston-London, 1995.

17. Zlatev, Z., Dimov, I. and Georgiev K., Three-dimensional version of the Danish Eulerian Model, Zeitschrift für Angewandte Mathematik und Mechanik, Vol. 76 (1996) S4, 473-476.

18. Zlatev, Z., Fenger, J. and Mortensen, L., Relationships between emission sources and excess ozone concentrations, Computers and Mathematics with Applications, Vol. 32, No. 11 (1996), 101-123.

A Model for Parallel One Dimensional Eigenvalues and Eigenfunctions Calculations

Antonio Laganà,[1] Gaia Grossi,[1] Antonio Riganelli,[1] and Gianni Ferraro[2]

[1] Dipartimento di Chimica, Università di Perugia, 06123-Perugia, Italy
[2] Istituto di Chimica, Politecnico di Bari, Bari, Italy

Abstract. The calculation of eigenvalues and eigenfunctions of one-dimensional cuts of reactive potentials is often a key step of scattering calculations of higher dimensions. Parallelized versions of related computer codes do not consider a parallelization at the level of individual eigenvalue calculations. In this paper we present an attempt to push the parallelism to this level and compare the sequential and parallel performances of the restructured code.

1 Introduction

The calculation of accurate eigenvalues and eigenfunctions of one dimensional (1D) cuts of multidimensional potential energy surfaces is the basic step of several quantum approaches to the many body problem and it has been discussed several times in the reactive scattering literature.[1, 2, 3, 4, 5, 6, 7, 8]

The 1D bound state equation in the generic coordinate r can be written as

$$\left[\frac{d^2}{dr^2} - U(r) + A\right] \phi(r) = 0 \tag{1}$$

where A and $U(r)$ are the mass scaled energy and potential. This is a typical 1D two-boundary points problem.[9, 10, 11] Most often this problem is solved variationally by expanding ϕ into a set of known trial functions and finding the roots of the system of algebric equations arising when the expansion is substituted into the Schrödinger equation and an averaging over r is performed. This problem typically dependends on a power of the size of the truncated expansion basis set (M) larger than 1. The parallelization of diagonalization routines is an active research area and libraries especially designed to distribute the calculation over concurrent processors are available.[12]

2 An alternative procedure

An efficient approach of the above mentioned family of variational techniques is the DVR method[13]. A proper choice of the expansion basis functions and of the collocation points minimize N the number of grid points (and as a consequence the size of the matrix to be diagonalized). An alternative approach is the one suggested by Cooley[14] determining step by step the value of the eigenfunction on a grid using an efficient recursive propagation algorithm. When using this approach the following integration formula

$$Y_{j+1} = 2Y_j - Y_{j-1} + h^2(U_j - A)P_j \tag{2}$$

can be used. In equation 2 h is the integration step while U_j, P_j, and Y_j are respectively equal to $U(r_j)$, $P(r_j)$, and $\left[1 - (h^2/12)(U_j - A)\right]P_j$. The first boundary condition requires that P_0 is zero and P_1 is a small arbitrary number. The other boundary condition requires that P_N is a small arbitrary number and P_{N-1} is equal to $P_N \exp\left[r_N\sqrt{U_N - A} - r_{N-1}\sqrt{U_{N-1} - A}\right]$. The latter equation results from the assumption that for $r \geq r_{N-1}$ the quantity $rU(r)$ vanishes as $r \to \infty$. The integration is carried out outward from r_0 to a given intermediate r_m point and inward from r_N to r_m. Since equation 1 is homogenous, the logarithmic derivative of the outward and inward solutions in the matching point m must be identical. Therefore, a correction to A can be formulated as $\Delta(A) = \left[(-P_{m-1} + P_m - P_{m+1})h^{-2} + (U_m - A)P_m\right] / \sum_{i=1}^{N} P_i^2$. Using each time the corrected value of A the process is repeated until the inward and outward logarithmic derivatives match (within the accepted tolerance).

An advantage of the method just outlined is that the computational load goes as N (the number of points of the integration grid) times N_v (the number of desired vibrational eigenvalues) while that of the DVR method goes as N^3. A further advantage of Cooley is that individual eigenvalue calculations are, to a large extent, independent computational tasks. Unfortunately, these calculations cannot be decoupled as independent tasks since the numerical procedure critically depends on the trial value of A. In the sequential code this is ensured by taking as a trial value of the ground state the lowest closed form solution of the harmonic oscillator (HO) approximating the actual potential around its minimum. For higher levels, instead, the trial value of A is set equal to the previously calculated next lower eigenvalue. If the eigenfunction calculated in this way has the wanted number of nodes it is retained, otherwise actions are taken to properly modify the trial value. The related computational code can be schematized as:

```
LOOP over the N_v levels
    IF current level is an already calculated one GO TO next level
    IF current level is a ground one
    THEN
        Take as trial energy the lowest HO eigenvalue
    ELSE
        Take as trial energy the next lower level
    END IF
    LOOP over the number of attempts
        Call COOLEY
        IF the solution has the right number of nodes
        THEN
            Memorize the eigenvalue and the eigenfunction
```

```
        GO TO next level
    ELSE
        Change trial value
    END IF
END DO
Send a message of no convergence
END DO
```

In this scheme the routine **COOLEY** is in charge of carrying out at a given value of A the recursive integration of equation 2 subject to the boundary conditions.

3 The parallel model

The recursive nature of the algorithm outlined above makes it impossible to implement a version of the code parallelized at this level. In the case of reactive scattering codes in which the **COOLEY** routine is embodied into a DO loop running over the grid values of the reaction coordinate (sector),[15] it is possible to adopt a higher level parallelism based on a task farm model assigning the whole calculation of eigenvalues and eigenfunctions of a certain sector to a given node of the used machine.[16, 17] This parallel organization can lead to efficiencies higher than 90% for typical scattering calculations (say Li + HF or similar reactions in the usual energy range of crossed beam experiments) when the code is properly optimized.[18] However, because of its fairly coarse grain nature, the proposed task farm model finds a limit in the size of the grid on which the eigenfunctions are defined (N) and on the number of solutions required (N_v). When both quantities N and N_v become large, node memory may become insufficient and a finer grain parallelization or a multi-level articulation of the task farm may be needed.

The advantage of making use of a parallel model articulated over more levels for reactive scattering codes has been already discussed in the literature.[18] In our case, a lower level of parallelism could be introduced if a vector of sufficiently accurate trial A values can be produced. The method we adopted to determine these trial values makes use of the semiclassical[19] formulation of the solution of equation 1. The semiclassical approach associates a continuous vibrational number to the classical action integral $\int_a^b \sqrt{A - U(r)} dr$ (with a and b being the inner and outher turning points, respectively ($U(a) = U(b) = 0$)). The classical action can be easily estimated once the potential has been calculated on an appropriate grid of points and a value of A has been selected. By performing this calculation for some properly chosen values of A and interpolating to integer values the vector of trial vibrational eigenvalues can be constructed. This procedure was incorporated into the **STRTVB** routine whose scheme is:

SUBROUTINE STRTVB

LOOP on a small arbitrary set of A values
    LOOP over the N_g grid points
        Step-integrate the classical action
    END DO
    Memorize the corresponding integral values
END DO
LOOP over the N_v levels
    Interpolate the classical action to integer values
    Memorize corresponding A values into the trial vector
END DO

Once the vector of trial energies is constructed, its elements can be used independently to start concurrent calculations of the eigenvalues refinement. For this reason a call to **STRTVB** has been placed just before the LOOP over the sectors calling **COOLEY**. As a result, the new scheme of the code is

Call **STRTVB**
LOOP over the N_v levels
    Get the initial energy value from the trial vector
    LOOP over the number of attempts
        Call **COOLEY**
        IF the solution has the right number of nodes
        THEN
            Memorize the eigenvalue and the eigenfunction
            GO TO next level
        ELSE
        Change the trial value
        END IF
    END DO
    Send a message of no convergence
END DO

As can be easily seen from the scheme shown above, by paying the modest price of running **STRTVB**, the calculation of a given eigenvalue and of the related eigenfunction is now an independent computational task. As a result, different eigenvalue calculations can be distributed as independent processes for concurrent execution among the nodes (or clusters of nodes) of a parallel machine by adopting, for instance, a task farm model.

4 Performance measurements

The parallel model adopted for our work is a task farm. In this model, one node (the farmer) takes care not only of running the main process and **STRTVB** but also of distributing, at the beginning, the vector of trial enegies. Work (the execution of **COOLEY**) to the workers is assigned dynamically by the farmer (*i.e.* new work is assigned when the previous execution is completed). Measurements of the performance of the parallelized code have been carried out using PVM on a Cray T3D by incorporating the code into a scattering reduced dimensionality quantum program. For the measurements reported here, a number of 400 sectors has been considered in order to average over the different computational situations associated with the different shapes of the reaction channel cuts when moving from the reactant to the product region. The number of calculated eigenvalues was varied from 8 to 24 and the number of nodes used was varied from 1 to 16.

Although the number of eigenvalues considered for the present measurements was contained within limits typical of fairly light systems, the method can be equally well used for larger sets of internal states as required by heavier systems at fairly large energy values (in this case N_v may well exceed several hundreds). Measured performance values are given in the Table. It is apparent from the Table that an increase of the number of nodes used always reduces the amount of computing time. However, it is also apparent from those numbers that there is a tendency to saturation when the number of nodes tends to equal the number of considered eigenvalues. This is due to the fact that, when the number of nodes increases, the load imbalance becomes larger. In the limit of a number of nodes larger than N_v it occurs even that some worker nodes do not receive any work to execute. This means that the optimum performance of the code is associated with the use of small ensembles of nodes. However, since for actual simulations of scattering processes the higher level (coarse grain) parallelism on sectors confines the lower level parallel calculations into small (with respect to N_v) cluster dimensions.

The Table shows also that the speedup slightly increases with the number of considered eigenvalues despite the fact that no optimization was introduced in the parallel scheme to the end of reducing communication times, memory size, data transfers and final load imbalance. Similar results are obtained when increasing N.

5 Conclusions

The main result of our investigation is that it is possible to decouple the calculation of eigenvalues and eigenfunctions of one dimensional cuts of many body potentials. This allows the introduction of a second (finer grain) parallelization level in many body scattering problems. In fact, the related code has been up to now parallelized at the level of different angles, different energies and different l values. The method discussed in this paper introduces an additional degree of

Table 1. SPEEDUP

Workers	$N_v = 8$	$N_v = 16$	$N_v = 24$
1	1.0	1.0	1.0
3	2.5	2.8	2.8
7	5.2	5.2	5.4
15	–	9.6	9.8

parallelization at the level of individual eigenvalue calculations. This gives to the computational approach an extra flexibility that can be used for increasing the performance of the code by adopting more articulated parallel models. This becomes necessary when the value of the physical parameters of the problem vary in a way that node memory becomes insufficient to deal with the eigenvalue problem using a basis set expansion approach.

6 Acknowledgments

Financial support from CNR (Italy) is acknowledged. AR thanks INFN for a grant.

References

1. J.C. Light, In *The Theory of Chemical Reaction Dynamics* ed. by D.C. Clary, Reidel, Dordrecht (1986) p. 215.
2. Y.M. Wu, S.A. Cuccaro, P.G. Hipes, and A. Kuppermann, Theor. Chim. Acta 79, 225 (1991).
3. J. Manz, Mol. Phys. 28, 399 (1974).
4. J. Manz, Mol. Phys. 30, 899 (1975).
5. J.N.L. Connor, W. Jakubetz, and J. Manz, Mol. Phys. 29, 347 (1975).
6. R.B. Walker, and E. Hayes, In *The Theory of Chemical Reaction Dynamics* ed. by D.C. Clary, Reidel, Dordrecht (1986) p. 105.
7. E.F. Hayes, Z. Darakjian, and R.B. Walker, Theor. Chim. Acta 79, 199 (1991).
8. D.C. Clary, and J.P. Henshaw, In *The Theory of Chemical Reaction Dynamics* ed. by D.C. Clary, Reidel, Dordrecht (1986) p. 331.
9. L. Fox, *Numerical Solutions of two-points Boundary problems in Ordinary Differential Equations*, Oxford, London (1957).
10. D.F. Mayers, *Numerical Solutions of Ordinary and Partial Differential Equations*, Pergamon, New York (1962), Chap. 7.
11. H. Heller, *Numerical Methods for two-points Boundary value problems: Shooting Methods*, Oxford, London (1957).

12. J. Choi, J. Dongarra, S. Ostrouchov, A. Petitet, D. Walker and R.C. Whaley, Lecture Notes in Comp. Science 1041, 107 (1996).
13. J.C. Light, I.P. Hamilton, and J.V. Lill, J. Chem. Phys. 82, 1400 (1985).
14. J.M. Cooley, Math. Comp. 15, 363 (1961).
15. A. Laganà, E. Garcia, and O. Gervasi, J. Chem. Phys. 89, 7238 (1988).
16. A. Laganà, E. Garcia, O. Gervasi, R. Baraglia, D. Laforenza, and R. Perego, Theor. Chim. Acta 79, 323 (1991).
17. R. Baraglia, D. Laforenza, and A. Laganà, Lecture Notes in Comp. Science 919, 554 (1995).
18. R. Baraglia, R. Ferrini, D. Laforenza, A. Laganà, MPCS96, 200 (1996); A. Bolloni, A. Riganelli, S. Crocchianti, and A. Laganà, *Parallel quantum scattering calculations applied to Dynamics of elementary Reactions*, Lecture notes in Computer Science (present issue).
19. L.D. Landau and E.M. Lifshitz, *Quantum Mechanics*, Pergamon, New York (1977), Chap. 3.

Sparse LU Factorization with Partial Pivoting Overlapping Communications and Computations on the SP-2 Multicomputer*

C.N. Ojeda-Guerra, E. Macías, and A. Suárez

Grupo de Arquitectura y Concurrencia (G.A.C.)
Dpto. de Ingeniería Telemática U.L.P.G.C.
e-mail: {cnieves,alvaro}@cic.teleco.ulpgc.es

Abstract. The problem of solving a sparse linear system of equation ($A \times x = b$) is very important in scientific applications and is still an open problem to develop on multicomputer with distributed memory. This paper presents an algorithm for parallelizing the sparse LU on a SP-2 multicomputer using MPI and standard sparse matrices. Our goal is to implement the parallel algorithm studying the dependence graph of the sequential algorithm which drives us to overlap computations and communications. So, this analysis can be performed by an automatic tool that helps us to choose the best data distribution. The paper analyses the effect of several block sizes in the performance results in order to overlap efficiently.

1 Introduction

The solution to sparse linear systems of equation can be carried out using two different approaches: direct methods and iterative methods. Direct methods are based on the transformation of the matrix A in a product of matrices, which follow specific conditions (LU factorization, QR factorization and so on), while iterative methods approach to the final solution after several steps, which are not previously known [7]. The solution of a sparse linear system using direct methods can be split into four steps [4]: analysis of the sparsity structure to determine a pivot ordering, symbolic factorization to generate a structure for the factors, numerical factorization and the solution to the set of equations. If matrix A is nonsymmetric, the LU factorization can be developed following different strategies. Most analysed one are based on the using of supernodes [3], [13] or on multifrontal approaches [2] which carry out computations on dense submatrices of the sparse matrix. Also, other well known strategies are based on the updating (for the iteration $k - th$) of the column (row) $k - th$ using the columns (rows) previouly computed (left-looking LU or fan-in) [5] or using the

---

* This research was supported by Fundación Universitaria de Las Palmas (Nogal Metal S.L.). This work is part of the project "Study of the communication and computation overlapping on the SP-2 multicomputer" (C4 -Centre de Computació i Comunicacions de Catalunya-).

column (row) $k - th$ to update the following columns (rows) (right-looing LU or fan-out) [12]. These last approaches use a combination of some form of Markowitz ordering to choose the pivot element from the uneliminated submatrix. The right-looking LU method exploits parallelism much better because, in every iteration, a piece of submatrix is updated.

This paper presents the numerical factorization step (LU factorization) using a methodology, which was studied in [11], to program dense linear algebra algorithms based on a modification of systolic algorithms. This methodology is not only effective for systolizable algorithms but it also works well for non-systolizable algorithms which transform sparse matrices. In previous work, a multicomputer with local connection among processors and a specific programming language, which allow us to design algorithms that are executed efficiently, were used. In this work, our algorithm was tested on a SP-2 multicomputer [9] using MPI library and C language to prove that our methodology works well in a multicomputer with a dynamic and indirect interconnection network.

The rest of the paper is organized as follows. In section 2, the sequential algorithm and the generation of computation and communication graph are discussed. In section 3, the embedding and the initial data distribution are defined. In section 4, the computation distribution in the processors of the SP-2 and the parallel algorithm are proposed. In section 5, some results are presented and finally, in section 6, some conclusions and the future work are shown.

2 Sequential Algorithm

Let $x(x_j)$ and $b(b_i)$ be two vectors of n elements and $A(A_{i,j})$ be a sparse, non-singular and non-symmetric matrix of $n \times n$ elements, where $A(A_{i,j})$ and $b(b_i)$ are given and $x(x_j)$ is a vector to be computed so that $A \times x = b$ [7]. In order to solve this system, some methods use the factorization of the matrix A in two triangular matrices (lower triangular L and upper triangular U according to $P \times A = L \times U$, where P is a permutation matrix), which eases the computation of the vector x instead of computing the inverse of the matrix A which is a more costly computation. So, the solution to the original $A \times x = b$ problem is easily found by a two step triangular solving process ($L \times y = P \times b$ and $U \times x = y$).

2.1 Generation of the Communication and Computation Graph

The first step in our methodology consists in the generation of the communication and computation graph of the sequential algorithm (graph G). In every iteration of this algorithm, the processes to be carried out and the necessary data are analysed. With this information, graph G is performed, in which any node represents a point in the iteration space of the algorithm (a process to be carried out in the specific iteration) and any arc represents the relationship among them (the data needed for the process above). An example of a sparse matrix and its communication and computation graph is shown is fig. 1.

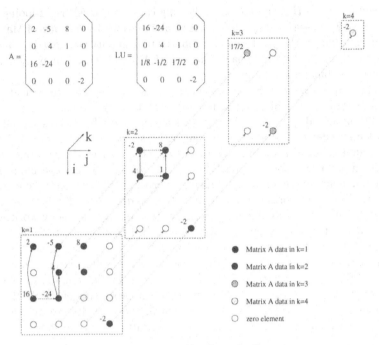

Fig. 1. Example of graph G

The arcs, in the direction i and j, represent the data of the matrices U and L respectively, which are needed in a specific iteration, and the arcs in the direction k represent the data which are needed among iterations.

3 Embedding and Initial Data Distribution

The chosen architecture, which executes the parallel algorithm, can be represented by a graph, where every node (processor+memory) is joined to one or more nodes by arcs (links). At this stage of the methodology, the embedding of graph G, obtained after the analysis of the sequential algorithm, is made on the graph of the processors (graph H).

Graph G has a lot of representations due to the sparsity of the matrix A and that the row k and the pivot row aren't the same row, for the different value of k. However, the data dependencies in the LU factorization have the same structure, so that, there are flow dependencies in the directions i and j, in the same iteration, and there are flow dependencies in the direction k, between consecutive iterations [1]. Based on these dependencies, a mapping of the data on the plane $\pi(i, j, k = n)$ is made (direction of the flow dependencies between iterations) which allows us to overlap communications and computations in the parallel algorithm, so that, the computation in one iteration can be carried out at the same time as the communication of the necessary data in the next iteration.

The problem with this mapping is that the number of arcs in the resulting graph is still very large (so we need a great number of communications -elements of L and U-). Guided by these results, a new mapping of the data is performed, from the plane $\pi(i, j, k = n)$ of graph G to the line $(i = n, j)$ avoiding the communications of the elements of U and the communications to search the pivot. With this new mapping the number of arcs in graph G, and consequently the number of communications in the factorization, is reduced so in every iteration, the LU factorization of a submatrix A, like if it were a complete matrix, is computed (in the submatrix, non-zero elements are stored) and the communications of the submatrix, for the next iteration, are carried out. Supposing that line $(i = n, j)$ were graph H, an embedding of graph G on the chosen architecture processors is made. In fact, this new mapping drives us the initial data distribution among the processors of the chosen architecture (column distribution -fig. 2-).

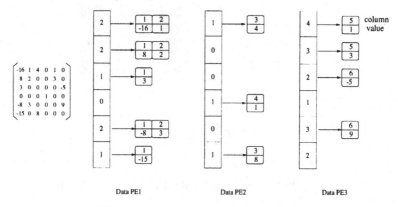

Fig. 2. Example of storing structure

4   Computation Distribution and Parallel Algorithm

Based on the embedding and using m *PEs*, the distribution of the matrix A is initially made in blocks of consecutive columns with size G, stored according to the explanation in the previous section. In every iteration k, the processor, which owns the column k, sends it to the rest of processors (fig. 3(a)). Once the communication finishes, all the processors compute column L_k and the processor, which owns column $k + 1$ (next pivot column), updates this column (fig. 3(b)). After all processors know which the pivot row is, a reordering (row k and pivot row) is made without interchanging. When this stage of computation finishes, the communication of column $k + 1$ (from the owner to the remaining processors) is overlapped with the computation of the elements of matrix A in every processor using pivot column k (in fig. 3(c) several examples of elements of L and U used to compute one element of A are represented by dashed lines).

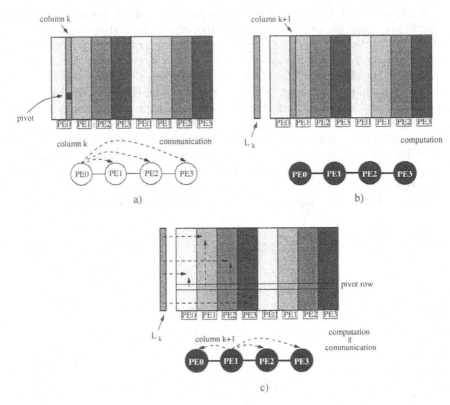

Fig. 3. Computation distribution in *LU* factorization

The parallel algorithm that computes the *LU* factorization takes into account: the embedding, the initial data distribution and the overlapping of communications and computations. However, the previous model can be improved increasing the communication granularity (sending more than one column of the matrix *A* at the same time -specifically, *P* columns, where *P* is a multiple of *G*-). In this way, in iteration *k*, *P* pivots are searched (in columns k, $k+1$,..., $k+P$), and that is why communications and computations can be overlapped more efficiently than before. Focus on the previous explanation, the parallel algorithm which computes the *LU* factorization, for a specific *PE x* is basically:

```
k=1
if x=1 then
    Pack columns k..k+P; Communicate columns k..k+P
else
    Communicate k..k+P
endif
do k=1,n-P,P
    Build L_k..L_{k+P} and Search the Pivot
```

```
if x is the Owner of columns k+P+1..k+2×P then
    Compute A_{k+P+1}..A_{k+2×P}; Pack columns k+P+1..k+2×P
    par
        Compute A_i (k+2×P<i≤n if column i∈x)
        Communicate columns k+P+1..k+2×P
    endpar
else
    par
        Compute A_i (k+2×P<i≤n if column i∈x)
        Communicate columns k+P+1..k+2×P
    endpar
endif
enddo
```

5   Experimental Results

The parallel algorithm was implemented on a SP-2 Multicomputer, with 14 processors and interconnection switch, using MPI library and C language (we didn't use any machine specific library function or any assembly code). We used the best compiler options: mpcc -O3 -qarch=pwr2 name.c. These options instruct the IBM C compilers to use the highest optimization level in generating Power2-specific code. We tried to use the system resource in as dedicated manner in order to minimize interference from the operating system and other user processes, but it wasn't possible (we used setenv EUIDEVICE css0 and setenv EUILIB ip).

In the parallel algorithm we used 64 bits numbers in the computation and point-to-point communication: MPI_Isend and MPI_Irecv (non-blocking primitives to overlap communications and computations). The type of the data to communicate, was MPI_INT + MPI_DOUBLE. We chose a set of Harwell-Boeing collection matrices [8] with different pattern to test our algorithm. Due to the previous restriction, our results are not encouraged because we have shared the High Performance Switch with other users. We tested the algorithm with different enviroment and obtained several measurements for the same values of G, P, number of processors and matrix. The average results for the best values of G and P are shown in the table of the next page.

Previously in [11] we studied the implementation of our method for generating parallel algorithms, with dense matrices, in the Transputer multicomputer. The architecture parameters of that multicomputer are very different than the ones of the SP-2. Specifically, in the SP-2 the communications can be done with a High Performance Switch instead of physical local links among processors. The experiment is interesting because of communication study for the SP-2 is critical and have been a subject of several recent papers [14], [10]. As far as we know, there are not publised results for parallel sparse LU on the SP-2 multicomputers. We have compared with other works on CRAY T3D [6], [12] (with very similar results for the same matrices), but they are different platform and it is not possible to take conclusions.

	Proc.	G	P	Time(sc.)
$steam2_{600 \times 600}$	3	100	50	0.3088
	6	50	25	0.2266
	12	50	25	0.1978
$sherman2_{1080 \times 1080}$	3	180	90	4.35
	6	180	30	4.099
	12	45	45	2.6050
$nos5_{468 \times 468}$	3	156	39	0.0885
	6	78	78	0.08607
	12	39	13	0.10670

	Proc.	G	P	Time(sc.)
$sherman1_{1000 \times 1000}$	4	250	50	0.4229
	8	125	25	0.3808
	10	100	25	0.3649
$jpw991_{991 \times 991}$	4	124	31	1.3265
	8	124	31	1.1534
	12	84	21	1.0099
$mcca_{180 \times 180}$	3	60	30	0.054
	6	30	30	0.0537
	10	18	9	0.0580

6 Conclusion and Future Work

In this paper the LU factorization with partial pivoting for sparse, nonsingular and nonsymmetric matrices, overlapping communications and computations has been studied. This overlapping can be made thanks to an effective initial data distribution. This initial data distribution is obtained after analysing the communication and computation graph of the sequential algorithm. In our previous work, a multicomputer with physical links among processors was considered, whereas in this work our methodology have been proved in a multicomputer with non-physical links among processors and current superscalar processors. The parallel algorithm was implemented on an IBM SP-2 multicomputer with 14 processors and a shared interconnection switch, which had a bad influence on the measurements.

The main target of our work is to develop an automatic tool which analyses the dependence graph of a sequential algorithm and helps us to carry out the best embedding (and initial data distribution) to overlap computations and communications. Focus on this target, we are parallelizing different numerical algorithm using our methodology to measure their efficiency.

References

1. U. Banerjee: Dependence Analysis for Supercomputing. Kluwer Academic Publishers. (1988)
2. Davis T.A., Duff I.S.: An Unsymmetric-Pattern Multifrontal Method for Sparse LU Factorization. RAL-93-036. Department for Computation and Information. Atlas Center. Rutherford Appleton Laboratory. (1993)
3. Demmel J.W., Eisenstat S.C., Gilbert J.R., Li X.S., Liu J.W.: A Supernodal Approach to Sparse Partial Pivoting. Technical Report CSD-95-883, UC Berkeley. (1995)
4. Duff I.S.: Sparse Numerical Linear Algebra: Direct Methods and Preconditioning. RAL-TR-96-047. Department for Computation and Information. Atlas Center. Rutherford Appleton Laboratory. (1996)
5. Duff I.S., Reid J.K.: MA48, a Fortran Code for Direct Solution of Sparse Unsymmetric Linear Systems of Equations. Tech. Report RAL-93-072. Rutherford Appleton Lab. (1993)
6. Fu C., Jiao X., Yang T.: Efficient Sparse LU Factorization with Partial Pivoting on Distributed Memory Architectures. IEEE Transactions on Parallel and Distributed Systems, vol. 9 no. 2 (1998) 109–126
7. Golub G.H., Van Loan C.F.: Matrix Computations. Second Edition. The Johns Hopkins University Press. (1989)
8. Information available in: http://math.nist.gov/MatrixMarket
9. Information available in: http://ibm.tc.cornell.edu/ibm/pps/sp2/sp2.html
10. Miguel J., Arrabuena A., Beivide R., Gregorio J.A.: Assesing the Performance of the new IBM SP-2. IEEE Parallel and Distributed Thecnology, vol. 4 no. 4 (1996) 12–33
11. Suárez A., Ojeda-Guerra C.N.: Overlapping Computations and Communications on Torus Networks. Fourth Euromicro Workshop on Parallel and Distributed Processing. (1996) 162–169
12. Tourino J., Doallo R., Asenjo R., Plata O. y Zapata E.: Analyzing Data Structures for Parallel Sparse Direct Solvers: Pivoting and Fill-in. Sixth Workshop on Compilers for Parallel Computers. (1996) 151–168
13. Li X.S.: Sparse Gaussian Elimination on High Performance Computers. PhD Thesis. University of California at Berkeley. (1996)
14. Xu Z., Wang K.: Modelling communication Overhead: MPI and MPL Performance on the IBM SP-2. IEEE Parallel and Distributed Thecnology, vol. 4 no. 1 (1996) 9–25

Use of Parallel Computing to Improve the Accuracy of Calculated Molecular Properties

Enrique Ramos[1], Wladimiro Díaz[1], Vicente Cerverón[1] and Ignacio Nebot-Gil[2]

[1] Departament d'Informàtica i Electrònica, Universitat de València
[2] Departament de Química Física, Universitat de València
{Enrique.Ramos, Wladimiro.Diaz, Vicente.Cerveron, Ignacio.Nebot}@uv.es

Abstract. Calculation of electron correlation energy in molecules is unavoidable in accurate studies of chemical reactivity. However, these calculations involve, a computational effort several, even in the simplest cases, orders of magnitude larger than the computer power nowadays available. In this work the possibility of parallelize the calculations of the electron correlation energy is studied. The formalism chosen is the dressing of matrices in both distributed and shared memory parallel systems MIMD. Algorithms developed on PVM are presented, and the results are evaluated on several platforms. These results show that the parallel techniques are useful in order to decrease very appreciably the time for calculating accurately the electron correlation energies.

1 Introduction

Quantum Chemistry is a highly computational demanding discipline that has been proved extremely useful in the qualitative and semiquantitative interpretation in chemistry. Calculations of Molecular Orbitals are almost a routine at present. They can found even in many experimentalist articles on chemical reactivity.

However, nowadays, the challenge relies on "chemical accuracy". Many efforts are devoted to calculate energy differences between different points of the same potential energy surface, or between different potential energy surfaces. These values represent relevant chemical magnitudes, such as reaction energies, activation energies or spectroscopic transitions. The challenge consists of calculating them with the same exactitude as the precision of the experimental values to be compared. Since experimental accuracy is nearly 1 kcal/mol, the calculations would be as accurate as 1 part per 10^5 to 10^7, depending on the size of the molecule.

In the field of the Computational Chemistry there are several applications taking profit from the parallel programming techniques. Parallel applications are more frequently found on shared memory multiprocessor (SMM) environments (Gaussian 92[3], Discover, Amber, Charmm, etc.) mainly because it is easier to adapt sequential programs, although there are several attempts to parallelize applications on distributed memory multiprocessor (DMM) systems[2].

2 Theoretical Background

The basis for almost all molecular calculations is the molecular orbitals (MO) calculated by means of the Hartree-Fock-Roothaan Self Consistent Field (SCF) procedure. However, the approximate nature of the monoelectronic potential in SCF procedure seriously limitates the quantitative applicability of its results. Correlated movements of the electrons in the molecule should be taken into account. This movement involves an energy, the correlation energy, E_{corr}, which is 100 to 1,000 times greater than the "chemical precision".

The methods for calculating E_{corr} are based on three different approaches: Configuration Interaction (CI)[4], Many Body Perturbation Theory (for instance, Möllet–Plesset MPn series)[4] and the Coupled Cluster (CC) theories[4].

Recently, others works have proposed several techniques to take into account the most of the E_{corr}. Two of these methods, due to their non iterative nature, are especially suitable for parallelization. The first one is based on a perturbative calculation over a SDCI wave function[1]. The second is based on the dressed matrices technique. With this method, the Hamiltonian matrix spanned by a model space (for instance, a SDCI, *i.e.* singly excited determinants –S– and doubly excited determinants –D– Configuration Interaction matrix) is 'dressed' or modified by an addition of the appropriate terms in the diagonal or in some rows or columns in order to incorporate the effects due to the outer space (mainly, triply excited, T, and quadruply excited, Q determinants). Then, the average value of this dressed hamiltonian is calculated. It has been shown that this is a very powerful technique to calculate E_{corr}[5–7]. We call this method Mean Value Total Dressing, MVTD.

Both methods can be programmed in a very similar way, and a large part of the resulting code, here called TQ2, is common. In this work we study the parallelization of the program TQ2 and the behaviour of the resulting code in both SMM and DMM environments.

2.1 Algorithm

The TQ2 program starts from a SDCI space from which all the determinants of the outer space TQ are generated. The algorithm generates each of the TQ determinants by means of a scan of the outer space indexes, α, and the following operations are performed on each α:

- Decomposition of α until all the elements, i, belonging to model space, $\mathcal{S}$, with a non zero coupling with α, are found.
- Calculation of each partial terms contributing to each coupled (α, i) pair.
- Other contributions according to the used mode.

In this way, only a scan on the α index allows evaluation of all the energy contributions. However, each α is defined by six (for the Ts) or eight (for the Qs), indexes, then until eight nested DO–loops are needed.

Since calculation of each partial term needs both the bielectronic integrals and SD coefficients, an indexation algorithm has been designed in such a way that a biunivocal correspondence exists between the indexes and the searched value. The indexation process is carried out through the first steps of the program by the subroutines INIRG, SD and related.

The loop on the symmetry for T is carried out in the T001 subroutine. The calculation of the contribution is performed by the subroutine T006 in the inner part. The loop on the symmetry for Q is carried out in the Q001 subroutine, analogous to T001, but now there are eight nested loops. Subroutine Q006 in the inner part of the loops calculates the contribution.

3 Program Parallelization

After analyzing the hot points in the sequential program, we have decided to parallelize the calls to subroutines in the inner part of the T001 DO-loops (T002, T003,T005 and T006). We have done the same for Q006.

In code parallelization we have followed a master-slave strategy with a dynamic distribution of the work. The main program (TQ2) performs the preliminary calculations (file reading, integral and coefficient indexation, etc.). Then, TQ2 initiates process execution on the slaves, by furnishing them with all the invariant information necessary to carry out their tasks. Slave initialization is the most expensive step of the process, since it involves the broadcasting of a large size message, which describes the SDCI reference space.

In T001 all calls to sequential subroutines T002, T003, T005 and T006 are replaced by a dynamic distribution algorithm of the tasks, in such a way that the work to be carried out is sent to the first empty slave. Then, the slave program performs the calculation carried by the parallelized subroutines. If no slave is available, the process waits until some processor notifies completion of its assigned task. When all the work has been carried out (all the loop indexes have been scanned with the sum of over), the master process requires the slaves for the intermediate results and then proceeds to sum the partial contributions.

For subroutine Q001 the same work distribution is implemented as in T001. When all symmetry indexes for Q have been scanned and the sum over the partial contributions has been performed, the master process notifies to slaves the program termination.

Slave initialization is an expensive process. In order to minimize its impact over the overall throughput, the slave program was developed in such a way that the calculation of the T and Q contributions could be carried out without making a distiction among them, according to the requeriments demands from the master process. The task to be carried out is determined by means of the message number sent by the master. The following types of messages have been implemented:

Message 1 Calculation starts. It receives the virtual machine configuration and the invariant data along the execution.

Message 2 Calculation of a T contribution. It receives all the necessary data, then calls the T002, T003, T005, and T006 subroutines, and performs the sum of the contribution to the partial accumulator. It communicates the master that the task has been carried out (message type 10).

Message 3 Sends to master the sum of all the T contributions calculated by the slave (message type 11).

Message 4 Calculation of a Q contribution. It receives the necessary data, then calls the Q002, Q003, Q005, and Q006 subroutines, and performs the sum of the contribution to the partial accumulator. It communicates the master that the task has been carried out (message type 12)

Message 5 Sends to the master the sum of all the Q contributions calculated by the slave (message type 13).

Message 6 End of the execution. Exit from the virtual machine and stop.

4 Results

Trial calculations with the developed parallel code were carried out on the following platforms:

1. Cluster of IBM RISC System/6000 370 workstations with AIX 3.2.5 Operating System and xlf 2.3 FORTRAN compilation.
2. SP1 Computer (first generation HPS) with Thin nodes. AIX Version 3.2.4 and Fortran–90 compiler xlf v3.2. The message exchange was performed with the standard PVM library (version 3.3.5) and TCP/IP on the switch.
3. SGI Origin 2000 with 64 processors R10000/195MHz nodes. The application was compiled with native SGI PVM library.

We have chosen as trial molecule the HF molecule with a very large basis set, a contracted basis set [5s,4p,3d,2f,1g] for the F atom and [4s,3p,2d,1f] for the H atom.

Tables 1, 2 and 3, show the results in terms of Execution Time, SpeedUp and Eficiency on the three plataforms. The results are the average of six executions runs for each machine and number of processors.

Results are presented in Figures 1, 2 and 3, they are respectively represented for each system, respectively, the obtained execution time,speed up and the efficiency (η), calculated as the speed up over the number of processors,as a function of numbers of processors.

5 Discussion

The main conclusions can be summarized as follows:

1. The algorithm is highly parallel, due to the large number of Ts and Qs which can be calculated independently, and this is demostrated with Itthe high values of efficiency reached in all three systems.
2. Comparison for the different systems shows that the SGI Origin 2000 with the native version of PVM has the best behaviour of the execution time, speedup values and efficiency. The maximum of speedup in this case is higher (nearly 8) . As the number of nodes grows, the values also grow.

Table 1. Execution Time in different systems for different number of nodes.

Processors	FDDI	SP1	O2000
2	712.93	638.96	148.90
3	363.80	349.25	76.59
4	248.91	241.11	52.57
5		186.51	40.99
6		154.77	34.20
7		135.91	29.51
8		120.37	26.51
9		110.55	24.03
10		107.03	22.64
11		90.90	21.47
12		88.43	21.05
13			19.97
14			19.30
15			18.76
16			18.59

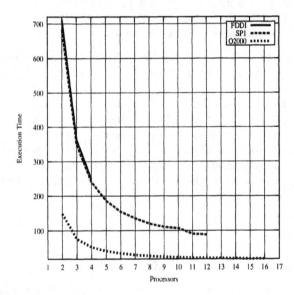

Fig. 1. Comparison of the Execution Time in different systems as a function of number of nodes.

Table 2. Speed Ups in different systems for different number of nodes.

Processors	FDDI	SP1	O2000
2	0.96	0.95	0.99
3	1.87	1.86	1.92
4	2.74	2.70	2.80
5		3.49	3.59
6		4.13	4.31
7		4.79	4.99
8		5.41	5.56
9		5.89	6.13
10		6.08	6.51
11		7.16	6.86
12		7.36	7.00
13			7.38
14			7.63
15			7.85
16			7.93

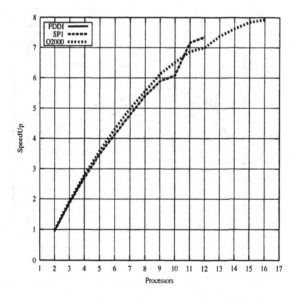

Fig. 2. Comparison of the Speedup in different systems as a function of number of nodes.

Table 3. Eficiencies in different systems for different number of nodes.

Processors	FDDI	SP1	O2000
2	0.48	0.47	0.49
3	0.62	0.62	0.64
4	0.68	0.67	0.70
5		0.69	0.71
6		0.68	0.71
7		0.68	0.71
8		0.67	0.69
9		0.65	0.68
10		0.60	0.65
11		0.65	0.62
12		0.61	0.58
13			0.56
14			0.54
15			0.52
16			0.49

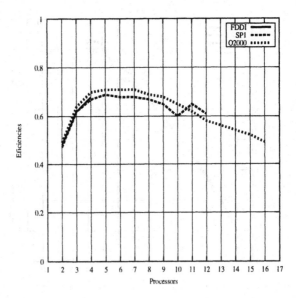

Fig. 3. Comparison of the Eficiencies in different systems as a function of number of nodes.

3. The decay in the efficiency curves is mainly due to the relatively small size of the molecule under study. It would be necessary a rather large molecule in order to bring a higher efficiency at larger values of the number of nodes.
4. The bottleneck of the algorithm is the information transfer. Efficiency is better for the fastest communication system, the newest version of the HPS.

In short, the results are better for the DMM systems than for the SMM ones, especially when compared to the SGI Origin 2000 system. Besides that, the speed up diverges more from the theoretical value at large values of the number of nodes. However, it can be pointed out that the algorithm has been designed for a DMM system, mainly in the message distribution, and it does not take benefit from the shared memory. Currently we are working in the optimization of the algorithm for SMM.

References

1. D. Maynau and J.L. Heully: Chem. Phys. Letters. **211**, 625, (1993)
2. M.W. Feyereisen and R.A. Kendall and J. Nichols and D. Dame and J.T. Golab.: Implementation of the Direct SCF and RPA Methods on Loosely Coupled Networks of Workstations. J. Comp. Chem. **14**, 818, (1993)
3. M.J. Frisch and G.W. Trucks and M. Head–Gordon and P.M.W. Gill and M.W. Wong and J.B. Foresman and B.G. Johnson and H.B. Schlegel and M.A. Robb and E.S. Replogle and R. Gomperts and J.L. Andres and K. Raghavachari and J.S. Binkey and C. Gonzalez and R.L. Martin and D.J. Fox and D.J. Defrees and J. Baker and J.J.P. Stewart and J.A. Pople.: Gaussian 92, Revision D.2. Gaussian inc., Pittsburgh PA. (1992)
4. McWeeny.: Ab Initio Methods in Quantum Chemistry. Part I and Part II. John Willey & Sons: New York. (1987)
5. J.P. Malrieu and I. Nebot–Gil and J. Sánchez-Marín.: J. Chem. Phys. **100**, 1440, (1994)
6. J.P. Daudey and J.L. Heully and J.P. Malrieu,: J. Chem. Phys. **99**, 1240, (1993)
7. J. Sánchez-Marín and D. Maynau and J.P. Malrieu.: Theor. Chem. Acta. **87**, 107, (1993)

A New Model for the Analysis
of Asynchronous Parallel Algorithms

Roda J.L, Rodríguez C., Sande F., Morales D.G., Almeida F.

Dpto. Estadística, Investigación Operativa y Computación,
Universidad de La Laguna, Tenerife, Spain
jlroda@ull.es

Abstract. The asynchronous nature of some MPI/PVM programs does not easily fit inside the BSP model. Through the suppression of barriers and the generalization of the concept of superstep we propose a new model, the BSP Without Barriers (BSPWB) model. The BSPWB parameters and their quality are evaluated on four standard parallel platforms: the CRAY T3E, the IBM SP2, the Origin 2000 and the Digital Alpha Server 8400. This study proves that the time spent in an h-relation is more independent on the number of processors than on the communication pattern. We illustrate the BSPWB model using two problem-solving paradigms: the Nested Parallel Recursive Divide and Conquer Paradigm and the Virtual Pipeline Dynamic Programming Paradigm. The proposed paradigms explain how nested parallelism and processor virtualization may be introduced in MPI and PVM without having any negative impact in the performance and model accuracy. The prediction of the communication times is robust even for problems where communication is dominated by small messages.

1. Introduction

The **BSP Without Barriers** model is proposed in the next section. In section 3 we estimate the BSPWB gaps and latencies in 4 representative platforms: an IBM-SP2, a Silicon ORIGIN 2000, a Digital Alphaserver 8400 and a Cray T3E using MPI. The use of the BSPWB model will be illustrated later in section 4. Subsection 4.1 concentrates in a Nested Parallel Recursive Divide and Conquer Algorithm. The model is applied in subsection 4.2 to a Virtual Pipeline Multistage Dynamic Programming Algorithm. The two examples cover two opposite communication scenarios: while the first one is coarse grain, the second corresponds to a fine-grain intensive communication situation. The computational resources prove that nested parallelism and processor virtualization can be introduced without negative impact in the performance and model accuracy.

2. BREAKING BARRIERS: The BSPWB model.

The execution of a PVM or MPI program in any processor consists in phases of computation followed by the communications necessary to provide and obtain the data for the next phase. Communication in this context means a *continuous stream* of messages. We propose a generalization of the BSP concept of superstep [5] to MPI/PVM programming that we call Message steps or "M-steps". In any M-step each processor performs some local computation, sends the data needed by the other processors and receives the data it needs for the next M-step. Processors may be in different M-steps at a given time, since no global barrier synchronization is used. The absence of barriers is the main difference with the BSP programming style. However, we assume that:

- The total number of M-steps R, performed by all the p processors is the same.
- Communications always occur among processors in the same step s.

To achieve these two goals, the designer can arbitrarily divide the computation stages in "dummy M-steps" at any processor.

An approach to the actual MPI/PVM time $t_{s,i}$ when processor i finishes its *s-th* M-step is the value $\Phi_{s,i}$ given by the **BSP Without Barriers** (BSPWB) model we propose here. We define the set $\Omega_{s,i}$ for a given processor i and M-step s as the set

$$\Omega_{s,i} = \{ j \, / \, \text{Processor } j \text{ sends a message to processor } i \text{ in step } s \, \} \cup \{ i \} \qquad (1)$$

Processors in the set $\Omega_{s,i}$ are called "**the incoming partners of processor i in step s**". The **BSP Without Barriers** (BSPWB) time $\Phi_{s,i}$ of a MPI/PVM program is recursively defined by the formulas:

$$\Phi_{1i} = max \, \{ \, w_{1,j} \, / j \in \Omega_{1,i} \} + (g \, h_{1,i} + L), \quad i = 0,1,..., p\text{-}1$$

$$\Phi_{s,i} = max \{ \Phi_{s\text{-}1,j} + w_{s,j} \, / \, j \in \Omega_{s,i} \} + (g \, h_{s,i} + L), \, s = 2,..,R, \, i = 0,1,..., p\text{-}1 \qquad (2)$$

where $w_{s,i}$ denote the time spent in computing and $h_{s,i}$ denotes the number of packets communicated by processor i in step s:

$$h_{s,i} = max \, \{ in_{s,j} @ out_{s,j} \, / j \in \Omega_{s,i} \}, \quad s = 1,...,R, \, i = 0,1,..., p\text{-}1 \qquad (3)$$

and $in_{s,i}$ and $out_{s,i}$ respectively denote the number of packets incoming/outgoing to/from processor i in the M-step s. The @ operation is defined as *max* or the *sum* depending on the input/output capabilities of the architecture. Gap and Latency values g and L can be computed as proposed in the next paragraph.

The formula says that processor i in its step s can not start the reception of its messages after it has finished its computing time $\Phi_{s\text{-}1,i} + w_{s,i}$ and so have done the other processors j sending messages to processor i. The formula charges the communication time of processor i with the maximum communication time of any of its incoming partner processors. The model assumes either that buffering capacities are large enough or that processors have the capacity of doing send and receives in parallel (@ = *max*).

Another issue to discuss is what is the appropriate unit size of a packet. This size depends on the target architecture. Our experiments prove that, more than a linear behavior, the communication time conducts according to a linear by pieces function on the h-relation size. There is always a slope for small size messages different from the slope for large messages. We define the **BSPWB** *packet size* as the size in which the time/size curve of the architecture has the first inflection point. Special gap g_0 and latency L_0 values have to be used for messages of sizes smaller than the BSPWB packet size. The total time of a MPI/PVM program in the BSPWB model is given by

$$\Psi = max \{ \Phi_{R,j} / j \in \{0,...,p-1\}\} \qquad (4)$$

where R is the total number of M-steps. Instead of bounding the time as if there were a hypothetical global barrier synchronization at the end of the M-step, the BSPWB model implies a synchronization of the processor with its incoming partners.

3. Estimation of the BSPWB parameters.

Some authors [1] estimate the BSP values of g and L by generating random h-relations. However, in every day algorithm practice, not all the h-relations have the same probability. There are certain communication patterns that occur frequently. Instead of random h-relations we decided to select for our study a set $\Pi = \{E, PP, OA, AO, AA\}$ of 5 communication patterns among those that most commonly appear in parallel algorithms: *Exchange (E), PingPong (PP), OneToAll (OA), AllToOne (AO) and AllToAll (AA)*. In an Exchange pattern, E, a certain number p of processors pairs simultaneously send messages of length m_E and immediately proceeds to receive the messages. In the more asymmetric PingPong pattern, PP, one of the processor in the pair sends a message of size m_{PP} and the other receives the message. In the OneToAll, OA, a processor sends a message of size m_{OA} to each of the other processors. Reciprocally, in the AllToOne pattern, AO, an incoming processor receives $p-1$ messages of size m_{AO} sent by the other processors. Under the AllToAll pattern, AA, each one of the p processors sends their message of size m_{AA} to all the other $p-1$ processors. Under the @ = + assumption, all these 5 patterns give place to the same h-relation if the following sequence of equalities hold:

$$h = m_{PP} = 2 * m_E = (p-1) * m_{OA} = (p-1) * m_{AO} = 2 *(p-1)*m_{AA} \qquad (5)$$

According to the h-relation hypothesis the communication time of these patterns for these messages sizes have to be the same. Our experiments prove that for any architecture, any pattern $\rho \in \Pi = \{E, PP, OA, AO, AA\}$ and any number i of processors, the time $Time_\rho(h)$ spent in an h-relation, for values of h larger enough than the **BSPWB** *packet size*, can be approached by a linear function:

$$Time_{\rho,}(h) = g_\rho(i)*h + L_\rho \qquad (6)$$

Figure 1 shows the variation of $g_\rho(i)$ expressed in sec/word. Observe that, except for the Digital 8400, the h-relation time of the other three machines is remarkably independent of the number of processors. However, the pattern influence in the h-relation time goes from a factor of 2 for the IBM SP2 to a factor of 4 in the less scalable machine: the Digital 8400. The slowest pattern in all the machines is the PingPong, since all the h bytes are sequentially sent through the output port. The other patterns benefit from the existence of different ports for input and output. It is remarkable the improvement of the OneToAll pattern with the number of processors. The authors in previous work have explained this phenomenon [3].

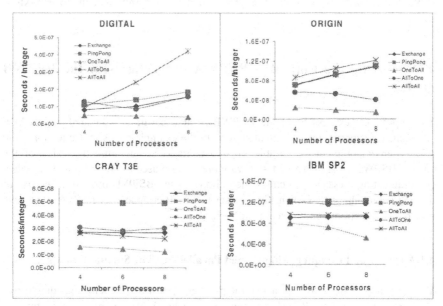

Fig. 1. Variation of the gap $g_{\rho,i}$ with the patterns and processors.

The **BSP Without Barriers** values of g and L at table 1 have been computed using linear fit on the average times $T_{average}(h)$ of the times $Time_{\rho,i}(h)$ obtained for $\rho \in \Pi = \{E, PP, OA, AO, AA\}$ and for the different number of processors $i \in H_\rho$:

$$T_{average}(h) = \sum_{\rho \in \Pi}(\sum_{i \in H_\rho} Time_{\rho,i}(h)/|H_\rho|)/|\Pi| \qquad (7)$$

where $H_\rho = \{2, 4, 6, 8\}$ for the Exchange and PingPong patterns, and $H_\rho = \{4, 6, 8\}$ for the OneToAll, AllToOne and AllToAll patterns. To produce the same h-relation size, message sizes m_ρ were chosen according to formula (5). In order to compare the 4 architectures we have preferred to express h-relation sizes in words. The negative values of L are due to the unsuitability of taking one word as unit packet size. Row labeled L_0 shows the latency value for 1 word message.

Table 1. Values of L_0, L and g for all the architectures.

	CRAY T3E	**DIGITAL**	**IBM SP2**	**ORIGIN**
L_0	0.00001	0.0000025	0.000025	0.0000085
L	3.59E-05	4.24E-03	4.51E-04	-3.20E-03
g	2.75E-08	1.28E-07	9.79E-08	6.65E-08

No doubt, it is interesting to have some data to compare current MPI releases with current BSP libraries performance. The BSP value of g for the IBM SP2 using the

Oxford BSP library in the same installation at C^4 is $g = 35E\text{-}8\ sec/word$ [2]. Since the Oxford definition of the h-relation is based in the operator $@ = max$ it has to be divided by two, $g = 17.5E\text{-}8\ sec/word$. Compare this value with the MPI value of $g = 9.79E\text{-}8\ sec/word$ in the table. The MPI is 1.8 times faster than the BSP Oxford Library.

4. Predicting the time of MPI/PVM programs with the BSPWB model.

To simplify the expression of the BSPWB M-step partition associated with a MPI program, we superimpose commented code to the example codes in sections 4.1 and 4.2. When uncommented, variable M_step contains at any time the value of the current BSPWB M-step. This M-step variable may be used as an additional tag when communicating messages, to check the validity of the BSPWB program. The use of this tag solves the well-known library-user tag conflict appearing in PVM that gave rise to the concept of communicator in MPI.

4.1 A Divide and Conquer using Nested Parallelism: The Sorting Example.

The qs function in code 1 is a natural parallel version of the classical quicksort algorithm solving the *AllToAll Sorting* of an array A of size n. We said that a problem is *AllToAll* if the initial input data is replicated in all the processors and the solution is also required in all the processors. The code is written using La Laguna C, a set of libraries and macros extending PVM and MPI with nested parallelism

```
1 void qs(int first, int last) {
2   int s1, s2, i, j;
3   if (NUMPROCESSORS > 1)
4     if (first < last) {
5       partition(&i, &j, &s1, &s2, first, last); /*A[k] ≤ A[q] k≤j< i ≤q */
6       PAR(qs(first, j), A + first, s1, qs(i, last), A + i, s2); /* M_step++ */
7     }
8     else quicksortseq(first, last);
9 }
```

Code 1. Parallel quicksort using the macro PAR.

capacities.

Procedure partition spends $B\ n$ time in dividing the array A in two intervals. When no processors are available the array is sorted in $C\ (n/p\ log(n/p))$ time using the call to *quicksortseq(first, last)*. The macro *PAR* divides in constant time the set of processors in two subsets of equal size and the variable *NUMPROCESSORS* is updated. At the end of the two parallel calls, the two split subsets swap the sorted arrays giving place to an h-relation with $h = s1 + s2 = (last\text{-}first+1)$ integers. After the exchange, they join together to form the original set. Thus, the exchange communication inside the

PAR macro creates a new M-step. There are *log(p)* of such M-steps. The time of the first step by any processor *NAME* is divided in the *log(p)* calls to *partition* plus the time spent sorting its chunk plus the time of the first exchange.

$$T_1 = \Phi_{1,NAME} = \Sigma_{i=0,\,log(p)-1} B\ n/2^i + C(n/p)\ log(n/p) + g\ 2\ n/p + L \qquad (8)$$

Only exchange operations take place after this first M-step:

$$T_s = \Phi_{s,NAME} = T_{s-1} + g(2^{s-1} n/p) + L \quad \text{for } s = 2,...,log(p) \qquad (9)$$

Substituting recursively, the total time is:

$$T_{log(p)} = \Phi_{log(p),NAME} = \Sigma_{i=0,\,log(p)-1} B\ n/2^i + C(n/p)log(n/p) + \Sigma_{s=1,\,log(p)-1} g(2^s n/p) + L \qquad (10)$$

The values of the computational constants *B* and *C* can be found in [4]. The model and actual time curves in figure 2 are so overlapped than can not be differentiated. The exception is the Digital 8400, which is the only architecture that does not scale.

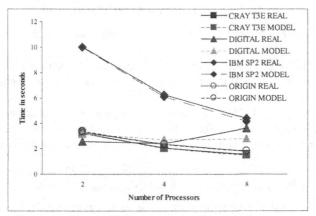

Fig. 2. Quicksort (7M integers) actual and model times.

4.2 A Pipeline Example: The Single Resource Allocation Problem.

On the opposite side to the former example, this section presents a fine-grain intensive-communication application. The function in code 2 uses *La Laguna Pipeline*, a set of macros and functions extending PVM and MPI. *La Laguna Pipeline* provides the programmer with a virtual pipeline whose size can be dynamically fixed by the user at any time. *La Laguna Pipeline* applies a cyclic mapping of the virtual processors in the actual machine. The code solves the Single Resource Allocation Problem (SRAP). The SRAP asks to map limited resources to a set of tasks to maximize their effectiveness. Assume that we have *M* units of an indivisible resource and *N* tasks. For each task *j*, function $f_j(x)$ gives the income obtained when a quantity *x* of resource is allocated to the task *j*. Let us denote by *Q[k][m]* the optimal income for the resource allocation subproblem constituted by the first *k* tasks and *m* units of resource. Applying the Dynamic Programming Principle to this problem leads to the following state equation:

$$Q[k][m]=max \{ Q[k-1][m-x]+ f_k(x) / 0 \leq x \leq m\} \}; Q[1][m]=f_1(m), m=0,...,M \quad (11)$$

This formula leads to a very simple sequential algorithm with time $O(N\,M^2)$.

The pipeline algorithm in code 2 uses $P = N+1$ processors. It assigns to virtual processor *NAME* the computation of the optimal values $Q[NAME][m]$ for all the resources m between 0 and M. The BSPWB requirement that *communications always occur among processors in the same step s* implies that processor *NAME* has to execute *NAME-1* dummy empty steps before the first reception. Thus, the last processor N performs $N-1$ dummy steps plus the steps inside the loop in lines 4-10. Each iteration of the loop is divided in two M-steps by the two communications at lines 5 and 7. There are $R = N-1+ 2 (M+1) = N + 2 M+1$ M-steps in this algorithm. For any step s and each processor *NAME* > 0 it holds that

$$\Omega_{s,NAME} = \{NAME\}, h_{s,NAME} = 0, \text{ for } s < NAME ,$$

$$\Omega_{s,NAME}=\{NAME\}, h_{s,NAME}=1, \text{ for } s = NAME+2m+1, m=0..M \quad (12)$$

$$\Omega_{s,NAME}=\{NAME-1,NAME\}, h_{s,NAME}=1, \text{ for } s = NAME+2m, m= 0..M$$

Since the BSPWB packet size of any of the considered machines is larger than the size of an integer, instead of using L and g we have to use the corresponding values L_0 and g_0 for small messages.

We have $\Phi_{s,NAME} = A (M+1)$ for all $s < NAME$, where A is the constant associated with the loop initializing Q in line 3. The first not dummy step takes place at M-step *NAME* when the first reception from the left neighbor occurs. According to (2):

$$\Phi_{NAME, NAME} = max \{ \Phi_{NAME-1, NAME-1} + w_{NAME,NAME-1}, \Phi_{NAME-1, NAME} +w_{NAME,NAME} \} + L_0 \quad (13)$$
$$= \Phi_{NAME-1, NAME-1} + w_{NAME,NAME-1}+ L_0 = \Phi_{NAME-1, NAME-1} + B + L_0$$

where B is the constant time spent in line 6. Substituting recursively, processor *NAME* starts its first non-dummy M-step *NAME* at time

$$\Phi_{NAME NAME}=(NAME-1)(B+L_0)+\Phi_{1,1} = (NAME-1) B+ NAME\, L_0+ A (M+1). \quad (14)$$

From this M-step on:

```
1  void transition () {
2     int m, j, QkMinus1_m;
3     for( m = 0; m <= M; m++) Q[m] = 0;
       /* for (M_step = 2; M_step < NAME; M_step++); */
4     for (m = 0; m <= M; m++) {      /* Ω_M_step,NAME = { NAME-1, NAME} */
5        IN_S(&QkMinus1_m);          /* M_step ++ ; Ω_M_step,NAME = { NAME} */
6        Q[m] = max(Q[m], QkMinus1_m + f(NAME, 0));
7        OUT(&Q[m], 1, sizeof(int));   /* M_step++ */
8        for (j = m + 1; j <= M; j++)
9           Q[j] = max(Q[j], QkMinus1_m + f(NAME , j - m));
10    }  /* for (M_step = 1; M_step<M+N; M_step++);*/
11 } /* transition */
```

Code 2. Simple Pipeline Algorithm for the SRAP. Code for processor NAME.

$$\Phi_{s,NAME} = \Phi_{s-1, NAME} + B + L_0 \text{ for } s = NAME+2\ m+1,\ m = 0..M \tag{15}$$

and for $s = NAME+2\ m,\ m = 1..\ M$ we have

$$\Phi_{s,NAME} = max\{\Phi_{s-1, NAME-1} +B,\ \Phi_{s-1, NAME}+C(M-m+1)\}+L_0=\Phi_{s-1, NAME}+ C(M-m+1)+ L_0 \tag{16}$$

where C is the constant factor associated with the loop in lines 8-9. The algorithm time $\Phi_{R,N}$ is obtained iterating the equations:

$$\Phi_{R,N} = \Phi_{N,\ N} + \Sigma_{i=0,M-1}\ \{(B + L_0) + (C\ (M-i) + L_0)\} + B \tag{17}$$

When only P processors are available, the last processor $P-1$ starts at time $\Phi_{P-1, P-1}$

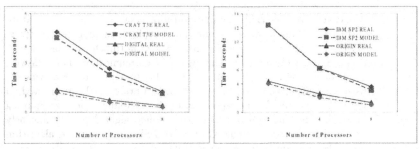

Fig. 3. SRAP (500 resources, 500 tasks) actual and model times.

Thus, the BSPWB complexity $\Phi_{R,N}$ on a P processor machine is obtained by multiplying the computing summand of formula *(17)* by N/P.

$$\Phi_{R,N} = \Phi_{P-1\ P-1} + (\ \Sigma_{i=0,M-1}\ \{(B + L_0) + (C\ (M-i) + L_0)\} + B\ )\ N/P =$$
$$= (P-1)\ B+P\ L_0+A\ (M+1)+((B+ L_0)\ M + (C\ (M+1)/2+ L_0)\ M+ B\ )N/P \tag{18}$$

Consult [4] for the values of the computational constants A, B and C. Figure 5 proves the prediction capacity of the model.

References

1. Juurlink B.H.H., Wijshoff H.A.G. *A Quantitative Comparison of Parallel Computation Models.* Proc. SPAA'96. 1996.
2. Marín, J. Martínez, A. *Testing PVM versus BSP Programming,* VIII Jornadas de Paralelismo, pp 153-160. Sept.1997
3. Roda J., Rodríguez C., Almeida F., Morales D.. *Prediction of Parallel Algorithms Performance on Bus Based Networks using PVM.* 6th Euromicro workshop on Parallel and Distributed Processing Madrid, Spain. IEEE Computer Society. Jan-1998.
4. Roda J.L, Rodríguez C., Sande F., Morales D.G., Almeida F. ftp://ftp.csi.ull.es/pub/parallel/BSPWB/constants.html
5. Valiant L.G.. *A Bridging Model for Parallel Computation.* Communications of the ACM, 33(33(8): 103-111, August 1990.

Portable Randomized List Ranking on Multiprocessors Using MPI

Jesper Larsson Träff[1]

Technische Universität München, Lehrstuhl für Effiziente Algorithmen
D-80290 München, Germany
email: traeff@informatik.tu-muenchen.de

Abstract. We describe a simple multiprocessor list ranking algorithm with low communication volume and simple communication pattern. With p processors the algorithm performs $< 4p$ (pipelined) communication rounds involving only point-to-point communication. For lists with N elements the algorithm runs in $O(N \ln p/p + p)$ time. Experiments with an implementation using MPI on a network of workstations and an IBM SP-2 comparing the algorithm to the well-known pointer jumping algorithm are reported. On the NOW the new algorithm is significantly better than pointer jumping. On the IBM SP-2 only the new algorithm was able to produce (modest) speed-up.

1 Introduction

The *list ranking problem* is a prototypical irregular problem of fundamental importance in the design of parallel graph algorithms under the PRAM model of parallel computation [4]. Many problems on trees and graphs can be reduced to list ranking, and the problem is of relevance in parallel computational biology and computer vision. Hence, the problem may serve as a *benchmark problem* for the feasibility of parallel combinatorial algorithms on parallel computers. In its simplest form the problem consists in computing for each element of a linked list the distance to the end of the list, ie. the number of links that have to be traversed to reach the last element of the list. Sequentially the problem is solved in linear time in the length of the input list; but the irregular nature of the problem manifests itself also in the sequential setting when solving very large problem instances [8]. In a parallel setting, where the list is divided among several processors, the problem is considerably more difficult, giving rise to algorithms with data dependent, irregular communication patterns. The problem is well-studied in the theoretical literature on parallel algorithm design [4], and has recently attracted considerable interest also from a more practical point of view [1, 3, 6, 7, 9, 11].

In this paper we describe portable implementations using the message passing interface MPI [10] of two algorithms for the problem and evaluate their performance on a small network of workstations (NOW) and on a powerful IBM SP-2 distributed memory multiprocessor. The first algorithm is the standard pointer-jumping algorithm of Wyllie [13]. Due to its simplicity this algorithm typically serves as a point of reference against which to compare other algorithms. As will be seen pointer jumping is not a very good algorithm for the NOW. The second algorithm is based on a different approach of ranking sublists on one processor by "folding" already ranked sublists on other processors into these sublists. Although also theoretically non-optimal, this algorithm has the advantage of a simpler communication pattern than the pointer jumping algorithm, and empirically it performs substantially better: on a NOW it is easily a factor of 5 faster. On the SP-2 only the new algorithm was able to produce speed-up, although limited.

The algorithms are implemented using MPI [10] for programming in a simple message passing model. The prime mode of communication MPI is by explicit point-to-point message passing, but in addition MPI provides a set of convenient collective operations. In contrast to other paradigms for portable parallel programming, like PVM [2] or BSP [12, 5], MPI does not force upon the programmer a particular virtual machine or programming style, although it is possible to use MPI for programming in a BSP-like style. The presence of collective operations makes MPI more flexible than BSP. Algorithm complexity can be measured in terms of basic MPI-communication operations, and local computation.

The list ranking problem is defined in Section 2. Sections 3 and 4 describe the two algorithms, and Section 5 gives a preliminary experimental evaluation.

2 The problem

Given a set of *list elements* each having a successor index pointing to some other element, or to a special *tail* element. Each element has at most one element pointing to it, and there are no cycles. Each element has an integer rank associated with it. The (inclusive) *list ranking problem* consists in computing for each list element the sum of the rank of the element itself and the ranks of all elements that succeed it. In addition a pointer to the last reachable element must be computed for each element. Note that in this formulation of the problem the set of list elements may contain several disjoint linked lists. By the second requirement each element will know after ranking to which list it belongs by having a pointer to the unique last element of that list. The special case of computing for each element the distance to the end of the list is obtained by setting the initial rank of all elements to 1. Finally note that lists are *singly linked*.

When solving the list ranking problem on multiprocessors the set of list elements is assumed to be distributed over a set of processors. The p processors, $P_1, \ldots, P_p$, have no shared memory and no common clock, but can communicate and synchronize by sending messages to each other. Each processor can communicate with any other processor through an interconnection network, the nature of which is left unspecified. The total number of list elements is denoted by N, and the number of list elements per processor, which we assume to be (roughly) equal, by n, eg. $N = \Theta(pn)$. The list elements are stored in arrays in some arbitrary order; in particular successor pointers and ranks are stored in arrays list and rank of size n, such that list[i] and rank[i] are the successor pointer and rank of the ith local list element. The list ranking procedures have the following MPI like prototype:

```
Listrank(Index list[], int rank[], int n, MPI_Comm comm)
```

Type `Index` represents a pointer to a successor element, and consists of the id (rank) of the processor at which the successor resides, and the index of the successor in the `list` array of that processor. Upon return `rank[i]` is the computed rank of the ith local element, and `list[i]` a pointer to the last reachable element. In the implementations of this paper an `Index` is a structure consisting of two integers. The `Listrank()` implementations can all be generalized to solve the more general *list scan* problem, in which the rank is of arbitrary type and some associative operation takes the place of addition.

Complexity is measured in terms of local computation and basic communication operations under the assumption of roughly synchronous operation of the processors. This assumption is only for the analysis; if needed synchronization can be enforced by appropriate `MPI_Barrier()` calls. The algorithms are randomized in the sense that a random distribution of the list elements over the p processors is assumed. This means that the probability of a list element at processor i to have its successor at processor j is $1/p$, independently of i and j. If this assumption is not fulfilled, the algorithms may run longer (but will still be correct). Alternatively, a random permutation of the list can be performed before list ranking.

3 List ranking by pointer jumping

List ranking by pointer jumping is done in a number of synchronized (super)steps. Each list element maintains a current successor and a current rank, the latter being the sum of the ranks of the successor elements up to but not including the current successor. In a superstep each element adds the rank of its current successor to its own rank, and updates its current successor to the current successor of the current successor. When the current successor points to an element which has already been ranked, correct rank (and last element pointer) has been computed, and the element does not have to be considered in subsequent supersteps. It is easy to see that the number of list elements "jumped over" doubles in each superstep, so that $\lceil \log_2 N \rceil$ supersteps are required. The algorithm can immediately be parallelized, since the list elements are treated independently of each other. The number of operations carried out in step $d, d = 1, \ldots, \lceil \log_2 N \rceil$, is $O(N - 2^{d-1})$ (since in step d the 2^d elements with distance $< 2^d$ to a last element have been ranked), so the total "cost" of the pointer jumping algorithm is $O(N \log N)$, in contrast to the linear number of operations required by a simple sequential algorithm. In this sense the pointer jumping algorithm is not (work) optimal. In a multiprocessor implementation accessing the information in the current successor elements is done by sending requests to the appropriate processors. A superstep requires 3 all-to-all communication operations. First each processor buckets its requests for current successor information and sends the bucket sizes to all other processors. Second the requests themselves are sent. Finally current successor and current rank are returned in acknowledgment to the requests. A request consists of a single integer (index in local list array) per list element. The information returned consists of index (2 words) and rank information. The extra space needed is about $8n$ words per processor; contrast this to the n words of the sequential algorithm.

There are two orthogonal improvements of the basic algorithm. For the special case of computing only the distance to the last reachable element, it is not necessary to send the rank of the current successor in every round, since, as is easily seen, this simply doubles in each round. Only when an element which has already been ranked is reached, does the rank of this element have to be sent. Hence, in all rounds but the last only the index of the current successor needs to be sent. This decreases the size of acknowledgment messages by one third. The other improvement consists in performing a local ranking on each processor after each superstep. On the assumption of a random distribution of the list elements this decreases the number of messages to be sent per round by a factor $1/p$. This version turned out to be by far the most efficient, and is used for reference in Section 5.

4 The fold-unfold algorithm

We now present a different list ranking algorithm. Let L be the global problem and L_i the set of list elements at processor i. Assume that the elements in each L_i have been ranked locally (the local rank of $x \in L_i$ is the rank of x treating each element having its successor outside L_i as a last element). Each L_i thus becomes a collection of sublists each with its successor outside L_i. By *folding L_i into L_j* we mean the following: each sublist in L_j having its successor in L_i has its rank updated with the rank of the successor sublist in L_i, and its successor updated to the successor of the L_i sublist; if the successor of the L_i sublist is in L_j the two L_j sublists are joined. We denote this operation by $\texttt{fold}(L_i, L_j)$. It runs in time proportional to the number of sublists of L_i folded into L_j by suitable bucketing of the sublists. The operation requires two communication steps, since processor j must first send a request (1 word) to processor i for rank information (3 words) for all L_j sublists with successor in L_i. The fold-unfold algorithm successively folds the sets L_k for $k = 1, \ldots, p-1$ into L_p and looks as follows:

1. For all $k \in \{1, \ldots, p\}$ do in parallel $\texttt{localrank}(L_k)$
2. For $k = 1, 2, \ldots, p-1$ do: for all $l \in \{k+1, \ldots, p\}$ do (in parallel) $\texttt{fold}(L_k, L_l)$
3. For $k = p, \ldots, 3, 2$ do: for all $l \in \{1, \ldots, k-1\}$ do (in parallel) $\texttt{getrank}(L_l, L_k)$

After the kth round of Step 2 all sublists in L_l have their successor in $L_i, i \in \{k+1, \ldots, p\}$, as had all sublists in L_k before round k. After completion of Step 2 final ranks for sublists in L_k can computed from the ranks of sublists in L_i. Correctness follows from these invariants. For the complexity we consider only the fold computations of Step 2; Step 3 is analogous.

Lemma 1. *The expected number of sublists per processor before round k is $\alpha = n \frac{p-k}{p+1-k}$.*

Proof. Before the first round processor $l, l \in \{1, \ldots, p\}$ has n list elements of which n/p have their successor in processor l. Hence the number of sublists is $n - n/p = n\frac{p-1}{p}$. Assume the claim holds before round k. In round k the α sublists in L_k are folded into $L_l, l \in \{k + 1, \ldots, p\}$. Since $1/(p - k)$ of these have their successor in L_l, the number of sublists in L_l becomes $\alpha - \frac{\alpha}{(p-k)^2} = \frac{\alpha}{(p-k)^2}(p - k + 1)(p - k - 1)$. Substituting for α yields the claim for $k + 1$.

In round k the sublists L_k are folded in parallel into all remaining subsets. Thus $O(n)$ words have to be communicated per round, giving an algorithm with running time $O(pn) = O(N)$, and no potential for speed-up. We solve this problem by *pipelining* the $\mathtt{fold}(L_k, L_l)$ operations. This is possible since processor k cannot start folding before round k. It suffices that processor k has received fold information from processors $1, \ldots, k - 1$ at round ck for some constant c. The pipelining also takes place in rounds, and works as follows: after receiving information from all lower numbered processors processor k waits one round and then performs the $\mathtt{fold}(L_k, L_l)$ operations one after another in increasing order of l, doing one fold per round.

Lemma 2. *At round* $2(k - 1) + i$ *processor k performs* $\mathtt{fold}(L_k, L_{k+i})$.

Proof. Processor 1 can start folding immediately, thus in round i performs $\mathtt{fold}(L_1, L_{1+i})$. Assume the claim holds for processors $1, \ldots, k - 1$. Then processor $k - j$ performs $\mathtt{fold}(L_{k-j}, L_k)$ in round $2(k - j - 1) + j = 2(k - 1) - j$. Hence processor k has received its last message (from processor $k - 1$) in round $2(k-1)-1$. It waits one round and in rounds $2(k-1)+i$ performs $\mathtt{fold}(L_k, L_{k+i})$.

Processor p has thus received information from all smaller numbered processors in round $2p-3$. An advantage of the pipelining scheme is that only point-to-point communication is called for.

Lemma 3. *The parallel time spent in exchanging messages in Step 2 is proportional to* $4n \ln p = O(n \ln p + p)$.

Proof. By Lemma 1 the number of words exchanged between processor k and $k + 1$ in round k is $4\frac{n}{p+1-k}$. Summing gives $4n$ times the pth harmonic number.

Theorem 4. *The fold-unfold algorithm solves the list ranking problem in $4p - 6$ communication rounds, each of which entails only point-to-point communication. The time spent in local computation and exchange of messages per processor is* $O(n \ln p + p)$.

The fold-unfold list ranking algorithm is non-optimal, but theoretically slightly better than the pointer jumping algorithm ($\log_2 N$ has been traded for $\ln p$). More importantly, the logarithmic overhead has been switched from a logarithmic number of phases (each having a non-negligible communication start-up latency) to a logarithmic overhead stemming from gradually increasing message lengths. An unattractive feature of the algorithm is that it is unbalanced; after the p first rounds of Step 2 processor 1 stands unemployed until Step 3. The extra space required by the algorithm is about $7n$ words per processor.

5 Experimental results

The algorithms have been implemented in C using MPI [10]. Experiments have been carried out on 1) a network of (different) HP workstations (80 to 125Mhz) connected via a standard 10Mbit/second Ethernet, using mpich version 1.0.12, and 2) an IBM SP-2 with 77 RS/6000 nodes; but only up to 32 67Mhz nodes were available. Running times are given in seconds, and are quite erratic on the SP-2; the machine at hand is run in batch mode and was often heavily loaded. The input lists are "random lists" generated by randomly permuting random local lists among the processors. Sequential running time is optimistically estimated as the sum of the times for locally ranking the locally generated lists. Results are reported for the best implementations of the two algorithms. For pointer jumping performing local ranking in each superstep gave an improvement of about 30% for 32 processors on the SP-2 compared to the standard implementation. The best version of the fold-unfold algorithm exchanges messages as described in Section 4; no explicit barrier synchronization was needed to make the pipelining work well. Attempts at enforcing division into rounds to prevent congestion by MPI_Barrier() calls lead to slowdown from 10% to 300%. Running times for fixed problem sizes for different numbers of processors have been measured, from which speed-up can be computed, see Tables 1 and 3. We have also measured the running times with problem size increasing linearly in the number of processors, ie. keeping $n \approx N/p$ fixed. The results are shown in Tables 2 and 4.

On the NOW the fold-unfold algorithm is clearly superior to pointer jumping, being easily a factor of 5 faster. Of course, none of the algorithms were able to produce actual speed-up, but with the limited communication capabilities of the Ethernet this was not expected. However, with the fold-unfold algorithm it is possible to solve problems larger than possible on a single workstation at a modest price: with 14 processors the "slowdown" for a list with 7000000 elements is only about a factor of 10 over the most optimistic estimate for the sequential running time. On the SP-2 the difference between the two algorithms is less striking, but significant. On the large problems fold-unfold is consistently a factor of two better than pointer jumping, and can better utilize the increasing number of processors. For $p = 32$ it gave speed-up close to two, both in the case where N was fixed, compared to the actual sequential running time (Table 3), as in the case where $N = np$ and sequential running time was estimated as p times local ranking time (Table 4). For the problem with $N = 4000000$ running times on the SP-2 differed a lot from run to run. For large problems where a straightforward sequential algorithm runs into trouble, a parallel algorithm might be of interest.

6 Discussion

We presented a new, simple list ranking algorithm for distributed-memory multiprocessors, and compared it to the well-known pointer jumping algorithm. On a network of workstations a significant improvement in performance was achieved. For an IBM SP-2 multiprocessor neither algorithms were good. Only the fold-unfold algorithm was capable of producing some small speed-up. On an Intel

		Pointer jumping						Fold-unfold					
N	Seq.	1	2	4	6	8	10	1	2	4	6	8	10
250000	0.58	0.75	2.67	9.21	16.59	41.65	64.04	0.93	2.88	4.44	5.07	9.84	11.65
500000	1.27	1.57	5.32	18.51	31.94	87.00	110.51	1.76	5.75	8.60	9.96	11.84	15.85
1000000	2.56	3.25	11.47	36.95	63.22	135.54	187.97	3.67	11.91	17.44	19.84	26.34	32.68

Table 1. Running times on the HP NOW for lists of fixed total length N for varying number of processors, and local list length $n = N/p$.

	n	Seq.	4	Seq.	6	Seq.	8	Seq.	10	Seq.	12	Seq.	14
Pj	250000	2.66	37.69	4.07	93.67	5.36	212.69	6.67	403.57	7.93	510.86	9.20	686.21
	500000	5.55	79.34	8.43	191.73	Out of Memory							
Fold	250000	2.69	16.91	4.01	29.71	5.33	50.97	6.62	68.30	7.90	94.27	9.18	126.34
	500000	5.55	35.29	8.46	66.13	11.34	97.21	13.82	143.72	16.75	179.10	19.22	211.76

Table 2. Running times on the HP NOW for lists with length proportional to the number of processors, $N = np$, for fixed local length n. The "sequential" running time is estimated as the sum of the running times for ranking a list of size n on each workstation.

Paragon [9] reports good speed-up of up to about 27 on 100 processors for problems of similar sizes to those considered here. However, it should be noted that even pointer jumping produced speed-up (up to 7 on 100 processors) on this machine. However, the Paragon had a better ratio between computation and communication speed than the SP-2. It would be interesting to test the performance of the algorithms of [9] on the SP-2. Reduction in problem size might lead to better algorithms. It is easy to devise a randomized scheme for reducing the list length by a factor of at least $1/2$ in only two all-to-all communication rounds. Such a scheme is currently being implemented. Space limitations prohibit thorough discussion and comparison to relevant related work [1, 7, 9].

References

1. F. Dehne and S. W. Song. Randomized parallel list ranking for distributed memory multiprocessors. *International Journal of Parallel Programming*, 25(1):1–16, 1997.
2. A. Geist, A. Beguein, J. Dongarra, W. Jiang, R. Manchek, and V. Sunderam. *PVM: Parallel Virtual Machine – A User's Guide and Tutorial for Networked Parallel Computing*. MIT Press, 1994.
3. T.-S. Hsu and V. Ramachandran. Efficient massively parallel implementation of some combinatorial algorithms. *Theoretical Computer Science*, 162(2):297–322, 1996.
4. J. JáJá. *An Introduction to Parallel Algorithms*. Addison-Wesley, 1992.

		Pointer jumping				Fold-unfold			
N	Seq.	8	16	24	32	8	16	24	32
2000000	5.58	10.18	7.45	6.03	5.33	6.36	4.47	3.59	3.04
4000000	11.34	19.18	15.91	16.48	14.55	14.05	9.49	7.22	6.11

Table 3. Running times on the IBM SP-2 for lists of fixed total length N for varying number of processors. For the large problem with $N = 4000000$ the sequential running time varied from 11.21 to 71.37 seconds.

	n	Seq.	8	Seq.	16	Seq.	24	Seq.	32
Pointer	1000000	21.09	33.28	41.51	58.71	64.93	111.36	86.90	133.68
	2000000	43.06	111.78	86.02	160.27	129.44	205.21	171.86	206.64
Fold	1000000	23.79	25.33	44.60	38.21	62.19	50.25	82.68	49.93
	2000000	42.82	50.24	85.98	71.73	129.27	91.05	172.84	103.59

Table 4. Running times on the IBM SP-2 for lists with length proportional to the number of processors and fixed local length n.

5. W. F. McColl. Scalable computing. In *Computer Science Today. Recent Trends and Developments*, volume 1000 of *Lecture Notes in Computer Science*, pages 46–61, 1995.

6. J. N. Patel, A. A. Khokhar, and L. H. Jamieson. Scalable parallel implementations of list ranking on fine-grained machines. *IEEE Transactions on Parallel and Distributed Systems*, 8(10):1006–1018, 1997.

7. M. Reid-Miller. List ranking and list scan on the cray C-90. In *Proceedings of the 6th ACM Symposium on Parallel Algorithms and Architectures (SPAA)*, pages 104–113, 1994.

8. J. F. Sibeyn. From parallel to external list ranking. Technical Report MPI-I-91-1-021, Max-Planck Institut für Informatik, 1997.

9. J. F. Sibeyn, F. Guillaume, and T. Seidel. Practical parallel list ranking. In *Solving Irregularly Structured Problems in Parallel (IRREGULAR'97)*, volume 1253 of *Lecture Notes in Computer Science*, pages 25–36, 1997.

10. M. Snir, S. W. Otto, S. Huss-Lederman, D. W. Walker, and J. Dongarra. *MPI: The Complete Reference*. MIT Press, 1996.

11. J. L. Träff. Parallel list ranking and other operations on lists. Technical Report SFB 124-D6 3/97, Universität des Saarlandes, Saarbrücken, Germany, Sonderforschungsbereich 124, VLSI Entwurfsmethoden und Parallelität, 1997. 69 Pages.

12. L. G. Valiant. A bridging model for parallel computation. *Communications of the ACM*, 33(8):103–111, 1990.

13. J. C. Wyllie. *The Complexity of Parallel Computation*. PhD thesis, Computer Science Department. Cornell University, 1979. Technical Report TR-79-387.

A Parallel Algorithm for the Simultaneous Solution of Direct and Adjoint Multigroup Diffusion Problems

E. Varin[1], R. Roy[1] and T. NKaoua[2]

[1] Ecole Polytechnique de Montréal, IGN-DGM,
P.O. Box 6079, Station Centre-Ville, Montréal H3C 3A7, Canada
{varin, roy }@meca.polymtl.ca
[2] Commissariat à l'Energie Atomique, DCSA-MLS,
P.O. Box 12, 91680 Bruyères-Le-Châtel, France
tnka@worldnet.fr

Abstract. In this paper, an acceleration scheme for the inverse power method based on the stationary properties of the Rayleigh ratio will be presented. Its practical use will be demonstrated by simultaneously solving the direct and adjoint multigroup diffusion problems. A parallel algorithm is developed using a repartition of both problems over two processors with a minimal communication effort. Speed-ups are given for a variety of problems on different computer architectures.

1   Introduction

The exact diffusion equation is discretized into G energy groups and the resulting direct equation has the following form for a given energy group g:

$$-\boldsymbol{\nabla} \cdot D_g \boldsymbol{\nabla} \Phi_g + (\Sigma_{t,g} - \Sigma_{s,g \to g})\Phi_g = \sum_{g \neq g'} \Sigma_{s,g' \to g}\Phi_{g'} + \lambda \, \chi_g \sum_{g'} \nu \Sigma_{f,g'}\Phi_{g'} \quad (1)$$

where summations are carried out over all the energy groups. The group-dependent input variables for this equation are:

 - D_g, the diffusion coefficients,
 - $\Sigma_{t,g}$, the total macroscopic cross section,
 - $\Sigma_{s,g' \to g}$, the scattering cross section from group g' to group g,
 - $\nu \Sigma_{f,g'}$, the production of secondary neutrons,
 - χ_g, the fission spectrum.

The goal is to compute Φ_g, the neutron flux eigenvector in the gth energy group, associated with the fundamental eigenvalue λ. In the multigroup formalism, the G equations result in a non-symmetric linear system that can be written as

$$(A - \lambda B)\Phi = 0 . \quad (2)$$

The corresponding adjoint system is:

$$(A^T - \lambda B^T)\Phi^* = 0. \tag{3}$$

The adjoint eigenvector Φ^* is often used as a weighting vector for perturbation theory or error assessment.

The DONJON reactor code [1] solves these multigroup direct and adjoint problems for the diffusion equation using the preconditioned power method.[2] An Alternating Direction Implicit (ADI) method is used to compute the system preconditioner. An acceleration strategy, called Symmetric Variational Acceleration Technique (SVAT),[3] has been developed and has proven to be quite effective for direct as well as adjoint problems.

When both the direct and adjoint eigenvectors are needed, they can be combined and used in the Rayleigh ratio, which is an estimate of the eigenvalue of both equations:

$$\lambda = \frac{< \Phi^*, A\Phi >}{< \Phi^*, B\Phi >}. \tag{4}$$

This definition of λ improves the eigenvalue convergence and its stationary properties can also be useful to compute extrapolation parameters required in the acceleration scheme.

In the following, a description of this acceleration technique using the Rayleigh ratio properties is presented. The parallel algorithm and communication efforts using PVM [4] are then presented. Comparisons for sequential calculations are made with SVAT results, in order to assess the correctness of the acceleration technique. Speed-ups are then given for different cases based on real reactor calculations.

2 Convergence Acceleration for Direct/Adjoint Problems

The general algorithm of the preconditioned power method developed for eigenvalue calculations is given by the following few steps:

- $\Phi^{(0)}$ given
- Evaluation of λ^k
- $r^{(k)} = (\lambda^k B - A)\Phi^{(k)}$; $k > 0$
- Solution of $M z^{(k)} = r^{(k)}$
- $\Phi^{(k+1)} = \Phi^{(k)} + z^{(k)}$

where M is a preconditioning matrix, that estimates A. This system is solved directly using an Alternating Direction Implicit splitting. One inner iteration per outer iteration is considered as sufficient for most problems.

In the algorithm, λ^k is a positive functional of $\Phi^{(k)}$ (for example, one could use any vector norm), but the convergence rate can be very slow. The estimate provided by Eq.4 will be chosen with an acceleration strategy based on the introduction of extrapolation factors, α, β, in the expression for the new eigenvector:

$$\Phi^{(k+1)} = \Phi^{(k)} + \alpha^{(k)} z^{(k)} + \beta^{(k)} p^{(k-1)}. \tag{5}$$

where $p^{(k-1)} = \Phi^{(k)} - \Phi^{(k-1)}$.

As in many other iterative schemes, the extrapolation factors α, β will be dynamically computed to find a stationary point of an appropriate functional, which usually is the new value of λ^k. This iterative algorithm can also be applied to the solution of the adjoint problem, defined by Eq. 3, in which the accelerated solution has the form:

$$\Phi^{*(k+1)} = \Phi^{*(k)} + \alpha^{*(k)} z^{*(k)} + \beta^{*(k)} p^{*(k-1)}. \tag{6}$$

Both eigenvectors will simultaneously be solved. The calculation of the extrapolation parameters is added onto the initial algorithm. The final algorithm is made up of a succession of free and "extrapolated" iterations. In free iterations, α and α^* are 1.0 and β and β^* are zero, which reproduce the original power method algorithm. The overall algorithm used to simultaneously solve direct and adjoint problems can be represented as shown in Fig. 1.

$\Phi^{(0)}$, $\Phi^{*(0)}$ given
Evaluation of λ^k (Eq. 4)
$r^{(k)} = (\lambda^k B - A)\Phi^{(k)}$ $\qquad\qquad\qquad$ $r^{*(k)} = (\lambda^k B^T - A^T)\Phi^{*(k)}$
Solve $Mz^{(k)} = r^{(k)}$ $\qquad\qquad\qquad$ Solve $Mz^{*(k)} = r^{*(k)}$
Stationarity of $\lambda^{k+1} = f(\alpha, \beta, \alpha^*, \beta^*)$
OR $(\alpha, \beta, \alpha^*, \beta^*) = (1, 0, 1, 0)$
Calculation of $\Phi^{(k+1)}$ (Eq. 5) $\qquad\qquad$ Calculation of $\Phi^{*(k+1)}$ (Eq. 6)

Fig. 1. Accelerated Algorithm for Direct and Adjoint Solutions

The number of free and accelerated iterations are controlled by the user; by default, 3 free iterations are followed by 3 accelerated ones. Similarities between this acceleration technique and a conjugate gradient method appear in the expression of the new iterates Eqs. 5 and 6, where the conjugate direction and the functional minimization are obtained simultaneously. As multigroup diffusion matrices are positive definite but non-symmetric, the Rayleigh Ratio technique is equivalent to the Bi-Conjugate Gradient Method with two extrapolation parameters only ($\alpha = \alpha^*$, $\beta = \beta^*$).[5]

3 Parallel Implementation

The DONJON reactor code is organized as a collection of modules that can be used to perform complex reactor simulations in a user-friendly environment. In that context, modules represent specific functionality and information is exchanged between them via data structures. The basic part of the modules allow the definition of the solution domain, the macroscopic properties and the solution of the multigroup diffusion equations. Particular modules have been developed to use the PVM message tool, mainly a module to initialize the calculation with *pvmfspawn* and two modules to send and receive data structures to and from different hosts.[6]

As both direct and adjoint eigenvectors are solved, the use of a two-processor "single program multiple data" model is the preferred choice. This model is included in the **INITP** module to begin the execution. The exchanges between hosts are realized directly inside the appropriate solution module named **FLUD-PAR**.

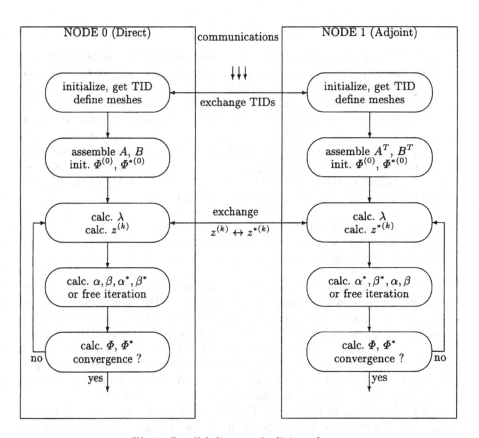

Fig. 2. Parallel direct and adjoint solvers

A minimum exchange option has been chosen. On each processor, the accelerated preconditioned power method algorithm is followed (See Fig.1). At every iteration, the adjoint information is only required for the eigenvalue calculation and the extrapolation parameter evaluation.

On every processor, two stacks containing $\Phi^{(k)}$, $z^{(k)}$ and $p^{(k-1)}$ and their adjoint equivalents are stored. The new residual estimate z (or z^*) is exchanged at every iteration as shown in Fig. 2. The communication effort is thus very limited and depends on the number of iterations. The new eigenvector estimates (Eq. 5, 6) are computed on both processors as well as the evaluation of the four extrapolation parameters, because they appear in the expression of $\lambda^{(k+1)}$.

Some calculations are carried out on both processors, instead of communicating the solution. This choice has been made because of the use of a cluster parallel machine, for which the communication time is very dependent on the net protocol and can vary during an execution.

4   Numerical Results

First, it is worth noting that the SVAT acceleration strategy has been validated against various benchmark problems and is also currently used in industrial calculations.[2, 3, 7] The numerical results presented here illustrate the new parallel implementation for simultaneous solution of direct and adjoint problems, and the validity of such calculations has been checked as compared with the current sequential version of DONJON.

The new Rayleigh ratio acceleration strategy presented above has been coded for both sequential and parallel algorithms. To test it, different cases were selected according to the computation effort and to the property of the diffusion equation. Three different configurations were used:

- One-speed diffusion equation over a CANDU reactor geometry,
- CANDU-6 reactor core as defined by the industry,
- HEU SLOWPOKE reactor core.

A CANDU-6 reactor is an heavy-water cooled reactor, composed of 380 fuel channels surrounded by a heavy-water moderator. The model used (see Ref. [7]) is composed of 21120 regions. A standard finite difference discretization is used. In industrial applications, CANDU-6 reactor are represented by two-group properties; in such a problem, the matrix A is a lower block-triangular matrix. The 2-group macroscopic properties are recovered from multigroup transport calculations made with the DRAGON code.[8] A one-speed problem was also considered because the resulting diffusion equation is self-adjoint.

A Highly Enriched Uranium (HEU) Slowpoke reactor is a pool reactor surrounded by ligth water, with a Beryllium reflector. Many calculations to represent this reactor were carried out in the last two years for macroscopic property generation as well as for reactor behavior.[9] A three-dimensional hexagonal representation of the reactor was made in DONJON and 6 energy group properties were generated with DRAGON. A total number of 50000 regions is needed. For that case, coupling between groups is large as the three last groups are thermal.

In a first part, comparisons with SVAT Technique are given. Parallel results are then reproduced.

4.1 Sequential Calculations

Only the CANDU geometry is considered here. For these two cases, sequential calculations are carried out using the SVAT acceleration strategy. For the sequential version of the Rayleigh Ratio Technique, direct and adjoint eigenvectors are solved together. The convergence criteria set on eigenvectors is:

$$\frac{\max\limits_{i} | \Phi_i^{(k-1)} - \Phi_i^{(k)} |}{\max\limits_{i} | \Phi_i^{(k)} |} \leq \varepsilon$$

The default value of ε is 10^{-4}. The calculations stop when both eigenvectors satisfy the criteria.

The SVAT Technique is a Conjugate Gradient method for non-symmetric systems as is the RRT method. Both techniques are used on a symmetric problem as an exception. In the one-speed case, every iteration has been accelerated. In 40 iterations, both methods lead to the same eigenvectors and eigenvalue as expected.

For the two-group case, the default acceleration strategy of 3 free and 3 accelerated iterations was used for both methods. As explained previously, the two-group case is a non-symmetric one. For the industrial CANDU-6 test, a precision of 10^{-4} has been used for eigenvectors and 10^{-5} for the eigenvalue.

Table 1 shows that both acceleration techniques give similar results. The use of the RRT is thus justified when both eigenvectors are required.

Table 1. Comparison of SVAT and RRT acceleration schemes for 2-group CANDU-6 reactor test

	RRT	SVAT
λ	0.979431	0.979431
# iterations	33	30
Error Φ	9.8E-05	4.7E-05
Error Φ^*	3.7E-05	4.7E-05

4.2 RRT Speed-Ups

For the three reactor cases chosen, calculations were performed with two processors on three architectures, all using PVM 3.3: two cluster computers composed of IBM Risc 6000 and HP 712 and one shared-memory parallel machine SUN SPARC 2000.

For CANDU reactor tests, speed-ups are very acceptable,(that is, much greater than 1.5) as seen in Table 2. To test the new strategy on a highly energy-coupled problem, HEU Slowpoke research reactor was chosen. ¿From Table 2, it is obvious that this problem is much more time consuming than the previous

ones. The results indicate that the speed-ups remain essentially constant even
for significant increases in problem complexity.

Table 2. Performance of the Parallel Acceleration Strategy

# Unknowns	Comm. MWords	HP 712 CPU Time Seq.	Speed-up	IBM Risc 6000 CPU Time Seq.	Speed-up	SUN Sparc 2000 CPU Time Seq.	Speed-up
1 × 21120	0.91	37 s	1.3	23 s	1.8	42 s	1.8
2 × 21120	2.61	116 s	1.5	88 s	1.9	118 s	1.9
6 × 54860	13.8	–	–	792 s	1.9	1337 s	1.7

The code was also implemented on a CRAY T3E. The UNICOS Multi Processor version of PVM routines was used successfully. This CRAY computer uses a 64-bit floating point representation. It can be limiting for large scale problems with large memory needs. But it allows a severe test of the algebraic calculations and an estimate of the truncation error done in using simple precision on 32-bit computers. It appears that results are strictly identical on CRAY and on SUN computers, which is really reinsuring of the chosen algorithm.

5 Conclusion

The use of the Rayleigh ratio allows the eigenvalue convergence to be very effective. Comparisons with SVAT sequential method show good agreement of the resulting eigenvectors and eigenvalues. As the communication effort is limited, speed-ups are very good whatever the architecture. Such an algorithm using only two processors with minimum communication is very interesting for users with limited resources, like a two-processor PC computer or a few processors availability in a parallel machine.

Extension of this work would be the use of the Rayleigh Ratio Technique to compute flux harmonics where direct and adjoint eigenvectors have to be known to use deflation. For numerical simulations involving system perturbations, this approach seems interesting because the direct flux map could be adjusted faster with the parallel direct/adjoint approach than with the usual sequential equivalent. The parallel implementation would be as simple as for the fundamental eigenvalue search presented here.

Acknowledgment. Part of this work is funded by a grant from the National Science and Engineering Research Council of Canada.

References

1. Varin E., Hébert A., Roy R. and Koclas J., "A Users' Guide for DONJON", Ecole Polytechnique de Montréal, IGE-208 (1996).
2. Hébert A., "Preconditioning the Power Method for Reactor Calculations," *Nucl. Sci. and Eng.* **94** (1986) 1-11.
3. Hébert A., "Variational Principles and Convergence Acceleration Strategies for the Neutron Diffusion Equation", *Nucl. Sci. Eng.*, **91** (1985) 414-427.
4. Geist A., Beguelin A., Dongarra J., Jiang W., Manchek R., Sunderam V., "PVM 3 User's Guide and Reference Manual", Report ORNL/TM-12187, Oak Ridge National Laboratory (1994).
5. Fletcher R., "Conjugate Gradient Methods for Indefinite Systems", *Lec. Notes in Math.* **506**, Springer-Verlag, Berlin Heidelberg New York (1976) 73-89.
6. R. Roy, Z. Stankovski, "Parallelization of Neutron Transport Solvers", Recent Adv. in PVM/MPI, Proc. Euro PVM/MPI-97, *LNCS* **1332**, Springer-Verlag, Berlin Heidelberg New York (1997) 494-501.
7. Varin E., Roy R., Baril R. and Hotte G., "Validation of DRAGON/DONJON Codes against CANDU-6 Reactor Operation Data", Joint Int. Conf. on Math. Meth. and Supercomp. for Nucl. Appl., Saratoga Springs (1997) 1539-1548.
8. Marleau G., Hébert A. and Roy R., "A Users' Guide for DRAGON", Ecole Polytechnique de Montréal, IGE-174 (1996).
9. Varin E., Noceir S., Roy R., Rozon R. and Guertin C., "Using Deterministic Methods for Research Reactor Studies", Fifth Int. Conf. on Simulation Methods in Nuclear Engineering, Montreal, 8–11 September 1996.

Author Index

Abu-Ghazaleh, N.   97
Addison, C.   36
Alexandrov, V.   323, 346
Almeida, F.   387

Baker, M.   63
Baraglia, R.   249
Barak, A.   44
Beisel, T.   180
Bolloni, A.   331
Browne, S.   257
Bubak, M.   3, 131

Carissimi, A.   137
Cerverón, V.   379
Chan, K.J.   338
Chetlur, M.   97
Clarke, D.J.N.   215
Clematis, A.   11
Corana, A.   11
Cotronis, Y.   145
Crocchianti, S.   331
Cunha, J. C.   105, 273

Dehne, F.   323
Delves, M.   161
Derakhshan, M.   153
Díaz, W.   379
Dimov, I.   346
Doallo, R.   304
Dongarra, J.J.   93
Duarte, V.   273

Espinosa, A.   19

Fagg, G.E.   93
Ferraro, G.   364
Ferrini, R.   249
Fischer, M.   231
Fish, R.S.   215
Folino, G.   27

Fuerle, T.   172
Funika, W.   3

Gabriel, E.   180
Geist, G.A.   74, 231
Georgiev, K.   354
Gibbons, A.M.   338
Gray, P.   83
Grossi, G.   364

Hatazaki, T.   188
Hiraki , K.   223
Hirsbrunner, B.   206

Iskra, K.   3

Karaivanova, A.   346
Keller, R.   180
Kemelmakher, M.   196
Kohl, J.A.   297
Krantz, A.   83
Kranzlmüller, D.   265
Kremien, O.   196
Krommer, A.   153
Krone, O.   206

Laforenza, D.   249
Laganà, A.   331, 364
Lancaster, D.   36
Lavi, R.   44
Loeffelhardt, C.   172
London, K.S.   93
Luque, E.   19
Łuszczek, P.   131

Macías, E.   371
Margalef, T.   19
Marinho, J.   113
Martins, P.   121

Maruszewski, R.   3
Matsumoto, T.   223
Medeiros, P. D.   105
Megson, G.M.   215
Morales, D.G.   387
Morimoto, K.   223
Müller, M.   52

NKaoua, T.   403
Nebot-Gil , I.   379
Nitsche, T.   281

Ojeda-Guerra, C.N.   371
Olesen, S.   83
Oliver, T.   36
Orlando, S.   289

Papadopoulos, P.M.   297
Pasin, M.   137
Perego, R.   289
Pias, M.   338
Prechelt, L.   52

Raab, M.   206
Rajasekaran, U. K. V.   97
Ramos, E.   379
Rau-Chaplin, A.   323
Resch, M.   180
Reussner, R.   52
Riganelli, A.   331, 364
Roda, J.L.   387
Rodríguez, C.   387
Roy, R.   403
Rytter, W.   338

Sande, F.   387
Sanders, P.   52
Schikuta, E.   172
Scott, S.L.   231
Sgherri, R.   249
Sharma, G.D.   97
Silva, J. G.   113, 121
Silva, L.M.   121
Spezzano, G.   27
Stankovic, N.   239
Stockinger, K.   172
Suárez, A.   371
Sunderam, V.   83

Taft, K.   323
Talia, D.   27
Touriño, J.   304
Träff, J.L.   395

Varin, E.   403
Volkert, J.   265

Wanek, H.   172
Webers, W.   281
Wierzbowska, A.   131
Wilsey, P. A.   97
Wismüller, R.   312

Zhang, K.   239
Zima, H.   161
Zlatev, Z.   354

Springer
and the
environment

At Springer we firmly believe that an international science publisher has a special obligation to the environment, and our corporate policies consistently reflect this conviction.

We also expect our business partners – paper mills, printers, packaging manufacturers, etc. – to commit themselves to using materials and production processes that do not harm the environment. The paper in this book is made from low- or no-chlorine pulp and is acid free, in conformance with international standards for paper permanency.

Lecture Notes in Computer Science

For information about Vols. 1–1404

please contact your bookseller or Springer-Verlag

Vol. 1405: S.M. Embury, N.J. Fiddian, W.A. Gray, A.C. Jones (Eds.), Advances in Databases. Proceedings, 1998. XII, 183 pages. 1998.

Vol. 1406: H. Burkhardt, B. Neumann (Eds.), Computer Vision – ECCV'98. Vol. I. Proceedings, 1998. XVI, 927 pages. 1998.

Vol. 1408: E. Burke, M. Carter (Eds.), Practice and Theory of Automated Timetabling II. Proceedings, 1997. XII, 273 pages. 1998.

Vol. 1407: H. Burkhardt, B. Neumann (Eds.), Computer Vision – ECCV'98. Vol. II. Proceedings, 1998. XVI, 881 pages. 1998.

Vol. 1409: T. Schaub, The Automation of Reasoning with Incomplete Information. XI, 159 pages. 1998. (Subseries LNAI).

Vol. 1411: L. Asplund (Ed.), Reliable Software Technologies – Ada-Europe. Proceedings, 1998. XI, 297 pages. 1998.

Vol. 1412: R.E. Bixby, E.A. Boyd, R.Z. Ríos-Mercado (Eds.), Integer Programming and Combinatorial Optimization. Proceedings, 1998. IX, 437 pages. 1998.

Vol. 1413: B. Pernici, C. Thanos (Eds.), Advanced Information Systems Engineering. Proceedings, 1998. X, 423 pages. 1998.

Vol. 1414: M. Nielsen, W. Thomas (Eds.), Computer Science Logic. Selected Papers, 1997. VIII, 511 pages. 1998.

Vol. 1415: J. Mira, A.P. del Pobil, M.Ali (Eds.), Methodology and Tools in Knowledge-Based Systems. Vol. I. Proceedings, 1998. XXIV, 887 pages. 1998. (Subseries LNAI).

Vol. 1416: A.P. del Pobil, J. Mira, M.Ali (Eds.), Tasks and Methods in Applied Artificial Intelligence. Vol.II. Proceedings, 1998. XXIII, 943 pages. 1998. (Subseries LNAI).

Vol. 1417: S. Yalamanchili, J. Duato (Eds.), Parallel Computer Routing and Communication. Proceedings, 1997. XII, 309 pages. 1998.

Vol. 1418: R. Mercer, E. Neufeld (Eds.), Advances in Artificial Intelligence. Proceedings, 1998. XII, 467 pages. 1998. (Subseries LNAI).

Vol. 1419: G. Vigna (Ed.), Mobile Agents and Security. XII, 257 pages. 1998.

Vol. 1420: J. Desel, M. Silva (Eds.), Application and Theory of Petri Nets 1998. Proceedings, 1998. VIII, 385 pages. 1998.

Vol. 1421: C. Kirchner, H. Kirchner (Eds.), Automated Deduction – CADE-15. Proceedings, 1998. XIV, 443 pages. 1998. (Subseries LNAI).

Vol. 1422: J. Jeuring (Ed.), Mathematics of Program Construction. Proceedings, 1998. X, 383 pages. 1998.

Vol. 1423: J.P. Buhler (Ed.), Algorithmic Number Theory. Proceedings, 1998. X, 640 pages. 1998.

Vol. 1424: L. Polkowski, A. Skowron (Eds.), Rough Sets and Current Trends in Computing. Proceedings, 1998. XIII, 626 pages. 1998. (Subseries LNAI).

Vol. 1425: D. Hutchison, R. Schäfer (Eds.), Multimedia Applications, Services and Techniques – ECMAST'98. Proceedings, 1998. XVI, 532 pages. 1998.

Vol. 1427: A.J. Hu, M.Y. Vardi (Eds.), Computer Aided Verification. Proceedings, 1998. IX, 552 pages. 1998.

Vol. 1429: F. van der Linden (Ed.), Development and Evolution of Software Architectures for Product Families. Proceedings, 1998. IX, 258 pages. 1998.

Vol. 1430: S. Trigila, A. Mullery, M. Campolargo, H. Vanderstraeten, M. Mampaey (Eds.), Intelligence in Services and Networks: Technology for Ubiquitous Telecom Services. Proceedings, 1998. XII, 550 pages. 1998.

Vol. 1431: H. Imai, Y. Zheng (Eds.), Public Key Cryptography. Proceedings, 1998. XI, 263 pages. 1998.

Vol. 1432: S. Arnborg, L. Ivansson (Eds.), Algorithm Theory – SWAT '98. Proceedings, 1998. IX, 347 pages. 1998.

Vol. 1433: V. Honavar, G. Slutzki (Eds.), Grammatical Inference. Proceedings, 1998. X, 271 pages. 1998. (Subseries LNAI).

Vol. 1434: J.-C. Heudin (Ed.), Virtual Worlds. Proceedings, 1998. XII, 412 pages. 1998. (Subseries LNAI).

Vol. 1435: M. Klusch, G. Weiß (Eds.), Cooperative Information Agents II. Proceedings, 1998. IX, 307 pages. 1998. (Subseries LNAI).

Vol. 1436: D. Wood, S. Yu (Eds.), Automata Implementation. Proceedings, 1997. VIII, 253 pages. 1998.

Vol. 1437: S. Albayrak, F.J. Garijo (Eds.), Intelligent Agents for Telecommunication Applications. Proceedings, 1998. XII, 251 pages. 1998. (Subseries LNAI).

Vol. 1438: C. Boyd, E. Dawson (Eds.), Information Security and Privacy. Proceedings, 1998. XI, 423 pages. 1998.

Vol. 1439: B. Magnusson (Ed.), System Configuration Management. Proceedings, 1998. X, 207 pages. 1998.

Vol. 1441: W. Wobcke, M. Pagnucco, C. Zhang (Eds.), Agents and Multi-Agent Systems. Proceedings, 1997. XII, 241 pages. 1998. (Subseries LNAI).

Vol. 1442: A. Fiat. G.J. Woeginger (Eds.), Online Algorithms. XVIII, 436 pages. 1998.

Vol. 1443: K.G. Larsen, S. Skyum, G. Winskel (Eds.), Automata, Languages and Programming. Proceedings, 1998. XVI, 932 pages. 1998.

Vol. 1444: K. Jansen, J. Rolim (Eds.), Approximation Algorithms for Combinatorial Optimization. Proceedings, 1998. VIII, 201 pages. 1998.

Vol. 1445: E. Jul (Ed.), ECOOP'98 – Object-Oriented Programming. Proceedings, 1998. XII, 635 pages. 1998.

Vol. 1446: D. Page (Ed.), Inductive Logic Programming. Proceedings, 1998. VIII, 301 pages. 1998. (Subseries LNAI).

Vol. 1447: V.W. Porto, N. Saravanan, D. Waagen, A.E. Eiben (Eds.), Evolutionary Programming VII. Proceedings, 1998. XVI, 840 pages. 1998.

Vol. 1448: M. Farach-Colton (Ed.), Combinatorial Pattern Matching. Proceedings, 1998. VIII, 251 pages. 1998.

Vol. 1449: W.-L. Hsu, M.-Y. Kao (Eds.), Computing and Combinatorics. Proceedings, 1998. XII, 372 pages. 1998.

Vol. 1450: L. Brim, F. Gruska, J. Zlatuška (Eds.), Mathematical Foundations of Computer Science 1998. Proceedings, 1998. XVII, 846 pages. 1998.

Vol. 1451: A. Amin, D. Dori, P. Pudil, H. Freeman (Eds.), Advances in Pattern Recognition. Proceedings, 1998. XXI, 1048 pages. 1998.

Vol. 1452: B.P. Goettl, H.M. Halff, C.L. Redfield, V.J. Shute (Eds.), Intelligent Tutoring Systems. Proceedings, 1998. XIX, 629 pages. 1998.

Vol. 1453: M.-L. Mugnier, M. Chein (Eds.), Conceptual Structures: Theory, Tools and Applications. Proceedings, 1998. XIII, 439 pages. (Subseries LNAI).

Vol. 1454: I. Smith (Ed.), Artificial Intelligence in Structural Engineering. XI, 497 pages. 1998. (Subseries LNAI).

Vol. 1456: A. Drogoul, M. Tambe, T. Fukuda (Eds.), Collective Robotics. Proceedings, 1998. VII, 161 pages. 1998. (Subseries LNAI).

Vol. 1457: A. Ferreira, J. Rolim, H. Simon, S.-H. Teng (Eds.), Solving Irregularly Structured Problems in Prallel. Proceedings, 1998. X, 408 pages. 1998.

Vol. 1458: V.O. Mittal, H.A. Yanco, J. Aronis, R-. Simpson (Eds.), Assistive Technology in Artificial Intelligence. X, 273 pages. 1998. (Subseries LNAI).

Vol. 1459: D.G. Feitelson, L. Rudolph (Eds.), Job Scheduling Strategies for Parallel Processing. Proceedings, 1998. VII, 257 pages. 1998.

Vol. 1460: G. Quirchmayr, E. Schweighofer, T.J.M. Bench-Capon (Eds.), Database and Expert Systems Applications. Proceedings, 1998. XVI, 905 pages. 1998.

Vol. 1461: G. Bilardi, G.F. Italiano, A. Pietracaprina, G. Pucci (Eds.), Algorithms – ESA'98. Proceedings, 1998. XII, 516 pages. 1998.

Vol. 1462: H. Krawczyk (Ed.), Advances in Cryptology - CRYPTO '98. Proceedings, 1998. XII, 519 pages. 1998.

Vol. 1464: H.H.S. Ip, A.W.M. Smeulders (Eds.), Multimedia Information Analysis and Retrieval. Proceedings, 1998. VIII, 264 pages. 1998.

Vol. 1465: R. Hirschfeld (Ed.), Financial Cryptography. Proceedings, 1998. VIII, 311 pages. 1998.

Vol. 1466: D. Sangiorgi, R. de Simone (Eds.), CONCUR'98: Concurrency Theory. Proceedings, 1998. XI, 657 pages. 1998.

Vol. 1467: C. Clack, K. Hammond, T. Davie (Eds.), Implementation of Functional Languages. Proceedings, 1997. X, 375 pages. 1998.

Vol. 1468: P. Husbands, J.-A. Meyer (Eds.), Evolutionary Robotics. Proceedings, 1998. VIII, 247 pages. 1998.

Vol. 1469: R. Puigjaner, N.N. Savino, B. Serra (Eds.), Computer Performance Evaluation. Proceedings, 1998. XIII, 376 pages. 1998.

Vol. 1470: D. Pritchard, J. Reeve (Eds.), Euro-Par'98: Parallel Processing. Proceedings, 1998. XXII, 1157 pages. 1998.

Vol. 1471: J. Dix, L. Moniz Pereira, T.C. Przymusinski (Eds.), Logic Programming and Knowledge Representation. Proceedings, 1997. IX, 246 pages. 1998. (Subseries LNAI).

Vol. 1473: X. Leroy, A. Ohori (Eds.), Types in Compilation. Proceedings, 1998. VIII, 299 pages. 1998.

Vol. 1475: W. Litwin, T. Morzy, G. Vossen (Eds.), Advances in Databases and Information Systems. Proceedings, 1998. XIV, 369 pages. 1998.

Vol. 1476: J. Calmet, J. Plaza (Eds.), Artificial Intelligence and Symbolic Computation. Proceedings, 1998. XI, 309 pages. 1998. (Subseries LNAI).

Vol. 1477: K. Rothermel, F. Hohl (Eds.), Mobile Agents. Proceedings, 1998. VIII, 285 pages. 1998.

Vol. 1478: M. Sipper, D. Mange, A. Pérez-Uribe (Eds.), Evolvable Systems: From Biology to Hardware. Proceedings, 1998. IX, 382 pages. 1998.

Vol. 1479: J. Grundy, M. Newey (Eds.), Theorem Proving in Higher Order Logics. Proceedings, 1998. VIII, 497 pages. 1998.

Vol. 1480: F. Giunchiglia (Ed.), Artificial Intelligence: Methodology, Systems, and Applications. Proceedings, 1998. IX, 502 pages. 1998. (Subseries LNAI).

Vol. 1482: R.W. Hartenstein, A. Keevallik (Eds.), Field-Programmable Logic and Applications. Proceedings, 1998. XI, 533 pages. 1998.

Vol. 1483: T. Plagemann, V. Goebel (Eds.), Interactive Distributed Multimedia Systems and Telecommunication Services. Proceedings, 1998. XV, 326 pages. 1998.

Vol. 1485: J.-J. Quisquater, Y. Deswarte, C. Meadows, D. Gollmann (Eds.), Computer Security – ESORICS 98. Proceedings, 1998. X, 377 pages. 1998.

Vol. 1486: A.P. Ravn, H. Rischel (Eds.), Formal Techniques in Real-Time and Fault-Tolerant Systems. Proceedings, 1998. VIII, 339 pages. 1998.

Vol. 1487: V. Gruhn (Ed.), Software Process Technology. Proceedings, 1998. VIII, 157 pages. 1998.

Vol. 1488: B. Smyth, P. Cunningham (Eds.), Advances in Case-Based Reasoning. Proceedings, 1998. XI, 482 pages. 1998. (Subseries LNAI).

Vol. 1490: C. Palamidessi, H. Glaser, K. Meinke (Eds.), Principles of Declarative Programming. Proceedings, 1998. XI, 497 pages. 1998.

Vol. 1497: V. Alexandrov, J. Dongarra (Eds.), Recent Advances in Parallel Virtual Machine and Message Passing Interface. Proceedings, 1998. XII, 412 pages. 1998.

Vol. 1501: M.M. Richter, C.H. Smith, R. Wiehagen, T. Zeugmann (Eds.), Algorithmic Learning Theory. Proceedings, 1998. XI, 439 pages. 1998. (Subseries LNAI).

Vol. 1503: G. Levi (Ed.), Static Analysis. Proceedings, 1998. IX, 383 pages. 1998.